GW00836596

MANAGING BUSINESS ARCHIVES

To Lesley and Michael,
colleagues, mentors and friends

MANAGING BUSINESS ARCHIVES

Edited by Alison Turton

*Published in association with
the Business Archives Council*

Butterworth-Heinemann Ltd
Linacre House, Jordan Hill, Oxford OX2 8DP

 PART OF REED INTERNATIONAL BOOKS

OXFORD   LONDON   BOSTON
MUNICH   NEW DELHI   SINGAPORE   SYDNEY
TOKYO   TORONTO   WELLINGTON

First published 1991

British Library Cataloguing in Publication Data
Managing business archives.
  I. Turton, Alison
  651.5

ISBN 0 7506 0211 2

Library of Congress Cataloguing in Publication Data
Managing business archives / edited by Alison Turton.
  p.   cm.
  'Published in association with the Business Archives Council.'
  Includes bibliographical references and index.
  ISBN 0 7506 0211 2
  1. Business records – Great Britain – Management.   2. Business
enterprises – Great Britain – Archives.   I. Turton, Alison.
II. Business Archives Council (Great Britain)
HF5736.M34 1991   651.5'0941–dc20   91–20212
                                                    CIP

Printed and bound in Great Britain.

Contents

Foreword

As a businessman and ninth generation Twining, with an invaluable, working archive, I commend this useful publication to all archivists and others responsible for the historical records of old-established companies. It is a book which is long overdue and has been commissioned by the Business Archives Council to meet the clear need for an authoritative guide to archival principles and practice in the business environment.

While the number of company archivists in the United Kingdom has multiplied dramatically in recent years there remains little published material, other than the journals and occasional leaflets produced by the Business Archives Council, which caters specifically for their needs and discusses the kind of issues which can confront business archivists. This is not to claim that the basic principles of archival administration are for the most part any different for a company archivist than they are for an archivist in a local record office, but the archivist in business will certainly require a range of extra skills and awareness if the interests of the company are to be properly served.

Managing Business Archives has drawn upon the expertise of many of the Council's supporters and friends. I know that it will be of use not only to company archivists, but also to the wider constituency of those who are responsible for collections of business archives in local authority repositories or administering the historical records of other kinds of institutions. If it enables or encourages companies or other organizations to make proper provision for the long-term preservation of their historical records, then the production of this book will have been more than worthwhile.

S. H. G Twining
Chairman, Business Archives Council

Acknowledgements

This book would not have been possible without the contributions and good counsel of a great many people. First and foremost I am grateful to the fifteen authors who have worked hard to meet my gruelling specifications and have mostly borne with good humour my editorial changes and suggestions. It is hard to compress into a brief chapter expert knowledge of a subject which merits an entire book of its own and I am filled with admiration for their concision and thoroughness. A major debt of thanks is also due to Richard Storey, University of Warwick, who read the entire manuscript and made many helpful suggestions which have markedly improved the content and layout of the book.

Many others have seen and commented upon individual chapters, thereby allowing the authors to draw upon a wealth of expertise. In this respect thanks are due to: Robert Akers, Camberwell College of Arts; Adrian Allan, University of Liverpool; Melanie Aspey, News International plc; Sheila de Bellaigue, Royal Archives; Tony Bish, Wellcome Institute; Michael Bottomley, West Yorkshire Record Office; Margaret Brooks, Imperial War Museum; Terry Buchanan, Royal Commission on the Historical Monuments of England; Alan Cameron, Bank of Scotland; Clare Clubb, The University College of Wales; Tom Collings, Camberwell College of Arts; Anne Dickson, Record Ability; John Dodd, The BOC Group; Peter Emmerson, Barclays Bank plc; Meryl Foster, Public Record Office; Sue Garland, Guinness Brewing; Henry Gillett, Bank of England; Tricia Goodyear, The Royal Bank of Scotland plc; Terry Gourvish, London School of Economics; Adam Green, Somerset Record Office; Edwin Green, Midland Bank plc; Ken Hall, Lancashire Record Office; Brett Harrison, Leeds District Archives; Bruce Jackson, Tyne & Wear Archives Service; Suzanne Johnston, Clare College, Cambridge; David Jones, Suffolk Record Office; Jacqueline Kavanagh, British Broadcasting Corporation; Chris Kitching, Royal Commission on Historical Manuscripts; John MacIntyre, National Library of Scotland; George Mackenzie, Scottish Record Office; Alan McKinlay, Centre for Business History in Scotland; Jane Moon, St Albans High School; Michael Moss, University of Glasgow; Phil Ollerenshaw, Bristol Polytechnic; John Orbell, Baring Brothers & Co. Limited; Jim Parker, Royal Commission on Historical Manuscripts; Hugh Peebles, Stirling University; Lesley Richmond, University of Glasgow; Keith Sweetmore, West Yorkshire Record Office; Marcia Taylor, ESRC Research Centre; Alistair Tough, Greater Glasgow Health Board; Geoffrey Tweedale, National Archive for the History of Computing; Alan Ward, National Sound Archive; Angela Weight, Imperial War Museum; Roger Whitney, National Film Archive; Philip Winterbottom, The Royal Bank of Scotland plc; and Nigel Wratten, Clerical, Medical Investment Group.

I am grateful to my present employer, The Royal Bank of Scotland plc, which has always encouraged my involvement with such professional bodies as the Business Archives Council and supported the activities from which this book has sprung. I must also thank Linda White, my secretary, who has, with great skill and patience, translated my scribblings and helped me to cope with the many and diverse problems which have beset the project. A final debt of gratitude is owed to my husband Stewart who has had to put up with endless hours alone. To our son, Calum, who arrived during the final stages of the editorial process, no thanks. He helped not at all.

Alison Turton

Biographical notes on authors

John Armstrong
Author of Chapter 2, 'The development of British business and company law since 1750'. BSc and MSc (University of London) in economics. FRHistS. Currently Professor of Business History at Ealing College, London, and Honorary Treasurer of the Business Archives Council. Former editor of *Business Archives* and currently editor of *The Journal of Transport History*. Co-author of *Business Documents: Their origins, Sources and Uses in Historical Research*, and contributor of articles and chapters on aspects of business and transport history to periodicals and books.

John Booker
Author of Chapter 14, 'Access policy'. BA (Durham University) in classics; MLitt (Durham University) in history; PhD (York University) in architectural history; and diploma (University of London) in archive administration. FRHistS since 1979. Archivist and Curator of Lloyds Bank plc since 1978. Formerly Assistant Archivist, West Sussex Record Office, and Deputy County Archivist, Essex Record Office. Former Honorary Assistant Secretary, Society of Archivists. External lecturer on business archives for the postgraduate archive diploma course, University College, London. Author of *Essex and the Industrial Revolution* (1974). Contributor of articles and book reviews to many professional periodicals. Book on the architecture of banking due for publication in 1991.

Derek Charman
Author of Chapter 10, 'The corporate archivist and records management'. Scholar of Pembroke College, Oxford, and MA (University of Oxford). International consultant in records and archives management; lectures on, and organizes training courses in, records management. Sometime tutor in history at Leicester University. Formerly County Archivist of Ipswich and East Suffolk; Archives Adviser to the Federal Government of Nigeria; Government Archivist of Kenya; and Co-ordinator Records Services, British Steel Corporation. Compiler of *Records Surveys and Schedules: A RAMP Study with Guidelines* (1984) for UNESCO. Contributor of articles on history, archives and records management to many journals, including *Journal of the Society of Archivists*, *Archives* and *Business Archives*. Awarded the Britt Literary Award by the Association of Records Managers and Administrators (US) 1980. Author of *The Leicestershire Golf Club 1890–1990* (1990). Founder member and first chairman of the Records Management Group of the Society of Archivists. Sometime president and secretary of the International Records Management Council.

Michael Cook
Author of Chapter 13, 'The use of computers'. University Archivist and Director of Archival Description Project, University of Liverpool. Formerly Director of National Archives of Tanzania (1964–6) and of the archival training course of English–speaking Africa at the University of Ghana (1975–7). Previously Chair of the Education and Training Committee of the International Council on Archives (ICA) (1984–8), currently corresponding member of ICA's Automation Committee, and member of the Executive Committees of the Information Technology Group and the Specialist Repositories Group of the Society of Archivists. Author of *Archive Administration* (1977), *Archives and the Computer* (1980, 2nd edition 1986) and *Management of Information from Archives* (1986). Co-author of *The Manual of Archival Description* (2nd edition, 1990). Several times consultant for UNESCO in archival development, for example in Southeast Asia (1973) and Caribbean (1980–1), and for the British Council in Turkey (1984) and Pakistan (1990). Since the setting up of the Archival Description Project in 1984 has concentrated on the provision of standards for description and data exchange, and the design of channels for this, forging particularly close links with Portugal and Spain.

Chris Cooper
Author of Chapter 9, 'The repository'. MA (University of Oxford) and diploma (University of Liverpool) in archive administration. Since 1986 curatorial officer in the Public Record Office. Previously Keeper of Manuscripts at Guildhall Library, London. Member of the Executive Committee of the Business Archives Council and former Treasurer and member of the Technical Committee of the Society of Archivists.

Veronica Davies
Author of Chapter 17, 'The business archivist as manager. BA (University of London) and diploma (University of London) in archive administration. Head of Information Services, Shell International Petroleum Company Ltd. Previous experience with the BBC Written Archives Centre; Surrey Record Office; India Office Library and Records; and the Imperial War Museum. Author of articles and reviews in *Records Management Society Bulletin, Records Management Journal* and *Journal of the Society of Archivists*. Contributor to the *Dictionary of Business Biography*. Course co-ordinator and lecturer on business archives for the postgraduate archive diploma course, University College, London. Records Management Consultant for the British Council assisting the Ugandan Government.

Helen Forde
Author of Chapter 12, 'Conservation'. BA (University of London) in history; diploma (University of Liverpool) in archive administration and PhD (Leicester University) on the history of early Derbyshire Quakers. Assistant Archivist, Nottingham City Archives from 1968 to 1972; Assistant Archivist, Library of the Society of Friends from 1978 to 1979;

and since 1982 Assistant Keeper at the Public Record Office. Currently Head of Conservation Department and editor of PRO readers' *Bulletin*. Honorary Secretary (1985–8), later Chairman (1988–90), of the Technical Committee of the Society of Archivists and currently external examiner at Camberwell College of Arts for final-year students and part-time lecturer on record office management for the postgraduate archive diploma course at University College, London. Contributor of articles and book reviews on conservation and conservation training to professional periodicals.

Stephen Freeth
Author of Chapter 11, 'Finding aids'. BA (University of Cambridge) in classics and diploma (University of London) in archives administration. Deputy Keeper of Manuscripts, Guildhall Library, London, from 1980 to 1986, and Keeper of Manuscripts, Guildhall Library, since 1986. Previous experience with Kent Archives Office and West Sussex Record Office. Author of various articles and guides on archives and on church monuments. Former member of the Executive Committee of the Business Archives Council.

Edwin Green
Author of Chapter 1, 'Business archives in the United Kingdom: history, conspectus, prospectus'. BA (University of Sussex) in history and MPhil (University of Sussex) in economic history. Group Archivist, Midland Bank plc, since 1974. Visiting Fellow in Business Studies, City University. Formerly research officer for the Insurance Records Survey, City University (1972–4). Co-author of *The British Insurance Business, 1547– 1970. An Introduction and Guide to Historical Records in the United Kingdom* (1976) and *Midland. 150 Years of Banking Business* (1986). Contributor to *Business Archives*, *Journal of the Society of Archivists* and the *Dictionary of Business Biography*. Deputy chairman, Business Archives Council, since 1984 and chairman of the management committee for the Council's Company Archive Survey (1980–4).

Serena Kelly
Author of Chapter 8, 'Business archive formats'. BA (University of East Anglia) in history and landscape archaeology and MA (University of London) in archive administration. MA thesis on the National Union of Women Workers 1895–1920. Deputy Archivist, Baring Brothers & Co. Limited. Previous experience with the Institution of Electrical Engineers, The Arts Council of Great Britain and the Business Archives Council. Contributor to the *International Directory of Company Histories* and author of 'Report of a survey of the archives of British commercial computer manufacturers 1950–1970'. Publications include *Men of Property – An Analysis of the Norwich Enrolled Deeds 1286–1311* (1983) and, with P. J. Corfield, 'Giving directions to the town, the early town directories' in *Urban History Yearbook* (1984).

Leonard McDonald
Author of Chapter 7, 'Legal, public relations, marketing, personnel and product records'. Trained as an archivist in pre-independence Central Africa and served in Rhodesia and Nyasaland from 1952 to 1964. Emigrated to the United Kingdom in 1965 and became one of the first professionally trained archivists to work in a business archive. Has served as Group Archivist at Pilkington plc since 1965, apart from a short spell as Archivist to the Bermuda Government in the 1970s. Contributor of articles on records management to Society of Archivists' publications and on archival matters to *Archives* and *Business Archives*. Author of the first course notes on business archives in this country for the Society of Archivists' Diploma on Archives Administration.

Michael Moss
Author of Chapter 6, 'Accounting records'. BA (University of Oxford) in history. Since 1974 Archivist of the University of Glasgow, which holds one of the largest collections of business records in Europe. Formerly worked at the Bodleian Library, Oxford, and later as Registrar of the Western Survey of the National Register of Archives (Scotland). Co-author of *Workshop of the British Empire:Engineering and Shipbuilding in the West of Scotland* (1977); *The Making of Scotch Whisky* (1981); *Shipbuilders to the World – 125 Years of Harland and Wolff 1861–1986* (1986); and *A Business of National Importance – The Royal Mail Shipping Group 1903–1937* (1982). Member of the Executive Committees of the Business Archives Council and Business Archives Council of Scotland and former member of the Council of the National Trust for Scotland.

John Orbell
Author of Chapter 3, 'The development of office technology'. BA (University of York) in economics and economic history and PhD (University of Nottingham) in economic history. Archivist and Records Manager of Baring Brothers & Co. Limited since 1978, with general responsibilities for the Baring Group, an international merchant bank based in London. Author of *A Guide to the Historical Records of British Banking* (1985), *A Guide to Tracing the History of a Business* (1987) and other books, articles and reviews in the fields of archives administration and records management, and business and economic history. A member of the Executive Committee of the Business Archives Council since 1980.

Lesley Richmond
Author of Chapter 5, 'Corporate records'. MA (University of Edinburgh) in Scottish historical studies. Since 1986, Deputy Archivist of University of Glasgow. Formerly Survey Manager of the Business Archives Council's Company Archive Survey and Group Archivist of Racal-Chubb Ltd, security specialists. Co-author of *Company Archives. A Survey of the Records of 1,000 of the First Registered Companies in England and Wales* (1986); *Directory of Corporate Archives* (1987); *The Brewing Industry. A*

Guide to Historical Records (1990); and *History and Computing 3* (1990). Editor of *Scottish Industrial History* since 1987 and contributor to *Business Archives*. Member of the Executive Committee and Library Adviser of the Business Archives Council since 1984 and member of International Council of Archives, Business Archive Committee from 1987 to 1990.

Bridget Stockford

Author of Chapter 4, 'Getting started'. BA (University of East Anglia) and diploma (University of London) in archive administration. Survey Officer and subsequently Survey Manager of the Business Archives Council's Company Archive Survey from 1982 to 1984 and Group Records Manager of Burmah Oil Trading Ltd from 1984. Co-author of *Company Archives. A Survey of the Records of 1,000 of the First Registered Companies in England and Wales* (1986) and contributor to *Business Archives*. Member of the Executive Committee of the Business Archives Council since 1988.

Alison Turton

Author of Chapters 15 and 16, 'Supplementing the collection' and 'The public relations uses of business archives'. MA (University of Cambridge) in history and MA (University of London) in archive studies. Company Archivist of House of Fraser Ltd from 1978 to 1983; Secretary-General of the Business Archives Council from 1983 to 1987; Company Archivist and Records Manager of Babcock International plc from 1987 to 1988; and Senior Bank Archivist of The Royal Bank of Scotland plc from 1988 to date. Researched and written several business histories and co-author of *Directory of Corporate Archives* (1987); *The Bitter with the Sweet. The History of Fletcher and Stewart 1838–1988* (1988); *A Legend of Retailing . . . House of Fraser* (1989); and *The Brewing Industry. A Guide to Historical Records* (1990). Contributor to professional periodicals, *Dictionary of Business Biography* and *Dictionary of Scottish Business Biography*. Member of the Executive Committee of the Business Archives Council since 1987 and editor of the Council's journal, *Business Archives. Principles and Practice*, from 1987 to 1991.

Business archives in the United Kingdom: history, conspectus, prospectus

Edwin Green

The nature of business archives

Most archivists will admit that they are in a minority profession. When answering polite enquiries about their occupation, they will be familiar with that blank look of incomprehension on the faces of their listeners. The work of archivists does not 'speak for itself' in the same way as the responsibilities of larger professional groups such as doctors, lawyers, accountants or teachers.

If archives work as a whole is not well known to the general public, the area of business archives is many times more obscure. Even within the history professions – teachers, curators and archivists themselves – few are familiar with the scope and content of business archives. This is not surprising, given the relatively small number of specialists in business archives. It is also the inevitable result of the traditional concentration in the history world on political, military, social and cultural topics rather than economic and business issues.

Increasingly, this relative obscurity is becoming both dangerous and inappropriate; if the business past remains in the shadows, the resources and priority attached to it will be permanently inadequate. At a time when the state continues to reduce its role and business plays a relatively larger part in national life, it is no longer appropriate that the heritage and archives of business should be so neglected. Enterprise, after all, is not the invention of only the very recent past.

In these changing conditions the business world and the history professions need a clearer view of business history in general and business archives in particular. The role of business history is a long-standing subject of exposition and argument, and we can expect that the new network of business history centres in the United Kingdom will (and must) clarify the identity of the discipline. Indeed one of the most baffling aspects of business history is the fact that after some 30 years of debate there are still no standard textbooks on the subject and precious little consensus as to its boundaries and content.[1] In business archives, on the other hand, such a consensus is within closer reach and attention can now be switched from justifying the existence and value of business archives to the practicalities of managing collections and making effective use of them.

To what extent is business archives a distinct subject, with its own identity? Clearly the work of a business archivist is not a separate, integrated profession; business archives are themselves part of a national network of archive institutions. In the United Kingdom the most familiar institutions are those record offices which are publicly funded and governed by public record statute or local authority legislation – at national level, for example, the Public Record Offices in London and Belfast and the Scottish Record Office in Edinburgh, and at local level the county record offices, city archives and local history collections attached to public libraries. Special repositories in the public sector, such as university archives, hospital records units and national museum collections, are also an important part of the British archives framework. In comparison, privately owned collections are less affected by legislative provisions and in general they are a less visible part of the archive scene. Nevertheless the archives of families, charities, societies and businesses are long-established and distinctive features of archive provision in the United Kingdom.

All these institutions are potentially the custodians of business archives. Moreover business archives cannot be defined in isolation from other archive resources. Like any other collection, the archives of a business are the record of decisions and change, structures and personnel, performance and results. The business might be a multinational corporation, a company, partnership or one-man enterprise. The archives are the evidence of the historical presence of an institution in the same way that departmental records are evidence of the existence and activities of a Whitehall ministry or that regimental records are witness to the constitution and campaigns of a military unit. In the business setting, as in any other organization, a high proportion of these records will be in paper form, but they might also include tape-recorded information, films, photographs and (increasingly) computer-readable media. Business archives, like those of other institutions, can be bulky, ill-kempt and profoundly dusty.

Equally the defined role of a business archivist does not differ fundamentally from that of the archivist in any other public or private institution. The business archivist is the guardian, keyholder and publicist for the collection in his or her care, in much the same way as the county archivist is the protector and go-between for the collections in a county record office. The training, professional disciplines and the vocabulary of the business archivist are also broadly the same as those employed in a public or private archive. Like his or her counterpart in a public record office, the business archivist adheres to such concepts as provenance of records and the preservation of original order. Consequently the types of classification and finding aids produced by a business archivist have much in common with the descriptive lists and catalogues available in the searchrooms of public record offices.

Not least, the archivist in business shares with other archivists the vocabulary and concepts of records management. In business as in any other area, records have a life-cycle from birth to ultimate disposal or permanent preservation. The business archivist is vitally concerned in the management of that cycle, identifying, appraising, scheduling records, devising retention periods and ensuring the orderly transfer of records between each stage of their cycle. These routines are again parallel to those of archivists and records managers in central or local government and other institutions. Here the business environment has played a pivotal role in the development of records management disciplines, with the result that the concepts and language developed by business have influenced usage throughout the archive community.

If the work of a business archivist is not a distinct profession, and if it shares the methods and vocabulary of archives in general, can it be claimed to have a separate identity and character? Perhaps the best test of this issue is to examine the origins and development of the subject. The following sections, using as a framework the history and traditions of business archives, show how their home environment, content and usage differ from other categories of records, and suggest how they require from the archivist additional skills and interests.

The prehistory of business archives

Among the archives of medieval and early modern institutions, there are plentiful examples of simple business records of the day-to-day dealings of merchants, shippers and financial middlemen. The records of Francesco Datini, a merchant of Prato in Italy in the later fourteenth century, are the most remarkable European example of this genre. Rediscovered in 1870, the Archivio Datini contains 140,000 letters, 500 ledgers and account books, and 300 other documents.[2]

In the United Kingdom the surviving evidence includes court case depositions which convey the methods and scale of enterprise in the early modern period. The 'Early Chancery Proceedings' series at the Public Record Office is a valuable source for the fourteenth to sixteenth centuries. Chancery exhibits include examples of merchants' trading accounts, and series from the High Court of Admiralty throw light upon shipping and shipbuilding in the fifteenth and sixteenth centuries.[3] In all these cases, however, the survival of business records has been incidental to the conscientious retention of records by courts of laws.

The true forerunners of modern business archives are those accumulations which were deliberately retained by a business unit for its own use. The purpose of retaining records in that way might be legal, fiscal, commercial or historical.

The guilds and companies of commercial centres such as London, Bristol and Norwich were conscientious in keeping records. The livery companies of London, which emerged in the fourteenth century as governing bodies over specific trades and occupations, maintained registers largely as a record of apprenticeship. The earliest of these series of registers, compiled by the Vintners' Company, dates back to the 1430s.[4] While such records do not reveal details of the day-to-day financial business in each trade, they are invaluable as evidence of the personnel and administration of the city's business community. The records of the Goldsmiths' Company, for example, have become a key source for fine art historians interested in the business careers of London goldsmiths and silversmiths.

While the livery companies retained records mainly as a membership register and rule book, other businessmen were retaining documents for commercial or tax reasons. Examples from the 1560s onwards include the customs farms in England and Wales, in which the crown leased the collection of duties on woollens, wines and luxury goods to entrepreneurs. In this foreshadowing of privatization, the customs 'farmers' were required to account to the crown for the collection of duties, their expenses and their profits. The crown in turn required to examine these records before assessing the rental for the next contract, with the result that copies of these business records have survived among state papers at the Public Record Office.[5] Similarly, whenever the crown placed the provisioning of its armies in the hands of private contractors, the business accounts of those contractors were eventually submitted to departments of state.

By the sixteenth century two recognizably modern reasons for retaining business records were in evidence. Firstly, any business which included an element of safe-custody or long-term contract could only operate effectively by keeping registers of its dealings. The Chamber of Assurances, established at the Royal Exchange in London in 1576, was known to have maintained a 'Book of Assurances'.[6] That register has not survived but it would have included specifications of marine insurance policies and the prototypes of life assurances. More tangibly, the London goldsmiths kept registers of gold, silver and jewellery left with them for repair or (increasingly after the English Civil War) safe custody. The ledgers of Edward Backwell, covering the period 1663 to 1672 and now held in the archives of The Royal Bank of Scotland, have a particularly important place in financial history; they demonstrate how the goldsmiths' business shifted from safe-custody services to banking transactions in the later seventeenth century.[7] The earliest records of other long-established London banks, such as Coutts and Childs, also reflect this transition from safe custody to banking business.

The second important impulse towards the retention of business records in the seventeenth century was the rise of the joint-stock company. The formation of these companies, which were owned by shareholders and operated according to agreed rules of business, introduced the responsibility to keep records of the company's proceedings and to report back to the company's shareholders. This was (and remains) a powerful influence upon record-keeping in business. The Levant Company, founded in 1581, left a continuous series of records until 1866.[8] Few records of the Russia Company (1555) and Barbary Company (1585) have survived but their great contemporary the East India Company gave birth to a major collection of business records. Founded in 1600, the Company dominated British interests in India and the Far East for over 250 years. From the outset it was meticulous and highly bureaucratic in its documentation, not only for the sake of its business operations but also in accordance with its duties to stockholders.[9]

Business archives in the eighteenth and nineteenth centuries

The themes of safe-custody and joint-stock regulation were both important ingredients in the development of banking and insurance from the late seventeenth century. In these two sectors, the presence of safe-custody services and joint-stock status were to produce the largest and some of the longest-established business archives in the United Kingdom. Uninterrupted series of insurance policy registers were produced by the Hand-in-Hand Insurance Company from 1696, the Sun Fire office from 1710 and the Royal Exchange Assurance from 1753.[10] With policy premiums being determined on a renewable 7-year basis, it was vital that the insurance offices retained details of their customers' property over a long period. Similarly bankers' loans, mortgages, investments and some bill transactions could be expected to have long renewable lives. Bankers, like the insurance companies, also required comprehensive records of their shareholders' investments and dividends; in some cases, their records were available for inspection by their customers and shareholders. Under these conditions the Bank of England was generating substantial series of business records immediately after its foundation in 1694, and the collection can fairly claim to be the longest-established business archive in use in the United Kingdom. North of the border the Bank of Scotland's archive is continuous from the date of the Bank's foundation in Edinburgh in 1695, while The Royal Bank of Scotland's collection dates from 1727.[11]

In England and Wales the 'Bubble Act' of 1720 brought joint-stock promotions in banking and insurance to a halt. Nevertheless, when the Bubble Act was eventually repealed in 1826, new joint-stock companies again proved very productive in terms of record-keeping. Whereas privately owned banks were not regulated as to the records they should retain, joint-stock banks and insurance companies were governed by the rules which they had agreed with their shareholders, and developed a complex machinery of documented accounting and decision-making. Indeed joint-stock companies were producing detailed retention schedules as early as the mid-Victorian period. In the 1870s, for example, the by-laws of the London Joint Stock Bank required 'That there shall be a fire-proof apartment in the Bank to be called the "Library" in which shall be arranged in convenient order for reference such of the Books as have been disused for six years and under, and another called the "Repository" for such as have been disused more than six years and are to be kept for a longer period'.[12] The by-laws also laid down specific and varying retention periods, including perpetuity for minute books, private ledgers, signature books, and letter books; 20 years for security books and customer ledgers;

10 years for cash books, acceptance books, and bill books; 6 years for pass books, stamp books and waste books; and 1 year for attendance books, bankers' payments, trial books and other sundries.

From the 1830s the formalized accumulation of business records became a feature of all types of joint-stock companies, including shipping companies, mining and exploration concerns, and the railway companies, with their massive clerical bureaucracies. In successive Companies Acts between 1856 and 1907 it became compulsory for a growing proportion of this documentation to be retained indefinitely (see Chapter 2).

The imperatives of joint-stock regulation and safe custody were not the only reasons why a business retained its records in the eighteenth and nineteenth centuries. Long-term documentation could be needed for commercial and industrial information. The voluminous archives of British brewers and distillers were partly retained as a working guide to recipes, output from different breweries and stills, and for tax reasons. Manufacturing concerns such as shipbuilders and locomotive engineers held on to their specifications and working drawings for the good practical reason that their customers would need replacement parts or repeat orders. For a company such as Chubb, which was manufacturing safes and other security equipment, a permanent record of mechanisms, keys and settings was in effect part of the product.

In contrast, by the nineteenth century some British firms were already retaining records with a view to posterity. This applied particularly to long-established family firms, where business records were the natural counterparts to genealogical information. Examples of this type of record-keeping included the archives of trading concerns such as Twinings, manufacturers such as Josiah Wedgwood & Sons (which opened its museum as long ago as 1906) and merchant banks, notably Barings and Rothschilds. Yet in these cases the accumulation of business records was not for antiquarian reasons alone. By the later nineteenth century all sectors of British business were anxious to celebrate their ancestry. In a period when advertising was increasingly elaborate, the heading 'Established 17XX' or '18XX' was perceived as a strong commercial advantage. These overt references to the business past began to feature in advertisements, company documents, and packaging, and were even engraved in stone over the doorways of commercial buildings.

For all these different motives, a significant number of British enterprises had accumulated major collections of business records by the beginning of the twentieth century. In each case the existence of the records was accepted as an integral part of the business. Pressure on storage space was not great, the cost of clerical labour was not usually heavy, and administrative structures (especially in joint-stock companies) were not ceaselessly changing in the late Victorian and Edwardian period. Nevertheless these collections were essentially for the private information of their parent companies, shareholders and customers. They were not yet on a public stage, any more than the archives of universities, hospitals, municipalities or other institutions were open to public view. Admittedly the records of government had been partly available for consultation since the nineteenth century; in Scotland there were search facilities at Register House as early as 1847, while in London the Public Record Office at Chancery Lane was opened in 1856. At the beginning of the twentieth century, however, these examples of archive provision remained exceptional.

New directions in business archives in the early twentieth century

From the early years of this century the appearance of an increasing number of company histories, mostly privately printed, presaged a change in the role of business archives. Historical studies of the Bank of England had been published as early as 1695[13] but after 1900 a great variety of other businesses celebrated their ancestry in this way. Francis Goodall's recent bibliography of business histories refers to only 340 company histories published before 1900. The equivalent number for the period 1901 to 1940 is 650.[14]

To modern business historians the contents of this vintage of company histories may seem antiquarian, supplying anecdote rather than analysis. These publications were nonetheless important for the future of business archives. Here were examples of long-standing company archives being employed in a public or semi-public fashion. Here were publications indicating that business archives had a historical value beyond the obvious commercial and legal necessities of record-keeping.

The multiplication of company histories at this level coincided with a new appreciation of the importance of business in economic history. For the first time business history was being considered as an option for serious study. In the United States, N. S. B. Gras and his colleagues at Harvard were using case studies in business history in the teaching syllabus of the Graduate School of Business Administration, an initiative that led to the formation of a special interest group, the Business History Society, in 1926. Meanwhile in the United Kingdom economic historians were already penetrating business archives as a source for studying the Industrial Revolution. This was a highly productive phase for research in economic history, and in the 1920s and early 1930s its output included the remarkable series of monographs published by Manchester University Press — G. W. Daniels, George Unwin, A. P. Wadsworth and Julia Mann on the cotton industry; T. S. Ashton on iron and steel; and Ashton and J. Sykes on the coal industry. At the very moment when businessmen were increasingly prepared to celebrate their companies' history in print, economic historians were demonstrating the importance of the business firm in economic history.[15]

Clearly it was not enough for businessmen and academics to agree upon the value of business archives and the utility of business history. Almost as soon as the business past became a recognizable cause, it also became a rescue mission. Economic historians were excited by the rich resources of business archives, and knew that the United Kingdom's pioneering role in industrial development made those resources unique. On the other hand, they were powerfully impressed by the risks which threatened the future of business collections. Neglect was already a real problem. In one of the great texts in business archives, George Unwin's preface to *Samuel Oldknow and the Arkwrights* recounts:

> The distribution of some eighteenth century weavers' pay-tickets by an adventurous boy scout to casual passers-by led Mr Arthur Hulme to obtain permission to explore the upper floor of this building [Arkwright's cotton mill at Mellor, near Stockport in Cheshire] and here on January 1st, 1921 . . . we found a great number of letters, papers, account books and other business records of every kind and size, covering the whole floor of a large room and partly hidden from sight by several inches of dust and debris. To all appearances the records had lain there for a century . . .[16]

Neglect was not the only challenge to accumulations of old business records. The mechanization of accounting, the replacement of ledgers by loose-leaf binders, the growing cost of office accommodation (especially in the City of London) and the loud rumble of recession in 1929–30 were all signs that business archives were under threat.

Economic historians were not the only ones to spot the danger. Some companies were already prepared to reduce the risks to their heritage. In the early years of the century the Bank of England had established a separate records office in Surrey and from 1933 J. A. Giuseppi was given special responsibility for the Bank's history and records. An 'Archive Committee' was appointed in 1938, with the objective of collecting records and statistics, and from 1946 the Bank of England maintained its own historical records section.[17] Elsewhere on the banking scene, Wilfred Crick and John Wadsworth based their history of the Midland Bank solidly upon primary archive sources.[18] On completion of that project in 1936, they systematically brought together into a central archive the collections which they had located throughout England and Wales.

The formation of the Business Archives Council

The proven historical value of business archives, balanced against the risks of neglect or destruction, now persuaded a group of historians and businessmen that a focus was needed to raise awareness of the subject. The foundation of the British Records Association in 1932 was an influence here, showing that diverse interest groups could rally round the flag of records preservation. The Association's main campaign, however, was devoted to the safety of manorial records and it could not be expected to embrace the special problems of business records. Consequently in June 1932 Eileen Power, professor of economic history at the London School of Economics, proposed to the School the formation of a 'Committee for the Study and Preservation of London Business Archives'.[19] Professor Power envisaged that such a Committee could compile a register of business archives in London, with the School's library acting as a depository for records at risk. These proposals won wider backing during 1933 (although the limitation to London business archives was not pursued), and on 11 May 1934 the inaugural meeting of the Council for the Preservation of Business Archives was held at the London School of Economics. The formation of the Council (renamed the Business Archives Council in 1952) was announced in a letter to *The Times* in June 1934.

In the evolution of business archives as a whole there was now a focus for effort and advice. The public commitment to compile a register of all business archives over 100 years old showed that the initiative was much more than a club of enthusiasts. So too did the Council's willingness to arrange for the deposit of business archives and its concern for questions of access to confidential records. The outcome, in the Council's first 5 years, was the creation of a card-index register based upon a questionnaire survey of old-established businesses.

This progress gave business archives an identity and personality rather earlier than other specialist areas in the archives community. The Council's aims and objectives were also remarkably far-sighted in the context of the 1930s. 'This was a world', Peter Mathias points out, 'without a National Register of Archives, where County Record offices were far from universal and where they existed did not usually acknowledge any responsibility for . . . business records'.[20] Although the effort to treat business archives as a serious case for study and preservation was almost without parallel, not only in the United Kingdom but throughout the world, that effort was essentially a private initiative. The Master of the Rolls and officials of the Public Record Office had been involved in the preliminary meetings of the Council but there was no question that it was an official or government-supported body. The Council – and the subject as a whole – was dependent upon voluntary efforts and subscriptions from a small group of banks, companies and other institutions. Consequently both in its first years and in the decade after the Second World War the Council survived on a narrow ledge of support. By 1951 there were only 51 members, including businesses and individual historians and archivists.

Business archives in the post-war setting

Bombing, shortages of paper, evacuation of offices and disposal of businesses had heavily increased the risks to all categories of records during the Second World War. The importance of registering archives, as advocated by the British Records Association and the Business Archives Council since the early 1930s, was never more obvious. In 1945 this approach was given extra impetus by the formation of the National Register of Archives (NRA), under the auspices of the Royal Commission on Historical Manuscripts. The NRA (together with its counterpart in Scotland formed in 1948) was designed as a directory to public and private collections throughout the country. Its main contributions came initially from local voluntary committees, gradually replaced by the growing number of county record offices and other local authority archives, but its remit also included the registration of private family papers and business archives. As a result the NRA began to play an important role in the dissemination of information about business collections. From 1959 to 1972 the annual list of *Accessions to Repositories*, published by the Royal Commission on Historical Manuscripts, included a special section on business records and from 1973 the Commission permitted the abstracting of all business entries for publication in *Business Archives*. Between 1965 and 1972 the Commission also produced a typescript guide to sources of business history in the NRA, and its *Secretary's Reports* provided descriptions of recently located business collections.

One of the Register's major contributions to the archive scene in the United Kingdom has been the way in which from the outset it treated all categories of records as part of the nation's inheritance of archives. In the post-war period this attitude also became more evident in county and municipal record offices; some (but by no means all) local archivists were now ready to accept business collections as gifts or loans from companies and firms. The outstanding example of this change of approach was the Guildhall Library in London, where in the 1950s Albert Hollaender treated the collection of business archives as a priority. This policy won the confidence of the City's business community, enabling the Guildhall Library to bring together the records of livery companies, insurance offices and a host of other business concerns. The result is that today the Guildhall Library offers the finest collection of financial archives anywhere in the world.

The example of the Guildhall Library was evidence that the archive profession now treated business archives as a recognizable part of its responsibilities. Even so by the early 1960s a keen researcher using the indexes of the National Register of Archives would have found remarkably few collections of business records on the Register. At the Business Archives Council the pre-war register had been supplemented from time to time and lists of business records held by public libraries were circulated to members; but the total number of entries remained small. Although hundreds of companies maintained valuable collections of records, only a very tiny number had taken the step of treating their archives as a distinct responsibility.

Admittedly the Council's business membership had increased markedly, from merely 9 in 1950 to 80 in 1965, yet in the majority of cases these memberships were messages of support for the aims of the Council rather than signs that business members had made specific provision for their archives.

At the same time, however, a new generation of economic historians was turning to the study of business history, with a more analytical, quantitative approach to the subject and higher expectations of the sources which they might find. Many of them were being commissioned for prestigious company histories – Charles Wilson on Unilever, Bill Reader on ICI, Theo Barker on Pilkingtons, Donald Coleman on Courtaulds, Barry Supple on the Royal Exchange Assurance and Bernard Alford on W. D. & H. O. Wills.[21] As users of business archives, these historians knew of the research and teaching potential of this category of records. Their students, with grant support from the new Social Science Research Council (SSRC), often chose research topics geared to business archives. Indeed, in a survey of research in economic and social history published by the SSRC in 1971, business history was specified as a key area of research opportunity.[22] Under this leadership, and at a time of expansion throughout higher education and research, the study of the business past now appeared to be a serious and well-supported option.

Surveys of business archives in the 1960s and 1970s

The heavyweight business histories published in the 1960s and 1970s were principally concerned with large and successful companies offering extensive in-house archives. Evidently these subjects were only a small section of the business past, and many historians and archivists felt that the records of medium-sized companies, small local firms and unsuccessful businesses also deserved attention. This concern for the typical and ordinary as well as the brilliant high-achievers in business was a theme of Peter Mathias's work on brewing, Peter Payne's studies of the rubber and steel industries, and Roy Church's work on a West Midlands hardware firm.[23]

The search for a broader spectrum of business archives was a vital ingredient in a series of surveys undertaken in the 1960s and 1970s. These surveys, based upon particular regions or industrial categories, have been major factors in the modern development of business archives. The registration of collections (which had been one of the Business Archives Council's original objectives) was the chief priority. Whereas the business archivists of the 1930s had been forced to rely upon questionnaires, the surveys of the 1960s and 1970s were more practical in their methods and results.

One of the earliest and most effective examples of these surveys was based at the University of Glasgow. When the Colquhoun Lectureship in Business History was established in 1959, it was expected that the jobholder would survey and rescue business collections in the West of

Scotland, an objective enthusiastically taken up by Peter Payne, who held the lectureship between 1959 and 1969. It was a 'hands-on' approach to business archives, sorting and listing records on site and where possible arranging for the deposit of records at Glasgow University, the Mitchell Library, Glasgow City Archives or other local record offices. At a time when the West of Scotland economy was under severe pressure, many important collections were saved from extinction. The initial results of the project were published in *Studies in Scottish Business History*, edited by Payne, in 1967.[24] It was significant that Payne's book set the results of his survey alongside case studies in business history — an integrated approach to business history and business archives which has been characteristic of Glasgow for a quarter of a century and which has recently been described as 'the Glasgow School of archive administration'.[25]

The impetus of the Glasgow project was maintained when the National Register of Archives (Scotland) (NRA(S)) took on responsibility for surveying in 1969. Although the Regional Surveys run by the NRA(S) between 1969 and 1977 were also designed to cover estate papers, it was inevitable that a higher proportion of their reports and deposits related to business. A remarkable series of large-scale rescues was carried out in the early 1970s, notably the transfer of the records of Upper Clyde Shipbuilders to the Scottish Record Office and Glasgow University in 1972. Government finance and co-operation were indispensable in this survey work. With the exception of the Public Record Office in Northern Ireland, which took in about 300 substantial collections of business papers in the 1950s and early 1960s, there had not been any comparable official involvement until then in the preservation of business archives in the United Kingdom. That involvement was eventually reduced but survey work still continues with official and private sponsorship under the auspices of the Business Archives Council of Scotland.[26]

In England and Wales a number of early survey projects were also university-based. Surveys of British records relating to the British Dominions (at London University's Institute of Commonwealth Studies), South East Asia (at Cambridge University), and the Middle East (Oxford University) were all initiated in the 1960s and early 1970s.[27] In each case they included lists of business archives as well as other categories of records, although they relied more heavily on questionnaires than the Scottish surveys had done. A survey of the West Riding woollen and worsted industries, which was financed by the Pasold Research Fund and completed in 1973, took a very different approach,[28] with a meticulous listing of the archives of about 100 companies of all ages and sizes. The vast majority of these collections had already been transferred to public libraries, museums and local history societies, but the survey was the first opportunity to identify and evaluate such a large haul. This type of regional, sectoral approach was also adopted in Coventry Polytechnic's survey of industrial archives in Coventry.[29] At the same time the insurance industry was sponsoring a major archival survey, which compiled and published lists of the archives of over 300 insurance companies and institutions,[30] and also secured the permanent retention of a number of major insurance collections.

Initially the Business Archives Council was not closely engaged in this strong upsurge of surveying activity. This was partly because it could not match the staff and resources of the university departments undertaking the surveys and partly because the Council seemed 'to be growing further away from its potential'.[31] An almost complete change of personnel in 1968 altered the Council's stance. Peter Mathias was elected chairman, and professional archivists such as Tom Ingram, David Avery, Len Mcdonald and Richard Storey were strongly represented in the reinvigorated Council. The business archivist, who had always been the junior partner to the historian and to the businessman in the Council's affairs, now took an executive role in the Council's development. Sam Twining of R. Twining & Co., whose family had been keenly interested in the Council since its foundation, became deputy chairman and succeeded Mathias as chairman in 1972.

From 1968 the Council reappraised its commitment to publications. Its journal, *Business Archives*, became a monitor for new activities and discoveries in the subject. Not least, the Council took an active role in surveying business records in particular industries. The first result was a survey of shipping records, published in 1972, followed by a survey of shipbuilding records (undertaken jointly with the Business Archives Council in Scotland) between 1975 and 1978.[32] A major survey of banking records, initiated in 1969, was revived in 1977 and completed in 1984.[33] In each of these cases the Council turned to the business world for finance for full-time survey work. From 1975 the Council's Advisory Service also carried out surveys and rescues of records at risk, with indispensable support from the Royal Commission on Historical Manuscripts. Over the past 15 years the service has completed surveys of several hundred businesses, including many small or medium-sized firms, and has also arranged the deposit of scores of important collections.[34]

Business archives in record offices

Survey activity in the 1960s and 1970s had introduced a new dynamic into the collection and availability of business archives, yet by the 1970s other factors were also broadening the constituency of the subject. Both the supply of, and the demand for, business archives were changing sharply in character. Whereas in 1960 relatively few collections of business archives had reached record offices, 10 years later a significant migration was under way. The *Guide to Sources of Business History in the National Register of Archives*, published in 1972 by the Royal Commission on Historical Manuscripts, listed over 400 business collections, of which the majority were already held in local record offices or university libraries. Thereafter the total multiplied rapidly, and by the late 1980s the NRA held details of the archives of nearly 15,000 businesses. Access to this immense resource had by then been greatly improved by the overhaul of the NRA's companies index, particularly through the introduction of computer-search facilities. In addition, business records were included in the Royal Commission's series of guides to sources in the NRA. One volume in the series has been devoted to textiles and leather and a forthcoming volume to the engineering industries.

The facilities and services of local record offices were also more widely known, as archivists took an increasingly public role in their communities. Some county archivists canvassed local businesses for deposits; elsewhere, as in the Hampshire and Kent areas in the 1980s,[35] surveys of business records by county record offices led to the rescue of the papers of many small local businesses. Other record offices established reputations as custodians of the records of particular industries. The Guildhall Library's special position *vis-à-vis* financial records has already been mentioned. Other examples included Tyne and Wear County Archives with its fine collections of shipbuilding records; Merseyside County Archives, whose shipping and shipbuilding collections have now been transferred to the National Museum and Galleries on Merseyside; Leeds City (now Leeds District) Archives, where the acquisition of textile industry archives had been part of policy since the 1960s; and Birmingham Reference Library, with its unparalleled collection of Boulton and Watt archives.

National repositories also became active collectors of business records. The National Maritime Museum had been receiving business records of the shipping industry since 1960, but in the 1970s its holdings greatly increased as companies such as P & O, Furness Withy and Lloyd's Register placed records on loan with the museum.[36] The Science Museum accepted a number of business collections, including the Pearson archives, while the Victoria and Albert Museum was especially interested in business records in the field of fine arts and design. Outside London the Public Record Office of Northern Ireland, the National Library of Wales and the Scottish Record Office all accumulated substantial collections of business archives and provided valuable co-operation to the various surveys of business records which were under way from the 1960s.

The universities played their part in the migration of business archives. In many cases their collecting activities were linked to the research activities of individual historians or departments. This had certainly been the case at Glasgow, where the Colquhoun Lectureship in Business History had been such an influence. By the 1970s Glasgow's archives of shipbuilding, engineering and other heavy industries had become an international resource. Similarly, at Liverpool University, the transfer of the Cunard collection was linked to the specialization in shipping history in the University's department of economic history.

In these examples the universities were mainly interested in pre-eminent collections. Other universities took a different approach, establishing archive centres for the acquisition of specific types of records, regardless of the size or importance of their originating companies. The Institute of

Agricultural History at Reading University was established in 1968 with the task of collecting the archives of agricultural engineers and other farming businesses. At Warwick University the formation of the Modern Records Centre in 1973 was designed primarily to attract records of labour and industrial relations (including the records of employers' associations), but it was also prepared to accept the records of twentieth-century companies where no other suitable repositories could be found.[37]

Archivists from all types of record office were adopting a more positive attitude to the value and potential of business archives and were taking active steps to ensure their preservation. This shift in attitude coincided with unprecedented changes in the economic landscape, and if archivists had not been able to respond in this period, large tracts of the British business scene would have been left unrecorded. Most of the collections described above were drawn from companies whose existence was under real threat in the 1960s and early 1970s, especially in the heavy industries. Not for the first or last time take-overs, rationalization and asset-stripping were putting records at risk. Property redevelopment and relocation of offices meant that even the most secure companies were capable of peremptory destruction of records. Yet this period also saw the rescue of some of the finest collections of business records, almost literally from the back of the lorry of the waste contractor. Upper Clyde Shipbuilders, Rolls-Royce and Jensen are only the better-known examples.

This great migration helped to create a new tradition in business archives, namely, the archivist employed by a record office but essentially a specialist in business archives. The arrival of large collections required him or her to develop new methods of listing bulky and technically complex series of records. The archivist needed to become familiar with management structures and objectives unlike any seen in central or local government. Above all, these sources demanded expertise in the format and interpretation of business archives (especially accounting and technical records) if future users were to have any chance of unlocking the potential of these records. In the 1970s and 1980s the contribution of this tradition in business archives has been enormous, to the point where archivists in record offices in the United Kingdom are as experienced in dealing with business records as anywhere in the archive world.

Important problems remain. Some record offices regard business archives as a low priority, even if their repositories are located in a heartland of economic and business history. Others, after initially taking in large volumes of business papers, found that they had neither the space nor the cataloguing resources to cope with a great backlog of complex business records. Some archivists justifiably complained that the usage rate for their new collections was so low as to discourage them from taking in similar collections (though this must surely be a risk with most high-volume sets of records). With business records, as with other types of private papers, the conditions of deposit and access can also cause difficulties.

None of these problems need be insurmountable, and in recent years there has been much greater realism in agreements between companies and record offices, particularly on the question of storage and conservation costs. Less easily overcome is the public archivist's isolation from the business environment which created the records – inevitable where a company has ceased to exist or where it is so transformed that it has entirely abandoned the original business reflected in the records. Yet where there is any continuity in the business, it is vital that the public archivist has an agreement with the depositing company. It is equally important that the donor business understands that a record office cannot, and will not, provide a research and information service as well as a custodial and listing operation. In these areas the transfer of a business archive to a record office is an incomplete substitute for an in-house business archive.

The archivist in business

Although institutions such as the Bank of England had made provision for their archives from the 1930s, it was not until the 1960s that a measurable number of businesses appointed full- or part-time archivists. In 1965 there were no more than a dozen such appointments,[38] but now 26 years later, there are at least 100 archivists in the field.[39] The archivist in business is an essential part of the identity of business archives, but it must be recognized that the tradition is still comparatively recent.

Appointments of business archivists in this period have been made for an extraordinary variety of reasons. In some British companies archivists have been recruited purely and simply to identify and safeguard a collection as an historical asset. This was the pattern in a number of companies where family involvement in the business was particularly strong. For most companies, however, their archives could not be isolated from the business itself; business records remained in use for a mixture of commercial, legal, administrative and other reasons.

In these conditions it was often a new or external factor which led to the appointment of a company archivist. At the John Lewis Partnership, for instance, the centenary of the business in 1964 was the spur. History projects were also an important stimulus for archives development at *The Times*. In other examples it was the *completion* of a company history which inspired the decision to recruit an archivist. The volume of enquiries, and the resultant drain on management time, was an important factor here. It has also been known for a company to establish a professional archives service as a security measure for the protection of the asset value of its collection. The public relations potential of business archives increasingly came into play in the 1970s, particularly where the employment of an archivist was linked to a museum and educational facilities, as at Colman's of Norwich and J. Sainsbury.

The most common denominator, however, was a business decision that an in-house archivist would contribute to, and perhaps take control of, the management of a company's records. Although in the 1960s and 1970s British companies were employing a variety of systems designers or organization and methods professionals to advise on their records systems, this expertise was usually devoted to records in current usage. Records management was needed to control documents throughout their life-cycle if a company was to stand any chance of identifying and retaining essential categories of business information. From the 1960s onwards many British companies appointed archivists with the specific responsibility for records management; examples include the British Steel Corporation, British Petroleum, Burmah Oil, the Bank of Scotland, and Guinness Brewing.

In the 1960s not all these appointments had been full-time archive posts. Archive responsibilities might be part-time or in combination with other duties – for example, in economics or public relations. Twenty years later, in contrast, the majority of in-house business archivists in the United Kingdom were full-time professionals with archive training or other relevant qualifications. The largest institutions could assemble small teams of archivists and records managers but the more typical unit was a single archivist with one or two archive and clerical assistants. Their ranking within a business organization was rarely linked to the type of career path followed by archivists in local record offices, and, while some companies treated their archive function as a managerial role, others saw the responsibility as a relatively junior clerical post.

Many of the problems confronting archivists in business paralleled those in any other record office. The archivist would almost certainly face a large backlog of unidentified business records, and would need to devise methods of storing, listing, and bringing them into use. Whether or not records management responsibilities had been written into the job description, the archivist would also wish to have the opportunity to appraise recently non-current records and prepare for the transfer of selected classes for archive retention. Above all, the archivist would need to understand the past and present administrative structures which were giving birth to the records of the business.

This much the newly appointed business archivist shared with any member of the archive profession. There was even common ground in the types of record which the archivist was now dealing with, especially if he or she had been familiar with business collections held in local record offices. Similarly any archivist who had grown used to the decision-making records of a government department, a local authority, a nationalized industry (or even a recently privatized company) would not be totally surprised by record-keeping practices in business.

The business archivist's appointment nonetheless differed crucially in the environment in which it was placed and the disciplines which were required of it. The profitability, cost-effectiveness and public profile of the business are the imperatives of that environment, and the company archivist cannot afford to ignore them or become isolated from their influence. The fact that a company has accepted the need for an archive service does not mean that it will stop looking for ways of making more effective use of that service. It is all the more important that the archivist has a strong sense of 'positioning' within the organization and can adapt to its methods of management and communication (see Chapter 17). This is vital to identifying those parts of the company whose records will be of strategic importance, but it is also vital to understanding the changing needs and perceptions within the organization. Most business archivists will acknowledge that their jobs have altered in character as the fortunes and interests of their employers have changed. The business archivist needs to be professionally watchful of these changes, constantly aware of their impact in record-keeping and their effect on the role of archive services.[40]

In these demanding circumstances the business archivist can expect to answer a wide variety of needs within the organization. In addition to records management duties and the physical care of business archives, there will be regular requests for legal and management information up to the highest level. The documentation and reasons behind relatively recent decisions are frequently in play in business strategy, and the archivist will often be dealing with highly confidential modern or *sub judice* material.

These are tasks that must be trusted to a member of the company and which the archivist is best placed to perform. The same constraint applies to the company's frequent need for information about former members of staff, shareholders or customers. In addition the modern business archivist is almost certain to be drawn into more public duties. Co-operating with public relations and marketing projects, supplying and editing text, and taking a full part in historical exhibitions and anniversary events help to bring business archives into meaningful use, and can also widen the constituency of support for the archive function. In the same way involvement in training programmes, whether for induction schemes or management education, ensures that the business archivist is appropriately and visibly part of the practicalities of business development.

These different roles, which are examined in more detail in other chapters of this book, show that the archivist in business has multiple tasks requiring all-round skills. Equally, in their custodial role few company archivists are responsible exclusively for business records. In any archive post they might expect to have care of documentary sources, photographs, sound and video tape, cinematographic films, microforms and computer output. In a business setting they might also find themselves overseeing picture, furniture and silver collections, along with accumulations of historical artefacts. These responsibilities may arrive by indirect or accidental routes, but in most business situations the archivist may be the best-placed person to give serious and sympathetic treatment to these varied aspects of the company's history. In these ways the duties of a modern business archivist can be unexpectedly broad in scope. The job, often with few resources at its disposal, needs ingenuity and adaptability. In the business archives community as a whole, these same qualities are now needed in responding to the growth of public interest in business collections.

The uses of business history: changing patterns of demand

Among the pioneers of business archives in the 1920s and 1930s, businessmen as well as academics assumed that the main users of business collections would be company and economic historians. This was, and remains, an important tradition in business archives. As more and more collections have become accessible, either in record offices or in company archives, increasing numbers of British and overseas historians have turned to these records as their primary sources. A small but steadily increasing number of postgraduate theses have also been built mainly on business archives, and visits to company archives have now become a regular part of induction courses for postgraduate historians. Not least the publication of business histories brings the message of the business past to a wider readership. Since 1977 between 10 and 20 new books have been submitted each year as entries for the Wadsworth Prize for Business History, an award administered by the Business Archives Council for outstanding work on British business history; and with few exceptions, this steady flow of new publications was the outcome of serious research on business archive sources.

Providing a service to these users is and will continue to form a significant part of a business archivist's work. Pressures within the higher education system and the attitude of grant-making institutions to business and economic history will obviously affect the number of new projects. It is also disappointing that as yet the world of management education has made little use of business history and business archives, even when company records offer an obvious testbed for management theory and issues in business strategy. Nevertheless the proliferation of business history units in universities and polytechnics can be expected to maintain or even increase the demand for access to business archives. Most of the projects of the Business History Unit, established at the London School of Economics in 1978, have been source-based; and the new units at Bristol Polytechnic, Glasgow University, Coventry Polytechnic, Manchester Polytechnic and Reading University are staffed by historians who are experienced users of business archives. Moreover the results of recent surveys of business records will make it possible for these users to take a more comparative cross-sectional approach to their subject; with potential access to many thousands of business collections, historians of enterprise are no longer confined to the traditional case-study approach.

These users will continue to look for access to business archives, and in some cases they will hope that the business archivist (whether in a public record office or company archive) will provide guidance and even supervision. In the 1980s a number of business archivists themselves contributed research input to business history projects; others had experience as company historians. As a reflection of this close relationship, historians are well represented on the committees of the Business Archives

Council and the Business Archives Council (Scotland), while archivists are represented on the management committees of a number of business history units. This alliance between business historians and archivists is likely to remain a characteristic feature of the business archives scene.

In the past two decades historians with other special interests than business history have also turned to business archives – not through fascination with a particular business but because those records offer information about the business's customers and local environment. From the 1960s fire insurance policy registers were used to analyse the capital and equipment employed by eighteenth- and early nineteenth-century manufacturers. In the case of small firms no other record of their operations has survived.[41] Similarly Joyce Bellamy, Philip Cottrell and other historians have investigated banking records, finding that this type of material is often as useful for non-financial information about customers and local conditions as it is for the more predictable financial material.[42] Fine art historians have taken a similar route, using financial records to fill gaps in the careers and patronage of individual artists and craftsmen.

This *lateral* use of business archives multiplied greatly in the 1970s and 1980s. Historians of labour have sought out company wage books and other personnel records,[43] while social historians have used these sources to study the role of women in employment. Historians of science have turned to the specifications and drawings generated by manufacturing firms. Historical geographers value business records for the voluminous information they offer on local, regional and international transactions. Business records have also proved their worth in the long-running debate over the links between business wealth and social elites in Victorian and Edwardian Britain.[44] Biographers of public figures have consulted business archives if their subjects had directorships or other connections in the business world.[45] Historians of architecture have also become serious users of business records, particularly where a company has inherited or commissioned large numbers of commercial buildings.[46]

In all these areas the business archivist is answering the requirements of different disciplines within history, where the priorities and methods of research might be markedly different. Yet perhaps the overriding feature of business archives usage in the 1970s and 1980s was the entry of users who would not describe themselves as historians in any case. Here the archivist may need to give an enquiry from a school project or group of enthusiasts as much care as an enquiry from an academic or postgraduate historian. That enquiry may relate to the family history of a former employee; it may come from a local civic trust interested in the history (or even archaeology) of a commercial building; or it may come from a hobbyist or collector interested in the design and specification of a ship, a railway locomotive or a motor car. Increasingly and in ever greater numbers that enquiry might come from a picture researcher working on a publication or television programme concerned with the business past.

The user-group for business archives today is probably much wider than that envisaged when companies first appointed archivists or deposited their papers in a record office. This could mean that the research requirements of the business and economic historians, which were for so long the uppermost considerations in the preservation of a business collection, will be increasingly shouldered aside by the demands of the non-specialist and the leisure user. For the business archivist this changing pattern of demand is the opportunity to ensure that the interests of all actual and potential were of a collection are taken into account – a heavy but necessary responsibility.

Business archives in the 1980s and 1990s: achievements and prospects

Changes in the uses of business archives have meant that such archives have been transformed from a narrow resource for historians into a multi-purpose information source. As a result, the business archivist is frequently overlapping and sharing with other disciplines, such as museum curators, librarians, information scientists, and (in appointments where there is demarcation) records management. In many if not most companies these neighbouring disciplines are given primacy over business archives,

In this context the business archivist should not be shy about the identity of the subject. There are strong and recognizable traditions in business archives – its early development as a specialist area in archives and economic history, the expertise developed by record offices in collecting business records, and the multiplication of effective archive facilities in companies. The business archivist can also point to solid achievements in the subject. The tradition of surveying and registering business records, in particular, has given the United Kingdom a range of public information about business archives which is unparalleled in the world and which draws increasing numbers of users from overseas. This achievement is at the same time an opportunity. International co-operation in business archives has increased markedly in recent years, partly through the International Council on Archives and partly as multinational companies have become the custodians of multinational archives. British experience in the survey of business records has a valuable role to play in this international dimension.

To build upon these traditions and achievements it is vital that the subject should have focal points of co-operation and development. Since its foundation in 1947 the Society of Archivists has acted as the professional association for all groups of archivists, playing an important part in establishing technical standards, providing for training and influencing conditions of employment. In particular the formation of the Society's Records Management Group in 1977 gave business archivists with responsibilities for records management a new forum for meetings, conferences and occasional publications for professional archivists. The Records Management Society, formed in 1983, caters specifically for records managers and information managers.

The Business Archives Council, together with its Northern and North Western branches and its sister Council in Scotland, remains a key point of contact for business archivists. In the 1980s the Council's publication programme has been the chief contributor to the literature of the subject, examining the principles and practice of business archives, as well as mapping out the available sources and showing how they may be used. Although the postgraduate diploma courses in archives include an option in business archives, the Council's short courses and residential course are effectively the only training tailored to business archivists.

The Council's recent surveys also offer pointers to the future development of the subject. In its surveying responsibilities the Council's Company Archives Survey was a complete break with the traditional sectoral or regional surveys. Established in 1980 and financed by the Economic and Social Research Council (the renamed SSRC), this major project surveyed the records of the oldest 1000 registered companies in England and Wales, regardless of their size or type of business. The outcome was the listing of the records of 674 companies and 1000 subsidiaries – an extraordinary array of manufacturing, commercial and financial companies, mining and transport concerns active both at home and overseas, companies in the arts and entertainment, and even social and political clubs. The survey was a properly cross-sectional view of British business in the nineteenth and twentieth centuries. The published results also differed from previous surveys by supplying profiles of the companies covered by the survey.[47] In effect the survey was adding an information and research role to the traditional work of surveying records and in many cases negotiating for their preservation.

The Company Archives Survey looked forward to a more active style of presenting business archives in which the user is given much more than a list of ingredients. This shift towards a larger research content in business archives can be expected to accelerate, fuelled by more widespread adoption of computer technology. As a species, business archives are inherently bulky and difficult to handle, and their sheer mass has often discouraged exploitation. In recent years, however, computer technology has transformed the outlook for business collections. On the one hand, archivists in record offices and in business are discovering that even relatively cheap micro-computer applications can simplify and speed up the tasks of listing, housing, and controlling their business archives. Database technology now offers huge scope for creating sophisticated finding aids and records management systems (see Chapter 13). On the other hand, computer applications offer the capacity and flexibility to unlock business sources which otherwise seem impenetrable. It is especially significant, both to archivists and to historians, that computer databases offer improved access to the myriad of individual transactions which are reflected in each set of business records. The user of business sources is often interested in only a single payment, a single person, a single event or decision; the construction and searching of computer databases brings that scale of enquiry within reach in a way which was impossible with most manual index systems.

In the 1970s the effort to produce a computerized index to fire insurance policy registers, in a major project financed by the Social Science Research Council, was an early and ambitious attempt to improve access to one of the richest collections of business archives.[48] The project demanded close co-ordination between archival and historical requirements. Since micro-computers have come into more common use in the 1980s, this type of technical support for business archives has become a much more realistic possibility. Archivists and historians are now experimenting with databases drawn from business archives both for research and teaching purposes. At Glasgow University a database built from the ledgers of Peter Denny is being introduced to a wide range of users, from postgraduates to evening classes, who would otherwise have found it difficult to deal with the original series of records.[49] Computers in teaching and research are playing an important role throughout the history professions, but few types of records are so suited to database presentation and analysis as business archives. The presentation of business archives in a more structured fashion, with the crucial support of computer technology, has an enormous potential.

Yet there remain areas of patchy progress and inadequate coverage. The records of small to medium-sized companies, which form the vast majority of business units, are poorly represented and highly vulnerable. Few such companies are in a position to make provision for their archives and most are not aware that their heritage may be of wider value and interest. These constraints also affect young companies, particularly in high-technology industries. Archivists may find it difficult to envisage 10-year old companies as suitable cases for treatment, but these offspring of the technological revolution are precisely the companies which will in time prize their origins and which will excite the interest of future historians. Moreover the business archivist cannot ignore the way in which some of the great names in British industry and commerce have yet to make any form of provision for their business archives; and some others have been prepared to abandon what progress had been made, destroying a long-term asset for a short-term saving. The privatization of state enterprises and utilities, many of them custodians of major collections of business and technical records, is a continuing cause of uncertainty. In all these areas there is no room for complacency over archive provision in business, especially in phases of economic turbulence and change.

In meeting these challenges it remains essential that the subject matter of business archives has strong traditions and a clear focus for new initiatives. In both the public and private sector the demands of business archives have created special skills and disciplines. Not least, the study of business archives is an identifiable cause within the history professions, with a great variety of adherents; its support comes not only from professionals in business archives but also from a growing body of sympathizers and allies in other subject areas. This variety of support is increasingly the strength of the subject and its greatest opportunity.

Notes

1   See, for example, D. C. Coleman, 'The uses and abuses of business history', *Business History*, 29 (1987), pp. 149–54; G. G. Jones, 'Where is business history?', *Business History Newsletter*, 13 (1986), pp. 3–4.

2   I. Origo, *The Merchant of Prato. Francesco di Marco Datini* (Cape, London, 1957).

3   *Guide to the Contents of the Public Record Office*, 1 (HMSO, London, 1963), pp. 7–44, 156–62.

4   Guildhall Library, Ms 15211/1. The wardens' accounts of the Mercers' Company (Mercers' Company Archives) date back to the 1340s. C. R. H. Cooper, 'The archives of the City of London livery companies and related organisations', *Archives*, 72 (1984), pp. 323–53.

5   For example, Public Record Office, E351/607–1268.

6   H. A. L. Cockerell and E. Green, *The British Insurance Business, 1547–1970* (Heinemann Educational Books, London, 1976), p. 4.

7   L. S. Pressnell and J. Orbell, *A Guide to the Historical Records of British Banking* (Gower, Aldershot, 1985), p. 4.

8   Public Record Office, SP 105.

9   J. Foster and J. Sheppard, *British Archives. A Guide to Archive Resources in the United Kingdom* (Macmillan, Basingstoke, 1982), pp. 257–8. The surviving records of the Russia Company are held at the Guildhall Library, London, classification L66.2.

10   These three series are deposited at the Guildhall Library, London; see also Cockerell and Green, *op. cit.*, ch 1.

11   Pressnell and Orbell, *British Banking*, *op. cit.*, pp. 6, 8–9, 94–5.

12   Midland Bank Group Archives, Q59–60.

13   T. A. Stephen, *A Contribution to the Bibliography of the Bank of England* (Effingham Wilson, 1897), pp. 5–10.

14   F. Goodall, *A Bibliography of British Business History* (Gower, Aldershot, 1987). Analysis kindly produced by Lesley Richmond, Library Adviser to the Business Archives Council.

15   P. Mathias, 'The first half century: business history, business archives and the Business Archives Council', *Business Archives*, 50 (1984), pp. 2–3.

16   G. Unwin, *Samuel Oldknow and the Arkwrights* (Manchester University Press, Manchester, 1924), pp. v–vi.

17   Information kindly provided by Henry Gillett, Archivist, Bank of England.

18   W. F. Crick and J. E. Wadsworth, *A Hundred Years of Joint Stock Banking* (Hodder & Stoughton, London, 1936).

19   The following section relies heavily upon Mathias, 'The first half century', *op. cit.*, pp. 3–9.

20   *Ibid.*, p. 3.

21   C. Wilson, *The History of Unilever*, 3 vols (1954 and 1968); W. J. Reader, *Imperial Chemical Industries: A History*, 2 vols (Oxford University Press,

1975); T. C. Barker, *Pilkington Brothers and the Glass Industry* (Allen and Unwin, London, 1960); D. C. Coleman, *Courtaulds : An Economic and Social History*, 3 vols (Oxford University Press, Oxford, 1969 and 1980); B. E. Supple, *The Royal Exchange Assurance. A History of British Insurance, 1720–1970* (Cambridge University Press, Cambridge, 1970); B. W. E. Alford, *W.D. & H. O. Wills and the Development of the UK Tobacco Industry, 1786–1965* (Methuen, London, 1973).

22 B. E. Supple (editor), *Research in Economic and Social History*, (SSRC, London, 1971).

23 P. Mathias, *The Brewing Industry in England, 1700–1830* (Cambridge University Press, Cambridge, 1959); P. L. Payne, *Rubber and Railways in the Nineteenth Century : A Study of the Spencer Papers* (Liverpool University Press, Liverpool, 1961); R. A. Church, *Kenricks in Hardware* (David & Charles, Newton Abbot, 1970).

24 P. L. Payne (editor), *Studies in Scottish Business History* (Cass & Co, London, 1967).

25 Michael Cook in *Society of Archivists, Computer Group Newsletter*, 8 (August 1988), p. 5.

26 M. Livingstone, 'Surveys surveyed', *Scottish Industrial History*, 7:1 (1984), pp. 5–7.

27 C. A. Jones, *Britain and the Dominions. A Guide to Business and Related Records in the United Kingdom concerning Australia, Canada, New Zealand and South Africa* (Hall & Co, Boston, Mass., 1978); M. Thatcher (editor), *Cambridge South Asian Archive* (Mansell, 1975); E. R. J. Owen and F. Dux, *A List of the Location of Records Belonging to British Firms and to British Businessmen Active in the Middle East, 1800–1950* (St Antony's College, Oxford, *c.*1973).

28 P. Hudson, *The West Riding Wool Textile Industry. A Catalogue of Business Records from the Sixteenth to the Twentieth Century* (Pasold Research Fund, Edington, Wiltshire, 1975).

29 J. Lane, *Register of Business Records of Coventry and Related Areas* (Lanchester Polytechnic, 1977)

30 Cockerell and Green, *British Insurance, op. cit.*

31 Mathias, 'The first half century', *op. cit.*, p. 12.

32 P. Mathias and A. W. H. Pearsall (editors), *Shipping : A Survey of Historical Records* (David & Charles, Newton Abbot, 1971); L. A. Ritchie, *Modern British Shipbuilding. A Guide to Historical Records* (National Maritime Museum, London, 1980).

33 Pressnell and Orbell, *British Banking, op. cit.*

34 See also J. Orbell, 'The Business Records Advisory Service of the Business Archives Council', *Business Archives,* 44 (1978), pp. 26–30.

35 S. Garland, 'The Kent Business Archives Survey : A case study', *Business Archives*, 55 (1988), pp. 49–60.

36 R. J. B. Knight, *Guide to the Manuscripts in the National Maritime Museum*, 2 (Mansell, 1980), section 3.

37 R. Storey and J. Druker, *Guide to the Modern Records Centre, University of Warwick Library* (University of Warwick, 1977), pp. 5–17.

38 From information generously supplied by Len McDonald.

39 Sixty-seven business institutions are listed as maintaining archives facilities in L. Richmond and A. Turton, *Directory of Corporate Archives*, 2nd edition (Business Archives Council, 1987).

40   R. W. Ferrier, 'The business archivist today', *Business Archives,* 50 (1984), pp. 37–42.

41   S. D. Chapman, 'Business history from insurance policy registers', *Business Archives*, 32 (1970), pp. 10–16; S. D. Chapman, 'Fixed capital formation in the British cotton manufacturing industry', in J. P. P. Higgins and S. Pollard (editors), *Aspects of Capital Investment in Great Britain. A Preliminary Survey* (Methuen, London, 1971), pp. 57–107.

42   J. M. Bellamy, 'Some aspects of the economy of Hull in the 19th century with special reference to business history' (PhD thesis, Hull, 1966); P. L. Cottrell, *Industrial Finance, 1830–1914. The Finance and Organization of English Manufacturing Industry* (Methuen, London, 1980), Chapter 7.

43   G. Anderson, *Victorian Clerks* (Manchester University Press, 1976).

44   N. J. Morgan and M. S. Moss, 'Listing the wealthy in Scotland', *Bulletin of the Institute of Historical Research*, 59 (1986), pp. 189–95.

45   For example, R. P. T. Davenport-Hines, *Dudley Docker. The Life and Times of a Trade Warrior* (Cambridge University Press, Cambridge, 1984).

46   For example, F. Locker, 'The evolution of Victorian and early twentieth century office buildings in Britain' (PhD thesis, Edinburgh, 1984).

47   L. Richmond and B. Stockford, *Company Archives. The Survey of the Records of 1000 of the First Registered Companies in England and Wales* (Gower, Aldershot, 1986).

48   D. Jenkins, *Indexes of the Fire Insurance Policies of the Sun Fire Office and the Royal Exchange Assurance 1775–1787* (Economic and Social Research Council, 1987).

49   N. J. Morgan, 'Sources and resources : the DISH Project at Glasgow', in P. Denley and D. Hopkin (editors), *History and Computing* (Manchester University Press, Manchester, 1987), p. 306.

2

The development of British business and company law since 1750

John Armstrong

The first stages of industrialization

The vast majority of firms that participated in the significant changes loosely labelled 'the Industrial Revolution' were partnerships. They were owned and controlled by a small number of individuals whose liability was unlimited (if the firm were to become bankrupt, their private assets, such as their house and furniture, could be seized to reimburse creditors). Bearing in mind that Britain was the first country in the world to industrialize and that this occurred with a minimum of government encouragement, much of the praise or blame for this radical economic transformation must be attributed to the individual entrepreneurs who built the factories, sank new mining shafts and developed new machinery.

One reason for the predominance of the partnership was that after 1720 the law made it very difficult for firms to take joint-stock form and to acquire limited liability. The great outburst of financial speculation in the early eighteenth century characterized by the South Sea Bubble, in which prospectuses were issued for implausible and impossible adventures, such as draining the Wash to recover King John's treasure and the manufacture of square cannon-balls, led to government over-reaction in the form of the Bubble Act of 1720, which effectively discouraged the formation of joint stock companies with a large number of transferable shares.[1] Partnerships had no separate legal personality, which meant that any judicial action had to be taken against, or in the name of, each and every partner individually, and their liability was unlimited. Such firms had frequently to be reconstituted when partners left or joined, and a new business name was announced in the local press. A good example of this is the number and range of partnerships in which H. O. Wills was involved in the late eighteenth and early nineteenth centuries.[2] In a period of 40 years (between 1786 and 1826) Henry Overton Wills was a member of 6 different partnerships, the longest of which lasted 15 years.

Raising capital during the Industrial Revolution

The partnership was the preferred method of organization in the late eighteenth and early nineteenth centuries, because it was capable of providing enough capital for most businesses to start up and subsequently expand. Although businesses were growing in size and scale, the average firm was still small by twentieth-century standards. As late as the 1830s a firm with 50 employees was well above the average size. Similarly, although the capital requirements of firms were rising, most could be met informally, without recourse to a formal capital market, through a partnership.

Capital is conventionally divided into fixed and circulating or working capital. Fixed comprises those assets which are used again and again in the manufacturing process, such as land, buildings, and machinery, whereas working capital represents those assets whose value is used up and repurchased for each batch manufactured, such as raw material, fuel, and labour. It used to be thought that fixed capital was the most important for firms during the Industrial Revolution, perhaps because it was obvious that new factory and mill buildings were being erected, new forms of machinery being installed and new types of power being harnessed to work them. However, more recent research has demonstrated that there was a concomitant increase in the need for working capital.[3] As a business grew, so did its need for stocks of raw material and coal, its wage bill, the amount of work in progress and the amount owed by its debtors for goods delivered but not yet paid for. In business, credit was expected and quite normally extended, often for long periods. Manufacturers and merchants alike had to wait several months for payment, and then often received it as an inland bill of exchange which carried another 90 days' credit. Many studies have shown that the proportion of the total capital requirement made up by fixed capital for a whole range of businesses was quite small, varying from less than 10 per cent in Crowley's iron business[4] to about 35 per cent in Soho Foundry, the steam engine manufacturing side of the Boulton and Watt partnership.[5]

Not merely was working capital the larger part of all capital required by most firms, but it was also the form which was catered for in the most formal manner. By the mid-eighteenth century Great Britain had a large number of private banks throughout the provinces, and a number of larger, more prestigious London banks. Each of these banks was quite small, being limited, like other businesses, to partnerships. They were linked through each country bank, having a London agent or corresponding bank, and most London banks kept accounts with the Bank of England. In this manner surplus funds from one area of the country could be channelled to regions in need of working capital. The country banks provided their local firms with working capital by means of loans, overdrafts and through discounting inland bills of exchange. Country banks preferred to lend for short periods, given the volatility of economic fluctuations which brought runs on the banks, as individuals and firms sought liquidity. Hence the banks were more favourable to lending against goods delivered or work-in-progress where there was a finite duration to the loan.[6]

Businesses could also finance circulating capital through trade credit. There were a range of customary networks whereby merchants or manufacturers with surplus funds lent to those in need. For example, wool merchants and brewers lent to farmers by buying their wool clip or barley crop while it was still in the field for later delivery and textile middlemen advanced cash to manufacturers to pay their labour or buy raw materials. Additionally firms commuted some fixed costs into regular payments, which became revenue items, just as some modern firms prefer to lease or hire expensive pieces of capital equipment. Thus there were a number of well-established methods of raising the working capital requirements of businesses, largely from outside the firm and through formal markets. This left entrepreneurs free to devote most of the capital they could raise to the purchase of items of fixed capital, such as land, buildings and machinery, which represented a minority of the total capital requirements of the firm. Money was often borrowed from family and friends, most commonly from fathers as an advance on an inheritance, through dowries brought by brides to their husbands, and via loans. Members of particular religious denominations, especially nonconformist Christian groups such as Quakers and Unitarians, quite normally lent or invested surplus sums with their co-religionists, as the usual business imperative of honesty in repayment was reinforced by a religious one.

Once the firm was established, the most normal source of additional fixed capital, and to a lesser extent working capital, was ploughed-back profits. As firms were partnerships, there were no shareholders needing to be paid regular dividends. Outsiders who lent money to the firm were usually content with a fixed interest return of 5 per cent per annum, as this had become the customary return, based on the Usury Laws, which forbade higher interest rates between Christians as exploitative. As most entrepreneurs were willing to restrict their drawings from the firm to a reasonable, in some cases frugal, level, funds were available from profits to expand the business. Hence partnerships were able to raise their capital requirements without the need to expand the number of investors, and so there was no real reason for them to seek joint-stock form. Contemporary business morality reinforced this view, for it was a widespread belief that the best guarantee of probity in business was for owners to be engaged in the running of the business, and so able to check on their employees, and to be personally responsible to their customers and creditors for all debts and liabilities. Thus, for a range of reasons, joint-stock form was adopted only by a very limited number of firms.

Early corporations

The main exceptions to the norm of partnerships were in transport. For shipowners it was normal to divide the cost of a vessel into 64 parts, with up to the same number of owners. This practice, legitimized under Admiralty Law, is explained by the relatively large amount of capital which an ocean-going ship represented and the high risk of total loss by storm, fire or shipwreck. It was common for owners to spread their risks by taking shares in a number of ships rather than having all their eggs in one basket. Turnpike roads, canals, docks and later railway companies, also needed to raise their capital from a larger number of individuals than was possible through a partnership, and so they required joint-stock form. Since this led to a divorce between ownership and control, it was considered prudent to seek limited liability. Additionally, many of these undertakings had to buy land before they could start work. They therefore needed powers to compel landowners to sell the appropriate plots, should they be reluctant. The proportion of fixed capital to working capital in such undertakings was high, and there was likely to be a significant gestation period between investment and earning sufficient revenue to pay a return. For these reasons such transport-orientated businesses usually sought joint-stock form.

There were two methods of obtaining legal personality as a corporation before 1844.[7] One was to petition the Crown to become a chartered company. The other was to obtain a private Act of Parliament. Both methods were expensive. The former required a petition to be drawn up in appropriate legal language, and large sums needed to be spent on gifts to the officials who controlled access to the Crown. A private Act of Parliament also needed to be drafted by suitably experienced draughtsmen, complete with maps, diagrams and supporting evidence, all costing money. A survey of existing transport modes was often carried out to support the case for the new project. In addition, in the unreformed parliament before 1832, the bill needed powerful sponsors who expected to be entertained and showered with gifts. Once in parliament, experts had to be retained to give evidence, opposition had to be overcome by more presents, and the promoters had to stay in London for several weeks at significant expense. Transport schemes could carry these parliamentary costs because they were relatively small compared to the total amounts of capital required. Once a company was formed, the capital requirement of transport improvements, and of public utilities, such as water supply and later gas undertakings, was usually raised by private or public subscription among local gentry, merchants and manufacturers who were likely to benefit from them.

There were also a few large-scale, long-established companies enjoying the privilege of joint-stock and limited liability. Mostly these were the result of monopolies granted by the monarch in return for an outstanding service, often financial. The Bank of England is a good example. It was established in 1694 and given a monopoly of joint-stock banking in England in return for a large loan made to the government. Other long-established companies had monopolies in trading with certain areas, such as the East India Company, the Russia Company and the Levant Company. The restriction to partnerships did not apply to the mining of the ores of non-ferrous metals such as tin and copper. In Cornwall and Devon, under Stannary Law, a number of partners could combine to work mines which required increasing amounts of capital as they became deeper. By the late eighteenth century the co-partnership of working miners had largely been replaced by wealthy investors, who took shares in the mine and received a proportion of the profits and whose shares had become freely transferable.

Small-scale businesses

However, these were the exceptions. The vast majority of businesses were sole traders or small partnerships. They were normally single-site operations producing one product or a range of closely related products based on a common technology or set of raw materials. The labour force was small enough to be known to the employer, and often the master worked alongside his 'servants'. This encouraged good industrial relations, as workers were able to air grievances in person to the owner and some employers took a direct, paternalistic, interest in their workers' welfare. There was no formal division of the management functions, as the sole proprietor looked after all aspects of the business: production, marketing, finance, and personnel. In some firms, however, there was a simple split between partners, usually where one individual had expertise in the technical and production sides and so concentrated on product development, production and quality control, leaving the other partner to concentrate on marketing, sales and book-keeping. For example, James Watt, Josiah Wedgwood and Richard Pilkington filled the technical role in their partnerships, while Matthew Boulton, Thomas Bentley and William Pilkington took on the commercial role.[8]

Many firms served a local or regional market, and the lack of depth of demand meant that there was little need for sophisticated marketing methods. The average worker's pattern of consumption was limited and not easily expanded. The only sector where anything recognizable as marketing in a modern sense took place was in the very small, luxury goods segment. For the few aristocrats and gentry with high incomes, leisure, and a desire to affirm social status through conspicuous consumption, firms like Wedgwood or Boulton advertised their wares and promoted them in auctions and exhibitions and by royal patronage. This segment of the market could afford to be fashion-conscious and to produce articles of high quality; price was less of a consideration and hence marketing costs could be absorbed. The vast majority of firms, however, marketed their goods with minimal promotion.

As most businesses were small-scale, with the entrepreneurs in close touch with the running of the firm and no statutory obligation to create records for outside agencies, there was a limited need for internal documentation. Some firms did generate vast amounts which have survived to the present, for instance the huge Boulton and Watt archive, mainly in the Birmingham Reference Library, and the Wedgwood papers, in Keele University Library. Most records were aids to memory, for instance, books recording amounts advanced to workers in order to ensure later repayment;

goods sent or delivered to customers which had not been paid for, in order to ensure future settlement; notes of receipts and payments, in order to calculate net profits which would need to be apportioned among the partners. In some cases large accumulations of correspondence have survived, to customers or suppliers, to and from workers, between partners, or even to friends and colleagues in firms in the same industry where some form of trade association existed.

For many firms legal documents still survive, for instance, deeds of title, partnership agreements, and papers relating to court cases. For a few firms there is evidence of carefully recorded experiments trying out new production techniques and raw materials. For others there are attempts to cost individual products in order to gauge profitability and pricing. Yet others endeavoured to calculate the costs and returns on a particular investment. However, the sparsity of such records compared to letter books, accounting records and others, suggests that these firms did represent best practice, and the majority of businesses were less systematic and sophisticated in their activities and record keeping. Given the close personal attention of the entrepreneurs to the day-to-day running of their businesses, there was little clear distinction between business and personal papers. In some cases this extends to the accounts, where, alongside legitimate business expenses, may be found the cost of a piano or a case of wine. Thus apparently 'personal' papers will quite often contain material relevant to the business's history, and vice versa.

The advent of joint stock and limited liability

Until 1825 the only way to establish a joint-stock company other than a private Act of Parliament or a Crown charter was to form an unincorporated company. This was a large partnership, with the direction and control vested in the hands of a number of trustees. The deed of settlement, which brought the business into being, endeavoured to limit the liability of its members *pro rata* to their proportion of the total capital. However, this only held good while all the partners were solvent, and if some became bankrupt, the remaining members assumed their liability. Hence it was not a wholly satisfactory solution and there was pressure for reform.

The first significant nineteenth-century change in company law came in 1825, when the Bubble Act was repealed. This seemed to clear the way for the joint-stock company. However, the legal status of companies formed without the benefit of either parliamentary or Crown approval was questionable in the courts, particularly whether they had a distinct legal personality and hence could sue and be sued in their own right. In practice this legal change affected only a small minority of businesses, since the vast majority remained sole proprietorships or partnerships. Some firms took advantage of the new Act, mainly for foreign mining, and a number of insurance companies sought legal personality, as the capital they required was much greater than a handful of partners could subscribe. Under the 1825 Act the Board of Trade was given the discretion to grant, under letters patent, most of the privileges of corporate status. Initially the Board of Trade only extended the right to sue or be sued in the names of the officers, not the whole panoply of corporate status; it also showed a partiality for certain types of industry, especially insurance, mines and public utilities. These powers were altered by further Acts in 1834 and 1837, but the practice remained restricted and expensive, and the Board was susceptible to behind-the-scenes canvassing by interested parties and hence was not totally impartial. There remained pressure for a drastic change in company law.

The introduction of joint stock

The 1844 Joint Stock Companies Act marked a radical break with past practice, as it made the acquisition of corporate status and joint-stock ownership legal, cheap and relatively easy, with a minimum of formality and documentation. It also put an effective upper limit on the size of partnerships, as all those with more than 25 members had to become companies. This change was prompted by the need to regularize the large number of *de facto* joint-stock companies that had been established before 1825 and to counter charges of Board of Trade bias.

To some extent the path had already been paved by banking legislation. In 1826 joint-stock banking had been opened to firms established outside a 65-mile radius of London, so restricting the Bank of England's monopoly to London and the home counties. In 1833 this privilege was extended to London itself, so ending the Bank of England's 140-year-old monopoly. The arguments for this extension of the principle of joint stock were that wider ownership would make for greater capital assets, which would allow banks to spread their geographical and industrial base and so offset their risks. Given the vulnerability of country banks in trade-cycle slumps, when large numbers suspended business either temporarily or permanently, because their assets were less liquid than their liabilities, it was thought that larger numbers of shareholders would make for a less volatile banking system, which might then counteract trade depressions rather than aggravating them. Some indication of the fluctuations in economic activity is given in Figure 2.1. The fear of malpractice was lessened by insisting that the banks' shareholders retain unlimited liability. Once the principle had been conceded for banking business, it was more difficult to continue to oppose it for non-financial firms. The failure in the various economic downturns, such as 1824–5 and 1834–6, of a number of the quasi-legal incorporated firms also convinced the government that some action was needed.

The solution chosen by parliament was disclosure of the activities, organizers and financial results of these firms via the information required

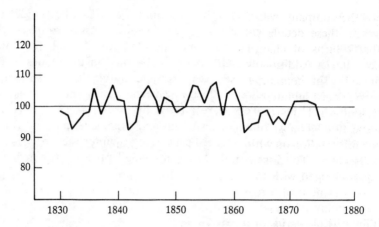

Figure 2.1   *UK industrial production, excluding building (Hoffman) deviations from trend, 1830–80.*
Source. *D. J. Coppock, 'The causes of business fluctuations', Trans of the Manchester Statistical Society, 127 (1959), reprinted in D. H. Aldcroft and P. Fearon, British Economic Fluctuations 1790–1939 (Macmillan, London, 1972), p. 191.*

in registration under the 1844 Act. If investors were better informed, it was argued, they would be likely to avoid the most speculative companies, and thereby reduce the number of such firms being formed and failing. Additionally, compulsory registration gave the government some possibility of regulating and controlling companies, to the same end. The pressure for reform was more legal than economic, and that it was not widely needed or wanted was demonstrated by the limited take-up of the privilege, both in the proportion of total firms and in the range of industries where it was adopted.

The 1844 Act required all existing firms with more than 25 members and transferrable shares to register. Additionally, the privilege of joint-stock and a separate legal personality were available to all businesses except those covered by the banking legislation. To qualify, the firm had to lodge certain documents with the Registrar of Joint Stock Companies (a position created by the Act) and pay specified fees, mostly in the form of stamp duties, which although substantial by the standard of the average weekly wage, were small in comparison to the costs of a private Act of Parliament. Registration was in two stages. Initially a number of subscribers obtained provisional registration by providing the Registrar with details of the name, purpose, address, and promotors of the company and a copy of any prospectus which was issued. Complete registration occurred when, in addition to the above, the Registrar received information on the amount and types of capital, both nominal and actually subscribed, a list of the subscribers with their addresses and occupations, a similar list of the directors, and a deed of settlement. In theory, if the deed contained any unacceptable provisions or failed to contain clauses on certain topics, it could be rejected and registration postponed or refused.

Once the company was formed, it had to notify the Registrar of any changes in these details within a specified period as well as making 6-monthly returns of changes in membership, and providing an annual balance sheet. Additionally the Act placed upon each company the responsibility of keeping books of account, registers of directors and members, board minute books and other documents – partially to provide the basis on which the returns to the Registrar were made, but also to allow the inspection of most of them by any shareholder or his nominee, to provide information on which shareholders could judge the performance of their directors. To disseminate this knowledge further, most of the documents lodged with the Registrar were open to the inspection of the public on payment of a relatively small fee. The significance of this Act, from the point of view of record-keeping is palpable.[9] Firms had to maintain a whole series of books within the company to comply with the Act. They had to provide regular returns to the Registrar, as well as disseminating some of the information, such as the balance sheet, to all the shareholders. For many public companies that have ceased trading the only records which survive are held at the Public Record Office among the records of the Registrar (see p. 125).

The 1844 Act marks a watershed, in the ease of obtaining joint-stock form and in the creation and preservation of a uniform set of documentation. The acquisition of limited liability, however, still required expensive and complex procedures. The take-up of corporate status was very restricted. Shannon calculated that only about 1,000 companies were created, of which insurance businesses and gas and water utilities were the largest groups, with about 20 per cent each.[10] Industrial companies were a small minority, and only shipping and cotton companies were prominent in this category. In part this was because most industries did not need to raise so much capital that they required to go beyond the traditional partnership. In addition, firms were unwilling to have much information about their business put into the public domain and believed that ownership and control should go hand in hand. Family firms were reluctant to see dilution of their ownership of the business in case it signalled a loss of control to non-family members.

The advent of limited liability

Given that so few firms took advantage of the 1844 legislation, it may seem strange that within a decade or so debate was initiated on the legalization of limited liability to complement joint-stock form, and that by 1860 limited liability had become easily and cheaply available to companies in all industries. The reasons for this radical change are complex. There was a belief that giving the workers the facility to invest in their employing firm would reconcile labour to capital and produce a more efficient and less disruptive workforce. There may have been a desire to try to increase the range of low-risk domestic securities. Foreign example was also a powerful motivator; limited liability already existed in other countries and British firms had taken advantage of these privileges by establishing themselves abroad rather than in the United Kingdom. The examples of France and the United States were cited, the former in 1853 and 1854 having over 20 British firms formed there. In order to keep British enterprise in the country, similar advantages had to be offered by British law.

The year 1855 is a key date in the development of company law because for the first time limited liability became cheaply and easily available by a brief Act which 'bolted on' provisions to the 1844 Act. In 1856 a new Act came into force, superseding both the 1844 and 1855 Acts and simplifying the procedure. This Act also lowered the maximum size of a partnership further than the 1844 Act, to no more than 20 members. Registration became a one-stage process, with a memorandum of association signed by seven members being lodged with the Registrar, stating the company's name and purpose. Initially most of the requirements of the 1844 Act in terms of record-keeping were incorporated in the 1856 Act, but many were missing from the 1862 Companies Act, which consolidated the legislation of 1856 to 1862. For instance, there was no longer any requirement to lodge a balance sheet with the Registrar, so that potential investors could not easily gain an idea of a company's financial position. Nothing in the body of the 1862 Act required the maintenance of board minute books, that accounts should be kept on the double-entry principle, or that minute books recording the proceedings of the general meetings should be kept. Although a number of valuable record-keeping recommendations were made in the model regulations appended to the Act, they only applied if the company did not stipulate to the contrary in its articles of association. Any firm could ignore these model rules simply by inserting a sentence in its articles, which is why the 1862 Act is often seen as much more liberal than its predecessors. In separate Acts, banks, insurance companies and co-operative societies were also granted the privilege of limited liability by 1862. All partnerships remained fully liable without limitation.

The period 1856 to 1862 saw radical changes in company law and, as in 1844, for largely non-economic reasons. The vast majority of firms were not requesting limited liability. That they did not feel the need to increase the number of members or to raise capital from a wider public is demonstrated by the relatively small proportion of total businesses which took corporate form in the 1860s and 1870s. Most were able to raise sufficient capital informally, and disliked the idea of disclosure or sharing ownership. The very mixed success of many proposed limited companies in the early period confirmed to investors and business owners that it was not a guaranteed method of increasing capital. Shannon calculated that about one-third of all limited companies in the period 1866 to 1883 failed to raise a large enough subscription from the public and so never traded. A similar proportion had only a brief life.[11]

Limited liability was adopted in those industries in which capital requirements were rising or where risks were high. For instance, in the cotton and iron and steel industries changes in technology and the appreciation that economies could be achieved through larger scale and the integration of different processes into one firm created a need for larger capitalization. There was a boom in the incorporation of Lancashire cotton businesses in the early 1860s and again in the mid-1870s. Both shipowning and mining ventures were perceived as hazardous because of the vagaries of weather and geology respectively; the desire to spread this risk among a large number of investors led to a boom in single-ship limited liability companies in the late 1870s and early 1880s and a multitude of mining businesses, mostly to operate abroad, in coal, iron, lead and copper in the early 1870s. In addition to these industrial concerns, a number of public utilities, such as water and gas companies, took limited liability, as well as a range of organizations such as political clubs, temperance taverns and skating rinks, whose purpose was less clearly profit-orientated.[12] These were not typical businesses. The majority of firms remained partnerships, often with complex arrangements to divide ownership among many family members, or sole partners.

The era of the company promoter

The 1860s and 1870s saw no great rush into corporate form by the majority of firms, whereas the 1880s and 1890s saw positive booms in company promotion. A rough guide to this phenomenon is the numbers of companies registered in each year, given in Table 2.1.

Table 2.1 Companies registered in England and Wales (average per annum)

1856–69	500
1870s	900
1880s	1,600
1890s	3,700
1900–14	5,200

Not all these registrations represented new business ventures which went on to grow and expand. About a third were stillborn, in that they were registered but a lack of further returns indicates they never started operations. Additionally, many of the companies registered were not *new* businesses but were partnerships converting into limited liability joint-stock form, a simple change of status. Some of the later registrations represented existing companies restructuring and reregistering for one reason or another, and so did not represent new firms, except in the purely legal sense. The total number of registrations does not even indicate the number of extant companies at any time. There was a growing trend to merge or amalgamate firms so that a number of nominally separate businesses were in fact jointly owned, sometimes under a holding company. Hannah estimated that over 1,700 firms disappeared in this way between 1888 and 1914.[13] However, the volume of registrations does give an approximate indication of the level of activity in company promotion.

The reasons for the growing acceptance of corporate form are complex and relate to both the internal changes taking place in the British economy and the altered external environment in which British business was operating. A number of events served to ram home the advantage of limited liability. One such was the failure of the City of Glasgow Bank in 1878. This bank still had unlimited liability, and when it failed, through fraudulent mismanagement, its liabilities were so far in excess of its assets that each shareholder was liable for twenty-seven times his original investment.[14] The switchback ride of the trade cycle, as illustrated in Figure 2.2, continued to lead to the failure of many firms in the downturns and the period 1873 to 1896, characterized as the 'Great Depression', encouraged the search for more stable forms of business organization.

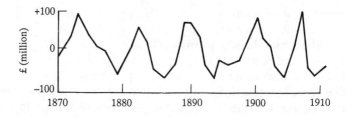

Figure 2.2 *Net national income at current prices (deviations).*
Source. *A. G. Ford, British economc fluctuations 1870–1914', Manchester School, 37:2 (1969), pp. 99–129, reprinted in D. H. Aldcroft and P. Fearon,* British Economic Fluctuations 1790–1939 *(Macmillan, London, 1972), p. 132.*

The growth of the formal capital market for domestic industrial shares also played a part. If a company wished to be quoted on the stock exchange, necessary pre-requisites were joint-stock form and limited liability. A number of factors pushed businesses into seeking such a market quotation and to switch out of partnerships. One was the increasing capital required to manufacture so as to extract maximum economies of scale. Increasingly processes were shifting to larger-scale production and some were moving from batch to continuous production. The brewing industry from the 1870s and soap manufacturing from the 1880s were examples of the former as the market for these products became less regional and more national. In soda manufacture the shift from the Leblanc process to the Solvay method meant a switch from batch to continuous production, and much greater capital to install pressure- and corrosion-resistant equipment.[15] Similarly the mechanization of cigarette manufacture with the use of the Bonsack machine shifted it from hand methods to near-continuous production of a uniform product, with a rise in capital requirements.[16]

The threat of intervention by overseas companies in the British economy caused some British firms to amalgamate to beat off the foreign challenge, for example, the merger of thirteen firms to form Imperial Tobacco in 1901.[17] In order to merge they needed to convert from partnerships to corporate form, and, once amalgamated, frequently went public to raise additional capital for further expansion. The use of the formal capital market was more acceptable to many family firms because they discovered a device which ensured no loss of control while raising additional capital: this was to issue debentures or preference shares to the public while retaining the whole of the equity in the hands of the family or original entrepreneurs. The stock exchange permitted this and investors preferred such scrip because it had priority to profits, usually had a fixed and guaranteed return and so seemed much less risky than equity. The advantage to the owning family was that holders of debentures and preference shares had no direct control over the business while they received their interest or dividends regularly. This left total direction in the hands of the original owners. Both Jesse Boot of Boots the Chemist and W. H. Lever of Lever Bros used this method to raise capital but retain control.[18]

Increased scale of production encouraged developments in methods of marketing. In the mid-nineteenth century the idea of giving a product a unique 'brand' name began to catch on in some industries, such as pipe tobacco, beer, and patent medicines. This was a necessary pre-requisite to advertising, and was often followed by posters or show cards at the point of sale. In the later nineteenth century a much wider range of consumer goods became branded – soap, drugs, meat extract, tea, bicycle lamps – encouraged by legislation allowing both words and designs to be registered as the unique possession of an individual firm. This in turn meant a proliferation of marketing effort, such as press advertisements, and posters on railway stations, horse buses and trams. As a result, by the turn of the century a number of well-known, heavily advertised, household names were selling throughout the country to a mass market to complement the scale of production.[19]

The 1880s and 1890s were the heyday of the professional company promoter who encouraged family firms to convert into public companies.[20] They often bought the firm outright for more than the current owners thought it worth, so allowing them to realize their assets and make a windfall profit. The promoter then launched the company on the public for a significantly larger sum than he paid, by buying suitable publicity and by ensuring the press 'talked up' the value of the company. Some promoters were only interested in making a fast killing and took no interest in improving the profit performance of the companies they floated. Others took a longer-term view and tried to vet the technical and financial condition of the firm, and to ensure that it was not over-capitalized, before going any further. Both types encouraged and facilitated the flotation of firms on the stock exchange.

Investors were willing to consider such securities because some of the traditional outlets for spare capital had become less attractive. For instance, the yield on government stock fell sharply in the last quarter of the nineteenth century; land was no longer a safe return, as competition from foreign-grown primary products caused world prices to plummet and farming rents were reduced or foregone; and railway shares and stock were suffering from lower yields as the railways' costs of extending into branch lines and improving the quality of their service were not matched by a concomitant increase in revenue. Foreign investment was an alternative outlet but it seemed, and was, higher risk and higher return. Home industrial and commercial stock looked more attractive as a result, and there was a rapid growth in the number of domestic manufacturing firms quoted on the stock exchange from about sixty in 1885 to nearly 600 by 1907.

The other device which encouraged small and family businesses to become corporations was the 'private company', which was implicitly recognized in the Companies Amendment Act 1900, when companies not issuing shares to the public were exempt from the need to issue a prospectus. Cottrell, however, considers some such private companies had 'been in existence since the . . . mid 1850s'.[21] They were explicitly recognized in the Companies Act 1907. By not offering shares or debentures to the public, keeping its shareholders below 50, and not transferring shares outside this group, a firm could qualify as a private company and then did not need to disclose information in a prospectus or balance sheet. To firms obsessed with secrecy about their processes, recipes, profits and even sales revenue, this provided the advantages of limited liability without the disadvantage of disclosure, and many family partnerships became 'private' companies. Another factor encouraging partnerships to become private limited companies was the introduction of estate duty in 1894, and the increase in its effective rates in the early twentieth century. Converting a family business to a company allowed the owner to give shares to his heirs in his lifetime. These *intra vivos* gifts, if made a specified period before the death of the donor, were exempt from estate duty.

The growth of large-scale industry

A greater willingness to adopt corporate form was coeval with a change in the structure of British industry. A multitude of small-scale firms competing vigorously, or endeavouring to restrict competition by trade and manufacturers' associations, was becoming more oligopolistic as mergers occurred.[22] Although affecting different industries in different decades, by 1914 businesses as diverse as banking, brewing, heavy chemicals, tobacco and sewing cotton were dominated by a few large-scale firms. Some causes were specific to the sector: for instance, breweries needed capital to buy public houses which were then tied to selling the products of the purchasing brewery, a form of forward vertical integration. However, there were also general trends at work. The increasing capital needed to produce efficiently led some firms to merge to become large enough to float on the stock exchange and so raise the capital. The actual or threatened competition from foreign firms entering the British market led some industries to unite. New technology led those firms working old processes to join defensively in the hope of competing. The desire to spread risk by having a national geographical coverage also prompted some take-overs.

The effect led to a process which has continued throughout the twentieth century. Firms increasingly became multi-site, with greater capital, larger market share and a national and international market orientation, trends that led to more complex managerial structures. The increasing quantities of fixed capital, plus more rapid technological obsolescence, meant a more sophisticated approach to depreciation was required. Greater complexity of production made costing more difficult at the same time that pricing had to be more precise, because competition in manufactured goods was increasing as countries such as Germany, the United States of America, Belgium and France exported finished goods. Increasingly firms needed to employ professional accountants to look after this side of their affairs, and were willing to do so because the establishment of chartered institutes provided a guarantee of capability and probity. Similarly, as production processes became more sophisticated, technically trained personnel became vital to install and maintain equipment. Firms recruited chemists and engineers or had their younger partners so trained. It was but a short step from this to a functionally specialized board of directors or set of senior partners, where each was primarily responsible for one area of the firm's activities – sales, production, research and development, or office management. This was compounded by the growing size and scale of firms, which made it impossible for one or two partners to control all operations. In some firms 'the third generation' argument began to apply, although it could be anything from the second to fifth generation in practice. Family members, grown rich from business, lost interest in further active wealth creation and preferred to live on the income and pursue more pleasurable pastimes such as politics, sport and socializing. In such cases family firms needed to recruit professional managers to bring back entrepreneurial vigour.[23]

Where firms grew large by amalgamation, they soon discovered that benefits in terms of reduced costs and competition and so increased profits did not occur automatically. Positive action was needed to cut out competing products, close the least efficient plants or ensure sales staff sold additional lines. As a result some companies which started out as loose federations of family firms, with large boards representing the constituent companies, established centralized offices or some form of executive committee. Once the reporting, costing and statistical practices of all the constituent businesses had been put on a common footing, this body then made the painful decisions on rationalization. Firms which failed to institute some such process usually were disappointed by the lack of additional profits. By the early years of the twentieth century the larger British firm had moved away from simple partnerships. It was a joint-stock, limited liability company, often with non-family, professional managers who had specific qualifications and expertise. It operated on more than one site, though making a related range of products, with a head office whose role was strategic and a functionally specialized board of directors.

Changes in company law, 1862 to 1913

These radical changes in business structure and organization were accompanied by a number of scandals involving company promoters and a general unease that the investor was not always getting a fair deal. As company promotion became almost synonymous with sharp practice, especially after the formation boom of the mid-1890s, the government moved to tighten up the content of prospectuses. Before 1900 there had been some attempts to outlaw fraudulent prospectuses (such as the 1857 Act to Make Better Provisions for the Punishment of Frauds committed by Trustees, Bankers and other Persons Entrusted with Property, which made the issue of a misleading prospectus a criminal act, and the 1867 Companies Act, which required every prospectus to declare all contracts entered into by the promoters and directors) but they had little effect. Even the 1890 Directors Liability Act, which made directors liable for any untrue statement in a prospectus, could be avoided, as the prosecution had to show that the directors *believed* it to be untrue and that they were not simply relying on reports from their professional advisers. As a result, the Davey Committee was set up in 1895 and its recommendations eventually found substance in the 1900 Companies Act, This insisted that every prospectus contain certain standard information (see p. 108) and was lodged with the Registrar prior to issue. Standardized prospectuses made it easier for investors to choose between companies as investment opportunities.

Financial information was essential to judge how well an established company was performing. However, following the 1856 Act, there was no requirement for companies to lodge a balance sheet with the Registrar, present it to a general meeting or pre-circulate it to members, except in the model rules, which could easily be avoided. Some companies provided their shareholders with a modicum of financial information but others failed to provide any. Accordingly the 1907 Companies Act required all public companies to lodge an annual balance sheet with the Registrar. The 1908 consolidating Act repeated this. However, there was no need to lodge a profit and loss account with the Registrar or circulate it to members, and the wording in the Act about what had to be disclosed in balance sheets was so vague that many remained paragons of concision: assets were not valued separately but lumped together and valued as a whole, tangibles and intangibles were not differentiated, and there was often no explanation of the basis of valuation.[24] Furthermore private companies did not need to send a balance sheet to the Registrar.

The government also tried to tighten up the responsibilities of directors. They had to ensure that the information stipulated by the 1900 Act was given in prospectuses. Similarly they had to ensure, after 1907, that balance sheets were filed if the company was not private. After 1900 the directors had to check not only that the company kept a register of all mortgages and other charges against the business (this had been required by the 1862 Act) but that it was open to public inspection, and all such charges had to be registered with the Registrar. In the 1862 Act only shareholders and creditors had access to such information and it had not been lodged with the Registrar. The intention after 1900 was that anyone could now see the data and this publicity would prevent malpractice.

During this period chairmen, on behalf of the board of directors, began circulating to shareholders a brief report on the year's activities before the annual general meeting. This practice arose partly in order to accompany the auditors' report, which the 1900 Companies Act required to be prepared and put before the shareholders. It was later given more formal sanction by the 1908 Companies Act, which in its model rules recommended that the balance sheet and auditors' report should be accompanied by a report from the directors on the state of the company's business and that the report should be circulated to all members as well as being laid before them in a general meeting. Most well-run companies adopted this policy and many used this directors' report as the basis for the speech given by the chairman at the annual general meeting which was often reported in the trade and financial press. However, the level of disclosure of information remained minimal through fear of competitors learning something to their advantage.

The First World War

The degree of economic effort needed to wage the First World War was unprecedented. It became a strategic necessity to maximize output and improve efficiency.[25] One result was that the government operated those industries which it believed would benefit from elimination of wasteful competition, or where it wished to give priority to war requirements. Additionally, and especially after the crisis over the supply of shells, the government became concerned with speeding up production and ensuring low levels of wastage to maximize output and efficiency. The government sponsored studies into industrial fatigue and the effect of breaks in work routine on the output of the labour force. These were to have an influence on the development of labour relations and personnel management in the inter-war period, just as direct government control led to calls for nationalization of the coalmines afterwards and new thinking emerged on the optimum method of structuring the railway system.

The war also brought significant changes in the finances of business. Excess profits duty, introduced in 1915, meant that for the first time business had to face a tax on its net income, which brought the government directly into the area of determining what constituted 'profits' and what were reasonable costs to set against income. This created a new requirement for record-keeping: books available for examination by the tax inspector. Because the government wished to prevent businesses making large profits on government work, they allocated some contracts on a cost-plus basis. Those businesses needed to justify their allocation of overhead costs to different products and at specific rates, which in turn meant they needed to introduce or refurbish cost accounting systems.

The First World War brought changes which led to new commercial opportunities after the war. Many improvements in production methods permeated post-war thinking, leading to more capital-intensive modes of production and higher levels of labour productivity, for example, greater use of machine tools, improved factory layout, the use of jigs, and standardization of components. In some cases whole new industries developed in the 1920s and 1930s were based on war-time-inspired improvements in technology, for example, the development of the aircraft industry and the associated growth in municipal and national airports.

The war also radically altered the relationship between management and its labour force. Government sought to keep labour disruption to a minimum and encouraged employers to recognize trade unions as one method of achieving this. In an endeavour to persuade organized labour to maximize output, government consulted eminent trade union officials and brought some into the government. This new climate was reflected in the number of trade unionists, which more than doubled between 1913 and 1920, with a similar rise in the proportion of the labour force belonging to trade unions. This recruitment bonanza was aided by the apparent success of union officials in negotiating flat-rate, cost-of-living rises for workers, giving the unskilled a larger proportionate increase. This encouraged the less well paid to join unions. There was an influx of women into employment and into jobs which had previously been perceived as only suitable for male workers. Women demonstrated their ability to cope with such tasks and, although in most cases their war-time employment was soon reversed when troops were demobilized and men reasserted their traditional right to particular types of occupation, the mould had been broken and the principle of equal ability had been established.

Concentration upon war work meant that firms had to cut their civilian production, disappointing customers at home and abroad. The long-term effects at home were slight: some brands of consumer goods never reappeared, and a few firms failed. Abroad, however, the impact was more drastic as foreign firms moved into the vacuum created by lack of British goods and commenced local production.

Business in the slump and recovery

In the 1920s and 1930s those industries which had been the basis of the industrial revolution were experiencing harsh conditions. Demand for cotton, coal, ships and iron products was declining at home and abroad, due in part to the arrival of substitutes – artificial fibres for cotton, oil for coal, aluminium for iron. These industries had made up a large proportion of British exports before the First World War, and when Britain's export trade declined, they were disproportionately hard hit. As firms endeavoured to cut costs in order to compete, they adopted more capital-intensive techniques, for example, mechanical coal-cutting and conveying, which led to increased labour productivity, but in turn meant less labour was needed to produce a given output. Overseas trade in these products was complicated by an over-valued pound sterling, which made British exports more expensive, as well as declining demand in many foreign countries, owing to local production usurping imports. At the same time other developed countries, such as the United States of America, Germany and Japan, were competing more aggressively even in markets which had traditionally been perceived as British. To protect infant industries developed during the First World War, when European exports were unavailable, many countries imposed or raised tariff barriers, aggravating high British prices and further reducing demand. In the 1930s these problems were compounded when even more rampant economic nationalism led to higher tariffs, quotas, and bilateral trade, and some currencies became non-convertible. This made exporting even more difficult, and there was no relief for the staple industries until the late 1930s, when rearmament began.

The reaction to these miserable conditions was predictable. A large number of horizontal mergers occurred in cotton textile manufacturing, shipbuilding, iron and steel making and coalmining. The situation was so bad that the government started to encourage rationalization, using the Bank of England as its agent and persuading the commercial banks to put up money.[26] Various bodies came into being, such as the Lancashire Cotton Corporation to merge and reduce cotton textile capacity. Between 1929 and 1932 it absorbed over ninety firms in the industry. The National Shipbuilders Security between 1931 and 1937 closed down over twenty yards. In some industries the government directly legislated mergers. The railways, for instance, were divided into four regional groupings by parliamentary Act in 1921, replacing more than 100 separate companies of 1913. In these declining industries there was a history of horizontal amalgamations, reduction of capacity, and permanent long-term unemployment for the workforce. Some firms made such good profits during the war that they were able to transfer large sums to reserve accounts, but did not inform their shareholders. When their trading activities failed to show a profit in the 1920s, they transferred these reserves back on to the balance sheet to give an overall 'profit'. Among these firms was the Royal Mail Steam Packet Co., which also had a complex arrangement of cross shareholdings the more to confuse the investor. When the secret reserves began to run out, the company had to reveal the true nature of its financial plight, leading to the prosecution of Lord Kylsant and the break-up of the group.[27] It is an indication of the rudimentary and unrevealing nature of many balance sheets and profit and loss accounts that these practices were not discovered earlier.

Although market conditions were more favourable for the expanding industries, such as motor vehicles, electrical goods and components, dyes, pharmaceuticals and other consumer goods, they too saw horizontal mergers and a great rationalization of capacity so that in many industries by 1939 a handful of firms dominated the sector, accounting for a large percentage of total output, employment and capital. The establishment of Imperial Chemical Industries in 1926 from a merger of the four largest chemical firms, some of which were the result of previous amalgamations, led to market leadership in Britain. The creation of Unilever in 1929 was the summation of a whole series of magpie mergers initiated by William Lever in the early years of the twentieth century, and created the largest British firm in soaps and fats. In the electrical industry a few giant firms emerged, such as Associated Electrical Industries and General Electric, to dominate the sector. Mergers were common in the dynamic sectors as well as the declining. In motor car manufacture there was a similar attrition of small-scale producers, either through merger or exit from the industry, so that by 1938 four firms, Morris, Austin, Ford and Standard, were producing over 80 per cent of total output.[28] Production-line methods meant small-scale producers were unable to compete on cost and price, and lost market share to the point where production ceased.

One cause for some of these mergers was foreign competition. Imperial Chemical Industries, for instance, came into being to operate against such large German and American firms as I. G. Farben and Du Pont. The British electrical industry was backward compared to foreign competitors such as Siemens or Allgemeine Elektrizitäts Gesellschaft of Germany or General Electric of America. In some cases the scale of production required to exploit new technology was so great that individual firms needed to amalgamate. Metal Box came into existence in the early 1920s as a merger of old-established tin-box makers. Once it saw the potential in mass-produced tin cans, using American technology, its sales grew rapidly, and throughout the inter-war period it continued to absorb other firms in an attempt to reduce competition and influence price.[29] Similar stories could be told in such other sectors as biscuits, photographic goods, or pharmaceuticals.

Between the wars marketing became of even more importance to firms, with greater scale of production, difficulties in many export markets and increased import penetration of the domestic market by foreign manu-factured goods. At the same time the range of media increased enormously, with the proliferation of the cheap, popular newspaper initiated in 1896 by the *Daily Mail*, the advent of cinema and continental-based commercial radio beamed into the south-east of England and the spread of electric signs. Consumer durables, such as the bicycle and radio, came within the purchasing power of many families. Those in work experienced rising real wages and aspired to improved living standards. To facilitate the sales of such consumer durables, hire purchase, pioneered by the Singer Sewing Machine Company in the nineteenth century, was often made available, so deepening the market. Increased emphasis was placed on fashion and the design of products to encourage premature obsolescence and repeat purchase, and real improvements in performance as a result of technological advances.

In addition to growing market share at home, some businesses became multinational, producing similar products in a number of countries. Unilever, Metal Box, Cadbury, Dunlop and Imperial Chemical Industries all initiated or pursued such a course of action.[30] One reason was to avoid tariffs on manufactured goods. Local manufacture with no transport or tariff charges, even at a lower level of output, might produce a cheaper product than one exported from Britain. In some cases the product was not amenable to long-distance transport, because of its low intrinsic value, and had to be manufactured locally. Metal Box, for example, established factories in South Africa and India in 1933 to manufacture empty tin boxes or cans. Some of these multinational investments were not particularly profitable – indeed some were loss-makers – but they pointed the way in which British industry was likely to proceed.

In the financial sector similar trends were at work. By the early 1920s there were less than 20 separate banking businesses. More mergers meant that by 1938 only about a dozen independent firms remained. This oligopoly was partly a response to the growth in size of business: if banks were to serve much bigger firms, the banks themselves had also to be bigger. Risks could be offset if there were many branches with a wide geographical and industrial range. Larger banks had greater reserves and could better weather any financial storm. In the inter-war period the commercial banks lent more to industries which were in need of reconstruction and refinance. In the declining industries business relied heavily on banks for working finance, and overdraft limits rose steeply. Public enquiries, like the Macmillan Committee, highlighted apparent shortcomings in the formal structure for financing British industry, and the commercial banks made some moves to remedy them.

Company law in the inter-war period

There were relatively few changes to company law in the inter-war period. During the war the nationality of all company directors had to be reported to the Registrar, as did their previous nationality if it had changed. This allowed the government to identify 'enemy aliens' who were running

British registered companies and give it the opportunity of interning the owners and seizing the business. The main changes in corporate law, including the 1928 Companies Act, came as a result of the Greene Committee, which sat in 1925 and reported in 1926. The main intention of the 1928 Act was to enforce disclosure on more topics and so ensure probity by publicity. Among its provisions were that shareholders had to receive a profit and loss account to accompany the balance sheet, though there was no requirement for it to be lodged with the Registrar. The contents of the balance sheet were specified in a little more detail – fixed and circulating assets had to be valued separately and the basis of the valuation made explicit; all loans to directors and officers of the company had to be declared, as did assets comprising shares in a subsidiary company or loans to it. Directors were also encouraged to declare their interest in other companies to their fellow directors. Finally, the 1928 Act insisted that prospectuses, when issued, should be certified as correct by the accountants as regards the previous 3 years' financial results. The 1928 Act also contained clauses laying down the sorts of minute books and accounts that a company should maintain. These were fairly simple requirements and every well-run company was already keeping such books as minutes of directors' and general meetings, and 'proper books of account' regarding sales, purchases, assets, liabilities, income and expenditure; members register; and directors register. The Act merely ensured that less well administered businesses came into line.

However, the 1928 Act, and the 1929 Act, which consolidated the company Acts passed since 1908, were not particularly innovative. Private companies, the vast majority of companies, remained exempt from the clauses about balance sheets and profit and loss accounts. The degree of disclosure in the financial accounts was still rudimentary, with a very low level of disaggregation, so that members were little better informed. Since the profit and loss account was not lodged with the Registrar, there was no access to it for intending shareholders or the public at large. Although directors were now supposed to declare their interests, it was only to their fellow directors, and company members remained in ignorance. It was ironic that the two greatest financial scandals of the inter-war period broke after these Companies Acts were promulgated – Hatry in 1929[31] and the Royal Mail Steam Packet Co. in 1930. There was no attempt to pinpoint the weaknesses in company law that these scandals indicated or to remedy them before the Second World War.

Business during the Second World War

The impact of the Second World War on British business was similar to that of the First World War. The demand for armaments of all kinds was, however, so great that civilian consumption was curtailed by rationing and shortages in order to allow firms to switch from consumer goods to armaments, and overseas markets were once again neglected. In order to maximize output of war materials the government again took greater charge of industrial production, directing labour into priority industries, encouraging and conscripting women into factories, and implementing the latest techniques and machinery to speed up production and reduce reliance on skilled labour. The range of goods produced was severely curtailed, standardization, interchangeability and automatic machine tools were the key to high output. The use of jigs, patterns and extreme division of labour allowed labour dilution, and the mass production methods developed in the inter-war period in the motor-car industry were applied to aircraft, tank and howitzer production. Small changes, such as the introduction of 'Yankee' pump action screwdrivers, accumulated into significant improvements, and pre-war resistance to such methods broke down in the atmosphere of common purpose.

As in the First World War, the government increased levels of taxation. In part this was intended to reduce civilian demand, in part to aid the government to finance the war. Excess profits tax was reintroduced and more vigorously collected than in the First World War, so that business had to pay a tax on its net earnings. However, unlike the 1920s, some form of profits tax was retained throughout the post-war period, although under different names, and hence business's ability to plough back was permanently impaired.

Similarly government increased excise duties on many goods, cutting back consumption. To compensate for declining civilian standards of comfort, businesses were encouraged to improve facilities at work. There was a proliferation of canteens, welfare officers, factory doctors and other such facilities, aimed at keeping the workers happy, healthy and productive. A further aid to maximizing output was the reduction of industrial disputes. Employers learnt to negotiate and be conciliatory rather than confrontational, a strategy aided by the appointment of Ernest Bevin, a prominent trade union leader, as Minister of Labour and by the general antipathy of the left to Hitler and his National Socialist policies.

The war was destructive of business records. Bombing was effective and widespread and incendiary bombs commonly used. The need for raw materials and the desire to save on imports led to salvage drives, and the pulping, for re-use, of many historical and current records. The war therefore caused significant lacunae in some business archive collections.

Post-war changes in company law

The financial scandals of the 1930s, combined with the economic changes brought by the war to bring about the establishment of the Cohen Committee to consider amendment of British company law. The outcome was the 1948 Companies Act, forcing companies to reveal to shareholders and the public their financial activities. It embodied all the previous provisions on disclosure in terms of the following: the contents of prospectuses; registers of directors, shareholders, and mortgages; memorandum of association and articles of association; and special and extraordinary resolutions. All these documents were to be maintained by the company, made available to creditors and shareholders free of charge, and opened to the public on payment of a nominal fee. Copies were lodged with the Registrar of Companies, and these were available for public consultation. In addition, the 1948 Act insisted on the profit and loss account, which the 1928 Act had required to go to shareholders, also being lodged with the Registrar. The contents of the statutory accounts were carefully specified in schedule eight, with rules about the disclosure of subsidiary companies' assets and how the accounts of holding companies and groups of firms were to be presented. This meant the shareholder with some financial understanding was better informed than ever before. Hannah[32] has pointed out that the 1948 Companies Act opened the way for the professional who could assess the market value of a company's assets, compare this with the balance sheet valuation and spot an opportunity to make money. The take-over bidder and asset stripper became a normal part of business in the 1950s and 1960s. However, private companies continued to be exempt from the necessity of lodging the balance sheet, profit and loss account, auditor's and directors' report with the Registrar, so these records remained outside the public demesne until the 1967 Act.

Concern over the secret reserves used by some companies in the 1920s to balance the books, led the 1948 Act to insist that the directors' report include details not merely of dividends declared but also any amounts carried to reserves. Also the remuneration of directors – salaries, pensions, gratuities – had to be shown in the accounts, as did their holdings of shares and debentures. Interests in contracts had also to be declared. The Act perpetuated previous requirements on record-keeping – each company had to continue keeping minutes of directors' and general meetings, account books giving 'a true and fair view' of the company, and the various registers. Finally, previous to 1948 the law had forbidden certain classes of individuals, for example, the directors, employees, officers or partners, from acting as the auditors for a company (except private companies). From 1948 only recognized auditors, members of professional accounting bodies, were to be allowed to carry out this work, to ensure that proper standards were maintained in the published accounts.

Post-war changes in industrial structure

Technological changes which originated in the inter-war laboratory or research department, such as the jet engine, radar, plastics, nuclear fission, antibiotics, and electronic computers, were to have a dramatic effect on the structure of British industry. After the war, for example, the development of fast, long-distance air travel, ended the reign of the ocean liners, except as cruise ships, and led to spectacular growth in airports, and the avionics, aero-engine and air-frame industries. Chemical production shifted into the manufacture of 'lights', especially a range of artificials, such as polythenes, plastics, polystyrenes and new artificial fibres which radically changed the textile and packaging industries and affected aspects of the building, motor and furniture industries.

The staple industries of the nineteenth century, in serious decline between the wars, received a brief fillip in the Second World War, only to face renewed competition and decline soon afterwards. The railways' share of goods traffic fell as motor lorries became larger, more fuel-efficient, and, with the opening of the motorway network from 1959, faster. In addition, demand for the goods they had traditionally carried, such as coal, iron and steel, was diminishing. As industrial estates developed out of town, road transport became more convenient where factories were some distance from railway termini. Although railways retained a greater advantage in passenger traffic, and increased their speed by bringing in 'inter-city' services with limited stops, the 125 diesel locomotive, and by electrification of some routes, the motor car and long-distance bus and coach were able to offer greater flexibility and lower price and so cream off some passengers. Employment on the railways, consequently, fell sharply, encouraged by technological improvements in signalling, one-man working, and greater automation. Similarly in the docks employment plunged with the introduction of such labour-saving methods as roll-on, roll-off traffic, containerization and the movement of bulk ores, grains, liquids and powders by pumping or by vacuum suction. At the same time most dock complexes moved downsteam to deep-water berths with greater space, as ship sizes rose, leading to vast acreages of derelict docklands suitable for redevelopment. Other 'old' industries, such as coal, shipbuilding and cotton textiles saw their output and employment continue to slump, as a result of substitute products reducing the demand for their commodities, the intensification of foreign competition, as in shipbuilding and textiles, and the implications of changes in consumer life-styles.

However, it was not merely the nineteenth-century industries which were in decline. Some of the newer industries also began to feel cold winds of change. Until 1960 their output and employment were generally booming, but thereafter some, like the motor-cycle industry, and later the motor-car and electrical consumer goods industries, began to face rationalization. In part this was a function of more aggressive marketing of foreign competitors, as European and Asian producers recovered from the effects of the war and ventured on to the world stage. These competing products were not necessarily cheaper, but were often technically superior to the British-made product. Japanese motorcycles incorporated features on small and medium-size machines which had previously only been available on large, expensive models or on racing versions. European and Japanese cars came fully equipped with items fitted as standard that were only found as 'extras' on British cars. They also proved more reliable and durable. In the radio and music-reproducing industries Britain was unable to keep up with miniaturization and rapid technical change leading to a succession of generations of music-playing equipment – hi-fi, stereo, transistor, solid state, cassette, compact disc and digital audio tape. Although Britain pioneered some of the technical breakthroughs and continued to produce some high-quality, high-price versions, her market share in the mass-produced segment declined sharply. Similar stories could be told in other industries, such as cameras and photographic equipment, household appliances and some light chemicals.

This general trend gave rise to the term 'de-industrialization' to explain Britain's plight. The more optimistic versions argued that the United Kingdom was moving to a service economy based on information processing, merchanting and financial services, and leaving dirty smokestack industry to the newly developing countries. This trend was seen as environmentally healthy, concentrating on high added value, and using brain power to design, organize and manipulate rather than make products. It was perceived as a normal economic evolution caused when levels of affluence increased, and the individual's marginal propensity to consume goods declined while that for services rose sharply. The pessimists saw Britain as high cost, under-capitalized and losing out on vital new technologies. The interrelatedness of these new production techniques meant that giving up production in one area was likely to increase the probability of being unable to compete in another. The scenario envisaged mass unemployment for the many, whose education and experience ill suited them for high-level brain work, while the few, in the white-collar and white-coat industries, enjoyed high material standards. Although to some extent de-industrialization was common to many developed countries, it went furthest in Britain, and had implications for the balance of payments which began to become manifest in the late 1980s.

The inter-war pattern of greater concentration continued. The market share of the largest 100 businesses continued to grow steadily, from about 15 per cent in 1907 to 42 per cent in 1980, according to Hannah, as monopoly and oligopoly became more common.[33] This came about by horizontal amalgamations, as, for instance, in the succession of mergers which led to most British motor car, lorry and bus-makers joining British Leyland by the later 1960s, or the amalgamations culminating in the 1960s with the juncture of General Electric, Associated Electrical Industries and English Electric to dominate the electrical industry.[34] Some firms went for diversification, deliberately absorbing businesses in unrelated fields to spread risks. For example, Imperial Tobacco, the largest British tobacco and cigarette business, began absorbing firms in the food industry, such as Ross and Youngs frozen foods, Golden Wonder crisps and Buxted chickens.

There was a growing belief that in some industries Britain was too small-scale a producer to compete with much larger foreign firms, and that the only route to greater competivity was growth in size through amalgamation. This was the basis of many of the mergers recommended by the Industrial Re-organisation Corporation, set up by the Wilson government of the mid-

1960s. Government also encouraged oligopoly in two other respects. In the post-war Attlee government a number of industries were nationalized, such as coal, railways, iron and steel, electricity and gas, making many of them monopolies. This pattern was repeated in the 1960s when another Labour government took other industries into public ownership – shipbuilding and aerospace – and in so doing created more monopolies. In theory governments were wedded to the belief that competition promoted the most efficient allocation of goods and services. Various bodies such as the Monopolies and Mergers Commission, existed to delay, examine, and even prevent, amalgamations if they were deemed to be contrary to the public good. However, it was rare for such mergers to be forbidden. In general, until the 1980s, governments sanctioned growth in size and scale. In the 1980s the Thatcher government espoused competition more whole-heartedly and began to 'privatize' a large number of nationalized industries or government holdings – Jaguar, British Telecom, BP and British Gas – but the amount of effective competition in, say, the telecommunications, gas, electricity and water industries was minimal.

Financial institutions

By the 1960s the stock exchange and merchant banks were primarily geared to home industrial finance in complete contrast to the formal financial markets of the 1860s. Not merely were merchant banks earning most of their profits from issuing, underwriting and promoting domestic industrial business, they were also acting as financial consultants to British business, advising on corporate structure, strategy and opportunities. Increasingly British firms were willing to call in outside experts, whether from banks, accounting or legal partnerships, to provide objective advice. This was partly a result of the continuing demise of family control of large firms, and the growth of professional management less concerned with trade secrets and more obsessed with a continuous search for efficiency.

The role of the City was given a great boost in the 1980s by 'big bang' and the privatizations. 'Big bang' was the opening up of the London stock exchange to electronic methods of dealing, international involvement and the abolition of restrictive practices and artificial job demarcation. It was intended to bring back investors who had turned to foreign exchanges and increase London's international role and prestige. The spate of privatizations gave much work to the merchant banks in issuing, underwriting, promoting, and arranging advertising. Such operations were expensive – the cost of launching British Gas in 1986 was £164 million and that of the BP share issue in 1987 £39 million. Until the slump in share prices in the autumn of 1987 Britain did indeed seem to be moving towards a larger financial service role.

The post Second World War period saw growing internationalization of business. This was not new, for Britain had exported goods, services, ideas and people on a large scale in the nineteenth century, but there were two novel trends. Firstly, British industry pursued the multinational path more aggressively. Secondly, there was a two-way flow as many foreign firms began investing in Britain. One component of the de-industrialization debate mentioned previously was that Britain seemed keener to invest in overseas manufacturing capacity than she did at home. Many large firms set up plants abroad to serve local markets or bought foreign firms rather than producing in the United Kingdom and exporting. In some cases this was justified by high local tariffs or the need to avoid costly transport charges but some voiced concern that it was a method of circumventing awkward unions to exploit foreign labour accustomed to lower wages and conditions at work. To the extent that such foreign profits were repatriated, they aided Britain's balance of payments, but there was also a belief that British jobs were being sacrificed.

The other side of the coin was the inward flow of investment from American, European and Japanese businesses. Again, of course, this was not new. There had been many examples of American multinational investment in Britain before 1914, both by establishing separate plants, and by buying British companies. In the early 1920s there had been a spate of American investment by firms flush with foreign earnings from the war: Boots, Vauxhall and Hedleys were bought by American parents, while Heinz, Chesebrough and Hoover established plants in Britain. This trend was repeated in the 1950s, and from the 1970s Japanese firms began opening plants partly as a tariff-free and local manufacture route into the prosperous European market, partly as a way of employing their vast balance of payments surpluses. During the 1980s, with the approach of the deadline for free transfer of factors of production between the 12 members of the European Economic Community (ECC), there was also European inward investment as firms strove to become big enough to cater for the whole of this market. The way ahead seemed to be for even fewer separate firms operating on a European-wide scale.

Compared to the 1948 Act, subsequent changes in company law were much less dramatic. In 1967 the status of the exempt private company was abolished, so that all limited companies now had to provide the Registrar with balance sheets, profit and loss accounts, auditors' and directors' reports, and much more information was available to creditors and the public. At the same time the rules about disclosure of individual directors' emoluments and shareholdings were tightened up, mainly because the wording of the 1948 Act had allowed firms to avoid its intention by submitting aggregate figures. To help identify potential bidders, particularly given the increased use of nominee shareholders, individuals and companies who owned more than 10 per cent of the total equity had to declare the fact. In 1976 the limit was reduced to 5 per cent.

The entry of Britain into the European Economic Community in 1973 brought changes in company law in order to harmonize statutory requirements throughout member countries. This began with the 1980 Act, which implemented the Second European Community Directive on company law, dealing among other things with the formation of public companies, allotment of shares and capital requirements. It also introduced the nomenclature of plc (public limited company) for publicly quoted companies and the notion of 'insider dealing', based on the confidentiality of privileged information, and tightened up the responsibilities of directors. The 1981 Act, which stemmed from the Fourth European Community Directive on company law, continued the process of harmonization. This Act also brought in new disclosure rules for one company owning shares in another, and new regulations on companies dealing in their own shares. Finally, in 1985, because so much new legislation had been introduced since the war, a consolidating act was considered necessary. It repealed the 5 companies Acts of 1948, 1967, 1976, 1980 and 1981 and restated the law in a more convenient form, with modern wording making it easier to read and understand.

Conclusion

There have been drastic changes since the mid-eighteenth century in both the nature and structure of British business and the scale and characteristics of its market. The market served by British businesses grew in size and wealth, as population and standards of living rose and as transport improvements created a national market, rather than a series of regional markets, and then a global market where British goods were sold almost as easily in Australia or Argentina as the United Kingdom. Growth in market size led to a need to produce on a much greater scale; hence the emergence of new production technologies which gave economies of scale and the need for greater capitalization. In order to ensure profitability and achieve these output levels, combination was popular. As output was growing in size, there was a concomitant need for large-scale marketing techniques to inform and persuade the consumer; hence the huge increase in the proportion of sales revenue devoted to this activity in the twentieth century.

As firms grew larger and more complex so did their need for formal documentation, as distinct from information carried in the heads of the partners. This led to a proliferation of types and quantity of internal records. In addition, for those firms which were joint-stock companies, the requirements of company law meant the creation, retention in the business and lodging in the public domain of a range of statutory records. For those companies that raised finance via the stock exchange – public or quoted companies – the rules of that body also imposed certain obligations to create some documents which were circulated to shareholders and deposited with the stock exchange.

SELECT LIST OF PARLIAMENTARY ACTS AND EVENTS RELEVANT TO CHANGES IN BUSINESS ORGANIZATION AND RECORD-KEEPING

1844   **An Act for the Registration, Incorporation and Regulation of Joint Stock Companies** – companies to be registered with and return certain records to the Registrar of Companies. A 'full and fair' audited balance sheet to be presented to each meeting of shareholders.

1847   **An Act to Amend an Act for the Registration, Incorporation and Regulation of Joint Stock Companies.**

1855   **An Act for Limiting the Liability of Members of Certain Joint Stock Companies** – introduced limited liability.

1856   **Joint Stock Companies Act** – replaced earlier legislation. Established separate registers in Scotland (Edinburgh) and Ireland (Dublin). Memorandum and articles of association to be lodged with the Registrar. Annual audit no longer mandatory.

1857   **An Act to make Better Provisions for the Punishment of Frauds Committed by Trustees, Bankers and other Persons Instrusted with Property** – made it a criminal act to publish or circulate any written statement or account a director knew to be false.

1858   **An Act to Allow Joint Stock Banking Companies to be Formed on the Principle of Limited Liability.**

1862   **Joint Stock Companies (Consolidation) Act** – consolidated previous legislation, and extended limited liability to insurance companies. All companies to retain a register of mortgages.

1867   **Companies Act.**

1869   **Limited Partnership Act** – allowed all partnerships to accept long-term loans at variable rates of interest, depending on profit (loss), effectively creating sleeping partners on the French model.

1878   Collapse of the City of Glasgow Bank stimulated adoption of limited liability.

1890   **Companies (Winding Up) Act.**

1890   **Partnership Act** – limited the number of partners to 20 (10 in the case of banks). Partnerships no longer automatically dissolved on the death of a partner.

1900   **Companies Amendment Act** – annual audit mandatory for all registered companies, directors no longer permitted to act as auditors. Required prospectuses and registers of mortgages to be lodged with the Registrar. The underwriting of share issues was made legal.

1907   **Companies Act** – distinguished between private and public companies for the first time and required that public companies annually lodge a balance sheet with the Registrar. Private companies able to appoint directors as auditors.

1907   **Limited Partnership Act.**

1908   **Companies (Consolidation) Act** – consolidated previous legislation.

1917   **Companies (Particulars as to Directors) Act.**
1928   **Companies Act** – required the circulation of accounts, including profit and loss accounts, to members before annual meetings, tightened the format of the balance sheet and required directors to supply lists of other directorships.
1929   **An Act to Consolidate the Companies Acts 1908 to 1928** – consolidated previous legislation.
1931   Royal Mail case stimulated pressure for publication of consolidated accounts by holding companies.
1939   Stock Exchange required companies seeking listing to publish consolidated balance sheets.
1948   **Companies Act** – made consolidated accounts and independent audit of all companies mandatory.
1948   Monopolies and Restrictive Practices Commission formed.
1967   **Companies Act** – required private companies to lodge balance sheets and profit and loss accounts with the Registrar and all auditors to be professionally qualified. Insisted on disclosure of individual shareholdings in excess of 10 per cent.
1968   City Panel on Take-Overs and Mergers formed.
1976   **Companies Act.**
1980   **Companies Act** – made United Kingdom legislation conform with Europe and introduced public limited company (plc) nomenclature for parent companies.
1985   **Companies Act.**

Notes

1 P. Mathias, *The First Industrial Nation: An Economic History of Britain 1700–1914* (Methuen, London, 1976) is an excellent introduction to this period and its issues.
2 B. W. E. Alford, *W D and H O Wills and the Development of the UK Tobacco Industry 1786–1965* (Methuen, London, 1973), pp. 15–100.
3 F. Crouzet, *Capital Formation in the Industrial Revolution* (Methuen, London, 1972) is a good introduction to this topic.
4 M. W. Flinn, *Men of Iron: The Crowleys in the Early Iron Industry* (Edinburgh University Press, 1965).
5 J. Lord, *Capital and Steam Power 1750–1800* (Frank Cass, London, 1966).
6 L. S. Pressnell, *Country Banking in the Industrial Revolution* (Oxford University Press, 1956) is still the best general survey.
7 One of the best expositions of company law is in P. L. Cottrell, *Industrial Finance 1830–1914: The Finance and Organization of English Manufacturing Industry* (Methuen, London, 1980), Chapter 3.
8 Lord, *op. cit.*; N. McKendrick, 'Josiah Wedgwood: an eighteenth century entrepreneur in salesmanship and marketing techniques', *Economic History Review*, XII (1960), pp. 408–33; T. C. Barker, *The Glass-makers: Pilkington 1826–1976* (Weidenfeld and Nicolson, London, 1977).
9 The influence of company law on document creation is discussed in

J. Armstrong and S. K. Jones, *Business Documents: Their Origins, Sources and Uses in Historical Research* (Mansell, London, 1987).

10 H. A. Shannon, 'The coming of general limited liability', *Economic History*, II (1931), pp. 267–91; and H. A. Shannon, 'The first five thousand limited companies and their duration', *Economic History*, II (1932), pp. 396–424.

11 H. A. Shannon, 'The limited companies of 1866 to 1883', *Economic History Review*, IV (1933), pp. 290–316.

12 See L. Richmond and B. Stockford, *Company Archives: The Survey of the Records of 1000 of the First Registered Companies in England and Wales* (Gower, Aldershot, 1988).

13 L. Hannah, *The Rise of the Corporate Economy*, 2nd edition (Methuen, London, 1976), p. 175.

14 R. N. Forbes, 'Some contemporary reactions to a banking failure', *Three Banks Review*, 121 (1979), pp. 42–57. R. E. Tyson, 'Scottish investment in American railways: the case of the City of Glasgow Bank 1856–1881', in P. L. Payne (editor), *Studies in Scottish Business History* (Frank Cass, London, 1967), pp. 387–416.

15 W. J. Reader, *Imperial Chemical Industries: A History*, Volume I: *The Forerunners 1870–1926* (Oxford University Press, 1970), Chapter 3.

16 Alford, *op. cit.*, Chapter 7.

17 *Ibid*, pp. 251–77.

18 S. D. Chapman, *Jesse Boot of Boots the Chemists* (Hodder and Stoughton, London, 1974); C. Wilson, *The History of Unilever. A Study in Economic Growth and Social Change* (Cassell, London, 1954).

19 See W. H. Fraser, *The Coming of the Mass Market 1850–1914* (Macmillan, London, 1981), and T. R. Nevett, *Advertising in Britain: A History* (Heinemann, London, 1982) for further discussion of the growth of demand and marketing activities.

20 The chapter on 'The rise and fall of the company promoter and the financing of British industry', in J. J. Van Helten and Y. Cassis (editors), *Capitalism in a Mature Economy* (Edward Elgar, Aldershot, 1990), pp. 115–38, deals with this topic in some depth. A case study is to be found in J. Armstrong, 'Hooley and the Bovril Company', *Business History*, 28: 1 (1986), pp. 18–34.

21 Cottrell, *op. cit.*, p. 65.

22 See Hannah, *op. cit.*, Chapter 2.

23 D. C. Coleman, 'Gentlemen and players', *Economic History Review*, 26:1 (1973), pp. 92–116.

24 See S. Marriner, 'Company financial statements as source material for business historians', *Business History*, 22: 2 (1980), pp. 203–35, for a detailed discussion.

25 For a general discussion of the economic effects of the war see A. S. Milward, *The Economic Effects of the World Wars on Britain* (Macmillan, London, 1970).

26 See Hannah, *op. cit.*, Chapter 3.

27 E. Green and M. Moss, *A Business of National Importance: The Royal Mail Shipping Group 1902–1937* (Methuen, London, 1982).

28 Reader, *op. cit.*, Volume II (Oxford University Press, 1975); C. Wilson, *The History of Unilever* (Cassell, London, 1954); R. Jones and G. Marriott, *Anatomy of a Merger* (Cape, London, 1970); R. A. Church and M. Miller, 'The big three: competition, management and marketing in the British motor industry, 1922–1939', in B. E. Supple, *Essays in British Business History* (Clarendon, Oxford, 1977), pp. 163–86.

29 W. J. Reader, *Metal Box: A History* (Heinemann, London, 1976).
30 See G. Jones, 'Multinational chocolate: Cadbury overseas, 1918–39', *Business History*, 26: 1 (1984), pp. 57–76, and 'The growth and performance of British multinational firms before 1939: the case of Dunlop', *Economic History Review*, 37: 1 (1984), pp. 35–53; and Wilson and Reader, *op. cit.*
31 D. J. Jeremy (editor), *The Dictionary of Business Biography*, 3, H-L (Butterworth, London, 1985), pp. 110–14.
32 Hannah, *op. cit.*, p. 149.
33 Hannah, *op. cit.*, Chapter 7.
34 G. Turner, *The Leyland Papers* (Eyre and Spotiswoode, London, 1971); Jones and Marriott, *op. cit.*

Further reading

J. Armstrong and S. K. Jones, *Business Documents: Their Origins, Sources and Uses in Historical Research* (Mansell, London, 1987).

R. Church (editor), *The Dynamics of Victorian Business* (Allen and Unwin, London, 1980).

P. L. Cottrell, *Industrial Finance 1830–1914: The Finance and Organisation of English Manufacturing Industry* (Methuen, London, 1980).

R. P. T. Davenport Hines (editor), *Markets and Bagmen: Studies in the History of Marketing and British Industrial Performance 1830–1939* (Gower, Aldershot, 1986).

W. H. Fraser, *The Coming of the Mass Market 1850–1914* (Macmillan, London, 1981).

F. Goodall, *A Bibliography of British Business Histories* (Gower, Aldershot, 1987).

L. Hannah, *The Rise of the Corporate Economy*, 2nd edition (Methuen, London, 1983).

S. Marriner (editor), *Business and Businessmen: Studies in Business, Economic and Accounting History* (Liverpool University Press, Liverpool, 1978).

P. Mathias, *The First Industrial Nation: An Economic History of Britain, 1700–1914*, 2nd edition (Methuen, London, 1976).

T. R. Nevett, *Advertising in Britain: A History* (Heinemann, London, 1982).

J. Orbell, *A Guide to Tracing the History of a Business* (Gower, Aldershot, 1987).

P. L. Payne, *British Entrepreneurship in the Nineteenth Century* (Macmillan, London, 1974).

P. L. Payne, *The Early Scottish Limited Companies 1856–1895* (Scottish Academic Press, Edinburgh, 1980).

S. Pollard, *The Development of the British Economy 1914–1980*, 3rd edition (Arnold, London, 1982).

S. Pollard, *The Genesis of Modern Management* (Penguin, Harmondsworth, 1968).

R. Pope (editor), *Atlas of British Social and Economic History Since 1700* (Routledge, London, 1989).

L. Richmond and B. Stockford, *Company Archives: The Survey of the Records of 1000 of the First Registered Companies in England and Wales* (Gower, Aldershot, 1986).

B. E. Supple (editor), *Essays in British Business History* (Clarendon Press, Oxford, 1987).

W. A. Thomas, *The Finance of British Industry 1918–1976* (Methuen, London, 1978).

3

The development of office technology

John Orbell

A review of the development of methods of recording, copying, communicating, organizing and analysing business information is a subject scarcely covered in published works and has escaped detailed research. Yet it is of indisputable importance to the archivist, providing invaluable insight into how business archives are created and accumulated and furnishing information which assists in dating, appraising and conserving records. In this chapter the definition of 'office technology' is a liberal one, extending well beyond conventional information technology to areas such as the development of the postal system and papermaking.

Recording information

Paper

Parchment was the earliest form of writing material used in Britain. Made from the skins of sheep, it was clumsy to handle and expensive, although not so in comparison with early paper. Yet parchment's greatest quality was its durability, which made it particularly suitable for legal documents such as property deeds, partnership agreements and indentures of apprenticeship. It only ceased to be used for these purposes in the last decades of the nineteenth century, although paper had begun to replace parchment for other uses in the later Middle Ages.

In the seventeenth and eighteenth centuries, when the business use of paper was increasing rapidly, paper was made exclusively by hand. The basic raw material (cellulose fibre) was rags, whose type determined the quality and colour of the paper produced. White rags – old sails of ships were one source and garments another – had to be used for white papers, as no bleaches were available until around 1800. Brown paper for packaging was made from any kind of rags and was thus cheaper and used in greater quantities.

The earliest handmade paper in England was produced by sorting and dampening rags and then leaving them to rot, a process quickened by adding lime (which imparted to the paper a creamy colour). The rags were then pulped by beating to reduce the raw material to its individual fibres, to clean, shorten and fibrillate the fibres, and to disperse them into a water solution. The resulting pulp or 'stuff' was then spread across the wire covering of a mould, which allowed the water to drain away leaving a film of cellulose. This cellulose film was placed in a press to remove surplus water, dried by hanging from a rope and later sized to give it strength.

Watermarks in paper have long been common, the first ones originating from Italy in about the thirteenth century. Each paper mill had its own distinctive marks, which varied over time, although sometimes the stationer's mark was used instead or as well. They were made by introducing into the mould designs fashioned from thin wire, so that some parts of the mould were higher and others lower than the ambient level. Thus when pulp was added to the mould, it would form around this wire pattern and the resultant paper would reflect the design through its thickness. For archivists watermarks provide an important means of dating records.

Early watermarks were of simple design, sometimes being just a letter of the alphabet or a simple symbol. During the eighteenth century they became more complex, especially in the production of security papers. At the end of the eighteenth century standard types of watermarks – often a *fleur de lys*, a fool's cap (later replaced by a seated Britannia) and a post horn all set in a complex shield with the manufacturer's monogram below – became commonplace, denoting size of sheet. These marks invariably appeared in the centre of the top half of the sheet with the manufacturer's or stationer's name in the second half, sometimes with the date below. Wove paper was watermarked more simply, as the smoothness of the paper was of paramount importance, with just the manufacturer's name at the bottom edge.

Towards the end of the eighteenth century tin foil shapes began to be incorporated into the wires creating a watermark design with relatively large lighter areas, although this practice was largely restricted to Continental Europe. In 1794 legislation required the incorporation of year of manufacture into watermark design if books made from this paper were to be exported without payment of duty, and this provides a fairly reliable means of dating. The legislation was repealed in 1811 but the custom prevailed. Date of manufacture, of course, does not necessarily reflect date of use, but studies have shown that it was uncommon for publishers to stock paper for more than 2 or 3 years, and this may well be applied to all areas of business. The first experiments in the use of coloured watermarks were successfully made in 1819 but were not then incorporated into security paper on account of the cost of doing so. They were revived again in 1885, but even then were not widely applied. A few studies have set out to list and describe watermarks, giving their date and manufacturer.[1] Inevitably most watermarks have been located in published works rather than in archives.

It was not until 1800 that white paper consumption in Britain began to expand significantly. All of it came from abroad until around 1600. By 1720 two-thirds was manufactured at home and the country was self-sufficient by around 1800 when annual United Kingdom production was around 600,000 reams. British manufacturers had improved the quality of their white paper as the century had progressed. From about the 1740s James Whatman had begun to make a good quality white paper with a hard, strongly sized surface to prevent the tips of quill pens digging into it. A further innovation, in the absence of paper with printed lines, was the manufacture in Britain in the 1770s of 'watermarked ruling', which guided users to write in straight lines.[2]

Of greater importance was the introduction, in the mid-1750s, of wove paper, used largely for printing and as high quality writing paper. Handmade, laid paper made in traditional wire moulds suffered from varying thicknesses and formed an unsuitable surface on which to print. It can be easily identified, if held up to the light, by its close fine lines, with a second series of lines, much further apart, running at right angles to them. Each line is the imprint of the wires in the mould. Wove paper, made in moulds with a cover made from woven wire cloth, lacked these lines and was especially smooth.

The greatest single improvement in the manufacture of paper occurred shortly after 1800. Until then century old methods still prevailed, based on highly skilled craft techniques, which meant that production was by hand and in small batches. In 1807 the Fourdrinier machine – named after the London stationer who financed its development – was making paper of satisfactory quality. According to contemporary estimates, the cost of making paper fell around 75 per cent, and by 1850 only about 10 per cent of British paper was made by hand.

In the early nineteenth century the principal source of cellulose for papermaking was still rags, but they were always in short supply and their quality was far from homogeneous, creating serious problems in manufacturing paper of consistent quality. Initially esparto grass provided a suitable substitute (first used in 1839 but not in significant quantity until the early 1850s). However, by the end of the century wood pulp was rapidly overhauling esparto grass as the principal source of cellulose fibre, as it was both cheaper and generally more suitable.

As the nineteenth century progressed, so the quality of paper declined. As early as the 1820s it was already recognized that this was the result of damage to fibres caused by papermaking machines – the use of alum in the size, the use of gypsum to ensure whiteness, and the excessive bleaching of rags. These shortcomings were seriously compounded by the use of poor quality fibre from esparto grass (from 1839) and wood pulp (from c.1860) which progressively created paper with shorter and shorter life spans. Paper made earlier than this, if properly stored and used, has almost universally survived in undiminished strength and freshness. However, the quality of paper made from inferior pulp can be substantially improved by chemical treatment during manufacture, although this seems to have been possible only from the second half of the twentieth century and then rarely carried out.

It is extremely difficult, even for an expert, to identify, one from the other, rag, wood pulp and esparto papers. However handmade papers are more easily distinguished from those made by machine. Handmade papers, when held up to the light, have light and dark patches, reflecting the high and shallow areas which are characteristic of such paper, however skilled the papermaker. A second tell-tale sign is that handmade paper has no grain, as the fibres are 'dispersed' by the movement of the mould during manufacture. A machine-made sheet will bend more in one direction than the other, reflecting the fact that the fibres are all aligned in one direction.

Writing instruments

Pencils are supposed first to have been made in the sixteenth century, following the discovery of graphite in Cumberland, England. Originally they comprised pure graphite wrapped in string or cedar wood and it was the Italians who first developed a wooden holder or casing. Many of the large pencil manufacturers were established relatively early – Staedtler in 1662 and Faber-Castell in 1760. Indelible pencils were patented in the United States in 1866. Nonetheless pencils were rarely used in business records on account of the ease of erasing the information they recorded.

The quill pen was the standard writing instrument in use before the first decades of the nineteenth century. Although cheap, the quill was difficult to use and required frequent sharpening until it would allow small writing without piercing the paper. Steel pens were introduced from the 1820s onwards and became widespread from the 1840s. Quills, however, remained popular – the Bank of England was still purchasing them in quantity in 1907. Both quills and steel nib pens were dip pens and were not easily portable, as an inkwell was required. Efforts were made to develop a pen with an ink reservoir at regular intervals throughout the nineteenth century, but it was not until the 1880s that the first practical fountain pen appeared. This was developed by L. D. Waterman of New York. It was, however, only in the 1900s that they came into common use.

Their successor, the ball-point pen, although patented in the last century and commercially marketed from 1885, only came into its own following the improvements of George Biro in 1938. He was the first to recognize the significance of quick drying ink, which was an important feature of the 'biro'. Biro perfected his pen during the early 1940s, and in 1945 the first commercially produced ball-point went on regular sale in the United Kingdom. By 1949 biro sales had outstripped sales of fountain pens. The first throw-away biro, priced at one shilling, was introduced into Britain from France in 1958; by 1959 annual sales totalled 53 million.

Typewriters

Speed was the chief reason for the attractiveness of the typewriter over the pen, legibility and the ability to make copies being secondary, though important, considerations. There were many early attempts to develop a typewriter, but the first machine of note was one developed by Sholes and

Gidden and marketed in the United States in 1874. Remington was the manufacturer and in 1876 the machine became known as the Remington Number One. This typewriter was neither technically reliable nor a commercial success, but its successor, the Remington Number Two, introduced in 1878, was much more satisfactory, although it suffered the disadvantage that it wrote 'non-visibly', so that the typist could not see what was being typed. This machine could write in both capitals and lower case and was equipped with a considerable number of sign keys. In the 1880s a succession of new models appeared, perhaps the most notable being the Caligrapher which, together with the Remington machines, were market leaders. The development of these machines was very rapid in the United States but much slower in Europe. The first machine of modern conventional design was the Underwood model, introduced in the late 1890s. It was the first successful 'visible' machine. A subsequent model introduced on to the British market in 1905 was the first to be fitted with an integral tabulator.

Standardization of the keyboard arrangement also gradually came about in the first decades of the twentieth century as the Universal Keyboard ousted those arranged by manufacturers' whim. The machines of the 1870s were capable of typing at the rate of 30 to 40 words per minute, or at about the same rate as fast handwriting. Thereafter speeds increased rapidly so that by 1887 Remingtons could claim that their latest typewriters could reach almost 100 words per minute. Mass production meant falling prices, but the typewriter's success was also due to the arrival, in the mid-1880s, of permanent inks to replace the earlier aniline inks, which were liable to fade. The typewriter was also an effective copying machine when carbon paper was used. Carbonated paper had been available from at least the early 1820s. However, the 'clean' carbon papers developed by American manufacturers in the last decades of the nineteenth century made poor copies when used with quills or steel pens because of the inadequate and uneven hand pressure applied. Thus carbons were restricted to marginal business tasks, such as making copies of receipts, bills of lading, orders and the like. The typewriter changed this, as the adequate and even pressure of its keys made good quality copies as well as several of them, a facility that was well appreciated from the early 1870s.

Typewriters were also vital in extending the application of duplication to produce mass copies. Handwritten stencils could not be used with typewriters as either ink-passing perforations were not made or, if made, tended to chop out entire letters. In 1886 Gestetner was experimenting with a more appropriate type of Japanese tissue called Yoshino, which eventually proved successful and was to form the basis of typewriting stencils up until the 1930s. Other improvements to the composition of the stencil itself followed, and from the 1890s an effective typewriter stencil was available for use in making clear, good quality, multicopies for the first time.

As the twentieth century progressed so machines were further refined. Perhaps the most significant development was the introduction of electric typewriters between the wars, the first commercially successful one being marketed by International Business Machines in 1935. However, in essence these were modifications of an old principle. It was not until the advent of the word-processor, first used in the 1970s and installed in huge numbers from the 1980s, that the conventional typewriter was ousted.

Inks

Since the eighteenth century there have been a huge range of writing inks, but they break down into three basic types. The earliest is carbon ink made from carbon mixed with gum. It is water-soluble and tends to fade. Iron gall inks, the most widely used in the nineteenth century, made from oak galls and copperas (iron sulphate), are very strongly acidic, and documents written with them tend to fade and to develop holes around the writing. They are not water-soluble. The third type, also made for the first time in the nineteenth century, is based on dyes, and was regarded as an inferior ink. It discolours easily and is affected by acids and alkalis.

Modern inks are made from a mixture of water-soluble synthetic dyes. Coloured writing inks – blue and red – were both well established in the nineteenth century, and, like other inks of the period, are liable to lose their colour. The inks used in ball-point, fibre or felt-tipped pens are also fugitive. Those used in early typewriter ribbons, consisting of dyes held in spirit or water and glycerine, and in early duplicating machines, are also unstable and prone to fade.

Addressing machines

Addressing machines were developed in the United States, using several individual inventions made between 1870 and 1909, when the basic machine was perfected. By this time brass embossed plates were the medium for recording the name and address and had replaced the rubber stamps which had been in use since the mid-1890s. These plates enabled addresses to be printed more sharply, so that they resembled typewriting. Improvements followed swiftly, so that by the early 1930s machines could automatically select address plates and control what information on the plate was printed. The addressographs, as these early machines were known, were not restricted to addressing envelopes but could also be used for entering information on card indexes and at the head of sheets from loose-leaf binders. They were subsequently used for heading invoices and similar records.

Copying information

Early practices

It was not until the last quarter of the nineteenth century that effective mechanical devices to make multi-copies of documents were introduced. Before then the copy clerk or 'writer' ruled supreme; if a copy was wanted it was made by hand and if many copies were required, many hands were needed. There were some early innovations. In 1655 at least one attempt had been made to make copies by pressing moist sheets against an original with wet ink. The polygraph or multipen, introduced in the late eighteenth century but never widely adopted, embodied a mechanical solution by linking the pen in use, by a series of levers, to other pens which then moved in tandem. It had first been introduced in the late eighteenth century.

James Watt's portable copying machine, patented in 1780, was, however, the most important innovation, and a much more serious competitor to the copy clerk. The letter to be copied was written in a special copying ink on a sheet of good quality writing paper and placed, when dry, in contact with damp tissue paper. The two were then held together in a screw press so that an impression was made in reverse on the tissue paper which could be read from the opposite side. It received a substantial, if belated, boost from the introduction of aniline dyes from 1856 (these gave copy letters their characteristic violet colour) and from the importation of strong, thin and transparent tissue paper from Japan during the mid-1860s. In its most refined form, letters were copied direct into copy books. The tissue page was dampened *in situ* with water from a brush, adjoining pages being protected by the insertion of sheets of oiled paper either side of the tissue. The letter to be copied was then laid on top of the tissue and the whole letter book closed and placed in a screw press for up to 30 seconds. By the mid-nineteenth century this system of copying had been widely adopted, but it produced only a few copies and demanded experienced operators.

Carbons, consisting of paper coated with oil and carbon black, were made as early as the 1820s, but they were never very popular until the advent of the typewriter (see p. 64).

Duplication

In the 1880s great advances in multicopying were made. In a sense the hectograph, Eddison's electric pen and the papyrograph had led the way but had never achieved any very great application. Most of these devices depended upon the principle of making fine holes in impermeable paper through which ink was then forced to form writing on sheets of paper below. The real breakthrough came with David Gestetner's invention of stencil duplicating. In 1881 he patented his Cyclostyle – a wheeled pen capable of making good ink-passing perforations through waxed paper sheets so that excellent reproductions of handwriting could be made from the master stencil.

The Cyclostyle seems to have sold well and its application was increased by two further refinements. One was an improved stencil based on Japanese 'Takamatsu' tissue paper, introduced in the mid-1880s, and the other was the invention of a more effective wheeled pen – the Neo-Cyclostyle – which was manipulated almost as easily as an ordinary pen. These, combined with the introduction by Gestetner of his upgraded duplicating apparatus, the Neo-Cyclostyle Duplicating Apparatus, ensured the very widespread adoption of duplicating as effective office technology in the 1890s. It was now possible to roll off a copy within 10 seconds and to make 2,000 copies from one stencil. A series of additional improvements were in place by about 1905, forming the basis of the modern duplicator: stencils which could be efficiently cut by typewriters were available before 1900; paste-like ink replaced fluid ink; automatic inking was introduced; and finally rotary machines were developed in which the stencil was fitted around a drum or cylinder which was turned by a handle considerably increasing speed of output. Indeed many models developed in the nineteenth century were still at work after the Second World War, while newer models were based largely on nineteenth-century technology.

Photography

Copying of records by photography was well established by 1914, but was never widely applied until it received a fillip from the introduction of microfilming output direct from computers. Photography was originally used to provide copies which could not easily or cheaply be made by other means – plans, drawings, diagrams, documents bearing signatures, handwritten accounts, tables of statistics, and so on – to provide facsimiles of guaranteed accuracy in case, say, of destruction of the original copy. The saving of storage space by miniaturization was very much a subsidiary by-product. In the early twentieth century microcopies were not referred to as such – 'for storing or filing purposes a good plan is to take a negative copy *en* miniature . . . and then to run out a positive enlargement as and when required – if ever'.[3]

One of the earliest machines marketed in the United Kingdom was the 'Photostat' which, like all equipment at this time, reproduced direct on to photographic paper. Records photographed could be as large as 26 by 19 inches, the largest print possible was 22 by 18 inches, and twelve copies could be made in about 20 minutes. Copies made in this way were 'negatives', with 'positives' being formed by photographing the negative. Early users were mostly in the engineering sector and included Babcock & Wilcox Ltd, Sir W. G. Armstrong Whitworth & Co. Ltd, British Thomson

Houston Co. Ltd and Daimler Co. Ltd. The film used until the 1950s was cellulose nitrate based and often unstable (see p. 190).

Photocopying

Photocopying transformed office copying procedures and in the late 1960s and 1970s largely displaced the conventional duplicators. The first xerographic image – the creation of an electrostatic image on a photo-conductive surface which was then transferred to paper – was made in the United States in 1938 by Chester Carlson. He later teamed up with the Haloid Co. of New York, known as the Xerox Corporation from 1961, and in 1949 the first machine was marketed. This was a crude manual machine, slow and dirty in its operation, known as the Model A. The first semi–automatic machine was launched in 1955, capable of making continuous copies on plain paper from microfilm originals. These early models were only modest successes.

The Xerox 914 Copier, the first automatic copier, followed 4 years later and could make seven copies in a minute. It was the first true photocopier and was an immediate success; 10,000 machines had been sold worldwide by the end of 1962. Thereafter development was rapid; the first desk-top copier appeared in 1963; and by 1968 60 copies per minute were possible. By 1970 the first automatic two-sided copier was introduced and in the mid-1980s the first colour copier was marketed. By 1988 the Xerox Corporation alone had manufactured world-wide 2 million machines. It is not yet possible to comment on the long-term durability of photocopies, but, in the short term, photocopies do tend to fade if exposed to daylight over an extended period and print can adhere to plastic or other similar surfaces. The wet chemical process common during the late 1950s and early 1960s used thick paper and produced uneven results.

Communicating information

Postal system

Crucial to the efficient running of trade and industry is reliable and fast, yet cheap, communications. For business, at least until recent years, the mainstay of such communications has been the postal service. The General Post Office came into being in 1657 with a monopoly, in theory if not in practice, in inland and overseas posts. Shortly afterwards, in 1661, the first date stamp was used to record time of dispatch. This was a simple date within a very small circle, and can sometimes be helpful to archivists in dating documents. The Post Office was very much a London-based affair, concerned primarily with long-distance posts carried along a relatively small number of main roads (6 in 1677) radiating from London and passing through many provincial centres.

In the late seventeenth century the phenomenally successful London Penny Post was established to collect and deliver London and suburban mail for one penny a letter or parcel not exceeding one pound in weight or £10 in value. Up until then it had been almost as easy to send mail from one end of the country to the other as it was to send it across the capital. By 1711 its official area of operation was up to 10 miles from Lombard Street in the City, although this was extended in 1794. Postmarks used by the London Penny Post were small heart-shaped stamps with 'MOR' for morning service and 'AF' for afternoon. Prepayment was compulsory, until 1794, and a triangular stamp, inscribed 'Penny Post Paid' and showing the initial letter of the sorting office, was also applied to the cover.

In the eighteenth century country postal services were improved by the reorganization of cross posts (those posts not originating from London but linking major provincial centres direct). The first ran from Bristol to Exeter in 1698. In 1765 legislation facilitated the establishment of penny posts outside London, as up until then the Post Office only carried mail to post towns but did not undertake to deliver to the addressees; only London had a local post. Dublin followed in 1773 and Edinburgh in 1773–4. Bristol, Glasgow and Manchester established them in the 1790s, when it was provided that any penny post could be extended beyond the former limit of 10 miles from the post's central location. By the 1830s penny posts operated across the country. In 1784 the first stage coaches carrying mails and operating to a strict timetable were introduced as an improvement upon the slow service provided by post boys carrying mails by horse, who had been increasingly liable to attacks by thieves. Speeds improved dramatically – the time to Edinburgh from London, for example, was reduced by 25 hours to 60. In the 1830s mail began to be carried by rail and by the mid-1840s all mail coaches on the London routes had been withdrawn. This was so on the cross country posts a decade later.

In 1794 the London Penny Post, perhaps the most vital part of the postal system, was overhauled. Receiving houses were given their own named stamps and date stamps showing the time in full. In 1840 the well-known reforms of Rowland Hill swept away inefficient practices and in particular the huge and complex variety of postal charges nationwide. No longer were charges to be based upon distance travelled and the number of sheets making up the letter but upon weight at the uniform charge of one penny per half ounce. Obligatory prepayment was also introduced, either evidenced by pre-paid letter sheets ('Mulreadys') or by adhesive postage stamps. This was the world's first stamp, the so-called Penny Black. The blacks were replaced by one penny reds about a year later, a move aimed at making cancellation more efficient and reducing opportunities for the fraudulent re-use of stamps. The Mulreadys survived for only a few months, after which they were replaced by plain embossed envelopes. These pre-paid envelopes were initially made from security paper with silk threads running through it, but in about 1860 this was replaced by watermarked paper. These reforms led to a dramatic increase in the amount of mail sent. Between 1840 and 1842 the number of chargeable letters sent in the United Kingdom increased from 75 to 196 million; in 1849, 329 million envelopes were sent. The bulk sending of mail was facilitated in the 1850s when postmarks bearing the word 'paid', together with the name of the Post Office and date, were applied as simple evidence of postage. In 1922 Britain introduced legislation to permit the use of franking machines and soon after the Post Office approved for use machines made by Pitney Bowes and Universal Postal Frankers Ltd.

The introduction of the postage stamp provides a means of precise or approximate dating of an envelope and its contents through reference to the annual stamp catalogues published by Stanley Gibbons Ltd. Postmarks, when they can be read, provide much better evidence for dating. These can be defined as any mark struck upon letters and other items passing through the post and can provide information on the place of origin and destination, the amount charged, weight, as well as date dispatched or received. There are an infinite variety and number of possible marks but they are well-documented in published works.[4] Stamps and postmarks are collectors' items and therefore can have considerable monetary value, thus creating a huge security problem for the archivist. In establishing values reference can be made to the appropriate stamp catalogue (published annually by Stanley Gibbons) and postmark literature.[5] Professional advice can be sought for items which are believed to have particular value, perhaps on an anonymous basis, from a reputable stamp dealer or auction house.

Foreign mails in early times were either letters of state or of merchants. By the end of the sixteenth century, all foreign posts had to be sent by the royal courier services, although some groups of merchants were allowed to carry their own. From 1619 the service was run by the Postmaster General for Foreign Parts, on some routes using official packet boats, so until the 1800s foreign mails were carried by a parallel service to the Post Office. So-called 'ship letters' were letters carried by ships other than the packets. From 1661, on arrival at British ports, shipmasters were obliged to hand over letters to the local postmaster, who stamped them with the local ship letter stamp, which marked the point of entry.

Sea voyages were very slow – the first packet voyage to Australia took 131 days in 1844! Steamships dramatically reduced sailing times and in the 1820s were carrying mail on short routes, such as across the Channel. By the 1840s mails could reach India in about 30 days.[6] However, it was the aircraft that truly revolutionized overseas mails. During the First World War air mail services were established for military use, and shortly afterwards scheduled services were introduced, the first between London and Paris. Charges were high, with a supplement of 12 pence per letter. In 1921 a part-air service reduced times to India from 27 days to 10, and by 1933 a regular service had opened from London to Singapore, to Australia by 1934 and to North America by 1939. By this time costs were fast coming down to a supplement of less than one penny per half ounce. Lightweight airmail stationery existed pre-war, but received a fillip during the war with special postcards for use by the forces, which were replaced by pre-stamped aerogrammes in 1942.

Envelopes

Until the advent of the envelope, letters consisted of a single sheet (or more) of paper folded so that the message was inside and the other, plain side carried the address. The letter was then sealed with a wafer (a small disc of flour mixed with gum and colouring which the writer moistened) or a wax seal impressed with a signet. The envelope as such, although in use on the continent, especially France, since the seventeenth century, was rarely used in the United Kingdom because postal charges were prohibitive and based in part on the total number of pieces of paper sent. Envelopes may first have been manufactured in the United Kingdom by a stationer called Brewer at Brighton as late as the 1820s.

The postal reforms of 1840, which meant that envelopes would no longer be charged, led to a notable increase in their use. Envelopes would then have been sold flat and folded and gummed by hand by the stationer or his customer. In 1845 Warren de la Rue patented an envelope-manufacturing machine which was improved further in 1850 to make gummed envelopes. It could turn out around 20,000 envelopes a day, considerably reducing costs. By 1876 John Dickinson & Co. were manufacturing 3 million envelopes a week, reckoned to be a quarter of United Kingdom output.

In the late-1850s production was mostly of 'pocket' envelopes, with the opening along the short edge, or 'bankers' envelopes, with the opening on the long side; also paper more resistant to wet, having a glazed appearance caused by burnishing against polished rolls, had been developed. In 1905 Millington & Sons acquired the United Kingdom rights from a United States manufacturer of the first 'window' envelopes marketed in this country. In the early 1930s lightweight airmail envelopes were being made, together with various types of easy fill and easy seal envelopes.

Telegrams

The telegraph's great advantage was that it allowed messages to be sent and received during the same working day. Anything not requiring immediate attention could be sent via the postal system at a much cheaper rate. Sending messages overseas was much slower and the telegram often replaced letters, although many businesses also confirmed telegraphic messages by post.

The first practical telegraph was patented in 1837, and the first to work over a substantial distance opened in 1839. From the late 1840s until the late 1860s 4 companies dominated inland telegraphy in the United Kingdom – the Electric Telegraph Co. (1846), the British Electric

Telegraph Co. (1849), the London District Telegraph Co. (1859), which was initially allowed to operate within a 4-mile radius of Charing Cross, and the United Kingdom Telegraph Co. By the early-1850s all the towns in the United Kingdom had been linked and by the late 1850s the network had reached such distant parts as the Channel Islands. By 1868 there were 110,000 miles of wire and 3,381 stations carrying over 6 million messages per year. Half originated from London – a good many from the Stock Exchange – and a further quarter from 15 other cities. However, letters still dominated; in 1865, for example, 151 letters were sent for every telegram.

From 1870 the business of most inland telegraph companies was transferred to the Post Office. A simple uniform rate was then introduced, at two-thirds the previous rate, which led to an explosion in traffic from 6.5 million messages in 1869 to 26.5 million 10 years later. Prices were steadily reduced and by 1900 some 90 million inland messages were being sent each year. From 1910, however, the inland telegraph declined as telephone usage expanded. In 1935, 35 million inland messages were sent and in 1970, 7.7 million. The inland service was wound up later that decade. One reason for this decline was the increasing use of telex.

The submarine telegraph was much more important to business than the inland telegram, as international mail was far slower than domestic mail. In 1851 the first submarine cable, between Dover and Calais, opened to public use, and by 1853 London was in direct telegraphic communication with the chief cities of Europe. By 1864 India was linked with Europe, although much of the line was overground, and 2 years later the first transatlantic line opened. Extension then moved forward at breathtaking speed, culminating in a line to Australia in 1872.

Competing technology was, however, around the corner. In 1907 Marconi's Wireless Telegraph Co. Ltd opened its first commercial overseas service, and during the next 17 years it opened circuits between London and the major cities of Europe as well as North America and Australia, although it was not until the 1920s that this technology began to make serious inroads into the business of the submarine companies. In 1956 the first transatlantic telephone cable was laid and was an immediate success. Others quickly followed. Telegraphy was to remain important throughout the 1960s but was effectively superseded in the 1970s by telephones and telex.

Telegram messages, whether inland or overseas, were delivered on printed telegraph company paper. Initially messages were handwritten but from the mid-1890s handwriting began to be replaced by a printed message on blue paper tape gummed to the form. Messages were still sent by morse, with typewriter-like keyboards perforating signals on to paper tape which then passed through an automatic transmitter. Receivers automatically printed on to tape. In 1915 E. E. Kleinschmidt and Markum of the United States developed the teleprinter and in 1921 the Post Office was experimenting with a similar machine, although it was not widely adopted in the United Kingdom until the early 1930s. Its advantage lay in its simplicity of operation, as Morse code was no longer the medium of transmission – the transmitting operator merely typed messages on an ordinary typewriter and the receiving operator had only to gum a typed slip on to the telegram form. The teleprinter also marked the beginning of telex with businesses installing their own machines and sending and receiving messages along dedicated telephone lines. This became a very significant means of international communications from the 1950s, and was only rivalled by facsimile messages in the late 1980s.

Telephones

Whereas the telephone did not in itself give rise to particular record formats, other than notes of telephone messages, it certainly led to a reduction in the number of letters which would otherwise have been sent. Moreover, the existence of telephone numbers on notepaper are often helpful to archivists in determining dates.

In 1876 Graham Bell patented his telephone technology and the telephone went into immediate business use in the United States. Application in the United Kingdom was slower, in order to protect the Post Office's investment in telegraphy, and in 1882 there were only 1,600 subscribers. During the 1880s most telephone systems in the United Kingdom were installed and managed by either the United Telephone Co. (London and South), the National Telephone Co. (Yorkshire, Midlands and Scotland), and the Lancashire and Cheshire Telephone Co., all of which merged together in 1898 to form the National Telephone Co. A national network was not immediately possible as the Post Office refused permission for inter-urban trunk lines. However, in 1884 these companies were allowed to develop oral communications to all parts of the country but were prohibited from transmitting written messages. Lines were opened from Edinburgh to Glasgow in 1884, from Manchester to Liverpool in 1885 and from London to Manchester in 1886.

The National Telephone Co.'s assets were acquired by the Post Office in 1911 and thereafter expansion of the telephone network was very rapid. Whereas in 1911 the number of telephone messages transmitted was 42.4 million, in 1913 the number had risen to an astonishing 486.5 million. By 1927–8 there were 1.6 million telephones installed in the United Kingdom, rising to 7.8 million in 1960, and to almost 14 million a decade later.

In 1889 the first experiment was made in sending telephone messages by submarine telephone cable and 2 years later the first international telephone service opened between London and Paris. Thereafter progress was very slow and in 1922 Britain was in direct telephone communication with only Paris and Brussels. Subsequently expansion speeded up and in January 1927 the first public service between this country and the United States was opened and 2 years later the first sustained telephone conversation between Britain and Australia was possible. These new links were based upon radio technology which was both insecure and vulnerable to atmospheric conditions. Long-distance international telephone calls were facilitated in 1956 with the opening of the first transatlantic submarine cable and cables connecting other parts of the world were soon laid. In 1962 the first telecommunications satellite, Telstar, was launched, and a year later direct dialling overseas was introduced, between London and Paris. However, the high cost of international telephone calls meant that most international messages were sent between businesses by telex via telephone lines.

Facsimile

The facsimile machine overtook telex as a means of business communication in the late-1980s, but its pedigree is surprisingly long. The principle upon which fax is based was developed in the mid–nineteenth century, but it was not until 1902 that the first photoelectric scanning fax system was demonstrated. This was especially suitable for sending copies of photographs, as text could be sent more cheaply by telegram or telephone. By 1910 newspapers in London, Paris and Berlin were swapping photographs by fax, using radio waves as a communications channel.

The first machines which could be connected to the public telephone network were introduced in the 1950s, and in 1966 the Xerox Corporation marketed the first facsimile machine designed specifically for business use. By the early 1970s there were 30,000 machines in the United States, but general innovation was delayed by the incompatibility of machines made by different manufacturers. Moreover these early machines were slow and unreliable; even in the 1970s it could take 6 minutes to send a single sheet of paper, making transmission costs very expensive.

Technical problems were solved with the innovation of digital technology in the late 1960s, which dramatically speeded transmission and improved resolution. However, problems of incompatibility only began to be solved from 1974, with the introduction of the first internationally recognized standards as laid down by a United Nations' forum. Falling costs in the 1980s, coupled with industrial disputes by postal workers, contributed to a boom in the use of fax in the United Kingdom. In 1987 there were 170,000 machines and the number had doubled by the end of 1988 to around 370,000, at a time when only 112,000 telex machines were in operation in the United Kingdom.

Unfortunately documents received on thermal paper machines are liable to fade over time – sometimes in less than 3 months – because of the paper's sensitivity to light and heat. These dangers are heightened when faxes are stored in plastic wallets. As a solution to this problem, machines using plain paper, and not paper treated chemically to facilitate transmission, were introduced in 1987 by Rank Xerox.

Organizing and analysing information

Books and binders

Account books and other volumes such as minute books, in their earliest form, were little more than printed books without the print. They were bound up by the same process. Given the costs of paper, they were prohibitively expensive, every page was used even if this meant devoting more than one account to a page, and margins were small. By the eighteenth century, if not before, firms of stationers manufactured a standard range of books – the 'guinea ledgers' marketed by the famous firm of Robinsons of Bristol were one such example. As well as these standard ranges, the production of custom-designed books enabled wealthier customers to continue with the same design for the same account book series over many years. Barclay & Fry of London was perhaps the best known firm specializing in this work. Its representatives covered the whole country, spreading the message that it would manufacture books to any size of paper, number of pages, style of binding, lettering on the spine, pagination, ruling, cover colour and so on, which its customers would specify. Repeat order could then be placed by citing a reference number, often written on the manufacturer's label on the inside front cover.

Loose-leaf binders were perhaps the single most significant development in the history of account and minute books. They had been introduced shortly before 1900 but only came into widespread use in the 1920s and 1930s. Initial reluctance to use them was born of fear of loss or theft of pages, and so early binders were equipped with sophisticated locking devices or had watermarked or machine numbered paper which might also carry the letterheading of the business. Loose-leaf binders had considerable advantages. Pages could be kept in strict alphabetical order, thus obviating the need for book or card indexes; clerical time was saved in not having to open periodically a whole new ledger; no pages went unused if incorrect allowances were made for the space of accounts when opening a ledger; contents could be typed; filled leaves could be removed to a transfer ledger – equipped with less stout covers on account of less frequent use – meaning that binders did not become too unwieldy. 'Card ledgers', where pages were held together on rods and not in binders, were a derivative of loose-leaf binders and also introduced around 1900 but not so widely used.

Filing systems

As the volume of business correspondence grew during the nineteenth century so filing systems became crucial. This was reflected in both filing equipment and procedures.

The age-old system of filing inward letters by date of receipt, pasting them into guard books and finding them by means of book indexes was largely redundant by 1900. As early as the beginning of the nineteenth century the so-called 'pigeon-hole' system had been recognized as an improvement. Letters were docketed with the name of correspondent, subject and date of reply, and then allotted a pigeon-hole according to name or location of correspondent. When non-current they were placed between boards, bundled up and stored, often in a deed box. Outgoing correspondence was kept separate, either in a press or in a copy letter book.

By 1900 other filing apparatus existed. The simplest held correspondence loosely in the pockets of an 'expanding alphabet case' or concertina file. A more secure method was making holes in the side or top of letters and placing them over spikes. The earliest such files were sold under the 'Shannon' trademark – a 'substantial board to which is attached a perforator, a double spring arch over which the letters are placed and a cover on which a spring presses to protect the letters from dust'.[7] The conventional 'manila' file appeared shortly before 1900, with letters 'being placed in a strong paper or linen cover (which can be had in various colours to distinguish departments, subjects, geographical division) on the back of which are placed metal strips which pass through corresponding holes pierced in the document, the ends of the strips being bent down over the top letter and held in place by a clip'.[8]

This apparatus reflected growing sophistication of filing procedures as separate files began to be kept for different correspondents and subjects. In these both outward and inward correspondence, arranged in date order, were kept on the same file, a procedure facilitated by carbon copies produced easily and cheaply by the typewriter. Indexes were often provided at the beginning of the file. Government departments with very large registries started to produce files from about 1905, but businesses only seem to have done so in large numbers after the First World War, when businessmen who had been seconded to the Civil Services during the emergency advocated the practice.

Where there were few letters from each of many correspondents, numerical systems were employed from the mid-nineteenth century until about the 1930s. In the earliest of these, well-established by 1900 and widely used by railway companies, each letter was stamped with the date of receipt and details of it entered into a letter register. Each letter was given a reference number and stored in that order. Replies carried this reference, in combination with the folio number of the copy letter book where a copy of the reply was to be found. Any subsequent incoming letter would be filed with the first letter, but to make the system work an index to the incoming letter register was vital. A typical reference on an outgoing letter was A2/16/1234, in which A was the department, 2 was the number of the copy-letter book, 16 was the number of the letter within the book, and 1234 was the number of the incoming letter(s). With the second system, all in and out letters with one correspondent were placed on the same numbered manila file, which was then kept in a numerical sequence with other files in the series. Files were then located by means of a card index. This was known as the 'vertical' system, in which files were held vertically in drawers rather than flat as had been standard practice in the nineteenth century.

In 1908, recognizing a market opportunity, the Roneo Company established a filing systems division. Its most noteworthy innovation was an alphanumeric system designed to reduce dependence on card indexes. In essence, filing was done in an approximate alphabetical order of, for example, customer name, but interspacing the files in the filing cabinet drawer were guide cards, each one covering certain letters of the alphabet (for example ABD–ANZ). Each guard card was also given a number corresponding to its place in the guard card sequence. On the guard card were written the names of the files which fell between its letters. These files were placed directly behind the card and each was given a number which was written both on the file and on the guard card. Thus files were arranged in approximate alphabetical order and within that order by number. They could be located by letter and returned by number, considerably reducing the chance of misfiling. A range of metal office furniture, including filing cabinets, card-index drawers and book racks, was introduced shortly after 1900 to accommodate new filing, especially vertical, systems. It came from the United States of America and was the product of the Art Metal Construction Co.

In attaching one paper to another a number of simple devices were applied from the mid-nineteenth century onwards. The oldest was by means of a stout steel pin. In the nineteenth century this was supplemented by a range of sophisticated brass and steel clips. The elastic band was patented in London in 1845, and was immediately advertised for use in bundling papers. However, rubber perishes and crumbles, often leaving a dark mark on papers in the process. Paper clips were patented in Germany in 1900 and quickly went into widespread use. Brass clips do not rust and can, with reasonable confidence, be left in place, as there is little danger of damage to the paper. Steel pins, of the nineteenth century and before, also seem to be resistant to rusting, but later steel paper clips are unstable and should be removed.

Adding and book-keeping machines

The first reliable calculating machine was developed by C. X. Thomas in 1820, but such machines were not used in significant numbers until the 1860s. By the 1870s they were being mass-produced and the first machine with a typewriter-style keyboard – the comptometer – was introduced in the United States in 1887. By 1900 several makes of key-driven machines were being marketed, culminating in 1922 with a machine which could automatically divide and multiply. Of greater significance to record-keeping were the key-driven 'adding and listing' machines of W. S. Burroughs, which, for the first time, produced a printed record of numbers and totals – either on rolls or sheets of paper or on printed forms. The first one was marketed in the early 1890s and by 1908 over 60,000 had been sold. Earlier machines had simply presented results on registers which had to be read off and written down.

Subsequently very large machines were developed for specific accounting applications such as book-keeping and billing. By 1905, for example, some machines could print two rows of figures simultaneously, or could print other information, such as page, invoice and policy number and so on. In the 1920s the range was extended to include book-keeping machines in which ledger narrative could be typed against the row of figures being listed and totalled. The first desk top electronic calculator appeared in 1961 and the first pocket calculator in 1972.

Tabulating machines and computers

The inaccuracies of logarithm tables supposedly gave rise to Charles Babbages' search, in the mid-nineteenth century, for a device for calculation by means of machine. His 'analytical engine' was an early but impractical form of computer which not only calculated but stored results for use in another calculation. It is the presence of memory which is one of the hallmarks of the computer.

By 1890 the first punched-card tabulating machine was speeding the analysis of data collected by the United States census, an innovation which managed to reduce data analysis from 7 years to 3. The answers to many census questions had been a straightforward yes or no, which could be recorded on a card simply by the presence or absence of a hole at a particular location. Thus data could be analysed by passing the cards through a machine which sensed the location of holes electro-mechanically. This principle was fundamental to data analysis up until the 1960s. These early machines were tallying machines, that is adding one to a total over and over, but soon they incorporated separate adding machines equipped with carrying devices into the tabulating machines. Thus armed, the systems began to undertake more demanding statistical tasks for large companies, in particular insurance and railway companies.

In 1904 what came to be known as the British Tabulating Machine Co. began marketing punch-card machines – known as Hollerith machines – in the United Kingdom, in 1905 renting (which remained normal practice for many years) its first to Woolwich Arsenal and three others to the giant businesses of Vickers, the Great Western Railway and the Lancashire & North Yorkshire Railway. It had acquired the rights to exploit in Britain and its Empire (other than Canada) the patents of the Tabulating Machine Co. of the United States (later International Business Machines, abbreviated to IBM), and so the machines it marketed were to be closely based on those of the American company until well after the Second World War.

Shortly after 1910 Powers Accounting Machines of the United States developed a punch-card machine which could print out its results; this was a major advance which enabled the machine to take on non-statistical tasks, especially book-keeping. Power Accounting Machines' British subsidiary, Accounting and Tabulating Machine Co. of Great Britain Ltd, in 1915 installed the first 2 machines in the United Kingdom, at His Majesty's Stationery Office and at the Prudential, followed by installations at Cadburys and Colmans in the following year. In 1923 a machine capable of printing letters as well as numbers was marketed in the United Kingdom for the first time. Thus punched card machines became completely accepted for business accounting.

In 1912 the data capacity of a punched card increased from 37 to 45 columns of information, a standard adopted by both the British Tabulating Co. and Accounting and Tabulating Co., the two companies which dominated the British market until well after the Second World War. The capacity of British Tabulating Co. machines increased further to 80 columns in 1928. Its rival, now trading as Power Samas, responded by producing a 26 column card machine in 1932 (increased to 36 columns in 1936), designed for small businesses, and upgraded its larger machine to 65 columns in 1936. The different card capacities of the two manufacturers were to create an enduring source of non-compatibility between their equipment.

Application of punched-card machines in the United Kingdom was slow. It received a spur during the First World War when munition factories acquired them, but even in 1917 the Hollerith machines were described as undoubtedly 'not well known'. Twenty years later *The Economist* reckoned that their high capital cost still made them too expensive for offices other than the very largest, despite their wide range of well documented applications – wages and sales analysis, stock control, valuations, and so on. However, the years from 1936 to 1939 were a time of boom, marking a huge increase in the use of such machines.

Tabulating machines created a mass of punched cards, batches for different tasks being distinguished by different colours. Where they did replace existing records, it was books of statistics, each line of which was replaced by a punched card. However, when produced to create statistics for internal consumption, there were few, if any, commercial or legal requirements to retain them long term. Where long-term retention was necessary the number of cards could be reduced by transferring data to 'summary' cards of distinctive appearance.

The first all-electronic machines for calculating purposes were developed in the United States and Germany for military use during the Second World War. The American machine, the so-called American Numerical Integrator and Calculator (ENIAC), had no moving parts (electronic valves were used in place of mechanical parts) and proved that automatic computation was possible. In 1948 IBM's Selective Sequence Electronic Calculator (SSEC) was the first computer to combine electronic calculation with stored instructions, and marked a big step forward. Using vacuum tubes, it was 250 times as fast as an earlier machine using conventional technology. However, the memory devices in the SSEC were electro-mechanical which reduced its effectiveness. This shortcoming was rectified in the early 1950s with the introduction of magnetic cores.

It was not until 1951 that the first commercial computer was put to use, not in business but in the United States Census Office. This was UNIVAC1. In 1952 IBM entered the market, with its 701 machine used mainly for government and research work, and rapidly came to dominate not only the United States but international markets as well; even by the beginning of the 1970s only indigenous companies in Japan and the United Kingdom were able to compete with IBM in their own markets. Britain had made an early start in computer development when in 1953 J. Lyons & Co. Ltd, the catering company, developed the first United Kingdom machine for its own use in accounting and payroll work. However, the application of the electronic computer in the United Kingdom should not be exaggerated. As late as the end of the 1950s, 90 per cent of the revenue of the British Tabulating Co. and Powers Samas was derived from conventional punched-card machines.

Innovation in computing, however defined, did not pick up until the 1960s. By 1967 there were about 10,000 machines at work in Western Europe and the number was doubling every 2 years. Worldwide, by 1970, about 100,000 computers had been installed. This increase came on the back of falling costs and improved education as to what could be achieved, and a rapid increase in the potential applications perceived by big business. Thus it was only in the 1960s that conventional punch-card machines were ousted by computers, although early computers still used the principle of punch cards for both input and output. Around 1960 it became possible to obtain printed output direct from the computer (until then a printed sheet was only obtained by passing output punched cards through a tabulator).

By 1970 five important functions for computers in the office (as opposed to the factory floor) had been identified. The first, and by far the most widely applied, was its use in undertaking routine clerical tasks, such as invoice writing and mailing and payroll preparation. Data analysis work then came second, providing information about stock levels, pricing, sales, costs and other important business variables. Design work in developing new products was the third function, and one of the earliest attempted; it could both assist in the perfection of a design and consider alternatives in order to identify the most cost-effective solution. The other functions were more specialized – facilitating operational decision-making by comparing input data against stored instructions, useful in such areas as stock control, and assisting management decision-making by establishing the effects of different courses of action.

Huge changes already under way, however, were to change computer technology during the 1970s and 1980s. In 1947 the transistor had been invented, and, on account of its small size and robustness, it was to replace the old thermionic valves used in electrical equipment up until then. The limitation to this 'miniaturization' was set by the fact that the components of circuits were individual items which had to be wired together, and wiring was bulky and vulnerable to human error. The solution lay in integrating all the components in one solid piece of material, which was achieved in 1958 with the development of the first integrated circuit – incorporated into commercial products from the early 1960s. Meanwhile another huge step forward had been made when in 1960 Fairchild Semiconductors developed the planar process, in which transistors were created in the surface of a wafer of silicon, making possible previously unimagined degrees of miniaturization and complexity in microelectric circuits. In 1965 it was possible to store 30 components on a 5 millimetre square silicon chip; by 1975 this had risen to 30,000 and by 1978 to 135,000.

This miniaturization was a key reason for ever-falling prices and ever-increasing computing capacity per machine. It gave rise to a whole new breed of computers. While big machines became yet more powerful and were increasingly dubbed 'mainframes', so smaller and smaller machines with more and more capacity – variously known as 'minis', 'micros', 'personal computers' (PCs) and 'lap tops' – became a vital part of the office. The first small machines began to appear in the office in the late 1960s and early 1970s, but it was only in the late 1970s that innovation in the United Kingdom became significant. During the 1980s they transformed the office.

A revolution, from the 1960s, in computer languages was as important to the increased application of the computer, especially PCs during the 1970s, as miniaturization. Languages such as Cobol (Common Business Orientated Language) meant that programs could now be written, not in machine code, but in structured English, which took program-writing away from a small band of technicians to a broader-based group of programmers and increasingly to the user.

In the late 1970s the idea of the computer and its associated technology, linked with other computers via telecommunications, was a source of fascination and concern, and gave rise to such expressions as the 'electronic' or 'paperless' office. In the early 1990s much of this technology is now in place and proven. Word-processing is very widely applied and has probably overtaken the conventional typewriter. The use of micros for accounting and data-processing, employing powerful and increasingly user-friendly database and spreadsheet software, is widespread. The linking of these machines in networks, enabling the sharing of data between different points of access, is commonplace. The mailing of messages in electronic form between networked machines within the office or between other locations, using the telecommunications network, and the storage of images of paper records on optical disc, are not widely applied, at least in the United Kingdom, but this is poised to change rapidly. The printing of letters, papers and reports has been massively improved by the widespread application of laser printers, colour photocopiers and desk-top publishing software. However, it is the co-ordination of all these different components, a factor dependent on capital but more so on the confidence and culture of the user, that has lagged behind what is possible, and it is this which will constitute the next great step forward in information technology.

Notes

1   E. Heawood, *Watermarks Mainly of the Seventeenth and Eighteenth Centuries* (Paper Publications Society, London, 1950). There is no publication covering the post-1800 period. See also E. Heawood, 'Use of watermarks in dating old maps and documents', *Geographical Journal* (May 1924), pp. 120–7.
2   Paper with watermarked ruling had been produced on the Continent since 1645 and had presumably been imported into Britain.
3   L. R. Dicksee, *Office Machinery. A Handbook for Progressive Managers* (Gee & Co, London, 1917), p. 104.
4   The best and most comprehensive work is reckoned to be R. C. Alcock and F. C. Holland, *The Postmarks of Great Britain and Ireland* (R. C. Alcock Ltd, Cheltenham, 1940). An abridged and revised edition is published under the title of *British Postmarks. A Short History and Guide* (R. C. Alcock Ltd, Cheltenham, 1977). Other important publications, all by J. A. Mackay, are *English and Welsh Postmarks since 1840* (J. A. Mackay, Dumfries, 1980), *Scottish Postmarks from 1693 to the Present Day* (J. A. Mackay, Dumfries, 1978) and *Irish Postmarks from 1840* (J. A. Mackay, Dumfries, 1982). Also of interest is H. C. Westley, *Postal Cancellations of London 1840–1890* (H. F. Johnson, London, 1950).
5   J. T. Whitney, *Collect British Postmarks. Handbook to British Postal Markings and their Value* (Longmans, London, various editions from 1979).
6   R. Hosking, *Paquebot Cancellations of the World* (R. Hosking, 1977).
7   L. R. Dicksee and H. E. Bain, *Office Organisation and Management* (Pitman & Sons, London, 1906), p. 43
8   *Ibid.*

Further reading

M. Adler, *The Writing Machine* (George Allen and Unwin, London, 1973).
Anon, 'Hollerith cavalcade. Fifty years of company history', *Tabacus*-British Tabulating Co. Ltd house magazine (May 1958), pp. 3–7.
K. C. Baglehole, A *Century of Service. A Brief History of Cable & Wireless Ltd 1868–1968* (Cable & Wireless, London, 1969).
H. Barty-King, *Girdle Round The Earth. The Story of Cable & Wireless* (Heinemann, London, 1979).
M. Campbell-Kelly, *ICL. A Business and Technical History* (Oxford University Press, Oxford, 1989).
C. H. Costello 'A quarter century's progress in management methods and business equipment', *Business Management*, 58: 1 (January 1933), pp. 120–5.
M. J. Daunton, *Royal Mail. The Post Office Since 1840* (Athlone Press, London, 1985).
R. B. Davidson, *A Guide to the Computer* (Longmans, London, 1968).
L. R. Dicksee, *Office Machinery. A Handbook for Progressive Managers* (Gee & Co, London, various editions from 1917).

L. R. Dicksee and H. E. Blain, *Office Organisation and Management* (Pitman & Sons, London, various editions from 1906).

J. S. Dorlay, *The Roneo Story* (Roneo Vickers, Croydon, 1978).

C. Evans, *The Making of the Micro. A History of the Computer* (Gollancz, London, 1981).

J. Evans, *The Endless Web. John Dickinson & Co Ltd 1804–1954* (Jonathan Cape, London, 1955).

R. Hills, *Papermaking in Britain 1488–1988. A Short History* (Athlone Press, London, 1988).

J. L. Kieve, *The Electric Telegraph. A Social and Economic History* (David & Charles, Newton Abbot, 1973).

A. Lambrou, *Fountain Pens, Vintage and Modern* (Sotheby's Publications, London, 1989).

S. H. Lavington, *Early British Computers and the People Who Built Them* (Manchester University Press, Manchester, 1980).

B. Morgan, *Total to Date. The Evolution of the Adding Machine. The Story of Burroughs* (Newman Neame, London, 1953).

H. Petroski, *The Pencil: A History* (Faber, London, 1990).

W. P. Proudfoot, *The Origins of Stencil Duplicating* (Hutchinson & Co, London, 1972).

H. Robinson, *Carrying British Mails Overseas* (Allen and Unwin, London, 1964).

F. Staff, *The Penny Post 1680–1918* (Lutterworth Press, London, 1964).

G. Tilghman Richards, *The History and Development of Typewriters,* 2nd edition (Science Museum, London, 1964).

H. C. Westley, *Postal Cancellations of London 1840–1890* (H. F. Johnson, London, 1950).

4

Getting started
Bridget Stockford

Defining a business archive

The archivist working within the business environment needs to understand that the term 'business archive' may have many different meanings. Within the business context the term will not necessarily mean the same as within the local authority context, and may vary from company to company. The reasons for the foundation and exploitation of a business archive will differ in accordance with the demands of the employing organization concerned, and a business archive must be managed in a way which satisfies specific and relevant criteria. There will also be a difference in the way that the term 'archive' is defined by the professional archivist and by the company itself. A priority task for the archivist who is 'getting started' is to formulate a definition of the term business archive that is understood and agreed by the employing company; the impetus for this definition should come from the archivist, not the organization.

A business archive, as defined by the professional, would comprise records no longer required for the routine administration of the company but which are nonetheless deemed worthy of permanent preservation on administrative, legal, fiscal, operational or historical grounds (see Chapter 10 for more detailed discussion of appraisal). These would include records showing precedent and original thinking, the development of company policy and practice, information relating to the organization and industry unavailable elsewhere, and records that illustrate changes in company business and direction. Some records which must be permanently retained on legal or administrative grounds are often controlled in perpetuity by the function that created them. These would include minute books and share records created by the secretarial department, accounting records generated by the financial function, and a wide variety of files which have had, or may have, relevance in ongoing legal disputes. It may be necessary to accept that in some organizations the control of this kind of record will never pass wholly to the company archivist. There will also be the material of obvious 'historical interest', such as letterbooks, advertisements, photographs and films and even physical objects such as packaging, posters, medals won at exhibitions and manufacturing equipment. Such artefacts are not, strictly speaking, archives, but their care will often fall to the business archivist simply because there is no more suitable custodian within the company.

It is important to realize that the company may, in the past, have defined the term 'archive' in its own particular way. The word may have been used to denote storage areas in the basement or roof, under the stairs or in garages at the bottom of the site. Such locations may have been used to store masses of accumulated paperwork, kept either on a 'just in case' basis or because no one will accept responsibility for throwing any records away. This situation will be most apparent in companies which do not have a problem with space or which have not moved site for many years. It is surprising how much valueless paperwork can accumulate in comparatively small storage areas. Records will range from important files of past directors to obviously irrelevant material such as additions to library stock, old staff vacancy notices or stocks of such publications as annual reports. More usefully, the term archive, as defined by the organization, will denote a separate storage area where records recognized as historically important have been set aside. The area may also contain records needed by departments on a long-term basis, and the two record areas might overlap.

The company may have in the past employed an 'archivist' who devoted a great deal of time to looking after certain historical records. This individual may have been a retired staff member who had a particular interest in the company's history, or a current employee who used historical information for such purposes as the production of staff magazines. Often these people will have done useful work – explaining names and organizational structures, compiling short histories of various companies, departments, products and processes, identifying people in photographs, and performing basic listing and indexing tasks.

Unfortunately work carried out by such enthusiasts may create as many problems for the archivist as it solves. Parts of the collection may have been physically arranged by subject or chronology, ignoring original order and provenance. Subject files may have been created to cover specific topics of interest, and these may have led to the removal of pages from files and letterbooks to bring the information together. Original material may have been annotated to explain obscurities in the text or to decipher signatures. This will make it impossible to re-create the original arrangement of the collection, and any finding aids should explain this.

Uses and benefits of a business archive

A company archive may be initiated either by the company itself, by a professional archivist who is temporarily employed on a specific task, or by outside organizations such as the Business Archives Council. It is important to realize from the outset that the archive must offer some positive benefit to the employing organization, as the keeping of historical records simply for their own sake will rarely prove adequate justification within a commercial concern.

The great value of archives to the company can be demonstrated in many areas. The most obvious use for archive material is in the public relations field. Uses include the provision of historical information for speeches or press releases, the reproduction of original material in nostalgic packaging and advertising, the compilation of leaflets detailing the company's history, or the creation of in-house museums or visitors' centres. Such use will be particularly heavy in relation to important anniversary celebrations. The various public relations uses of business archives are discussed more fully in Chapter 16.

There are, however, other important uses of a business archive, particularly in the field of management information. There is often a regrettable tendency among managers to ignore the past and concentrate exclusively on future developments. As a result, in some cases the wheel is reinvented or important questions are answered inaccurately, with adverse financial consequences, simply because past actions have not been taken into account. An archive can provide information on specific past policies, strategies or decisions to determine their relevance to current problems. Properly organized, a company's archive becomes the company's corporate memory. This memory becomes particularly important when rapid promotion or staff turnover means that the archives are the only source of long-term knowledge, which may allow present managers to avoid previous strategic errors and to rediscover products, processes, assets and markets.

An efficiently organized archive should be able to provide answers to management questions in many areas when there is a need to look beyond current records – corporate issues, such as a capital restructuring, the sale of long held assets and the reissue of articles of association; staff queries such as those relating to the pension rights of long-serving individuals or claims for past accidents; or marketing issues, such as trademark disputes and development of sales campaigns. Engineering companies require old plans and specifications when manufacturing spare parts for machinery delivered years before and quality control records are needed to answer potential legal claims against faulty products. Banks need recourse to old customer ledgers or safe-custody registers in checking claims to supposed dormant balances or deposited valuables. Pharmaceutical and other 'research and development' based companies may need to retain test and patent records for protection against legal claims. Extractive companies may save resources by consulting the results of basic field work undertaken much earlier, yet relevant to reappraisal in the light of modern technology.

The archives can often provide the only information available about long dormant subsidiaries or past organizational structures and long-term links with customers, countries and subsidiary or associate concerns. Such archives could include details of early contacts and trading links, photographs of early operations and premises, and information on founding staff. They can provide background information for those who deal with such outside agencies as regulatory bodies, law-makers and special interest groups to place the company's policy in its proper context. They can supplement the specialized legal resources of the company by determining facts or historical patterns and relationships in support of legal claims and legal positions. These are not everyday queries, but when they do occur, it is essential that they are answered as speedily and accurately as possible – delay may be expensive in administrative or monetary terms.

In addition, the archive should become a central tool in any internal staff training and education. It should be obligatory for all new management recruits to gain an understanding of the general history of the organization and the development of its business. Indeed a sense of history can be used to strengthen corporate identity and promote employee loyalty. The company's history should be advertised at all levels, beginning with lectures to new entrants, and continuing with articles in house journals and small in-house displays of interesting memorabilia. Some organizations positively encourage staff to consult the central archive resource in order to settle such internal administrative queries as alterations in holiday entitlement or working hours, by reference to the historical context.[1]

Positioning within the organization

Once the company has decided to appoint a professional archivist, the archive department will have to be slotted into the company's organizational structure. The positioning of the department will depend on the projected use of the archive, although it is possible that the archivist will be placed in an illogical reporting structure simply because of the position and function of the interested party who has initiated the appointment.

The secretarial department is the most common home for the archive department, as both areas have an interest in maintaining records. The company secretary is responsible for the presentation and maintenance of all records retained in compliance with the Company Acts, such as minute books and share records. Thus he or she will appreciate the need to retain, locate and produce past company documentation. An advantage of this reporting line is often direct access to main board executives. However, it might be that the main thrust of the archive work is towards public relations activity – either aimed internally at helping the sales and marketing department, or externally at shareholders and the general public. In these cases the archive function will be placed in the marketing or public relations departments. Equally, if archive material is going to be used in the design of current products, then the archivist will report to design personnel.

Alternatively, the archives may be expected to operate alongside other areas in the organization already disseminating information. This is usually a library function, thus providing an opportunity to implement a fully integrated information system; or, more rarely, the computer function. Occasionally archives are positioned within the central services department, which manages the space within the building, providing facilities such as microfilming, telecommunications and so on. The only rationale for placing the archive service here would be if it were to play a central role in managing masses of stored paperwork. This is rarely the case, unless archives are merged with a records management function.

There is therefore no 'correct' place for the archive department. Its position within the company will depend both on the purposes for which the archives were established, and the constraints of current organizational structures. The new archivist should not be shy of recommending a suitable placing.

However, the important consideration is not where the service is placed but at what level the archivist reports. When the archive function is new and often poorly understood by general management, it is essential that the archivist has high level management support when formulating an archive policy and implementing the new procedures in practice. This is particularly important if the archivist's job is not graded above junior management level. It is preferable that the new archive function should report as close to director level as possible, to ensure that its aims are taken seriously by the rest of the organization.

Formulating an archive policy

The establishment of a company archive policy is the most important task that faces the newly appointed archivist. It is essential that the archive service has a definite role and authority within the company, and that its objectives are clearly defined and understood by other employees. The rationale underlying the new archive function, its importance to the organization and mode of operation should be officially stated; but can only be formulated after the archivist has gained a knowledge of both the archive and the company. Such matters should be set out in an archive policy document, drawn up by the archivist and accepted as official company policy. The composition of the policy will not be the first task to be undertaken and will take some months to complete; during this time normal archive activities should continue, but at a level which allows the archivist to formulate and test various elements of the policy.

The policy document can consist of several sections, the most important being the policy statement, which should clearly outline the fact that records are important company assets, and that it is a matter of official company policy that they should be effectively managed. It is essential that this statement is discussed and approved at senior management level, and preferably minuted by the main board as official company policy. This is an invaluable back-up when attempting to 'sell' the archive concept to management and employees, although the use of high level authority to demand co-operation should only be considered as a last resort.

The policy statement is only the first element of the policy document which should contain several other sections, as appropriate to the specific company and archive service. The first section should comprise an explanation of the aims of the newly created service giving brief reasons for its establishment. This may be the place to define terms used in the document such as 'archives', 'records' and 'appraisal', and to clarify who is responsible for which type of record and who has control over their use. For example, a departmental manager may be responsible for all records used by his department, while the archivist is responsible for all records selected for permanent preservation. This section should also include a description of the range and contents of the archive.

The policy document should outline the services that the archives will offer to departments and individuals within the company. These will include the identification and collection of historical material, and the provision of information from this resource for such purposes as management information and public relations work. The collecting policy and procedures should be detailed, outlining the rights of the archive to collect relevant material and the ability to dispose of such material that is not deemed to have any archival value. This should also reinforce the fact that physical transfer of records to the archive is accompanied by a simultaneous transfer of authority over the records to the company archivist, and discuss the use of any forms used in the transfer of records to archives. It will also state that the records will be listed and information incorporated in catalogues or indexes held by the archives, or input on to the archive database, and explain that they will be held in a secure and environmentally suitable storage area. It may be worth stating that simple preservation and conservation work may be undertaken, such as refiling in acid-free files and boxes, as this may be an important factor in convincing individuals to deposit records in the archive.

The policy document should also discuss the ways in which information can be retrieved from the archive. Conditions of access will need to be detailed. Do you allow originating departments direct access to their own records, or do all loans have to be made via the archivist? Will they need to fill in forms and do they quote their reference number, or that of the archivist? Do records have to be integrated into the archive catalogue before access is granted, or can files be found from their list? Again, how should requests for information, rather than requests for records be treated? Make it clear if requests need to be in writing and explain any factors which may cause a delay in answering queries such as a backlog of uncatalogued records. It is also important to determine conditions of access for the general public, and these may be outlined in the policy document.

The archive policy document can include examples of all forms used, legal criteria affecting the retention of company documents, or a timetable of actions to be taken in conjunction with the establishment of the archive. Although the policy statement should remain unchanged, unless the authority for the archive changes, the rest of the document should remain under constant review. Any alteration in procedures or additional services, should be reflected in an updated policy document. The document will be widely distributed and available to new users of the archive, and should therefore remain current.

A policy document should contain the following elements:

1   *Authority.* State the authority of the archivist to exercise his/her powers and perform the duties and assume the responsibilities necessary to

achieve the objectives of the archive programme. May quote the board minutes setting up or redefining the function.

2   *Purpose.* State the purpose that the archive function fulfils within the organization. This will include the provision of historical information, the collection and cataloguing of records and the promotion of the company history.

3   *Definitions.* Define terms used in the document, e.g. 'archives', 'records', 'appraisal', 'repository', 'access', etc.

4   *Administration background.* Detail the positioning and responsibilities of the archive function:
   • Position within organization.
   • Responsibilities of archivist to the company archives.
   • Duty of employees to co-operate with the archivist to ensure that (a) guidelines and procedures drawn up by the archivist are followed, and (b) records are not destroyed without reference to the archivist.

5   *Archival activities.* Explain how various activities and procedures are carried out by the archive function.
   • Acquisition.
   • Listing, including any use of computerization.
   • Research and the provision of information.
   • Access.
   • Preservation and conservation.

Selling the policy document

Having completed the policy document, it is important to ensure that all the statements and procedures it contains meet with the approval of your senior manager. It is often easy to upset political sensibilities without being aware that they exist, or to implement policies which act against established working practices. Secondly, if possible, make sure that the policy statement is approved by the main board – which may mean a personal presentation to the board. Once this high level approval has been gained, the next step is to hold a meeting of departmental heads to sell the concept of the archive, the reasons for its establishment and its potential benefits. This meeting should be chaired by the archivist's senior manager, to underline the high level support that the function enjoys.

Such a meeting should cover the following points: firstly, a definition of the term archives, for laymen not professionals; secondly, an explanation of why the archive function was created, outlining the problems that existed before the appointment of the archivist; and thirdly, the intended plan of campaign. This plan will fall into two areas – work to be done in the archives, and work to be carried out in the departments. Although many historical records may have already been centralized, other material worthy of permanent preservation will also be held by departments, both in offices and storerooms. Thus the plan of campaign will outline a timetable for visiting departments and identifying records of interest which they hold. The meeting with departmental heads should outline the eventual results of these efforts and the benefits that will accrue to the company. Finally, it is a good idea to send the audience away with a task to perform, such as sending in a list of the location of any interesting records that they hold. Such a meeting underlines the fact that this is a new function, affecting all areas, with high level support. It also provides a useful forum for answering general questions.

It is inevitable that this meeting will need to be followed up with a series of one to one meetings, to cover managers not present at the group meeting. You should also encourage managers to arrange mini-presentations with their departmental staff, in this way you should have been able to contact almost all employees. It is a time-consuming task, but time spent on explanation will be amply repaid by the enhanced understanding and enthusiasm of company staff.

Resourcing the archive department

An important issue to resolve is that of resources. There is a great temptation to offer to 'make do' with a low level of resources, in order to help the project get off the ground. However, this becomes self-defeating in the end, for if the archivist copes without help for 6 months, it is difficult to justify more resources later.

The level of assistance offered will affect the ability of the department to respond rapidly to queries in the crucial formative months, which in turn will affect the regard in which it is held by other departments and personnel. Thus it is important to ascertain the level of assistance the company is offering, and to define the level of assistance needed. There will usually be a gap between the two, but is is helpful to be aware of this as soon as possible, in order to begin campaigning for the resources required.

The following questions need to be asked. 'What level of automation can I use – does the budget allow for the provision of a computer, the necessary software and support?' 'What secretarial assistance can I count on, especially in view of the number of lists that will be generated?' 'Does a separate budget exist for the provision of archive quality boxes, photographic envelopes, etc?' 'Do I have money to spend on publications, conferences, subscriptions, travel?' 'Do I have access to such facilities as reprographics?' Initially the archive department may not control a separate budget, but it is useful to ensure that the function bearing the cost of the archives is aware of its real needs. It is also important to find out when the next budgeting round begins in order to secure early approval of the archives' expenditure for the following year.

As well as establishing the financial framework of your function, it is important to clarify any other areas of doubt. These may range from minor concerns, such as receiving visitors and offering lunch, to the allocation of suitable repository facilities. Lastly, make sure that you have a suitable office area to work in, as near to the archives as possible without being directly sited inside the repository.

Another task to undertake at an early stage of employment is that of creating an information resource, covering both professional and company matters. On the professional side, now is the time to join bodies such as the Business Archives Council and the Society of Archivists (see Table 4.1). Begin to build up a library of their publications (see Table 4.2), and search through back copies for information on any helpful pamphlets which may be available. Buy all the relevant British Standards Institution (BSI) recommendatons, as it is always helpful to know what standards the archives should be aiming for. Find out the names of other business archivists and make contact with them. Use any information and literature they found helpful. Such publications may not appear to have any immediate relevance, but may be needed to answer queries at short notice, as well as to provide information on general professional developments.

Table 4.1   *Professional societies connected with archives*

Name and address	Activities	Membership categories
Business Archives Council 185 Tower Bridge Road London SE1 2UF	Promotion of the preservation and exploitation of business archives and of the study of business history. Publications.	Individual Institutional Corporate
Society of Archivists Information House 20–24 Old Street London EC1V 9AP	Professional society for qualified archivists: formulating strategies and discussing issues that affect all aspects of archive work. Publications.	Individual Student
British Records Association 18 Padbury Court London E2 7EH	Co-ordination and encouragement of the work of various individuals and bodies engaged in the preservation and use of historical records. Publications.	Individual Institutional
Business Archives Council (Scotland) c/o The Archives The University Glasgow G12 8QQ	Promotion of the preservation of business archives and the study of industrial history in Scotland. Publications.	Individual Institutional

Table 4.2 *Academic and professional journals related to archives*

Name	Publisher	Content	Frequency
British			
Business Archives	Business Archives Council	Articles on the administration of business archives and business history; book reviews; bibliographies; lists of deposited records.	Biannual
Journal of the Society of Archivists	Society of Archivists	Articles on the administration, use and content of local government, business and specialized archives; book reviews; notes on topics of interest.	Quarterly
Archives	British Records Association	Articles on the nature and use of archive collections and repositories in the United Kingdom. Book reviews.	Biannual
Business History	Frank Cass & Co. Ltd	Articles on aspects of British and overseas business history. Book reviews.	Quarterly
Foreign			
The American Archivist	Society of American Archivists	Articles on the administration and use of archives – research perspectives and case studies – and the international archives scene. Book reviews.	Quarterly
Archivaria	Association of Canadian Archivists	Articles on the administration and use of archives, including case studies concerning particular documents. Book reviews.	Biannual
Archives and Manuscripts	Australian Society of Archivists	Articles on the administration, use and content of archives in Australia. Often useful on matters of professional principle. Book reviews.	Biannual
Archivum	International Council on Archives (K. G. Saur)	Issues devoted to particular topics or proceedings of conferences concerning archives administration. International and multilingual.	Occasional
Business History Bulletin	Hagley Museum and Library	Case studies of the development of specific business archive services.	Biannual

They also serve to remind the business archivist that he or she is not alone, and that a professional world exists, and is relevant.

There is also a great deal that can be done in respect of building up an information resource relating to the employing organization. Collect any pamphlets or books already written about the company's history – both the main company and any subsidiaries or associates. Acquire a complete back run of annual reports and of any staff magazines produced – these will give invaluable background information on the organization, including dates of major events or policy decisions and an indication of the growth of the organization. Ask for any current corporate or marketing brochures, to give you a perspective on what the company does today. Contact the personnel department for past and present organization charts. Make sure that you are added to any circulation lists for daily presscuttings, staff notices and staff magazines. Bring together any existing employee reminiscences and use any suitable staff magazines or circulars to pensioners to encourage people to contact the archives. Finally, before embarking on any detailed listing, use the information resources you have gathered. Any finding aids will be made infinitely more valuable if the archivist knows why certain files were created by certain functions in certain departments at a particular time.

Compiling a job description

A useful task to undertake after 2 or 3 months have elapsed is to prepare a job description. Although the archivist will have been given an initial job description or brief on joining the organization, it is certain that this will omit many of the tasks now added to the original remit. This is also an ideal time to clarify the archivist's responsibility for certain areas, and will provide an opportunity to judge where these areas overlap with other departments. It is useful to remember that you may be taking over functions and duties previously exercised by another department or member of staff, and it is important to resolve any conflict of interest from the beginning. Behave tactfully in order to avoid building up any long-term resentment towards your appointment. It is important to define the requirements needed by the archives, and to draw up a job description and work programme within the first few months of joining the organization. Management will give greater attention to the new function during the early months and is more likely to be receptive of new ideas and requests; this is the time when the archivist's role and the ground rules under which the archivist operates are established. It is easier to get things right at the beginning than to correct mistakes after many months have passed and attention is directed elsewhere.

Planning

One of the most important skills that the lone business archivist must acquire is that of managing a varied selection of projects to utilize time and available resources efficiently. It is also important to direct effort with an eye to any relevant company expectation or requirement. There must be a balance between developing an archive policy, raising the profile of the service and undertaking the essential work of listing the archives. The size of the organization will also need to be taken into account, as this will affect planning of this kind. It is easier to formulate a strategy for dealing with the needs of a compact organization with well-defined procedures than a complex structure where different departments may have developed in-house systems at variance with one another.

Preliminary survey

Before any detailed listing is performed, it is important to conduct a survey of all records involved. This should cover all storage locations, access conditions, quantities and types of record. While there may be a main archive area to which you control the key, there may also be off-floor storerooms, strongrooms, disused offices and roof spaces that house record accumulations. It is useful to make contact with the building services manager, security guards or maintenance staff, who may know of unclaimed accumulations of records, and hold relevant keys. This survey should be extended to all companies, departments and sites, despite the cost in time and money of travelling. If the archivist cannot visit other sites, it is important that an employee at these locations conducts an outline survey and alerts the archivist to any problem areas.

The survey should identify what quantity of records exist and where. It should note the type of record (volumes, files, photographs or films) and the condition (clean, dirty, badly boxed, inaccessible). The results of the survey and discussions held with departments and other interested personnel will be drawn together to provide a planned timetable of future work. This will give a structure to work to which will need to be agreed by the archivist's line manager. It is important to explain how much work is involved in listing a collection, as it is often easy for the layman to assume that listing is a quick and simple task. This timetable should also be compiled with the needs of the organization in mind, e.g. it is pointless listing files in detail if the urgent task is to clear the basement prior to a move.

The timetable should cover all the known sites of record collections and give proposed dates for listing each area. Areas could include both the headquarter site, which is employing the archivist, and allied subsidiary sites around the country. With subsidiary sites, it is necessary to ascertain the official attitude to the archive holdings. Are they to be listed *in situ*, for example, or will selected holdings be transferred back to the main collection? Once the timetable is drawn up, the task of listing can begin. The compilation of finding aids is discussed in Chapter 11.

Creating and maintaining staff interest

It is essential that the archive department maintains a visible profile within the company. It is all too easy, after the initial effort of creating the function has passed, to become very inward-looking, concentrating on listing and cataloguing. This will have a detrimental effect on the archive department, minimizing its apparent value to the company and making it vulnerable to economic cutbacks and closure. As adverse economic pressures can directly affect the organization's commitment to the archive resource, it is essential that the archivist does not lose sight of the company's strategic policies and that work patterns are changed to take note of new priorities, while keeping long-term goals in mind.

After the initial interest created by the establishment of the post of archivist has subsided, what should follow? The most potent weapon is enthusiasm for the collection and its uses, and the most effective way of using this weapon is by personal contact: the archivist should talk to anyone who shows the slightest sign of interest in the archives – the chairman, senior and middle management, junior clerks or maintenance staff. Once staff are aware of the existence of the archives, they will be more likely to contact you with any historical query, to send down any interesting records turned out during office moves, or to notify you of any sacks of rubbish that 'look interesting.' Offer to show anyone and everyone around the archives, irrespective of whether or not full catalogues exist. Ensure that interesting photographs or 'old' handwritten ledgers are easily available, to illustrate that archives are not dirty or boring. This is the ideal opportunity to explain basic archive principles, stressing the fact that all records are now controlled and cared for. This will encourage any hoarders of interesting material to pass it on to the archives in the knowledge that it will be looked after. If such people are reluctant to pass over their personal collections, note their names and approach them at regular intervals.

The next step is to write articles for any internal staff magazines that are circulated among present and past employees, describing the archive collection and outlining the company's history. Use this medium to appeal for old photographs, reminiscences or artefacts. Utilize any vehicle for reaching a wider audience, such as providing information for shareholder literature.

In addition, the archivist should offer to speak at any internal training courses, particularly those where new recruits enter the organization. Make sure that all historical enquiries are answered as quickly as possible.

It is important to be as helpful as possible, as the reputation of the archives will quickly spread by word of mouth. It is useful, when you know both the archives and the organization, to send lists of relevant and interesting documentation to specific departments. Keep an eye out for appropriate corporate functions, anniversaries, visits or events, and volunteer any helpful information. Prepare a short history of the organization, a selected sector of business or even a specific site, which can be supplied in typescript to interested parties. It is not essential to have the archive collection fully listed before carrying out any of the above; a working knowledge of the records should suffice. Any delay in answering a query can be accompanied by an explanation of the work consequent upon establishing a new archive, and this education can be as valuable as any other.

Professional ethics

Business archivists should seek to maintain standards in their professional relations with their employer, colleagues and researchers. However, the clarification of these standards, and their enforcement demands a central professional organization with some disciplinary powers. This does not yet exist, although discussions have been held within the Society of Archivists since 1977.[2]

All archivists share aspects of a professional code of ethics, particularly those related to the use and care of records. There is, however, a basic difference between the environment and philosophy of the business archivist and the record office archivist. The record office has responsibilities both to the depositors and users of the records that it holds, while the business archivist's first responsibility must be solely toward the employing organization. Thus the criteria for administering and exploiting the collection will be detemined by the needs of the business, as there can be little justification for the storage of records which are of no value to the company, or the devotion of excessive time and resources to the maintenance and supervision of searchroom facilities for the public. A business archivist certainly has a duty to ensure the physical well-being of those company records with an administrative, legal, operational or historical value, whether by campaigning for an environmentally suitable repository or challenging dangerous instructions from a line manger. Even so, in business such responsibilities may be compromised by the need to use records for display or publication under less than ideal conditions, or to utilize storage environments which do not conform to BSI standards.

The following are, however, ethical standards that the business archivist might adopt, and these should be explained to the employer at the outset. If the organization is suitably educated as to the professional responsibilities of the archivist, the need to guard against suggestions that would contravene them is less likely to arise.

The business archivist should have:

- belief in the corporate ownership of company records,
- awareness of the confidentialities and sensitivities of business,
- awareness of the priorities and needs of the employing organization,
- respect for the integrity of the records,
- commitment to the care and and preservation of the records,
- commitment to educating the employer as to the special needs of the archive resource,
- enthusiasm for exploiting the archive resource in line with company needs,
- commitment to *bona fide* historical research within the terms of access allowed by the organization,
- impartiality towards researchers, except when the outcome of that research may not be in the best interests of the business,
- willingness to discuss professional topics with colleagues, especially those in similar establishments.

The business archivist should not:

- impose his own interests onto the management of the archive resource,
- publish work based on company information without informing his employer,
- expect the business to respond to all external research enquiries if resources are limited,
- expect that all procedures and environmental conditions conform to professionally accepted standards.

Notes

1 L. N. Poole, 'Administration and other internal uses of a company archive: the John Lewis Partnership', *Proceedings of the Annual Conference 1984* (Business Archives Council, 1984), pp. 61–75.
2 Such a comprehensive code of practice was first mooted by the Society of Archivists in 1977, but a final text has yet to be agreed by the profession at large. Alternative codes were produced, circulated and discussed in 1981; the issue was revived in 1988 and continues to be examined.

Further reading

A. Cooke, 'A code of ethics for archivist: Some points for discussion', *Archives and Manuscipts*, 15:2 (1987), pp. 95–104.
N. Johnson, 'Further thoughts on a code of practice', *Journal of the Society of Archivists*, 8:2 (1986), pp. 93–4.

L. McDonald, 'Ethical dilemmas facing an archivist in the business enviroment: the constraints on a business archivist', *Journal of the Society of Archivists*, 10:4 (1989), pp. 168–72.

J. Orbell, *The Uses of Business Archives*, Record Aids 2 (Business Archives Council, 1983).

5

Corporate records

Lesley Richmond

The corporate records described in this chapter are defined as those produced and retained by a business in the process of acting as a 'corporation', as a body regulating itself in its administration, organization and operation as a legal business. Such records include statutory and legally created records, except those governing the financial affairs of the business. The creation of these records by a business has been determined either by the owners of the business or by statute, and they document its formation, regulation and dissolution. The majority of the records in this group were originally created and retained on behalf of the company by its owner or chief clerk and subsequently by the company secretary and/or the company registrars. As companies have grown by acquiring other businesses and forming their own subsidiary and associated companies, it is usual to find that a collection of business records was not created by one single company but by many. This is especially true in the case of corporate records held under the control of the parent company's secretary who also acts in that capacity for many other companies within the group. Subsidiary and parent company records require to be distinguished from each other.

The company secretary is the person concerned with keeping a company's statutory books and generally supervising the administration of its affairs. A company secretary, among other duties, keeps the minute books for board and general meetings, maintains the share registers, completes annual returns for the Registrar of Companies and arranges dividend and interest payments. He or she has specific responsibilities and holds a senior position in a company. In some large companies the book-keeping duties of the company secretary are carried out by an outside body specializing in the work, such as registrars, while in small companies the company secretary may only be employed by the company part-time.

The legal constitution of a business dictates the type of records which are created to regulate that business. There are three main types of business organization: sole traders, partnerships, and registered companies.

Sole traders

The sole trader, the original entrepreneur, has been and remains the main type of business in operation in the United Kingdom. Sole traders usually operate on a small scale, and so produce few records. A negligible amount of record creation is required by statute as a pre-requisite to trading and a minimum to regulate the business. There were exceptions: sole traders such as brewers and distillers, for example, had to apply for a licence to brew or distill. There were and are still restrictions within certain trades and professions. It is a legal offence for an unqualified person to act as a solicitor in a civil or criminal matter or to set up as a doctor, or to sell game, wines or spirits without a licence. Other records created by a sole trader exist to document or prove an association or arrangement with a third party – legal records, patents, trademarks, agreements and licences.

Few documents were created to help run the business. A sole trader was usually in full control of a business and carried out the many managerial roles, such as sales, finance, production and personnel, and knew all the information required for each function and so did not create many records as *aide-mémoires*. Occasionally a sole trader may have kept a diary or correspondence, which will often be the only surviving material relating to the structure and organization of the business concerned. Such records may reveal the sales techniques, manufacturing process or financial procedures which were in use, and should be permanently preserved in their entirety, unless the correspondence is of a very routine nature, in which case it can be weeded or sampled.

Since 1973 sole traders and other small businesses, if their turnover exceeds a certain statutory limit, are required to be registered for Valued Added Tax (VAT), and such registration documents may be these traders' only corporate records. Sole traders were not required to register details of their activities until February 1916, when the Register of Business Name Act was passed as a war-time measure. From 1916 to 1982 sole traders wishing to carry on a business under a name other than their own surname had to register the trading name, the name of the proprietor, the address and the business function with the Register of Business Names. The Act was difficult to enforce and many businesses never made returns. The register was abolished in 1982 and a sample of its registration documents for a selection of businesses registered in 1916–17 and every 10 years from 1921 until 1981–82 was made and placed in the Public Record Office in class BT 253.

Partnerships

Partnerships, like sole traders, have been a significant form of business organization since commercial and manufacturing enterprise began. Partnerships consist of two or more people owning and controlling a business. A partnership in England and Wales has no separate legal personality, the partners usually being personally liable (unlimited) for debts and other liabilities. A Scottish partnership has a separate legal personality, although it does not have all the attributes of a legal person. In Scotland a partnership can contract in its own name while in England it cannot. Partnerships are formed by a deed of co-partnership or a partnership agreement.

There was no limit, at common law, to the number of persons who might carry on a business in partnership, although where the number of partners was large, it was impossible for them all to have an active part in its management. It was usual in such cases to place the management of the partnership with a small body of directors, who alone had the power of binding the firm up to specified limits. This applied not only between the partners themselves but also to creditors, whenever the members were too numerous to act. The undetermined definition of 'too numerous' was removed with the passing of the 1862 Companies Act, which stated in section 4 that no partnerships consisting of more than 10 members were to be formed for the purpose of banking, or of more than 20 members for the purpose of carrying on any other business. If a partnership exceeded the maximum number, the members had to incorporate themselves. Since the passing of the 1967 Companies Act firms of solicitors, accountants and stockbrokers have been exempt from this limit.

Subject to agreement, a partnership is automatically dissolved on the death or bankruptcy of a partner. When partners left and/or new partners entered a business, an announcement to that effect, including the new business name, was made in the *London Gazette* or *Edinburgh Gazette* and often in the local press. Ordinary partnerships have been governed since 1890 by the Partnership Act of that year, and between 1916 and 1982 such firms had to register with the Register of Business Names if they did not carry on business under a name which consisted of the true surnames of the partners.

Limited partnerships were introduced in 1907 and have been governed by the Limited Partnership Act of that year. They are similar to ordinary partnerships except that certain partners have liability limited by the amount they contribute on joining the partnership. Limited partners cannot dispose of their share or withdraw it, take part in the general management of the business, bind the firm, dissolve the partnership or object to the introduction of another partner. There must be at least one general partner with unlimited liability. Since their introduction, limited partnerships have had to be registered with the Registrar of Limited Partnerships and provide and keep up to date the following information: the firm's name; general nature of the business; principal place of business; full names of the partners; term of the partnership; date of commencement; a statement that the partnership is limited, which names the limited partners; and the amount paid by each limited partner and manner of payment. This information can be inspected at the Companies Registration Office in Cardiff, London, Edinburgh and Belfast.[1]

Records of partnerships

The main corporate records created by partnerships are articles of co-partnership or partnership agreements and minutes of partners' meetings.

Partners' attendance registers, diaries and correspondence are less commonly found.

Partnership agreements and deeds of co-partnership and settlement

The articles of co-partnership or partnership agreement comprise a legally binding contract laying out the limits and obligations of the partners, such as liability for debts and managerial activity. The names and occupations of the partners are specified, and the removal or addition of a partner brings an agreement to an end and a new one is drawn up. Partnership agreements identify the partners of a company at any given time, define their areas of interest and indicate their financial stakes in the business. These are therefore historically important and should be permanently preserved. Deeds of settlement were used to form large partnerships, known as unincorporated companies, under which members agreed to take shares and abide by the regulations of the firm, before the passing of the 1844 Joint Stock Companies Act. The assets of the 'company' were vested in trustees through the deed of settlement, and the shareholders were co-partners. The management of the 'company' was entrusted to directors, provision was made for the transfer of shares, and each shareholder was liable for only a proportion of any liabilities. Deeds of settlement are also historically important, defining the operation of such entities, and should therefore be permanently preserved.

Partners' meeting minutes

There is and has never been any statutory obligation for partners to keep minutes of their meetings, and in small businesses this was rarely done. In larger partnerships a permanent record of decisions was usually kept in order to arbitrate in the event of a dispute or as a reminder of past policy. Partners' meeting minutes, if recorded, state the place of the meeting, the names of the partners present, and the identity of the chairman and senior partner, and give a very brief account of decisions reached, often without any background information. The minutes kept by different partnerships can vary greatly between firms and with time. They are usually to be found in manuscript form in bound volumes. Partners' meeting minutes should be permanently preserved, as they record the activities and financial and other information about a partnership which is not generally available elsewhere.

Partners' attendance registers

Partners' attendance registers are very rare, and at their simplest record the attendance of partners at meetings. They can also contain other details, such as a record of fines for non-attendance. If such supplementary information exists or no minutes survive, these registers should be permanently preserved, as they give some indication of how the business was conducted, where meetings were held, the names and numbers of partners present, and so on.

Partners' diaries

An active member of a partnership sometimes kept a diary recording business and personal events. Along with notes on the weather, sermons heard and family illness, details of potential and actual sales, visitors to the business, new projects and product ranges, sales, purchases, costs, employees, continental and home sales tours, and so on, were recorded for the partner's own personal *aide-mémoire*. Such a daily or weekly record was usually maintained in a small notebook or in a pre-printed diary. They are rare, but where they are extant they can often be the only surviving material relating to the structure and organization of a business, and therefore should be permanently preserved.

Partners' correspondence

Correspondence between partners, if it survives, can provide valuable information about the organization, sales techniques, manufacturing processes, or finances of a business. Partners' incoming letters would most commonly have been filed in yearly bundles, although they were sometimes arranged in bundles by subject covering several years, or alphabetically by sender. Copies of outgoing letters survive less frequently, but have a greater chance of survival where they were bound into volumes or copied straight into wet-copy books. In some instances the draft reply to a letter is to be found endorsed on the original, along with notes on action taken. Partners' correspondence should be retained in its entirety unless it is of a very routine nature, in which case it can be weeded or sampled.

Companies

Companies can be created by royal charter, by specific Acts of Parliament, or, since 1844, may be registered under the Companies Acts (see Chapter 2). A company, unlike a partnership, is a separate legal entity with rights and duties distinct from those of its members. The liability of its members may be limited by shares or guarantee or may be unlimited. A company has perpetual succession in that its existence is maintained by new members who replace those who have died or transferred their interest, unlike a partnership, which is no more than a sum of its members. For the purposes of this chapter the corporate records created by different types of companies will be considered to be identical unless otherwise stated. Certain other commercial and professional organizations, such as some insurance companies, housing associations, building societies, friendly societies, and industrial and provident societies, must register under such statutes as the

Building Society Acts 1874, 1894 and 1939 and the Industrial and Provident Society Acts 1893–5 and 1913.[2] These are not companies in the strictest sense, but are commonly known as companies and for the purposes of this chapter can be considered as such.

Chartered companies

These are incorporated by the grant of a charter from the Crown. Until the nineteenth century joint-stock companies were founded either by the grant of a royal charter or the passing of a special Act of Parliament. Some of the most famous trading concerns of previous centuries, such as the Bank of Scotland and the Hudson Bay Company, were founded by such a royal incorporation and are still in existence, while others, such as the East India Company and the South Sea Company, have long since ceased trading. More recently charters have tended to be reserved for the incorporation of special non-commercial organizations such as universities, professional bodies and national charities. There is no restriction on the number of members in this type of company and, unless otherwise stated, the members are not personally liable for the company's debts. Patented companies, founded by letters patent, also exist, and their liability is unlimited unless the terms of the letters patent state otherwise.

Statutory or parliamentary companies

Such companies are incorporated by special Acts of Parliament. This form was frequently used in the nineteenth century for the formation of public utilities such as railway, gas, electricity, canals, docks and water companies, which required special powers, such as the compulsory purchase of land. Statutory companies required a minimum of two members, and a member whose shares were not fully paid up could be liable for the company's debts. The powers of statutory companies were defined in the Acts by which they were created, and additional Acts were required to modify them. This made such companies very inflexible and they are now uncommon. As a result of nationalization in the mid-twentieth century, most statutory companies were taken over by public corporations and public boards.

Cost book companies

These were incorporated for governing the working of metal-bearing mines or tinstreaming in Cornwall and Devon, and are basically partnerships. Members, known as adventurers, had unlimited liability for all the company's debts. The companies were originally governed by local custom and subject to the jurisdiction of the Stannary Courts. Jurisdiction has been vested in the County Courts of Cornwall since 1896, and the rules governing them are set out in the 1869 and 1887 Stannaries Acts. These companies are now extremely rare.

Registered companies

Such companies are incorporated under the Companies Acts, the first of which was passed in 1844. A registered company does not require to have a share capital unless it is a trading company. The 1980 Companies Act provided for three basic types of registered companies (companies limited by shares, companies limited by guarantee and unlimited companies) and two basic forms of companies (public and private).

Companies limited by shares

These are the most common type of company incorporated with the intention of making a profit in the United Kingdom, and have been the most popular form of company since the passing of the 1856 Joint Stock Companies Act. The liability of their members is limited to the amount, if any, unpaid on their shares.

Companies limited by guarantee

These are usually incorporated for the purpose of carrying on business as trade protection and mutual insurance societies; trade associations; political, social, athletic and other clubs; and charitable organizations where there is no intention to make a profit. The liability of their members is limited to an amount specified in the company's memorandum which the members guarantee to contribute to the assets of the company if it should go into liquidation. A large number of guarantee companies obtain a dispensation from the Board of Trade to have 'limited' removed from their name. Before the 1980 Companies Act these companies might either have been private or public, but following the passing of this Act no new guarantee company with a share capital could be formed.

Unlimited companies

Such companies do not have any limit on the liability of their members for debts. In 1844 the first Companies Act laid down that companies could become incorporated with unlimited liability. The Joint Stock Companies Act of 1856 only granted incorporation with limited liability to companies other than banking and insurance concerns. Limited liability was extended to these companies in 1858 and 1862 respectively. Over 1,960 unlimited companies were registered between 1844 and 1856, of which 455 reregistered under the 1856 Act as unlimited companies between 1856 and

1865. In comparison, only 88 new unlimited companies registered in this same period. Few companies were subsequently incorporated with unlimited liability, and many companies originally constituted as such were reregistered with limited liability following the disastrous collapse of the unlimited City of Glasgow Bank in 1878, and the passing of the 1879 Companies Act, which conferred such power. Since the passing of the 1980 Companies Act all unlimited companies must be private companies; they are exempt from filing annual accounts, directors' reports and auditors' reports with the Registrar of Companies, and can be formed with or without a share capital.

Public and private companies

From the passing of the 1907 Companies Act until the enactment of the 1980 Companies Act, all companies were public companies unless they could satisfy the requirements relating to private companies, namely, that the rights of their members to transfer their shares were restricted; that the number of their members, excluding past and present employees, was limited to 50; and that any invitation to the public to subscribe for shares was prohibited. Since the passing of the 1980 Companies Act, following the Second EEC Directive on Company Law Harmonization, a private company is defined as being any company that is not a public company. A public company must state in its memorandum that it is a public company, end its name with 'public limited company' or 'plc', and have a minimum share capital of £50,000. As a private company does not require a large amount of capital and as it cannot seek public investment it has always been the preferred type of company (about 97 per cent of companies registered in the United Kingdom in the late 1980s were private companies), and this has had an important bearing on record-keeping. Until 1948 a private company was not required to include its accounts with its annual return to the Registrar.

Exempt private companies

These existed from 1948 until abolished by the 1967 Companies Act. They had the following characteristics: no company held any shares or debentures; no person except the holder had any interest in any of the company's shares or debentures; the number of persons holding debentures was less than 50; no company or other corporate body was a director of the company; and there was no agreement whereby the policy of the company could be determined by persons other than directors, members, debenture-holders and trustees for debenture-holders. Such companies were exempt from filing annual balance sheets, profit and loss accounts and printed copies of certain resolutions and agreements with the Registrar of Companies – hence their name. Exempt private companies did have the option under the 1967 Companies Act of becoming unlimited companies if they wished to preserve their financial privacy.

To form a company, certain documents must be registered with the Registrar of Companies, namely, a memorandum of association; articles of association; a list of persons who have agreed to be directors (only required for public companies); the written consent of the directors to act (only required for public companies); a statutory declaration that the requirements of the Companies Act have been complied with; a notice of the registered office address; and the particulars of the directors and secretary. A company continues to exist indefinitely until such a time as it is dissolved and becomes defunct. There are 3 ways in which a company can be dissolved: the Registrar of Companies can strike a company from the Register and so dissolve it if satisfied that it is no longer trading or a company can be dissolved by going into voluntary members' liquidation or compulsory liquidation ordered by the Court. Its affairs are wound up and its name removed from the Register of Companies. When the name of a company is removed from the Register, it is entered in the Register of Defunct Companies.[3]

Records of companies

Companies create a wide range of corporate records in complying with statutory and legal requirements.

Prospectuses

A prospectus is a printed offer of shares to the public, generally or selectively, inviting them to buy shares or debentures in a company. This can be an initial issue of shares on the formation of a company or one of many subsequent issues made by a company to raise new capital. Since 1900 every prospectus has had to contain such standard information as the names, addresses and descriptions of the signatories of the memorandum of association and of the directors, any vendors of property to the company (specifying their remuneration), any preliminary expenses or payments to a promoter, any charges for underwriting, and all material contracts. Prospectuses must also state the purposes for which the company was formed, the uses to which the capital was to be put, the amount of capital to be issued and the issue price of the shares or debentures. They usually contain the names and addresses of the company's bankers, solicitors, auditors, share brokers, company secretary, overseas agents, consultants and correspondents, and the address of the registered office of the company. Usually there is also a statement to attract the investor concerning the profitability of the company, its history and its past and future markets. The prospectus must be lodged with the Registrar of Companies, and it is the directors' responsibility to ensure that it complies with the law.

Prospectuses should be kept for the lifetime of a company, and subsequently retained permanently, as they record the intention of a company at a given time and show how the company viewed its progress to date. It should be noted, however, that prospectuses are only statements of intent drawn up to attract investors, and until 1900 there was no effective legislation to ensure that they were honest. During the twentieth century they have become increasingly more reliable. The quantity of information contained within prospectuses and their appearance has also varied with time: they have grown in length and detail from 2 or 4 sides of folded paper at the turn of the century to 10- to 15-page booklets from the 1960s. Despite their problems as a historical source, they are one of the quickest ways to discover the names of the company's solicitors, auditors, brokers and bankers, which can provide a lead to the possible whereabouts of other records relating to the company in question.[4]

Certificates of incorporation

These documents, the birth certificates of a company, have been issued by the Registrar of Companies to all new companies since 1844, once those companies have fulfilled the various conditions laid down by the Companies Acts. They give the recipients the legal status of a 'company'. In order for a public company to start up in business, a trading certificate has to be issued. A copy is placed on the company's file at Companies House. The original must be kept for the lifetime of a company, but once a company has ceased to exist, it has limited research value, although it may be the only record of a company's exact name. Such certificates are not bulky and should, on balance, be retained permanently. If a company changes its name, the Registrar issues a change of name certificate, which should be treated in the same way as a certificate of incorporation.

Memoranda and articles of association and deeds of settlement

The memorandum of association is filed with the Registrar of Companies upon the registration of a company and is open to inspection by anyone at any time at Companies House. It lists the following information: the name of the company; its nationality (whether its registered office is in Scotland, England, Northern Ireland or Wales); its objects; a statement that the members have limited liability; the amount of authorized capital; and the number and amount of shares into which the capital is divided. These details are followed by an association and subscription clause, which states the names, addresses, and descriptions of subscribers and the number of shares taken by each. A company is bound by its memorandum but may alter it by special resolution, a copy of which must be sent to the Registrar. The objects of a company tend to be stated in very broad terms in order that its activities remain within its governing rules.

The articles of association contain the internal regulations for the management of a company's affairs, and they are registered when a company is formed. They govern the rights of members among themselves and set out the manner in which a company must conduct its affairs. The articles are subject to the memorandum of association and must not contain anything illegal or *ultra vires*. They can be altered by the company by special resolution at a general meeting.

Deeds of settlement were submitted to the Registrar of Companies under the 1844 Joint Stock Companies Act to obtain incorporation as a joint-stock company, and from 1844 to 1856 were the equivalent document to the articles of association. Deeds of settlement and early memoranda and articles of association were often large manuscripts of over 50 pages of foolscap, but by the end of the nineteenth century most companies were using a standard printed format. The 1856 and 1862 Companies Acts laid down non-mandatory model regulations for articles of association.

Jordan & Sons Ltd, established in 1863, were company registration agents, seal engravers, printers and publishers, and account book manufacturers of Chancery Lane, London, and produced forms to meet all the statutory requirements of companies in respect of the Registrar of Companies. These included draft printed forms of memoranda and articles of association for the use of solicitors and others involved in the formation of companies, and printed forms containing the model memorandum and articles of association laid down in the Companies Acts. Printed resolutions amending the original articles are usually to be found in both a company's general meeting minute book and loosely in copies of or with the memorandum and articles of association.

The memorandum and articles of association of a company and all admendments must be kept for the lifetime of a company, and subsequently should be retained permanently. These documents specify the objects of a company and the regulations governing its affairs, which are invaluable to the understanding of the inner corporate workings of a company. These records can survive in bulk, but only one copy of each need be retained.

Directors' meeting minutes

A director of a company is an officer of that company. The board of directors is the effective management committee of a company limited by shares. The members of the board represent, in theory at least, the interests of the shareholders by whom they are elected. The chairman of the company usually presides as chairman at these meetings and the company secretary usually takes the minutes and maintains the minute books. It was not until the 1908 Companies Act that it became a legal necessity for a company to keep minutes of its board meetings, although the vast majority of companies had, before that date, written into their articles of association that regular meetings of the board should take place and that the minutes of such meetings were to be kept and duly signed. Minutes were kept as a permanent record of decisions made and survive more often than other corporate records.

In the nineteenth century minutes were generally written in longhand in large bound volumes, but gradually, during the twentieth century, typed minutes began to be produced, and they were either pasted into bound volumes or placed in files. Directors' copies of minutes are often to be found separately as loose sheets together with the agenda and papers for such meetings. The destruction of individual directors' copies of minutes, which can create bulky series of duplicated records, should be considered if marginalia are insignificant.

Minutes vary greatly in detail from company to company and over time. Detailed minutes can explain business policies; suggest management style; record events in a company's history, such as the opening of new buildings, the issue of annual accounts and applications for employment; and provide information from which sales and production trends can be deduced. Less detailed minutes may give only brief summaries of the meetings, recording the principal decisions taken and none of the preceding discussion. The frequency of directors' meetings varies between companies and over time and a series of minutes can be very bulky or very scant. The covers of directors' meeting minute books are often to be found secured by a lock, as the minutes recorded the private affairs of the company and were only accessible to the directors, company secretary and auditors. However, all minutes of directors' meetings, no matter how brief they are, should be kept for the lifetime of a company, and subsequently be permanently preserved, as they record the principal management decisions made by a company.

Often boards of directors form sub-committees to look into or control certain aspects of a company's activity, such as finances, sales, training, or overseas development. The minutes of these committees should also be preserved.

Board meeting papers

The supporting papers presented at full board and committee meetings by directors, managers, research teams and such like should be permanently preserved, as they often contain detailed information which can help explain the reasoning behind policy decisions that is not contained in the board minutes. These papers were usually distributed loose or as individually bound reports with copies of the last board minutes and agenda for the next meeting. They may be presented by individual directors who have a special area of interest, either by function (finance, sales, marketing, public relations, employee relations, etc.) or by geographical area (Asia, Northern Europe, South America, etc.), and can be regular or occasional features on the agenda. What they have in common is that their contents are never reported in full in the minutes and rarely even appear in summarized form. They are considered as supplementary to the minutes themselves, although they are rarely appended to the board minutes and often do not survive. They began to be produced by the larger companies in the 1920s, and have become very bulky in recent years. They are usually duplicated among the files of individual directors and the company secretary. Weeding duplicated material is recommended, although it should be borne in mind that such action may break up a series of directors' records and destroy marginalia written by individual directors.

Shareholders' meeting minutes

General meetings consist of members (ordinary shareholders) of a company. Other shareholders, such as those holding preference and deferred shares, can hold class meetings and produce their own minutes, e.g. 4 per cent preference shareholder meeting minutes. The first Company Act of 1844 required that directors of companies made up a balance sheet at least once a year, and presented it to the shareholders in general meeting. Since then a limited company must by law hold an annual general meeting (ordinary general meeting) in each calendar year, notice of which must be given to all members. Extraordinary general meetings can be called by directors with due notice, and by members holding not less than 10 per cent of the paid-up capital. The 1856 Company Act required that the minutes, resolutions and proceedings of general meetings be recorded in appropriate books. It is the responsibility of the company secretary to record and maintain the minutes of the general meetings. According to statute the business conducted at an annual general meeting must include the appointment of the directors and auditors, the presentation of the accounts by the directors and the reading of the auditors' report. Such meetings also normally deal with the remuneration of the auditors and the payment of dividends, and consider the annual report. The annual general meeting usually ratifies decisions already taken, presents accounts and summarizes changes in the company without debate.

General meeting minutes are to be found either in a separate series of volumes or entered in the directors' meeting minute book – chronologically or in a separate section at the back of the volume. During the lifetime of a company the originals of the minutes must be kept at the registered offices of a company. The minutes of such meetings may appear to be of less historical value than board meeting minutes, but they should be permanently preserved after the dissolution of a company, as they provide information about the activities during the year, auditors, the annual accounts, and changes in the company during the year. Sometimes the chairman gives a summary of the principal events of the past year, which can be most useful to researchers. Even when the minutes give no information that cannot be obtained elsewhere, signed copies of the annual report may be interleaved with the minutes. It is not unusual to discover that a company changed from recording the minutes in a separate volume to including them with the directors' meeting minutes and *vice versa*. As general meeting minutes are open to the scrutiny of members, many companies maintained separate general and directors' meeting minute books, so that the private affairs of the company remained so. It is also common to find interspersed in these minute books, or located separately, documents and printed papers such as resolutions and chairmen's speeches presented at the annual general meeting. These papers should also be permanently preserved.

The minutes of other shareholders' meetings, such as those of preference shareholders, should be preserved, where they exist, as they record the decisions taken at class meetings.

Rough minute books

At board, general or committee meetings the minute secretary takes rough notes, sometimes in shorthand, in order to be able to compile a set of minutes to be presented at the next meeting as a true account of the proceedings. Occasionally these notes were made in bound volumes called rough minute books, which were often prepared in advance, with the agenda items laid out, apologies for absence noted, resolutions drafted and so on. Any surviving notes of meetings taken by the minute secretary or rough minute books can be destroyed if they contain no further information than that contained in the signed minutes.

Agendas and agenda books

Agendas lay down the items to be discussed at board, general or committee meetings. Agendas were kept in a separate volume or issued with the papers for the meeting. Occasionally agenda books double as rough or scroll minute books. If they contain information not recorded in the minute books, they should be permanently preserved; if not, they can be destroyed.

Attendance books

Attendance at board and general meeting minutes by directors and shareholders respectively was recorded in books or on sheets of paper signed by all those in attendance. Such records have little historical value, as attendance at meetings was usually recorded in the minutes of the meetings, and they can therefore be destroyed. Occasionally attendance records merit retention as exhibition items if, for example, the names of the attenders are of national renown or took part in a historically significant meeting.

Proxy forms

If members cannot attend the annual general meeting of a company, they are entitled to return a form appointing a proxy to attend and/or vote in their place. These forms have no historical value and can be destroyed a year after the meeting has taken place.

Shareholders' circulars, and notices of and resolutions passed at general and class meetings

Master copies of circulars sent to shareholders, notices of general and class shareholders' meetings and printed copies of resolutions passed at such meetings should be retained for the lifetime of a company and subsequently permanently preserved. Copies of these records often survive in bulk, but only one copy of each need be retained. Copies of resolutions passed at general and class shareholders' meetings must be sent to the Registrar of Companies and are kept on the company's official file.

Annual reports

It was first suggested in the model rules for the proper running of a company recommended by the 1908 Companies Act that a report under the names of the directors of a company be sent each year to members and to other people who requested it. Since 1928 all public companies have had to create and circulate a directors' report and send a copy to the Registrar of Companies. Private companies have only been required to produce such a report since 1967. The annual report contains certain documents required by law since 1928: an audited copy of the company's balance sheet and profit and loss account; the auditors' report; the directors' report for the year, which must also conform to the requirements of the Companies Acts; a notice convening the annual general meeting; and, where a company has subsidiaries, group accounts. The annual report may also contain a chairman's review and photographs of a public relations nature.

The directors' must report on the company's affairs and give details of the following:

- Dividends recommended.
- The names of directors.
- The principal activities of the company and its subsidiaries.
- Any substantial difference between the market value and book value of land or interest in land held by the company.
- Significant alterations in fixed assets.
- Any proposed transfers to reserves.
- Details of shares and debentures issued during the year.

- Any interest that a director has in a contract with the company.
- Each director's interest in shares and debentures as shown in the register of directors' interests, with comparative figures for the beginning of the year.
- An analysis of turnover.
- An analysis of profit or loss before tax.
- The average number of persons employed per week.
- Any other matters necessary to a proper appreciation of the company's affairs which are not harmful to the operation of the company or its subsidiaries.
- Details of political and charitable giving.
- Details of exports where they exceed a certain amount.
- Total remuneration paid to employees where there are more than 100.
- Any rights of directors to acquire shares and debentures.

Corresponding figures for previous years must also be given.

If the company is a holding company, then it must also include the audited consolidated balance sheet and profit and loss account for the group. Other information regarding the company's affairs, including photographs of new premises and products, has been common since the 1960s. Such information is intended to act as an aid to the uninformed investor or member, and often includes cashflow statements, bar charts and pie charts showing how income is derived from various sources and how it is expended.

The chairman's report or review is often included in the annual report. This is a personal message from the chairman to members, originally given orally at the annual general meeting, in which the company's fortunes in past and future years are surveyed and prospects for the future anticipated. The chairman's statement gives an indication as to how the directors view a company's progress at any given time, and is often reported in the financial sections of contemporary newspapers. The value of the financial information presented in the annual report is discussed on p. 145. The remaining information in the report summarizes the activities of the company over the past year, and varies in usefulness from company to company. A signed copy of each annual report, if they survive, should be kept for the lifetime of the company, and such reports are of sufficient historical value to be permanently preserved once the company ceases to operate.

Since the late 1960s it has been common for public companies to issue interim reports to shareholders and the media, with the intention of keeping them abreast of the progress of the business. They are usually small and give little more than the unaudited results for the first half year, with comparative figures for the same period the preceding year, usually indicating the improvement or deterioration in the figures which will be revealed in the forthcoming annual report. One copy of an interim report should be permanently preserved.

Directors' contracts

The 1967 Companies Act specified that companies must keep, in an appropriate place (the registered offices or the principal place of business), details of service contracts with directors. Where the contract is in writing, a copy must be kept, and where it is not, a memorandum setting out its terms must be retained. The contracts must be open to inspection on every business day for at least 2 hours, free of charge to all members of the company. Such contracts contain details about the remuneration and duties of the director concerned which are not often available elsewhere. Directors' contracts should be permanently preserved.

Directors' and secretaries' correspondence

The administrative correspondence of a company, dealt with by the company secretary, manager or a director, was kept by many businesses until the 1960s in the form of letterbooks, often with in-letters and out-letters forming separate series. Usually out-letter volumes survive where in-letter files have been lost or destroyed. While it is impossible to weed bound letterbooks, it may be practical to weed correspondence files. Letters dealing with policy and non-routine matters should be kept, and routine letters destroyed, although it is impossible to lay down hard and fast rules as to selection.

The correspondence and papers of the chairman, directors and senior managers of a company should be preserved if such documentation survives. Many senior businessmen consider their files and papers to belong to them personally, and arrange for them to be destroyed or to be removed when they retire or otherwise leave a company. Recent developments in the aftermath of the Guinness/United Distillers affair and new rulings on the liability of non-executive directors will have ramifications on the preservation of these records. Such material requires to be reviewed, and routine correspondence and duplicated papers weeded, as it forms a bulky but important source for understanding policy-making and the workings of business and businessmen.

Registers of directors and secretaries

The 1844 Joint Stock Companies Act laid down that companies must make an initial return to the Registrar of Companies of the names of their directors, notify any changes and make the list freely available to shareholders at the company's registered offices. The 1856 Act omitted these conditions, and the 1862 Act, which tried to repair the omission, did so in a way which made the requirement avoidable by most companies. It was not until the passing of the 1900 Companies Act that it once again became a legal requirement for companies to maintain a register of directors and secretaries, giving names, former names, addresses, nationalities (since 1917), business occupations, dates of birth (since 1948 for public companies only) and other directorships held, with the date of appointment and the date of resignation. Copies of the register have to be sent to the Registrar of Companies, who must be notified of any changes. This information is therefore available on a company's file at Companies House or one of the national public record offices for the 1844 to 1856 and post-1900 periods. The register must be kept for the lifetime of a company and as it gives details of the directors within and outwith the company in question, it should be permanently preserved.

Registers of directors' shareholdings or interests

The 1928 Company Act required all directors to state to their fellow directors the other companies in which they were shareholders or directors, in order to reduce the likelihood of corruption. These statements are often to be found in board minute books. Shareholders, however, remained unaware of possible conflicts of interest until the passing of the 1948 Companies Act, which demanded that every company must keep a register showing the number, description and amount of shares and debentures of the company or its subsidiary companies held by its directors or held in trust for them, or of which they have some right to be holders. Directors are obliged to notify the company in writing of all shares and debentures that they hold, cease to hold, or acquire the right to purchase in the company or a subsidiary. The register has to be open for inspection at the company's registered office or wherever the register of members is kept, and must be produced at the annual general meeting and remain open and accessible throughout. This register should therefore be retained for the lifetime of the company. It should be subsequently permanently preserved, as it lists the shareholdings held by a director of a company, which would be very difficult and time-consuming to discover from other sources. It should also be noted that no copy of this information is kept by the Registrar of Companies.

Shares

A share is a single unit of the common fund of a company known as the share capital. Shares establish the rights and obligations of the owners of a company, its shareholders, the persons who have promised to subscribe a sum of money to the company's capital in return for a portion of any profit which has accrued. The share capital is divided into shares of equal amount which must have a nominal value. Shares are transferable freely in public companies, although private companies restrict the right to transfer. The total of the company's share capital to be issued, the authorized or nominal capital, is stated in the memorandum and articles of association of the company. More capital cannot be issued until a resolution to that effect is passed at a general meeting. However, directors may consider that not all the nominal capital is required to be called up, and decide to offer a lower amount of capital for subscription, which is known as the issued capital. The conditions, described in a company's prospectus, upon which shareholders subscribe for their shares usually allow for only a portion of each share to be paid on application, a further amount on allotment and the remaining amounts on fixed dates. Many companies only require the amounts due on application and allotment immediately, the remaining portion only being called up in accordance with the authority given to the directors in the company's articles of association. The paid-up capital is that part of the issued capital in respect of which the company has received payment. The uncalled capital is that portion, if any, of the issued capital which the company has yet to call up but for which the shareholder is still liable. If a shareholder falls in arrears with his or her payments, the company has the right to forfeit the shares.

Ordinary shares

The ordinary or equity capital is held by ordinary shareholders, who are entitled, in the absence of deferred shares, to the balance of the distributed profit and in a winding-up to the balance of assets. The prefix 'A' or 'B' to shares normally denotes some curtailments of the rights customarily or legally attached to those shares. In the majority of cases 'A' shares are non-voting shares, frequently issued when the majority shareholding of a company wish to raise additional risk capital without a commitment to a fixed annual dividend or a dilution of control. Frowned on by the Stock Exchange, these issues are now rare – being at their most popular between the 1880s and 1960s – as institutional shareholders are reluctant to take up shares where there are no voting rights and they would possess no element of control.

Founders or deferred shares

The holders of founders or deferred shares are only entitled to a dividend if the dividend on the ordinary shares reaches a predetermined amount. Such shares are not common in the late twentieth century. They were often held by the nineteenth-century promoters or managers of companies – hence their name.

Preference shares

These shares give certain preferential rights over other types of shares in a company. There are different types and therefore different rights. The two main rights usually enjoyed by these shares are the right to preference in payment of dividend and the right to preference in repayment of capital in a winding-up. Holders are entitled to receive a dividend which is expressed as a percentage of the nominal amount of the share (for example a 2½ per cent preference share) when a dividend is declared. Such shareholders are not entitled to the whole dividend every year but to preferential treatment when a dividend is declared. Unless it is otherwise stated, it is cumulative: if no dividend is declared, arrears are carried forward and paid before any dividend is paid to ordinary shareholders. Preference shareholders have no voting rights unless a dividend is passed.

Share application forms

When someone wishes to purchase shares on a new issue, they submit a formal letter of application to the company, stating the number of shares they require. *Pro-formas* of such letters are usually published with the prospectus. The company then allots shares to the applicant, although not necessarily the number requested. The application forms have no historical value and can be destroyed when a company ceases to exist.

Share allotment letters

Following an application for shares, a company allots them on a predetermined basis set out in the prospectus. When a company makes a capitalization issue of shares, otherwise known as a bonus or scrip issue, it allots new shares to existing members in proportion to their existing holdings fully paid-up, such as one new share for 2 existing shares. The allotment under both types of issue is made by means of a letter which entitles the recipient to a certificate for the number of shares stated in the letter. These documents are of no historical value and can be destroyed once the company has been dissolved.

Renounced letters of acceptance and renounced letters of allotment

A company can raise new capital by a rights issue, inviting existing shareholders to acquire additional shares. The right might be, for example, one new share for each three shares previously held, and the price of the new share is usually lower than it would be in the open market. The shareholder can normally sell the right to a third party, and does not need to take up new shares. A letter of renunciation can be sent to the company to forgo the right either completely or in favour of another person. The originals of these letters should be kept for the lifetime of a company, and can be destroyed following the winding-up of a company.

Registers of members or shareholders or share register

The 1844 Joint Stock Companies Act laid down that every company had to keep a record of its members or shareholders, and every piece of company legislation since that date has maintained this stipulation. The register records the names and addresses of members, particulars of their shareholdings, and often the occupation or status of the shareholder. The register is vital for the work of the company secretary in issuing dividends, offering new share issues and sending out notifications to members about the annual general meetings. Share ownership is determined by entry in the register. If shares are held jointly both names are entered. Where there is a trust, the names of the trustees are entered, except in Scotland, where it is possible for the trust's name to be entered. The register also records the dates of beginning and ending of membership, and the amount paid up on shares. The register must normally be kept at the registered office or some other office which has been notified to the Registrar of Companies. Today many companies have turned over their share transactions to other firms specializing in registrar work. Since 1844 the register has been required to be open to members for free inspection and to non-members for a nominal sum during business hours, and therefore must be kept for the lifetime of a company.

The register of members should be preserved permanently as it contains detailed information about shareholdings which is not obtainable elsewhere. The registers of ordinary and preference shareholders and debenture-holders, however, can be very bulky, especially for large companies. The information recorded in them is in any case available, for all companies dissolved after the mid-1960s, in the microfiche copy of the company's annual return to the Registrar of Companies, which contains a list of shareholders. For public companies registered in England and Wales before the mid-1960s, and all companies registered in Scotland, a selection of annual returns is to be found in the dissolved companies files in the Public Record Office and the Scottish Record Office (see p. 125). This means that the share registers of all deceased companies registered in Scotland and all public companies registered in England and Wales could be destroyed as a space-saving exercise. However, careful thought is required before doing so, as such action would mean destroying the only source for detailed research into a company's shareholding structure.

Share ledgers

Share ledgers contain the share accounts of members of a company, and are therefore accounting records. They can form a very bulky series, and until the mid-twentieth century were usually contained in large bound volumes, often split into alphabetical sections by members' surname, e.g. A–C, D–G, and so on. In the late 1950s loose-leaf ledgers were introduced. By 1900 a system of combined register of members and share ledger had been introduced, arranged to record the number of shares each member held, the inclusive distinctive numbers of these shares, and the amount called up and paid up on the shares, showing at a glance the exact state of each member's share account. Combined registers of members and share ledgers should be treated as share registers, but a separate series of share ledgers could be destroyed after a company is dissolved.

Combined registers

Combined registers, introduced about 1900, consist of one volume combining sections for the register of share applications and allotments, register of directors and secretaries, register of directors' holdings, register of share transfers, register of members and share ledger, register of debentures, annual returns and so on. They should be preserved permanently.

Share certificates

The share certificate is evidence of ownership of shares but is not a negotiable instrument. Ownership is determined by entry in the company's register of shareholders, and certificates are usually issued under the company seal. Share certificates can be very colourful and highly illustrative, with fine engravings depicting a factory site, shop, product or related symbol, such as a locomotive, ship, or even advertising. Renounced and cancelled share certificates and share-certificate books, either wholly or partly used, with cancelled certificates occasionally attached, can be voluminous. Cancelled share certificates can be destroyed after a year, and renounced share certificates after a company has been dissolved. A selection of interesting share certificates might be retained for use in historical exhibitions and publications.

Share transfer forms

When a company share is sold or otherwise disposed of to another person, the right of ownership is required to be transferred formally. This is effected by the completion of a transfer form, which is then sent, together with the share certificate, to the registered office of the company. On receiving the transfer form, signed by the seller, the company will enter the buyers name in its share register, delete that of the seller and issue a new certificate. The share transfer forms should be retained for the lifetime of a company or for 12 years if microfilmed, and can be destroyed after a company ceases to exist, as they have no historical value.

Share transfer registers

The majority of public and large private companies kept share transfer registers into which details of share transfers were entered, usually from the original transfer documents. The register served as a means of checking the register of members and was invaluable to company secretaries when compiling the annual return for the Registrar of Companies and presenting transfers to directors' meetings for adoption. The keeping of such a register has never been a legal requirement, and for companies with a low rate of share transfer it was not a necessity. Share transfer registers need not be kept beyond their administrative usefulness.

Dividends

A dividend is a share of a company's profits distributed to a shareholder, the amount received depending on the number of shares held. Dividends are optional payments made at the discretion of the directors, unlike the interest payments due on debentures. Articles of association usually provide for dividends to be declared by the company in general meeting, by ordinary resolution, but shareholders cannot declare more dividend than the directors recommend. These dividends are usually referred to as final dividends. Dividends are always expressed as a percentage of the nominal value of the shares, whatever the category. The rate for preference shares is normally predetermined, e.g. 4 per cent preference shares. The amount of dividend issued on ordinary and deferred shares depends on the funds available and the amount of profits the directors decide to distribute. Articles of association also usually provide for the directors to 'pay' and sometimes even to 'declare' interim dividends without the need for a resolution in general meeting.

Dividend warrants entitle the recipient to a sum of money which can be obtained from a bank. These warrants should be kept for 12 years after date of payment, and then destroyed, as they have no historical value. Dividend mandates give a company the authority to pay dividends direct into a shareholder's bank account. Originals should be kept until the account is closed, and can then be destroyed.

Dividend lists or sheets record the distinctive numbers of the dividend warrants, the name of the shareholder, the dividend, amount of the warrant and other information. These lists were often bound into a large volume, and sometimes separate dividend warrant registers recording the numbers of the warrants were also kept. Neither series of records have any historical value and both should be destroyed.

Debentures

A debenture is a document setting out the terms of a loan. The ability of a company to issue debentures depends on its power to borrow, which is usually stated in the objects clause of its memorandum of association. The clause may also limit the amount which may be borrowed. When a company issues debentures, the people buying them are lending money to the company rather than buying shares in it. A debenture may be secured by a fixed or floating charge or a combination of both. A fixed charge or mortgage is a charge on specific assets of a company, such as property or interests in property, and it is usually referred to as a mortgage debenture. A debenture-holder secured by such a charge ranks as a secured creditor in a winding-up of a company. A floating charge is a charge on a company's general assets, such as book debts, cash or stock. A floating charge becomes a fixed charge when a company ceases to carry on a business, or is wound up, or on the occurrence of some event specified in the terms of the debenture. A debenture-holder secured by a floating charge has certain disadvantages, and is a deferred creditor in a winding-up of a company. The debenture deed is held for the debenture-holders by trustees appointed by the directors of the company but independent persons. The deed states the terms of the loan, when it becomes repayable and the powers of the debenture-holders. The trust deed itself should be kept for the lifetime of the company and is of sufficient historical interest to be preserved permanently thereafter.

Issuing debentures is a popular way of raising money for limited companies, as the debentures, unlike shares, can be redeemed by the company and are also freely transferable. Usually companies issue debentures in the form of debenture stock, as that facilitates the transfer of part of a holding. All charges must be registered on the company's file at Companies House. Debenture-holders receive annual fixed interest, which must be paid or provided for before any dividends can be paid to share-holders. On the winding-up of a company, debentures secured on a fixed charge are paid out of the asset charged. Those secured on a floating charge also have a preference after the Inland Revenue and the Depart-ment of Health and Social Security. Actions of debenture-holders held in the Chancery Division and filed by the Registrar of Companies (Winding-up) Department are to be found for the period 1891 to 1922 in the Public Record Office in class J 14.

Debenture application forms

Debenture application forms, like those for shares, should be kept for the lifetime of a company. Thereafter they can be destroyed.

Registers of mortgages, charges or debentures

Each company since 1862 has been required by law to keep a register of all charges on its property by way of mortgages, fixed or floating debentures, bills of sale and so on. These charges must also be lodged with the Registrar of Companies, otherwise they are void. The register of mortgages, also known as a register of charges or debentures, contains full details of each charge: a general description of the property, the persons involved, and the amount of the charge. This must be kept at the offices of the company and must be open for inspection by members of the company and creditors for a fee. This register should therefore be retained during the lifetime of a company. However, as details about the charges are to be found on the company's files at Companies House and on the dissolved company files in the appropriate public record office, the register could be subsequently destroyed in the case of public companies.

Registers of debenture-holders

Companies are not required by statute to maintain a register of debenture-holders, but the debenture trust deed usually stipulates that one will be kept. Such a register must be kept at the company's registered offices or some other office, the location of which must be notified to the Registrar of Companies, where it is to be open for inspection by members and others. The registers, which record the names and addresses of debenture-holders, can be destroyed 7 years after the redemption of the stock, and need not be considered for preservation beyond this date.

Debenture stockholders' meeting minutes

It is common, either in the trust deed or in the conditions on the debentures, to provide for meetings of debenture-holders with the power to vary the terms of the security or to generally sanction alterations. Where minutes for these meetings exist, they should be retained for the lifetime of the company and preserved permanently thereafter as a record of the policy underlying any alterations. Such minutes are not usually found with a company's other corporate records, as they do not belong to the company, but in the offices of the debenture trustees or their successors.

Seal books

It is a requirement that all limited companies have a common seal, known as the company seal, which is administered, preserved and protected by the company secretary. The name of the company must be engraved on the seal. The seal is used to authenticate all contracts made by the company which would be required to be by deed if entered into by a private person: service contracts, share certificates, title deeds and so on. A company is required to keep a seal book to record details of the documents sealed by the company seal and the signatures of two directors authorizing its use. The utilization of the seal is also often recorded in the directors' meeting minutes. The seal book is required to be kept during the lifetime of a company. It should also be retained permanently, as it records details about leases, property purchases, trust deeds, patent applications, service contracts for agents, directors and so on, not all of which are recorded in detail in the directors' meeting minutes. Where all entries in a seal book are duplicated in a minute book, the former could be destroyed

Annual returns

Every company registered under the Companies Acts since 1844 must each year, within 42 days of the annual general meeting, file an annual return with the Registrar of Companies. The return must contain details of all shares and debentures in issue, any changes in the amount of the ownership of these since the date of the last return, and particulars regarding the directors and secretary; and include all balance sheets and documents required to be attached that have been presented to members in general meeting since the last meeting. As copies of these returns are kept by the Registrar for all live companies and a sample is kept for dissolved public companies in England and Wales and all companies in Scotland, any surviving copies of public company annual return forms in loose or bound form can be considered for destruction.

Company registration files

The files kept by the Registrar of Companies on each registered company contain all the documentation (returns) that companies are required by statute to send to the Registrar. These are held by the Companies Registration Office in England and Wales for 20 years after the company's dissolution, and are then either destroyed or transferred to the Public Record Office, Kew. The files of returns made to the Registrar by all companies registered under the 1844 Joint Stock Companies Act and those registered under the 1856 Companies Act which were dissolved prior to 1860 are to be found in class BT 41. The information to be found in this class should include the name, purpose and address of the company; the names of the company's promoters and their solicitors; a prospectus; and details of capital, issue and allocation of shares and balance sheets.

The files for companies dissolved after 1860 and registered in England and Wales under the 1856 Act and all subsequent Acts are held in BT 31. The documents to be found in these files usually include:

1   Memorandum and articles of association with amendments.
2   A copy of the certificates of incorporation and changes of name.
3   A nominal share capital statement.
4   The location of registered office and the register of directors.
5   Selected annual returns and balance sheets.
6   Liquidation and dissolution documents.[5]

The equivalent files of dissolved companies registered in Scotland are located in the Scottish Record Office in BT 2, and for companies registered in Northern Ireland in the Public Record Office of Northern Ireland in COM 40.

Liquidation

The process of liquidation is the winding-up of the affairs of a company, leading to its dissolution. It can indicate insolvency (compulsory winding-up) but is also to be applied to the winding-up of a company by its shareholders (voluntary winding-up) when, for instance, the purpose for which it was originally formed has been completed. The Returns of final winding-up meetings, a copy of the court order for a compulsory winding-up, or a certificate of notice in the *London Gazette* or *Edinburgh Gazette* of winding-up, must be sent to the Registrar of Companies.

Appointment of liquidator

Until the Companies (Winding-Up) Act 1890 liquidators were not required to file accounts with the Registrar of Companies. From 1890 to 1932 these accounts have been preserved separately in the Public Record Office in class BT 34, but from 1933 they are to be found in the company file in class BT 31. When a periodic distribution of funds is made to creditors, the accounts are maintained by the Department of Trade and Industry.

Conclusion

Corporate records, in comparison with other business records, are simple to identify and are relatively uniform among companies as a result of the legislation which created them. Standard guidelines can be followed in appraising and preserving them. On the whole, the bulky series which exist can be sampled, weeded, or destroyed. It is not difficult for researchers to understand and use corporate records. The major problem with such records arises from the conglomerations of the records of subsidiary companies which can exist among the records of a parent company. The resulting difficulties of indentification can often be compounded by the fact that although a company's registration number is a unique identifier, its name is not.

Notes

1   The addresses of the four Companies Registration Offices are as follows: Companies House, Crown Way, Maindy, Cardiff CF4 3UZ; Companies House, 55–71 City Road, London EC1Y 1BB; Exchequer Chambers, 102 George Street, Edinburgh EH2 3DJ; and Companies Registry, 43–47 Chichester Street, Belfast BT1 4RJ.
2   The Chief Register of Friendly Societies, 17 Audley Street, London WIY 2AP, maintains a register of these organizations see T. M. Aldridge, *Directory of Registers and Records*, 4th edition (Oyez Longman, London, 1984), pp. 87–90 for further details of information available.
3   The register is maintained by the Registrar of Companies, and a microfiche copy can be consulted at the four Companies Registration Offices.

4 For further help in locating the records of a business see J. Orbell, *A Guide to Tracing the History of a Business* (Gower, Aldershot, 1987), pp. 17–30.

5 See *Registration of Companies and Businesses* (Public Record Office Information Sheet No. 54, n.d.) for further details.

Further reading

J. Armstrong and S. Jones, *Business Documents. Their Origins, Sources and Uses in Historical Research* (Mansell, London, 1987).

Peter Emmerson, *Records Retention*, Record Aids No. 3 (Business Archives Council, London, 1983).

F. Gore-Brown and W. Jordan, *Handbook on the Function, Management and Winding-Up of Joint Stock Companies*, 30th edition (Jordan & Sons, London, 1909).

D. Hirasuna, *A Historical Review of Annual Report Design* (Cooper-Hewitt Museum, The Smithsonian Institution's National Museum of Design, New York, 1988).

Jordan & Sons, *Secretarial Administration* (Jordan & Sons, London, 1984).

M. S. Moss, *Business Records and Business Failure* (Society of Archivists Information Sheet No. 1, 1984).

Public Record Office, *Registration of Companies and Businesses* (Public Record Office Information Sheet No. 54, n.d.).

P. Tovey (editor), *Pitman's Dictionary of Secretarial Law and Practice*, 4th edition (New Era Publishing Company, London, 1929).

D. T. and M. T. Watts, 'Company records as a source for the family historian', *Genealogists Magazine*, 21:2 (1983), pp. 45–54.

6

Accounting records

Michael Moss

Many archivists find accounting records more difficult to evaluate than any
other class of material, largely because they have never had an opportunity
to consider how they can be used as historical evidence. Similarly those
with commercial experience who find themselves the custodians of archives
may understand book-keeping methods but lack the historical perspective
to place them in context. For any archivist, whether professionally trained
or not, it is simply not enough to know the difference between various
types of accounting records, for appraisal must depend in part on content
as well as context. Every organization will create some sort of accounting
records, however rudimentary, during its lifetime, since almost every
activity has a financial expression which, except for the most trivial, will be
recorded. For any organization, whether it be a multinational group, a
small family firm, or a local charitable body, such records of individual
transactions form the basis of any accounting system.

Before attempting to select accounting records for permanent preservation, the archivist must be aware of the chronology of an enterprise's legal
status, which determines the range of information the records contain. In
the nineteenth century the partnership structure, however large, provided
a very flexible legal status (see Chapter 2) which allowed the individual
members to put a whole variety of transactions, unrelated to core business,
through the books. It is possible to find details of the cost of construction of
private houses, purchases of furnishings and daily necessities, and
charitable giving in the partners' personal account with the firm. This was
because the capital of partnerships was composed largely of the credit
balances on the individual partners' personal accounts on which they could
draw at will to meet their private needs. When an enterprise became a
limited liability company, with shares replacing credit balances, this
practice usually stopped.

Preliminary records of account: invoices received and rendered

These have different names, depending on the period and the part of the
country. In Scotland from the sixteenth century to the eighteenth century
they were often described collectively as precepts. Many archival lists refer
to them as 'accounts and vouchers' or bills. Today most organizations only
retain them for the statutory periods (6 years for revenue expenditure and
10 years for capital expenditure) before destruction, but large accumulations

are regularly encountered in old-established concerns where space is not at a premium, particularly estate offices and country legal practices. It might seem logical to apply current practices and destroy all such records that are found in archive collections. Immediately the archivist is faced with a dilemma; many accounts and vouchers from the eighteenth and nineteenth century are beautifully printed, incorporating vignettes of the shop or factory, normally very accurate representations – unlike the more generous artists' impressions to be found in the trade press.[1] They also contain detailed information not to be found in other accounting series. For many specialist historians, such as those of architecture arnd gardening, they are an invaluable source, providing crucial evidence. For company historians they represent a treasure trove of illustrations for exhibitions and brochures. Consequently, in reaching a decision about retention, the archivist must take into account the age, the provenance, and the information they contain. Any archivist who was foolish enough to destroy the accounts rendered by a notable craftsman, or the vouchers of an eighteenth-century bookseller, would deserve all the opprobrium that would be heaped upon him. On the other hand, an archivist who recklessly committed long runs of shelving to the accounts and vouchers of a mid-twentieth-century manufacturing company would have difficulty in justifying the decision to auditors. These are extreme and obvious examples of the discretion required of archivists in reviewing this class of accounting material.

More difficult to assess are long runs of accounts and vouchers for large landed estates, which often provide essential testimony to changes in a local landscape or built environment and precise dates and costs for sales, purchases and investment in fixed assets; they can also provide a day-to-day narrative of a firm's transactions that is difficult to reconstruct from the ledgers and other books of account. Accounts and vouchers sometimes also furnish information about changing terms of trading, such as the move from credit to ready money, business addresses, and names of partners and directors.

Usually invoices received, if they survive, are stored in neat bundles tied with string and organized in date order by year. Each invoice is invariably endorsed with a reference number to a page in the book of prime entry (the first account book) in which they were entered, a brief description of the transaction and the account total. Sometimes they are stored in separate bundles. Very occasionally they are to be found pasted into guardbooks. Invoices rendered are usually kept in separate bundles or registers and certified when paid, and endorsed with similar information to invoices received. Uniquely among accounting records, there may be a case for sampling accounts and vouchers, preserving those with billheads that contain important visual evidence. The well-known and heavily exploited John Johnson collection of printed ephemera at the Bodleian Library contains a large proportion of such material. However, directly an account or invoice is removed from its original context, the quality of its evidence as an accounting record is debased.

Single- and double-entry explained

Single-entry accounts

From mediaeval times the individual records of debit or credit transactions contained in the invoices received and rendered were recorded in single-entry account books which merely listed and totalled both types of transactions. Single entry was common until the mid-eighteenth century, when it began to be replaced rapidly by the double-entry system of book-keeping.[2] Single entry continued to be used well into the nineteenth century by small unsophisticated businesses, by trustees of estates, and by public authorities and institutions. Single-entry accounts, although adequate, could only provide a single balance (credit or debit) for the outcome of the activities undertaken by the organization for the period under review. It was very difficult to arrive at a picture of the state of an enterprise. The relationships with customers and suppliers could only be analysed by the laborious comparison of debit and credit transactions sometimes many pages apart. Their simplicity, however, should not be grounds for destruction. If they are found for a relatively late period in the nineteenth century, they provide important evidence in themselves of the persistence of the system. Single entry was also used a good deal by craftsmen, for example, goldsmiths and cabinetmakers, and by clubs and societies. In these cases the needs of specialist historians in part dictate selection criteria.

Double-entry book-keeping

There is a debate about the timing of the general adoption of double-entry book-keeping (the 'Italian system') in Britain.[3] Some scholars have chosen a date early in the nineteenth century, while others believe its use was widespread, at least among larger concerns, by the middle of the eighteenth century. The essential feature of the double-entry system is that every transaction has a twofold effect. For example, if a business purchases an item for £100, its stock rises by this amount, but at the same time either its cash resources fall by the same amount or there is a balancing increase in its liabilities. In consequence, the sum of the debit balances always equal the sum of the credit balances. The accounting records of a firm employing a double-entry system can be subdivided into 4 separate types:

- Books of prime entry.
- Journals.
- Ledgers.
- Accounts.
- Other records.

Books of prime entry

In the double-entry system most transactions enter the system via books of original or prime entry. The books of prime entry vary in name and function over time from sector to sector and from company to company. When the double entry of book-keeping was devised in the fourteenth and fifteenth centuries in Venice, there was just one book of prime entry, the memorial or waste book.[4] By the eighteenth century this had been subdivided for convenience into separate volumes for invoices and receipts, particularly in larger concerns with many hundreds of transactions. Writing in 1799 Benjamin Booth, an American merchant who had moved to London, identified 7 books of prime entry – the cash book; bill book; invoice book, inward; bought book or book of imports; invoice book, outward; day book, or book of exports; and the waste book.[5] A century later George Lisle recommended in his *Accounting in Theory and Practice*, just three books of original or prime entry – the cash book, the invoice book and the day (purchase) book.[6] Volumes bearing these titles and variations of them will be encountered among the records of any old-established business. Like all other accounting volumes, these are usually labelled and numbered on the spine. They have survived because they were the only legally admissable evidence of a transaction. Since books of original or prime entry recorded all transactions that were made by a concern from the very largest to the smallest, the detail provided can often be considerable. The most commonly encountered books of prime entry are waste books, cash books, day books and bill books.

Waste books

From the seventeenth century details were transcribed from receipts and invoices into a single book of prime entry, the waste book. At the end of each entry the transaction was summarized for posting to the journal or the ledger. Each entry was referenced back to the receipts and invoices and forward to the next book of account. As other books of prime entry were devised, towards the end of the eighteenth century, the waste book became obsolete, but many firms continued slavishly to use it.[7] Very few long series of waste books survive, but the occasional volume often turns up and is worthy of retention.

Cash books

These books are often encountered in large numbers even for firms of a moderate size. They contain a complete record of all cash (and bank) transactions, whether debit or credit, ranging from trivial expenditure on travel to the sale of a large item paid for in cash. Normally, but not always in Britain, sums received or debtor transactions marked 'Dr' are entered on the left and prefixed by the word 'To'. Sums paid or creditor transactions marked 'Cr' are entered on the right and prefixed by the word 'By'. The pages of cash books are ruled with a number of columns, depending on the nature of the business and its book-keeping system. The first column usually contains the date, followed by a description of the transaction, and then by either a single column for the amount or, more commonly, by several columns that analyse the transaction into type, goods, charges, sundries, and so on. In addition, there is usually a column with a page reference to the journal through which the cash-book entries are formally incorporated into the double-entry system. In manufacturing companies the job or batch number to which the transaction related may also be quoted, linking the accounting record directly with the production records – the job books, order books and technical drawings (see Chapter 7).

Figure 6.1 represents facing pages from the cash book of Scotts Shipbuilding Co. of Greenock in the West of Scotland. The first two columns on the left give the date, the third the description of the transaction, the fourth the method of receipt/payment, and the fifth the sum in question. The first entry on the left-hand side for 14 November 1862 is a payment of £7,017 16s 4d from the Compagnie Générale Trans-atlantique of Paris, part of the cost of vessels being constructed by Scotts at Greenock and at St Nazaire in France. This was posted to page 296 of the journal (see Figure 6.3).

Since transactions are posted to the journal and then the ledger, there is a temptation for archivists to destroy all cash books. However, in most double-entry systems the detail of transactions entered in the cash book is rarely repeated in the journal. This is particularly true for sundry expenditure or purely cash transactions such as a partner's personal expenditure from his capital account. Although this is not a good argument for retaining all cash books where they relate to concerns of local or national importance or to industrial/commercial sectors where there is high-user demand, the archivist should examine the content in comparison with the other books of account before making a decision.

Private cash books

In addition to the main cash book, some businesses maintained separate cash books for cash transactions of a confidential nature; for example, partners' salaries, commission paid to third parties, and so on. These form part of the private accounting series and are usually locked (*see also* Private ledgers, p. 144).

Petty cash books

These were introduced in the late nineteenth century when suppliers of daily necessities of an organization began to demand payment in cash rather than on account. If a great number of small transactions had been entered in the cash book, the cash book would have quickly become overburdened. Petty cash books usually contain details for very trivial transactions, such as the purchase of stamps, fares for travel, stationery and food. They can almost always be safely destroyed, as they merely account in detail for small sums of cash which appear on the payments side of a cash book.

Day books

These are almost invariably found in enterprises that had a very large number of daily transactions, for example, stockbrokers and auctioneers, and provide details of the cost and price of a transaction – say the cost of selling goods for a client, the commission charged to the client, and the price paid by the customer. Sales day books and purchase day books also formed an important part of the accounting system of many manufacturing enterprises. They do not contain any record of cash transactions which would appear in the cash book, but day book entries, like those in cash books, often contain far more detail than can be found in either the journal or the ledger.

Figure 6.2a, for example, is a page from day book no. 1 of Andrew Barclay Sons & Co., locomotive builders and general engineers of Kilmarnock in Ayrshire. The book is arranged into 6 columns: the first on the left gives the job number of the product, the second the page number in the ledger, the third the name of the customer or supplier, the fourth the quantity, the fifth the cost per item, and the sixth the total price. Job 1899 was for a 2 foot 5 inch gauge tank locomotive, with 4 wheels coupled and 2 trailing wheels, as per contract numbers 310 and 311 (i.e. 2 locomotives) for Kerr Stuart & Co. of London, invoiced 12 December 1878 for £610. This was posted to page 18 of ledger no. 1 (Figure 6.2b). This transaction appears in the left-hand side of the ledger page for Kerr Stuart & Co., 20 Bucklesbury, London, under the legend 'Goods', indicating that Andrew Barclay & Co. had supplied some items to the company but offering no explanation. There is a reference (186) back to the day book, which contains the detail of the contract. In the right-hand side of the ledger page are payments to Andrew Barclay by Kerr Stuart, including 2 for the locomotives, £450 in a 3-month bill of exchange on 22 November 1888 and the £160 balance in cash on 5 December, which has been transferred from the cash book.

The destruction of the Andrew Barclay day books would have resulted in the loss of important information for a well-defined user community – the railway and locomotive enthusiast. In some manufacturing businesses the cost of transactions entered in the day book are supplemented by separate cost book series, showing how the cost was made up, for example the cost of all the materials, wages and overheads that went into the 2 locomotives.

Dr		Cash			
1862	To	Balance from October	33	13	7
Nov 1	"	Royal Bank	30	"	"
"	"	do	500	"	"
" 2	"	Barnett & Co	703	9	10
3	"	Royal Bank	13	"	"
4	"	do	2983	"	"
"	"	do	10	"	"
5	"	do	13	"	"
6	"	Ross Brothers 2nd Instalment No 95	2900	"	"
"	"	Royal Bank	43	17	"
"	"	do	115	"	"
"	"	do	320	"	"
"	"	P Henderson & Co to 4c of Bastias Engines	1000	"	"
7	"	Royal Bank	845	"	"
8	"	do	1760	"	"
"	"	do	83	"	"
"	"	Greenock Foundry Co	320	"	"
10	"	Royal Bank	58	"	"
11	"	J S Begbie	5000	"	"
11	"	Royal Bank	126	16	"
12	"	do	120	"	"
"	"	do	1466	13	4
"	"	Barnett & Co	16	"	"
14	"	Compagnie Generale Transatlantique	7017	16	4
"	"	Exchange & Commission a/c	20	18	4
"	"	Royal Bank	100	"	"
18	"	do	235	"	"
"	"	Barnett & Co	1600	"	"
19	"	do	10	"	"
"	"	Royal Bank	270	"	"
21	"	do	856	"	"
22	"	do	1610	"	"
"	"	Barnett & Co	600	"	"
24	"	do	1500	"	"
"	"	do	2050	"	"
26	"	Royal Bank	25	"	"
27	"	do	65	"	"
28	"	do	50	"	"
		Carried Forward £	34470	4	5

Figure 6.1 *Facing paces from the cash book of Scotts Shipbuilding Co. The left-hand page contains debitor, 'Dr', transactions or sums received, and the right-hand page, creditor, 'Cr', transactions or sums paid.*

Cash   Cr.

		Account	Detail	£	s	d
Nov	1	By C C Scott	Order Miss McGowan	20	"	7
"	"	do Paid him		10	"	"
"	"	Building Yard. Railway account minerals		2	11	7
"	"	do Painters wages		1	8	"
"	"	Greenock Foundry Co Paid them		500	"	"
"	"	Bills Payable C T & S		703	9	10
3	"	Insurance Account J C Hunter		12	8	2
"	"	C C Scott paid Him		1	"	"
4	"	do Order on Edinburgh Marine		17	"	"
"	"	do paid him		10	"	"
"	"	Bills Payable M L & Co		1297	17	3
"	"	do P McC & Sons		1212	2	10
"	"	do A G K		456	19	2
5	"	Building Yard Iron Bought at Sale		14	12	5
6	"	do Ps W McLellan & Co a/c		43	17	"
"	"	Royal Bank Lodged		2900	"	"
"	"	John Robb & Co paid them for Timber £3.10.8		112	"	"
"	"	Greenock Foundry Co on a/c of Scotias Engines		1000	"	"
"	"	do paid them		320	"	"
8	"	E B Maclean paid Him		40	"	"
"	"	Hugh Maclean "		25	"	"
"	"	Thomas Nicol "		27	10	"
"	"	L Clark to account		24	"	"
"	"	St Nazaire Building Yard, R. Agnew		3	"	"
"	"	Building Yard R Wilson		10	"	"
"	"	do Coopers account		15	"	6
"	"	do Henry Ker do		17	11	11
"	"	do J Lyon paid Him		3	"	"
"	"	C C Scott Carters Wages		1	14	"
"	"	do G Lang		1	10	"
"	"	do Gardner		1	10	"
"	"	do Order on A B Murdoch		385	"	"
"	"	do Gardner		3	13	4
10	"	do Paid Him		50	"	"
"	"	J D Scott "		8	"	"
11	"	Bills Payable T & B		5000	"	"
"	"	Building Yard J Phillip Oak Timber		126	16	"
12	"	do part Freight pr "C 80"		47	10	"
		Carried Forward £		14426	2	7

186

7th December 1888

		Brot forward					148	11	4
2024	46	Britannia Eng Wks Coy. Kilmarnock To 2 Bevil wheel castings	1	22	4	10/-	17 2	-	17 2
2016	159	W & A Ruddd, Kilmarnock To 1 Sm " Bearing studd.					- 2 - - - 3		- 2 3
1956	35	Ganchalland Coal Coy. Gatston To 12 Sted punched					1 17 6		1 17 6
2032	49	8th Gilmour Anderson & Coy. Kilmarnock To 1 Brass Valve seal facing old value					9 .		9 .

1899	18	12th
		Kerr Stuart & Coy. London
		To 2' 5" Tank Locomotives. 4
		  wheels cupled. 2 trailing wheels
		  as per contract No' 310 & 311
							610		610 .. ..

2011	15	Cowdenbeath Coal Coy. Cowdenbeath To 1 Air Pump Bucket & guard casting	10	"	"	4/-	6 . ..		6 .. ..
2053	188	R. Stuart, Stonehouse To Brass ashes	4	4	..	" 4/	3 7 2		3 7 2
2015	175	Portland Forge Coy. Kilmarnock To Repairing value 2 new blades	..	"	"	"	" 3 8		" 3 8
1940	101	14th D Proctor & Coy. Kilmarnock To 1 Steel screw, & cast iron mat for lathe as per contract					5		5 .. ..
		Carry forward					776	8	1

Figure 6.2   *Pages from (a) day book no. 1 and (b) ledger no. 1 of Andrew Barclay Sons & Co., locomotive builders and general engineers of Kilmarnock, Ayrshire.*

18

Kerr Stuart & Co, 20 Bucklersbury, London

1886   1886

Date			Fol	£	s	d	£	s	d	Date				£	s	d	£	s	d
1886										1886									
Nov.	19	Goods	4	30	..	..	30	..	..	Nov.	22	Cash		30	..	..	30	..	..
Dec.	31	"	16	5	..	..	5	..	..	1887 Jany	7	"		5	..	..	5	..	..
1887 March	31	"	36	6	13	4	6	13	4	April	2	"		6	13	4	6	13	4
June	9	"	55	70	15	..				June	15	"		40	..	..			
							70	15	..	July	7	"		30	15	..	70	15	..
1888 Oct	12	Goods	167	6	13	4				1888 Oct	11	Bill 2 m/d		264	..	..			
Nov.	20	"	179	529	..	..					25	" "		265	..	..			
Dec.	12	"	186	610	..	..				Nov.	7	Cash		6	13	4			
											22	Bill 3 Yd		450	..	..			
							1145	13	4	Dec.	5	Cash		160	..	..	1145	13	4
1889 May	1	Goods	239	550	..	..				1889 May	18	2 Bills @ 3 months							
	17		245	51	9	2						Balance		550	..	..			
							601	9	2					51	9	2	601	9	2
1890	18	Balance		51	9	2						Credit	500	5	5	..			
April	18	Goods		30	..	..					31	" "		1	5	..			
May	5	"	288	21	5	6				1890	20	Cash	5	46	4	2			
	16	Balance		..	7	..				Mar	25	Cash		25	..	..			
											3			25	..	6			
							103	1	8	April		Credit	507	..	7	..	103	1	8
1891 May	16	Balance		..	7	..	..	7	..	May	16	Balance	written off	..	7	..	..	7	..
										May	16	"		..	7				

Dr.   Cowdenbeath Coal Co, Cowdenbeath   Cr.

From 16

Date			Fol	£	s	d	£	s	d	Date			Fol	£	s	d	£	s	d
1895 Dec	20	To Goods	272	..	6	..	..	6	..	1896 Jan	29	By Cash & dis	143	..	6	..	..	6	..
1896 Feb	12	" "	289	39	10	..				April	29	" "	153	300	11	3			
	20	" "	292	303	15	..	343	5	-	May	26	" "		33	6	9	333	18	0
Apl	4	" "	306	1	3	5	344	8	5	April	20	Bal Goods	57	3	2	..			
May	15	" "	322	3	..	..	347	8	5	May	31	Bal. Allow	592	6	3	3	343	3	3
Sept	29	" "	390	..	17	9	348	6	2					..	10	..	344	13	3
										July	29	" .. dis	161	2	13	5	347	6	8
										Oct	29	" "	171	..	17	9	348	4	5
							348	6	2	April	30	" Disct af	1	..	1	9	348	6	2

In some archival textbooks day books are grouped together with journals. This is misleading, as they form a distinct record of prime entry, unlike the journal, which is a book of secondary entry.

The journal explained

All transactions in the books of prime entry must be posted to the ledger. In the case of a small enterprise with few transactions they may be posted direct, but in most enterprises they are posted from a journal, or 'arranger', as it was often termed in the nineteenth century. This volume stands between the cash book and other books of prime entry and the ledger. It also records any transfers between ledger accounts, for example, when profit or loss is transferred from the balance of one ledger account to the profit and loss account. In the journal all transactions of the same kind are 'arranged' sequentially in date order and gathered together, often alphabetically, under appropriate headings, with an indication of which sums are to be carried to the debtor side and which to the creditor side of the ledger. There are simple and complex entries. Simple entries are those where a credit entry has only one debit entry and *vice versa*. A complex transaction is one in which a credit entry has more than one debit entry, or *vice versa*, representing cash received. In the journal many pages of entries in the books of prime entry may be reduced to a summary of a few lines. Transactions were summarized in this way to stop the ledger becoming overburdened with detail. Like the cash book, the journal is ruled into several columns, the first normally containing the date, and the second a reference forward to the ledger page and in some cases also a reference back to the book of original entry in different colour ink.

Figure 6.3 is a page from the journal of Scotts Shipbuilding and Engineering Co., which includes the payment from the Compagnie Générale Transatlantique, originally entered on the page of the cash book shown in Figure 6.1. At the end of each month trial balances were often struck for all the accounts in the ledger to which transactions had been

Figure 6.3   *The payment to Scotts Shipbuilding Co. from the Compagnie Générale Transatlantique on 14 November 1862 in Figure 6.1 was posted to page 296 of the journal, shown here as the first entry on the page. This page contains entries for debitors and creditors arranged by ledger headings for the month of November 1862. Like the cash book, it is ruled into columns. The page numbers in column 2 refer to the ledger. Column 3 contains the ledger headings, and column 4 the detail of the transaction, where these have been grouped together, as in the case of the numerous cash transactions described as sundries which are to be posted to the ledger heading 'Building yard' – in other words shipyard. In this example the journal entry contains more information than the cash book, as the bald entry Compagnie Générale Transatlantique has been annotated with '4 and 5th inst Engines', indicating which part of the contract the payment was for. This transaction was posted to page 145 of the ledger (see Figure 6.4).*

296

November 1862

		Cash Dr To Sundries						3500	17	7
14	145	Compagnie Generale Transatlantique						7017	16	4
	146	Exchange and Commission a/c						20	18	4
	151	St Nazaire Building Yard						1674	14	10
25	157	Loan Account						5000	"	"
29	142	Building Yard, Iron Slabs &c						"	13	"
								45221	"	1

	123	**Sundries Dr To Cash**					
1	142	Building Yard	Railway a/c Minerals	2	11	7
		do	Painters Wages	1	8	"
5		do	Iron Bought at Sale	4	12	5
6		do	P. N. McLellan & Co a/c	43	17	"
8		do	Wages	2446	1	6
		do	R Wilson	10	"	"
		do	Coopers a/c	15	"	6
		do	Henry Ker	17	11	11
		do	J. Lyon paid him	3	"	"
		do	J. Phillips oak Timber	126	6	"
11		do	part Freight pr "BV"	47	10	"
12		do	Gratuity to Captain of "BV"	8	"	"
		do	Dues on Iron	2	"	"
		do	Insurance paid Royal	16	"	"
		do	P. Christie & Co Carving No. 93	100	"	"
14		do	Singleton for Wood	61	15	9
18		do	Gas Accounts	18	11	"
19		do	H. Kalle & Sons Hair a/c	43	13	"
		do	C. Turner & Sons Varnish	34	10	"
22		do	Wages	2398	5	3
		do	R Wilson	9	"	"
		do	R Barclay Cartage	1	13	9
		do	Move. Forriers a/c	2	13	1
		do	Thos Davis Frett Cutter	2	17	9
		do	G Beattie a/c	1	1	"
		do	H. Watt Refreshments	1	5	"
24		do	J. McGown a/c	1	19	"
		do	Dock Entry Money "Extra	1	"	"
		do	Sr E Ransome a/c	65	13	11
		do	Railway "	1	5	10
		do	Allan & Mann "	1	5	6
28		do	J Lyon to Account	50	"	"
				5550	18	9

posted to ensure that they had been entered there correctly. As all transactions in the ledger from which the accounts are prepared are summarized in the journal, including adjusting entries which do not appear in any book of prime entry, journals should be considered for preservation as integral to the archive of an enterprise.

Private journals

Journal entries of a particularly confidential nature, for example, entries which would have allowed clerks to compute the profits or losses of a business are sometimes consigned to a separate 'private' journal. These form part of the private accounting series and are usually locked (*see* Private ledgers, p. 144).

The ledgers explained

The ledger is the central record in double-entry book-keeping, where all the transactions of an enterprise are classified by every activity in which the enterprise is engaged, by the property it owns, and for every person or concern with which the enterprise deals on credit. The name of each account is written at the top of the page and the relative transactions entered below. Periodically, usually when accounts were prepared, each account was balanced off, with the debit balances carried down on the left and the credit balances carried down on the right. Each transaction is referred back to the journal. Even where the transaction has not been summarized in the journal, the entry in the ledger may not be as full as that in the journal. The individual accounts appear in no particular order and when a page has been filled the account is continued anywhere else in the book where there is space, with the continuation page given at the foot. So that the book-keepers can find the individual accounts nearly all ledgers have indexes. These are sometimes to be found bound in at the front of the volume but more commonly in separate index books which can easily become detached from the ledger.

Normally in partnership ledgers the partners' capital and current accounts appear first in the volume, followed by impersonal or nominal accounts, e.g. for fixed assets, stocks, wages, materials, services, cash, charges and expenses. After these entries come individual customers' and suppliers' accounts, with the profit and loss account at the end. The ledger accounts were usually balanced annually, but sometimes half yearly or quarterly. Before this was done, the book-keepers normally tried to secure payment of as many outstanding customer invoices as possible and settle accounts with suppliers. This explains the occasional survival of series of printed letters requesting settlement of accounts. At the nominated date, more often than not related to the date of the formation of the enterprise rather than the calendar, each account was balanced and sales and cost of sales and expenses transferred to the enterprise's profit and loss account, and the balances of assets and liabilities carried forward.

Figure 6.4 shows facing pages from the ledger of Scotts Shipbuilding & Engineering Co. of Greenock, showing the account of Compagnie Générale Transatlantique. Each transaction is described in the fifth column on each side, and referenced back to the journal in the third column. These page references do not specify to what volume of the journal they relate, which has to be deduced from the date. The payment of £7,017 by Compagnie Générale Transatlantique, which appears in Figure 6.3, was entered on the right-hand or 'creditors' side on 14 November 1862, and is described simply as 'Cash', with no indication as to what the payment was for. Scotts balanced their ledgers annually.

During the nineteenth century, despite the book-keeper's attempts to summarize transactions in the journal, the ledgers, particularly for larger concerns, grew in size. They sometimes became so heavy that the clerks found them almost impossible to lift. One solution to the problem was to split up the ledger, by dividing the entries alphabetically, for example, A-L and M-Z. More commonly, by the end of the century, ledgers were divided by type of accounts and/or by function.

Nominal/impersonal ledgers

These ledgers contain all the accounts which do not relate to an individual or a concern, such as those for fixed assets, stocks of material, services, wages, property, and possibly profit and loss. The title on the outside of these ledgers varies from firm to firm. If the archivist encounters nominal/impersonal ledgers, there should be a complementary series of personal ledgers.

Personal ledgers

These contain customers, suppliers and sometimes partners' personal accounts. They are not always called personal ledgers; more commonly they are simply titled general ledgers and appear in older concerns to be the continuation of the initial ledger series. Where a concern had many customers, the personal ledger was often further subdivided alphabetically, by customers and suppliers or by geographical region. Such ledgers have a variety of names, for example, customers' ledgers and goods outward ledgers, or suppliers' ledgers, inward ledgers or goods received ledgers, or bought ledgers, country ledgers and foreign ledgers. Where ledgers were subdivided in this way, it was common practice to keep the accounts relating to the management of the enterprise in a separate series known as private or partnership ledgers.

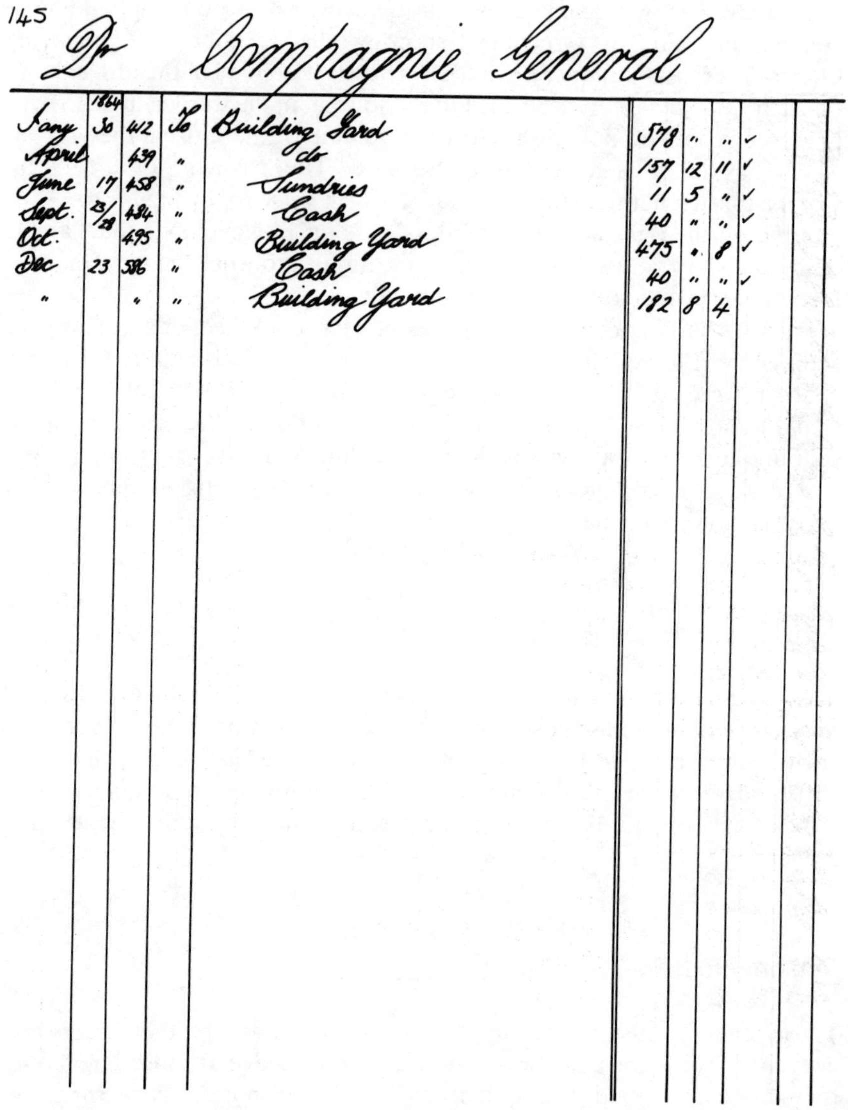

145

Dr Compagnie General

	1864							
Jany	30	412	To	Building Yard	578	"	"	✓
April		439	"	do	157	12	11	✓
June	17	458	"	Sundries	11	5	"	✓
Sept.	23/28	484	"	Cash	40	"	"	✓
Oct.		495	"	Building Yard	475	.	8	✓
Dec	23	586	"	Cash	40	"	"	✓
"		"	"	Building Yard	182	8	4	

Figure 6.4 *The page for the account of Compagnie Générale Transatlantique with Scotts Shipbuilding Co. from the firm's ledger.*

Transatlantique 145

					£	s	d	
1862								
Feby	7	237	By	Cash	4845	11	4	✓
March	12	244	"	do	18376	4	9	✓
May	30	254	"	do	7825	14	10	✓
June	26	262	"	do	14843	11	4	✓
July	2	270	"	do	3841	11	8	✓
Augt	30	276	"	do	19675	9	8	✓
Oct	"	288	"	do	11334	13	"	✓
Novr	14	296	"	do	7017	16	4	✓
Dec	23	302	"	do	20291	12	4	✓
1863								
Feby	10	317	"	do	14455	8	11	✓
March	31	325	"	do	16910	17	10	✓
April	14	334	"	do	6508	18	2	✓
May	19	342	"	do	7017	16	4	✓
"	"	349	"	do	11330	13	1	✓
June	30	351	"	do	26906	2	8	✓
July	"	365	"	St Nazaire Building Yard	7	18	5	✓
"	"	358	"	Cash	9900	19	9	✓
August	7	368	"	do	1267	6	6	✓
Sept	15	376	"	do	1017	16	5	✓
Oct	31	383	"	do	15655	10	8	✓
Novr	17	392	"	do	23310	17	9	✓
1864								
Feby	16	416	"	do	3508	18	2	✓
Mar	4	426	"	do	1188	2	4	✓
April	3/28	423	"	do	11420	1	5	✓
May	6	443	"	do	10478	19	10	✓
June	26	453	"	do	7914	17	"	✓
July	13	460	"	do	15192	16	"	✓
Aug	16	471	"	do	554	"	"	✓
"	"	477	"	Transatlantique [&] Bond a/c	13340	"	"	✓
Oct	7	488	"	Cash	446	14	9	✓
Decr	10/20	508	"	do	19984	8	"	✓

Private ledgers

These ledgers contain all the accounts relating to the management and ownership of an enterprise, for example, the capital account, partners' accounts, balance sheets, profit and loss accounts, and depreciation account.[8] They also sometimes contain confidential accounts, providing the financial details of agency agreements, product licenses, and contracts. Since they contain private or secret information, these ledgers were nearly always secured with locks and stored in safes apart from the other accounting records. They were often supported by separate series of private cash books and journals. The archivist should always enquire if private accounting records were kept. They should always be considered for retention. Even where private ledgers exist, balance sheet and profit and loss accounts may have been kept elsewhere in balance books or in the bundles of annual accounts rather than in the ledger itself.

Loose-leaf ledgers

Although for the archivist and historian bound ledgers provide a conveniently complete record of the transactions of an enterprise, they had many drawbacks for the book-keeper. It was almost impossible to keep accounts in alphabetical or continuous order, and regular reference to the indexes was required to locate ledger entries. In addition, in a ledger which remained open for several years, there were inevitably accounts that were no longer active. The compilation of materials and contract accounts demanded complex cross-referencing. The solution to these obstacles was loose-leaf ledgers and automated accounting systems.

Although loose-leaf ledgers were introduced in the 1890s and mechanical automated accounting systems became available in the 1920s, they were not generally used in the United Kingdom until the mid-1950s, except by the larger clearing banks and insurance companies. Their advent may have helped to solve the difficulties of book-keepers, but for archivists they cause many problems. Sheets were stripped from ledgers when complete and stored in bundles; the bundles are invariably insecurely tied and over time they come apart and the contents scatter. When automated, using mechanical computation methods, impersonal or nominal account titles are sometimes converted to codes, making interpretation impossible without a list of the codes used. The advent of loose-leaf ledgers often led to the closures of all the previous ledger series with the exception of the private ledgers.

Annual accounts

Balance books

E. H. Jones, a Bristol accountant, in his well-known book on double-entry book-keeping – *The Science of Book-Keeping*, published in 1831 – advocated keeping a balance book which exhibited the balances (the sums standing at the credit or debit) of all the accounts of the ledger on one or two folios to create a balance sheet.[9] This system was adopted by large enterprises with disparate activities, a large number of customers and suppliers, and many partners. When the balance sheet in the balance book had been struck, the statement signed by all the partners was often attached, declaring that it presented a 'true' picture of the enterprise's financial position. They occasionally survive and should be considered for retention. They were usually replaced in the 1880s by separate balance sheets and profit and loss accounts.

Balance sheets and annual accounts

Balance sheets were created every 6 months or each year. They show in a summary form the state of the enterprise. On the left, marked 'Cr', are the liabilities, usually starting with the capital, followed by other long-term liabilities such as loans and debentures, reserves and provisions, then by current liabilities (accounts owing to suppliers, short-term bank advances, etc.) and then the profit (if there is any) to be distributed to the shareholders or partners. On the right hand, marked 'Dr', are the assets of the enterprise – fixed assets, stock, loans made by the enterprise, investments, and current assets (accounts due from customers, cash at the bank, etc.) and the loss (if there is one). The profit and loss entries in the balance sheet are usually explained in a separate profit and loss account, detailing how the final figure was achieved. More commonly today (and sometimes in the past) the balance sheet is laid out in vertical format on one page, with the assets (fixed and current) listed first and below the liabilities (creditors due within one year – current liabilities – and creditors due after a year). At the bottom are to be found details of capital and reserves. This vertical form of balance sheet is now fairly standard in printed annual reports, as it can be more easily understood.

The production of annual accounts, even for a small enterprise, is a time-consuming process, requiring a good many supporting papers, for example, showing how the value of the fixed assets has been calculated and listing accounts owing to suppliers and due to customers. Since auditors and the Inland Revenue need to know how balance sheet entries have been achieved, these working or supporting papers are often stored together with the internal balance sheet and profit and loss accounts. In some larger concerns these were bound up into volumes, sometimes termed 'Bibles'

(Figure 6.5). In the absence of other corporate records, the annual accounts and working papers often provide the only information about new issues of shares and debentures, admittance of new partners, partners' capital, loans negotiated, contracts undertaken, property, plant, and investments purchased and sold, loans advanced, departmental performance, and profit and loss.

Although the 1844 Companies Act insisted that all limited liability companies should present a 'full and fair' balance sheet to shareholders at each annual meeting, this injunction was abandoned 12 years later in the Companies Act of 1856. A model set of accounts was, however, retained as an appendix to the Act. Some limited liability companies, particularly those acting for the mutual benefit of a group of investors, had such requirements built into their articles of association, and some extended partnerships had similar provisions in their contracts of co-partnership. Limited liability did not become popular until towards the end of the century, after the collapse of the City of Glasgow Bank in 1878 had demonstrated the horrendous consequences for partners who were not protected in this way.

With the growth of limited liability, measures were taken to tighten the legal framework in which they operated. In 1900 it became compulsory for all companies to have their accounts audited annually, and from 1907 all public companies were required to file with the Registrar of Companies an annual balance sheet containing 'a summary of its capital, its liabilities, and its assets, giving such particulars as will disclose the general nature of such liabilities and assets, and how values of the fixed assets had been arrived at'. It was not until 1929 that limited liability companies were required to publish separate profit and loss accounts, and also to circulate balance sheets and the directors and auditors reports to shareholders at least 7 days before the annual meeting. The 1948 Companies Act required companies that had subsidiary or associate companies to consolidate their accounts and all auditors to be independent of the company.

Since then further legislation has compelled more and more information to be disclosed to shareholders. Balance sheets and profit and loss accounts required to be filed with the Registrar of Companies are usually referred to as 'company accounts' to distinguish them legally from internal accounting records. Individual practice has often been in advance of the minimum standards set at every stage in the legislation. By 1899 George Lisle in *Accounting in Theory and Practice*[10] had no doubt that 'full and fair' balance sheets with profit and loss should be prepared by all companies, whether protected by limited liability or not, for the benefit of shareholders and partners.[11]

Figure 6.5 *In some instances, all the information needed to compile the published balance sheet was bound into volumes nicknamed appropriately 'Bibles'. From 1901 William Beardmore & Co., the Glasgow steel-making, armaments and shipbuilding company, adopted this practice. This is the title page from the volume for 1923 listing the contents. Parkhead, Mossend, Dalmuir, Paisley, Anniesland, Coatbridge, and Van Street, were all individual manufacturing plants.*

INDEX

The published or printed balance sheet and profit and loss account invariably contain much less information than the internal balance sheet.[12] If they survive, both should be considered for retention. Internal working papers are often to be found with the signed copies of the company accounts, and these should also be considered for retention. In recent years the working papers, particularly for large companies, have become bulkier and bulkier, and can be weeded without loss of evidence. Since the internal accounts contain commercially sensitive information, they are normally stored in a secure place under the control of the company secretary or finance director. In concerns where financial direction was or is provided by an outside firm of accountants, these papers are often retained in the accountants' strongroom and should be recovered by the archivist. It should never be assumed that printed annual accounts survive in the company registration file at Companies House.

In the balance sheet there are entries drawn from record series which are either not accounting records proper or do not form part of the principal books of account. On the liabilities side details of capitalization, dividends paid and outstanding secured loans are made up from shareholders' registers and dividend ledgers, and registers of mortgages and debentures. On the debtors' side entries for fixed assets and investments in other enterprises are computed from registers of property and plant and registers of investments. After 1948 consolidated accounts were made up by reference to the accounts of the holding company and its subsidiaries, and the only record of how the consolidating accounts were prepared may be contained in the auditors' working papers.

Profit and loss accounts

These are subsidiary to the balance sheet, detailing how the profit or loss figure has been arrived at. They bring together profits from the different activities of an enterprise and losses and other items that must be set against them. Income and profits are normally shown on the right-hand side and expenses and losses on the left-hand side. Profits will normally include not only profits on the trading activity of an enterprise but also dividends received from investments, interest on cash at the bank, and rents from property. Items to be set against the profits before the declaration of the result for the year will include not only losses on any part of the enterprise, but also directors' fees and expenses, audit fees, provision for the depreciation of property and plant and the writing off of any capital losses. The resulting sum is the net profit or loss. From 1886 the estimated income-tax liability was deducted to show the profits net of tax. Since interest on mortgages, debentures and any repayments must be met before any dividend payments, it is usually deducted before the sum available for distribution is shown.

Financial records of subsidiaries and divisions

Subsidiary companies and divisions normally keep parallel accounting series to the owning company. These records used to be kept by the subsidiaries, but more commonly today are integrated with the parent company's accounting procedures. In the last 20 years, although company names may still be used for trading purposes, many subsidiary companies have been liquidated. The financial records of these companies are often to be found along with those of the parent.

Other accounting records

Apart from the core financial records, there are many other subsidiary series of financial records. The following are the most commonly encountered.

Bill books

Until recently every would-be book-keeper, accountant and bank clerk, had to learn by rote the legal definition of a bill of exchange – 'a bill is an unconditional order in writing addressed by one person to another, signed by the person giving it, requiring the person to whom it is addressed to pay on demand, or at a fixed or determined future time, a sum certain in money, to or to the order of a specified person or to bearer'. In other words, a bill of exchange was a legally binding commitment to pay a stated sum at a future date (commonly 3 or 6 months later) for goods received, and by so doing provided vital credit. The bill was in two parts, with one half held by the payee and the other by the payer. The payee could sell his interest in the bill at less than its face value to a third party, who would then become responsible for collecting the money from the payer.[13] This practice, known as discounting, became common at the end of the eighteenth century, when some large merchant houses, particularly in London, began to specialize in such transactions, and played an important part in the development of commercial and merchant banking.[14]

From at least the sixteenth century until relatively recent times bills of exchange were one of the commonest methods of payment for goods and services. Entries in accounting records often refer to payments by bill in a number of months (abbreviated to 'mo'). Although sums received or disbursed on the discharge of bills appear in the cash books, most enterprises that used bills regularly kept separate registers of bills receivable and payable to remind them when payment was due and to whom bills had been discounted. These are sometimes contained in one volume and sometimes split into two series by type – receivable and payable. They are rarely bulky and should be considered for retention, as they provide information about the intermediaries used by a concern to finance its business. Bills of exchange themselves do not often survive, but where they do, they should be retained, as they can shed light on the source and use of credit.

Bank pass books

Related to the cash books of any enterprise are bank pass books, usually small volumes, often attractively bound and embossed in gold letters with the name of the bank. Larger firms often held accounts with more than one bank. Apart from their curiosity value, they usually contain little information except a record of deposits and withdrawals. Turnover of cash in a bank account, unless the pass book gives details of the nature of the transactions, provides little useful information for the historian. They can usually be destroyed but, like accounts and vouchers, can often provide attractive exhibition items for the corporate archivist.

With the introduction of automated accounting systems in the 1920s bank pass books began to be replaced by printed statements. These are often to be found in great quantities and can be safely destroyed, providing they do not fall within the prescriptive 6-year period required by the Inland Revenue.

Cheque books and returned cheques

Unusual cheque books are often encountered, but unless they can be used as exhibition items because of the quality of their lettering and illustration, they are of little interest as historical evidence. Equally, returned cheques should also be destroyed at the end of the prescriptive period of 10 years. It should be noted that historic cheques are collectors' items, and they therefore have a financial value unrelated to their archival usefulness.

Cost books

In some firms further explanations of product/transaction costs are to be found in a separate series of cost books, detailing the cost of components or types of material used, overheads (such as use of power and the plant, office/management services, etc.) and labour. They may also show selling price and thus profit (loss), along with any special terms (for example, discounts) provided to the customer. Occasionally, and this is often the case in firms engaged in the manufacture of large and complex products such as ships, detailed comparisons of costs and estimates were compiled in a further series. All these records are an invaluable source for the researcher and should be considered for retention. As they give details not provided in the financial accounts, they are usually cross-referenced by job/order numbers with job/order books and contracts, and by stock numbers to stock books.

Wages/salary books

These are technically financial records, detailing individual payments of wages/salaries to individual employees/managers, which are usually only aggregated in the journal and ledgers. For employees they sometimes also show the wage rate or grade, how the wage was made up, and often, but not always, against which contract the wage should be charged. In large firms with hundreds of employees they can be very extensive. However, they rarely survive as complete series, but when they do, they should be considered for permanent retention, as they provide vital information about incomes not to be found elsewhere. In larger companies separate salary books for senior managers/directors were maintained and kept by the company secretary or senior book-keeper rather than the wages department. Until recently, wages/salary books were the only personnel records kept by many firms.

When National Insurance was introduced in 1911, employers were required to make weekly contributions for each employee on the payroll. These were often recorded in the wages/salary books from which annual returns to the Inland Revenue were made up. Since employers' National Insurance contributions always rank in front of all other creditors of a business in event of bankruptcy or liquidation, documentation is often retained for long periods, as in the case of tax. Between 1966 and 1971 there was a poll tax, levied as a flat rate surcharge on employers' National Insurance contributions, known as Selective Employment Tax (SET). As it was refunded to all industries except services and construction, it gave rise to considerable arguments and disputes. Records relating to National Insurance should never be destroyed without prior consultation with the relevant department.

Plant/property registers

Balance-sheet entries for the book value of fixed assets were often supported by plant/property registers. Although the net book value of plant and property appears in the ledger, separate registers were required to provide details of written down/depreciated values, as well as a full description of each item. They are an important accounting record, which should be considered for retention (see Chapter 7), and are often to be found in the office of the master of works or plant/property supervisor.

Registers of investments and loans

These list a firm's investments in other concerns and loans. They contain details of the purchase price of investments, payments of dividends and interest, repayment of loans, annual valuation of investments and sums realized on sale of investments. These registers were normally kept by the company secretary or lawyer, along with the share certificates and other relevant legal documentation.

Tax and excise records

Tax returns and papers

Partnership financial accounting was made more complex by the introduction of income tax in 1799. From the outset allowances could be made for children, interest on debts, annuities and life insurance, and general business expenses. In 1802 the income tax was reorganized into the familiar 5 schedules (A, B, C, D and E), with differing allowances and deductions. At the end of the Napoleonic war in 1815 the government no longer needed additional income to fund spending on armaments and income tax was abolished. It was reimposed in 1842 as a component in the shift to free trade. The 1842 tax was modelled on its predecessors, being divided into 5 schedules, with provision for allowances and deducations. The allowances in schedule D (under which most business profits were assessed) were open to different interpretation. For example, wear and tear or depreciation of machinery was allowed in London, but not in Scotland. Wear and tear or depreciation represents the amount by which a machine or building has fallen in value during a year, owing to the effects of its use, the elements and its age. Wear and tear allowances were sanctioned generally from 1878 at set rates for different types of assets. From 1886 business profits were taxed at source and payments to partners and dividends to shareholders paid out of profits net of tax. Directors' fees were also taxed at source. Annual variations in profit were to be compensated for by making the assessment on a 3-year average.[15]

Legacy duty was introduced in 1694 and replaced by death duties in 1894. These required partnerships to be valued by external assessors on the death of a partner, since the balance-sheet entry of a partner's capital bore little relation to market value. The valuation was usually arranged through the family lawyer.[16]

In 1915 excess profit duty was imposed on business profits which had risen greatly since the outbreak of war. This tax continued until 1921 when it was replaced by corporation profits tax, which was abolished in 1924. Corporation tax was not reintroduced until 1965.[17]

Occasionally personal tax returns from the nineteenth century survive. These can usually be destroyed, but only with the permission of the company secretary or financial director. However, income tax returns from the business itself should be considered for retention, as they provide details of profits declared for tax which often differ from those in the annual accounts. Where returns and papers relating to excess profit duty and corporation profits tax survive, these merit preservation, since these taxes were assessed on a complex formula, taking into consideration pre-war profits and wartime capital expenditure. They help to explain how profit figures for the war years, 1914 to 1919, and immediate post-war years were calculated.

After 1965 it was common for external firms of accountants to calculate corporation-tax liability and complete the returns. Gradually, from the 1970s, as United Kingdom and foreign corporation tax became more complex, separate tax departments were established by larger concerns. Papers relating to corporation tax remain active for long periods, often beyond the 25-year period prescribed by the Inland Revenue in the United Kingdom. They are rarely made over to archivists, even after the liquidation of an enterprise, as the settlement of tax claims may take several years after closure. Tax papers, even for small businesses, can be very bulky. Some of them are undoubtedly of historical interest, particularly where an industry is in dispute with the Inland Revenue about various special allowances and charges.

Indirect taxation and price control

Administratively the most onerous fiscal burdens for any enterprise have always been indirect taxes imposed on raw materials or products. Customs and Excise duties have been used as means of raising government revenue since mediaeval times. Most of these duties were progressively abolished in the decade that followed the repeal of the Corn Laws in 1846 and the move to free trade. The most enduring were excise duty on alcoholic drinks, whether manufactured in the United Kingdom or imported. The financial and other record-keeping practices of firms making or selling dutiable goods has largely been dictated by the requirements of the Customs and Excise.[18] In approaching the records of firms whose business falls into this category the archivist should seek expert advice.

Indirect taxation re-emerged with the imposition of tariffs on certain classes of imported goods from 1920 and, more generally, from 1932. Records relating to the payment of tariffs from this period rarely survive, but correspondence concerning the tariff is sometimes encountered and merits preservation. At the outbreak of the Second World War the government introduced price controls on certain essentials to prevent inflation and, at the same time, imposed a purchase tax on luxury items, whose prices were allowed to find their own level. Because of post-war shortages, controls remained in force until the early 1950s. Purchase tax continued until the introduction of Value Added Tax (VAT) between fiscal years 1971–2 and 1973–4, following Britain's entry into the European

Economic Community. VAT with a few exceptions (notably children's clothes and books) was imposed on all goods and services provided by enterprises above a relatively low minimum turnover. Because VAT is paid on every transaction, the Customs and Excise – responsible for its collection – require firms to retain a mass of financial information for a minimum of 7 years and to make detailed returns. Price controls were reimposed in 1964 as part of the Labour government's anti-inflationary policy and continued in force until 1970; they were reintroduced at the end of the Conservative government's period in office in 1974 and were not abolished until 1979.[19] Correspondence relating to policy towards purchase tax and VAT should be considered for retention, along with details of negotiations concerning price levels during periods of control. It cannot be guaranteed that such papers will automatically find their way into the Public Record Office. For the corporate archivist such papers can help explain the performance of a company and its subsidiaries since 1939.

Recent developments in accounting practice

Management accounts

Price controls, particularly during the periods of high inflation in the 1960s and 1970s, forced many concerns to improve their financial management. Although the concept of using accounts as a management tool (to gauge performance and to judge cash and capital requirements) probably dates back to the eighteenth century, forecasts were rarely formal. In the inter-war years some companies began to include future estimates of budget, turnover, sales, investment and profit and loss in their board papers. The preparation of such financial projections became common among even small companies in the 1960s, and are now a matter of course. Today the core document in such accounting forecasts is the business or corporate plan, nearly always a highly sensitive document. If the corporate archivist finds such planning documents, they should be considered for retention as they explain management thinking and financial expectations.

Computerized accounts

Since the 1960s, accounting procedures have been transformed by the introduction of computers. The ability of mainframe computers, and more recently micro-computers, to store, sort and rapidly retrieve large quantities of information has rendered manual book-keeping obsolete from the largest to the smallest enterprises. The only records to be kept in either paper or on microfilm/fiche are invoices received and issued, and in most organizations these are destroyed at the end of the statutory periods of 6 to 10 years. Even the balance sheet and profit and loss account can be generated on the computer.

Although the central accounts are held on computer, a vast amount of print-out is generated, either in paper or microfilm/fiche format, listing such things as creditors, debtors, sales, material costs, fixed capital expenditure and so on. These print-outs are usually unintelligible to the outsider, with complex coded entries and lack of adequate reference. They are intended for management use and in no sense replicate the traditional books of account, even if the titles ascribed to them suggest that they do. All that can usefully be preserved from such electronic systems are the internal annual accounts, which in most organizations continue to be retained in their paper form with a growing mass of supporting documentation. If possible, the archivist should get a member of the accounts' staff to identify the piles of print-outs which were used to produce the trial balances for the preparation of the annual accounts and to form the basis of the audit, and these should be considered for retention.

It has yet to be proved whether it is worth preserving any of the machine-readable data itself. For any large enterprise this will occupy a large amount of computer filestore or a large number of demountable disks or tapes. It is doubtful that, with the exception of the record of prime entry, they contain any useful information for either the corporate archivist or the historian, but expert guidance should be sought before they are destroyed. The most likely accounting records to be stored in the newly available CD-ROM format are receipts and invoices, which can safely be destroyed after the statutory periods.

Appraising accounting records

Since double-entry accounting systems are designed to be perfectly complete, they are difficult to evaluate for permanent preservation. A business historian, conducting an in-depth financial analysis of a company, will regret the disposal of any record, as the details posted to the ledger may be insufficient to explain the nature of a transaction. Few archivists, even those employed by companies themselves, can contemplate such wholesale preservation. In the past some archivists, not understanding financial records or the needs of historians, were tempted to keep samples of long series of volumes whether they related to each other or not. Such a procedure is equally unsatisfactory. For many small concerns it is probably sufficient to keep only the annual internal balance sheets and profit and loss accounts and the ledgers. However, many small businesses were in the past much larger, and care must be taken not to destroy financial records without enquiring into previous experience.

For any business of importance, either locally or nationally, selection must be based on an evaluation of record-keeping practice by a careful examination of the contents of the different series to determine, for example, the amount of information posted from the journal to the ledger. Wherever possible ledgers and the corresponding journal series should be retained; in others the cash books and day books should also be kept. Supporting documentation, such as investment registers, tax papers, and financial forecasts, usually survive only for larger enterprises.

Cataloguing accounting records

When accounting records have been selected for preservation, they should be sorted by class, i.e. ledgers, journals, day books, and so on. When ledgers have been divided, they should also be sorted by type, i.e. nominal/impersonal ledgers, personal ledgers, and so on. Care should be taken to ensure that such series do belong together. In concerns where amalgamations have taken place, old accounting records often become confused, as they were not necessarily labelled with the name of the firm to which they relate, and there is always a risk of attributing them to the wrong firm. Clues to provenance can often be found in the individual accounts, particularly those relating to partners, capital and property.

Sorting out such confusions can be a laborious and time-consuming task and it often takes a reader with specialist knowledge to identify a series. In the final list or catalogue the private ledger and ledger series should be placed first, then the journals, then the books of prime entry and finally invoices, if these are to be preserved. If the indexes are loose within the ledger, these should be taken out and catalogued separately, possibly with a linking reference next to the ledger to which they relate. Should this proposed ordering not be adopted and another selected, the system chosen should be applied consistently to all collections, so that readers will know where in a list or catalogue to expect the required class. Fortunately for the archivist, accounting systems, when they have been established, are remarkably enduring, often lasting over a century.

Inevitably there will be some accounting records that do not seem to fit any obvious grouping but are nevertheless worth preserving. These tend to be subsidiary ledgers opened experimentally. Such unallocated volumes should be grouped together. A 3-part reference number is desirable to accommodate any additional volumes that may be transmitted. The list or catalogue should provide the class title and for each item the opening and closing dates, along with any additional information provided on the volume itself, such as original title and number. The outside dates of ledgers are hard to find because individual accounts were opened and closed at different dates; partners' accounts and nominal accounts usually span the whole lifetime of a volume. Under no circumstances should accounting records simply be classified as books of account and listed in date order. This confuses the reader and causes difficulties in the search room. Figure 6.6, by way of example, shows the listing of the ledgers of Scotts Shipbuilding and Engineering Co. held in the Business Record Centre in the Archives Department of the University of Glasgow. Since the collection is held under charge and superintendance of the Keeper of

Reference

GD. 319			
	LEDGERS: SHIPYARD & ENGINE WORKS		
	Date		
2/1	1780–1784		
2/2	1802–1804		
2/3	1825–1827		
2/4*	1857–1864	No. 2	
2/5*	1865–1866	3	
2/6*	1868–1876	4	
2/7*	1877–1883	5	
2/8*	1884–1888	6	
2/9*	1889–1891	7	
2/10*	1896–1898	9	(Shipyard)
2/11*	1899–1901	10	
2/12*	1907–1911		(Shipyard)
2/13	1912–1916	15	(-do-)
2/14*	1916–1920	16	
2/19*	1918–1922	17	
2/16	1859–1883	No. 1	(Greenock Foundry Co.)
2/17	1884–1901	2	(Engine Works)
2/18	1902–1912		(-do-)
2/19	1913–1922		(-do-)
2/20*	1916–1918		(Foundry)
2/21*	1919–1926		(-do-)
	* water damaged		

Figure 6.6 *Listing of the ledgers of Scotts Shipbuilding and Engineering Co.*

the Records of Scotland, it has a Scottish Record Office class code and number GD (Gifts and Deposits) 319.

Accounting records and the user

For accounting records, like many other classes of business records, there are few users who are interested in the history of enterprise itself. Therefore, in order to justify committing long runs of shelf space to these records, the archivist in both the private and public sectors must encourage other researchers to exploit the information they contain. At a scholarly level there are many potential users, but academic historians, like archivists, are notoriously badly trained in the use of accounting records. Many assume, erroneously, that because accounting records contain numbers, they can only be employed for quantitative analysis. However, accounting records also contain dates and written descriptions of transactions which can provide important evidence for the chronology of historical events and names of participants. Records from the early modern period have been used to construct indices of prices and in the modern period to reconstruct the dynamics of an individual's lifetime wealth-holding.[20] Even such academic uses, valuable as they are, cannot alone justify the permanent retention of more than a sample of such record series; the principal users must be historians engaged in family, local, and specialist researches.

For the family historian accounting records can provide information about employment, investments, property ownership and relationships, and for the local historian a wealth of information about a locality often extending far beyond the enterprise to which they relate. The accounting records of a rural supplier will, for example, contain names and addresses of customers, sometimes providing the only information about the occupant of a farm or a house. Shopkeepers' accounts will provide fascinating details of personal expenditure. By far the largest users of accounting records, and all other classes of business records, are specialist amateur historians interested in such diverse historical subjects as gardens, the development of gunpowder manufacture, locomotives and railways, ships and sea and inland waterway transport, and costume, to name but a few. Some of these interest groups, like those concerned with locomotives and ships, are well-defined; their needs must necessarily influence selection criteria, as they do other classes of business records, particular technical drawings. The archivist cannot expect such historians to use accounting records unaided; they have to be encouraged to consult them and helped to find their way about the different classes of records, as with any other category of archives.

Conclusion

Sadly, for the archivist, there are no hard and fast rules for the preservation of accounting records. Although the double-entry system is a precise art, practice varies from one firm to another and one product to another, with different levels of information about transactions in the various classes. In making an appraisal, as with any other group of records, criteria for selection must be based on provenance which will suggest likely usage. There is, however, a hierarchy of importance in accounting records, beginning with:

- The annual accounts and supporting papers.
- Ledgers/journals.
- Books of prime entry.
- Other financial records. In this miscellaneous group there are some records meriting preservation (e.g. bill books, cost books, wave/salary books, registers of plant and investments) and others which can be destroyed (e.g. bank pass books and cheque books).

Archivists responsible for collections of business records must learn to find their way around accounting series, and, for want of anyone else, educate readers in their use. Otherwise their employers can quite properly question why so much expensive shelf space is occupied by records that are rarely consulted.

Notes

1 See, for example, M. L. Turner and D. G. Vaisey, *Oxford Shops and Shopping* (Oxford Illustrated Press, Oxford, 1972).
2 This type of account is discussed in M. S. Moss, 'Forgotten ledgers, law, and the business historian: Gleanings from the Adam Smith Business Records Collection', *Archives*, XVI (1984), pp. 358–9.
3 Although Professor B. S. Yamey has argued in 'Some topics in the history of financial accounting in England, 1500–1900', in W. T. Baxter and S. Davidson (editors), *Studies in Accounting* (Sweet & Maxwell, London, 1967), p. 17, that few businesses adopted double entry until the early nineteenth century, this does not seem to be the case, and few examples of single entry are to be found among the records of enterprise. The exceptions are financial records of trustees, to be found in legal offices and those of public authorities and institutions.
4 These developments are described in R. Brown (editor), *A History of Accounting and Accountants* (C. E. C. Jack, Edinburgh, 1905), pp. 173–202.
5 B. Booth, *A Complete System of Book-Keeping by an Improved Mode of Double Entry* (Wells & Co, London, 1789), p. 7. This book usefully provides examples of each type of record, with detailed instructions as to how they were to be used.
6 G. Lisle, *Accounting in Theory and Practice* (W. Green & Sons, Edinburgh, 1899), pp. 23–5.
7 For a description of their use, see B. Booth, *op cit.*, pp. 24–5.
8 For a more detailed consideration see M. S. Moss, 'Forgotten Ledgers etc.', *op. cit.*, pp. 358–72.
9 E. T. Jones, *The Science of Book-Keeping Exemplified in Jones's English System of Single and Double Entry and Balance Books* (Edward & Jones, London, 1831).
10 G. Lisle, *op. cit.*, pp. 74–6.
11 A helpful guide to the development of the accounting requirements of the Companies Acts is to be found in C. W. Nobes and R. H. Parker, 'Chronology of the development of company financial reporting in Great Britain, 1844–77',

in T. A. Lee and R. H. Parker, *The Evolution of Corporate Financial Reporting* (Thomas Nelson & Son, London, 1979).

12   S. Marriner, 'Company financial statements as source material for business historians', *Business History* XXII (1980), pp. 203–35; J. R. Edwards and K. M. Webb, 'The influence of company law on corporate reporting procedures, 1865–1929 – An exemplification', *Business History*, XXIV (1982), pp. 259–79.

13   A. McNeil, *Bills of Exchange, Cheques and Promissory Notes* (William Green & Sons, Edinburgh, 1904).

14   L. S. Pressnell and J. Orbell, *A Guide to the Historical Records of British Banking* (Gower, Aldershot, 1985), pp. xvii-xix.

15   B. E. V. Sabine, *A History of Income Tax* (George Allen & Unwin, London, 1966), pp. 26–41, 60–3 and 70–1. This is the only comprehensive guide to the history of income tax in the United Kingdom.

16   W. D. Rubinstein, *Men of Property – the Very Wealthy in Britain Since the Industrial Revolution* (Croom Helm, London, 1981), pp. 15–16.

17   B. E. V. Sabine, *op. cit.*, pp. 164–6, and A. Sked and C. Cook, *Post-War Britain – Political History* (Penguin Books, Harmondsworth, 1984), pp. 203, 205.

18   M. S. Moss, 'Books for the excisemen? – the records of the Scotch whisky industry', *Proceedings of the Annual Conference 1985* (Business Archives Council, 1986), pp. 51–6.

19   These events are described in the economic sections of A. Sked and C. Cook, *op. cit.*

20   See N. Morgan and M. S. Moss, 'Wealthy and titled persons – the accumulation of riches in Victorian Britain: the case of Peter Denny', in C. Harvey (editor), *Business History: Concepts and Measurements – Business History*, 31: 3, (1989), pp. 28–47; and N. Morgan and M. S. Moss, 'Urban wealthholding and the computer', in P. Denley, S. Fogelvik and C. Harvey (editors), *History and Computing II* (Manchester University Press, 1989), pp. 186–92.

Further reading

J. R. Edwards, *Company Legislation and Changing Patterns of Disclosure in British Company Accounts 1900–1940* (Institute of Chartered Accountants in England and Wales, London, 1981).

J. R. Edwards, *A History of Financial Accounting* (Routledge, London, 1989).

E. Jones, *Accountancy and the British Economy: The Evolution of Ernst & Whinney 1840–1980* (Batsford, London, 1981).

T. A. Lee and R. H. Parker, *The Evolution of Corporate Financial Reporting* (Thomas Nelson & Sons, London, 1979).

R. H. Parker, *Understanding Company Financial Statements* (Penguin Books, Harmondsworth, revised, 1989).

7

Legal, public relations, marketing, personnel and production records

*Leonard McDonald**

All businesses, no matter their size or legal status, create records other than those described in the previous two chapters. The records discussed in this chapter are common to most businesses, and include legal, public relations, marketing, personnel, manufacturing and technical records.

Legal records

Statutory records which are created and retained by a business under the Companies Acts have already been discussed in Chapters 5 and 6. However, businesses occupy buildings, employ people, carry out commercial or industrial activities and meet various legislative requirements – all of which can generate legal records.

Real estate records

Most businesses rent or own premises. Expansion, either through mergers or internal growth, will often lead to the leasing or purchase of further offices, shops, factories and warehouses anywhere in the United Kingdom or overseas.

Title deeds, conveyances and leases

Property ownership is supported by title deeds and other legal documents which often predate the firm itself. When the property is sold, they are generally handed over to the new owner. If the land has been registered at the Central Land Registry under the terms of the Land Registration Act 1925, there is no administrative need for the firm to keep the original deeds. However, they sometimes contain information of interest to a business. An accumulation of title deeds, conveyances and leases will often include accompanying maps and plans which clarify the description of the land being conveyed; such maps are of value to a corporate archivist, but they should not be separated from the deeds, unless these are to be

* I am grateful to Michael Moss and Lesley Richmond for commenting upon and revising the text of this chapter.

with the titles for an individual property, e.g. mortgages, which are an important source for information on the financing of a sole trader, partnership or private company.

Title deeds, which take a variety of forms, were generally in Latin until the early eighteenth century and in English thereafter. Their recognition can be achieved with the aid of two useful publications by Cornwall and Dibben.[1] The arrangement and description of title deeds can be time-consuming and it is a matter for each archivist faced with a large accumulation to decide how detailed the finding aids should be.

The disposition of title deeds can present problems because of their bulk and the fact that their historical value is limited to the area (county, city, town) in which the property is situated, and this may be remote from the firm's administrative head offices. Should it be decided to dispose of the title deeds, it is generally preferable to deposit them with the relevant local record office rather than place them with the record office in the locality of head office. Care must be taken to ensure that other legal documents, such as contracts of co-partnership (see p. 103), are removed from bundles of title deeds which are so deposited, and that notes of relevant transactions in mortgages are taken before deposit.

Register of deeds

An aid to listing title deeds may be available in the form of a terrier or register of deeds, or progress of titles in Scotland. A typical register will contain some of the following information:

1   The number of the bundle in which a deed is packed.
2   The date of the deed.
3   Parties to the deed.
4   The parcels of land described.
5   The tenure.
6   The purchase price, or the yearly rents and the date payable.
7   Remarks.

Estate and property companies often kept registers of all their transactions in volumes known as cartularies. These cartularies and registers should be retained for the life of the company, even if the property is registered and the deeds themselves are dispersed, because they form a valuable source of information on the company's land and property transactions.

Property valuations

Property valuations are often commissioned at the time of a merger, share issue or rating appeal, or for balance-sheet purposes. They rarely contain historical information that is not available elsewhere, e.g. in the plant and property registers (see p. 163), and can be destroyed. However, from the

1890s printed valuations for sale often included photographs and descriptions of the premises, and these should be retained.

Rent and repair records

Rent and repair records usually consist of one file for each house or other property occupied by a tenant, and do not have an historical value, as most of the paperwork deals with the maintenance of the premises; so they can be destroyed once they are of no further administrative use. The costs incurred will in any case be found in the firm's financial records. Notable building projects, however, should be identified and considered for retention. Where firms were substantial property owners, this information will be recorded in rent and repair registers, analogous to product records (see below). These should be considered for permanent preservation, as they will provide information about the management and occupation of commercial and factory premises and houses not readily available elsewhere.

Estate records

Large companies are often significant landowners, sometimes owning big industrial and housing estates. Such estates were sometimes managed through subsidiaries or even completely independent companies. Correspondence files, rent books and corporate records relating to such estates require to be identified and permanently preserved.

Inventories and plant and property registers

Inventories, listing, valuing and fully describing fixtures and furnishings, were drawn up from time to time by professional valuers and formed the basis for the plant and property registers. These registers provide descriptions of property (buildings) and plant (machinery, furnishings, furniture and so on), with details of the original contract, written down/depreciated values, and disposal prices. This financial information is often also to be found in full or summary form in the internal balance sheet. Plant and property registers should be permanently retained.

Architectural records

Architectural drawings of the firm's own buildings are usually held in the clerk of works' office or estates department which need them for their day-to-day activities, or by the architect who designed the premises. Corporate archivists should make efforts to recover such drawings from architects, as they can save a company considerable sums of money if a building is altered or extended, and can in any case be attractive display items. They should be retained for at least the lifetime of the building. When a property is sold, they are usually handed on to the new owners.[2]

Insurance policies

Fire insurance was one of the earliest forms of business protection. Early policies listed the fixtures in a building, indicating the location of boilers, open fires, lighting and any inflammable materials such as pitch, as well as the contents, in great detail. Such policies, if they survive, should be permanently retained as they can contain much useful information.[3]

If a business collection does not include such policies, they may exist in the archives of its insurance company. Some of these have been deposited in public archives, e.g. those of the Royal Insurance Company Ltd at the Guildhall Library in London. From about the middle of the nineteenth century policies ceased to contain detailed information, and these, along with modern policies, can be destroyed.

Litigation records

Limited liability companies, partnerships in Scotland, and individuals as partners in England, can sue and be sued in both civil and criminal courts. They must defend themselves, their patents and trademarks, their expertise and trade secrets against attack by others, and be prepared to justify their actions and operations at any time in the courts. The documentation thus created, including transcripts of any court cases, can contain a large amount of information about the firm (and sometimes its competitors) not easily available elsewhere. Although in law they form part of the property of the firm, such records are often held by lawyers who may have deposited them with a local record office. A corporate archivist should always discover if legal papers relating to the enterprise or its subsidiaries exist and where they are held. With the exception of such trivialities as receipts and invoices, legal papers should be identified and retained. Care should, however, be taken, as invoices (bills of charges) may be the only surviving evidence of an important court case or other dispute.

Included in the category of records of litigation are evidence and reports created in response to government investigations – such as those of the Monopolies and Mergers Commission, originally established in 1948, or the Price Commission, established in 1973. Monopolies and Mergers Commission reports usually contain a considerable amount of historical information compiled by the companies concerned. All evidence and reports should be permanently preserved, particularly as they can save a company considerable cost in any subsequent enquiries.

Where a company does business in the export market, there may also be Customs and Excise investigations by foreign governments into the importation of the firm's products in relation to and in competition with those produced locally or by companies in other countries. In both cases the records will contain nearly as much information about the firm as a prospectus, and will provide additional information on its products or the company's marketing operations in overseas countries.

Agreements and licences

Companies, whether they operate on a small- or large-scale, will negotiate agreements with other companies and inventors for mutual manufacturing and trading. There may be a wide range of records dealing with marketing and agency agreements and contracts for the purchase of raw materials and goods. Joint-venture and merger agreements, where they exist, will chart the evolution and record the growth of the business. These are formal documents – the basis of their legality is the signed original and they must be kept for the term of the agreement – and will be recorded in a limited liability company's register of seals (see p. 124). They should also be permanently preserved, as they are of considerable historical value, showing how the company developed and exploited its expertise, with whom it traded, and where it thought its most important spheres of influence lay.

Patents

The Statute of Monopolies 1623 was the first English statute to refer specifically to patents for inventions, granting an inventor exclusive use of his invention over a period of normally 16 years. Initially these patents formed a small part of all patents granted by the Crown, but the legislation soon became too cumbersome to cope with the growing pace of technological development during the Industrial Revolution, and widespread demands to reform the law finally forced the promulgation of the Patent Law Amendment Act 1852. Under this Act the grant of a patent had to be followed within 6 months by the filing of a specification. Parts of this Act proved unsatisfactory, and a new Patents, Designs and Trade Marks Act came into force in 1883, requiring a specification to be filed within 9 months and checked by the Patent Office before the patent was granted. Further amendments took place between 1888 and 1949, and attempts were subsequently made to harmonize the laws of different countries. The United Kingdom became a signatory to the Patent Co-operation Treaty in 1970 and the European Patent Convention in 1973.[4]

Patent records can contribute materially to the history of science and technology. Some patents were very significant, forming the basis of fundamental changes to manufacturing processes and bringing great wealth to Britain and the companies controlling them. Patents for inventions were enrolled on the Patent Rolls until 1853, after which date they were merely entered in a register kept at the Patent Office. Patent records can be found outside the company at the Patent Office and the British Library.[5]

Early grants were made with letters patent and until 1878 all patents were engrossed on parchment with the Great Seal of the Realm in wax attached at the foot by a silken cord. These patents are often to be found in custom-made wooden boxes. In 1878 a wafer Great Seal was substituted for the wax seal, replaced in 1884 by the wafer seal of the Patent Office. All patents contain basic information, such as the date filed, its number, the title of the patent, and the name, occupation and address of the patentee. Expired patents must be carefully appraised, and examples of important inventions should be kept by the corporate archivist. They are sometimes useful as exhibition items.

Printed specifications

By the late eighteenth century it was common for a detailed specification to be included in the patent, and after the 1852 Act it was an essential pre-requisite for full registration. The specification gives a technical description, with sketches and plans where necessary, of the invention and an explanation of what is new about the process or product. Printed provisional and final specifications should be kept, although a complete record exists at the Science Reference Library, a division of the British Library. Samples may be used for exhibition purposes.

Certificates of registration and renewal of patents

Patents are granted for a term of years (varying in each country), and owners must register them on payment of a fee to protect them against misuse by others. Patents can be renewed for a further term on the issue of a certificate of renewal of patent. Certificates of registration and renewal of patents can be destroyed after the final expiration of the patent.

Licences and assignments

Businesses sometimes allow other firms to exploit a patent, design or trademark by granting licences. The licence, being a legal document, defines the agreement between the parties as to the extent of the permissions and the method of compensation. In the case of a limited liability company it would be engrossed by the company seal and recorded in the register of seals. Its most common use is when the holder of a patent or trademark allows another firm to work it in an overseas country.

An inventor can assign his patent to a manufacturer, which gives the latter the right to make and sell the product, usually on the payment of a fee or royalty to the inventor. If the invention to be patented was made by an employee, the patent is taken out in the inventor's name as well as that of the company. The employee's patent rights are subsequently assigned by the employee to the company in a separate legal document. In the same way an inventor can offer a patent to a manufacturer, and the rights to develop the process and manufacture under the patent can be purchased after assignment. Even if the information contained in licences and assignments is available in other records, e.g. the board minutes or the register of seals, these documents should be permanently preserved, as intellectual property rights are now the subject of considerable debate and litigation.

Trademarks

The Trade Marks Registration Act 1875 first established the right to register a trademark. It was incorporated into the 1883 Patents, Designs and Trade Marks Act, and then subsequently separated from patent law in 1905. The law of registered designs was separated in 1949. Sometimes a trademark has become a generic term for a product, such as 'Hoover' and 'Thermos'. Companies closely control the way in which their marks are used. The Coca-Cola Company, for instance, protects the use of the words 'Coca-Cola' and 'Coke', and even its familiar bottle was registered as a trademark in 1960. Trademarks are sometimes allowed to lapse, but companies also spend heavily to defend them, and very often registration abroad is dependent on the owners of marks being able to prove their commercial presence in that country by showing how long their products have been sold there. Trademarks can be found outside the company at the Public Record Office and the Trade Mark Office.[6] Since 1787 the law has afforded some protection for the originators of designs, the first Design Copyright Act being passed in 1839. The Design Registry was initially maintained by the Board of Trade but the function passed to the Patent Office in 1875. Registers of designs up to 1910 have been transferred to the Public Record Office.[7]

Trademark and design-registry documentation is rare within a business, but where original artwork and papers and correspondence explaining the reasoning behind the trademark and design survive, they should be permanently preserved. This is particularly important when a company's advertising claims early registration or longevity for a trade name, trademark or design, as the Advertising Standards Authority may require proof for that claim.

Public relations and publicity records

The role of public relations and publicity is frequently misunderstood. They both use similar forms of advertising but for different purposes. Publicity is concerned with promoting a firm's products or services – whether it is selling radios or home loans. Public relations, on the other hand, is much more concerned with promoting the image of the company. A good image means that investors will continue to buy the company's shares, the consumer will trust it enough to believe its advertising, and, if its image is one of progress and competence, it will have less difficulty in recruiting and retaining able employees to ensure its successful continuity.

News releases

News releases to the media go to the local, national and trade press, and to radio and television. Major press events will include, for example, the publication of the annual report and accounts, and the announcement of a new product or a new business initiative. These records should be permanently retained, as they are an important source for understanding how a company viewed itself and how it wished to be viewed by others.

Company brochures

Many businesses have produced glossy brochures illustrating their geographical and product spread and issued pamphlets to specialist audiences, e.g. recruitment brochures. Such brochures are worthy of permanent preservation, although, since the 1960s, they have tended to become more general and are perhaps less useful now as a source of information.

Newspaper cuttings

Newspaper cuttings about the company and its product base are often compiled by a business's public relations department or by outside press-cuttings agencies. Sometimes these cuttings are held in guardbooks or on date-stamped sheets of paper. They are worthy of permanent preservation.

Photographs, films and videos

Films dealing with companies and manufacturing processes, which exist from the turn of the century, served both a public relations and a publicity need. The intention was to persuade the customer to like the product and trust the company that made it. British firms started to use commercial radio stations on the continent from the end of the Second World War and, from the 1960s onwards, commercial television became an increasingly important advertising medium. All films and videos produced by a business should be permanently retained in an appropriate format. Public relations departments produce vast quantities of photographs. As a rough rule of thumb all pre-1960s photographs (both prints and negatives) should be retained, and a selection only of those dating from 1960 if large accumulations survive.

In-house publications

In-house newspapers, news sheets and internal news releases are an important source of information on the internal workings of a business.

They became popular in the aftermath of the First World War as a means of informing employees of corporate developments and staff activities. Initially they tended to be people-orientated, with news of individual staff and departmental activities, and were often compiled in duplicated typescript. In recent years, however, the news is more about company achievements and promotions, and they are produced as glossy, printed magazines. They should be permanently preserved. Copies are often to be found in local libraries or in the hands of former employees.

Sales and marketing records

Businesses sell a vast range of products and services as varied as chocolate bars and insurance. The documentation of trading covers the whole cycle, for example, from manufacture to distribution to the wholesaler, and onwards to the retailer and the consumer. A large manufacturer can have a chain of depots or warehouses from which products are distributed. Attached to that depot will be a number of salesmen who keep in contact with the customer and usually provide some kind of continuing service. Their reports to head office on the amount of goods sold, their reception at customer level and so on, enable the marketing department to assess market penetration. Centrally kept statistics, whether they be for the sale of manufactured goods or services, help management not only to calculate the firm's share of the market but also to forecast future production and sales effort.

In the export market there may be a chain of local offices staffed with the company's own personnel, or local commission agents. Evidence of first sales in a country is sometimes very important. In the registration of trademarks, for instance, a foreign government has been known to seek evidence of earlier trading. Expansion, in the face of local manufacture, may also require the company to demonstrate a long history of local trading.

Dealership and agency agreements

Dealerships and agencies are a form of sub-contracting in which a main firm appoints another to act on its behalf. Dealership and agency agreements are legal documents which allow businesses to delegate part of their business operations to others. Many traders have historically used local agents to act for them in parts of Britain distant from their headquarters and more especially overseas. Agents usually had wide powers to act on behalf of the principal firm, while dealerships were usually restricted to marketing and selling a product produced by the principal firm. Dealership and agency agreements define the services to be performed, the geographical area to be covered, the basis of the remuneration and other aspects of the relations between the firms. They are also a source of information for the marketing strategy of a business, the geographical extent of a business's trade and a product's distribution, and the administration of overseas markets.[8] Non-current dealership and agency agreements with related papers are worthy of consideration for permanent preservation.

Customer status records

Customer status records exist in various formats, such as status cards, files, notebooks, and so on. They record the state of the customer's ability to pay, the discounts negotiated (based on the annual quantity of goods purchased), the names and addresses of their senior management, and any other information thought to be useful to the sales team. Such records may be supplemented by reports of customer visits by the company's own sales representatives and senior sales management, and papers on pricing structures, based on the costing records (see Chapter 6). Some trade associations also circulated annual credit-rating lists to members. All these records are sensitive during their active lifetime and should be considered for permanent preservation, either in their entirety or sampled, as they can be an invaluable source of information on how sales were achieved and the creditworthiness of competitors and customers.

Product design and packaging

Since the late nineteenth century the design and packaging of products has been an important part of a business's sales and marketing strategy. Examples of new product designs, labelling and packaging, including documentation concerning their introduction, should be considered for permanent preservation, particularly as display items. As an artform in its own right, the typography and subjects used to illustrate packaging are a useful commentary on social mores.

Product sales literature

Businesses have produced sales literature, describing and illustrating their products and services, since the late eighteenth century, when handbills and trade cards were distributed to potential customers. Since the 1960s the quantity and frequency of such literature has grown rapidly. Sales departments have traditionally published price lists and catalogues, and often issued a series of trade circulars. These, which can be used for dating the introduction of new patterns, products and services, have become increasingly sophisticated in recent years. A selection of product specifications, price lists, catalogues and trade circulars should be permanently preserved. It is common for businesses to keep details of competitors' prices and products, usually in the form of catalogues and price lists. A selection of these should also be considered for permanent preservation.

Market surveys

During the twentieth century the science of market surveying has evolved, and market surveys by home and export departments can contain a great deal of unique economic information about the localities concerned. These reports often contain statistics showing market penetration by product and by value, at home and overseas. Sometimes such statistics are gathered and presented independently. Market survey and statistical reports should be permanently preserved. They are sometimes to be found with the board papers in large companies.

Advertising records

In the business of selling, the term merchandising covers those activities which push the product or service towards the consumer. This is different from advertising, which aims to pull the consumer towards the product. Advertising supports the sales force and serves to educate the public about the benefits of a service or how a product works and how it should be used. In assessing the value of a company's advertising records it is worth considering whether its sales department is marketing-orientated or product-orientated. A marketing-orientated company is one which makes a popular product or provides a service that is in demand in direct competition with similar companies. The merchandising activities of such companies are aimed direct at the consumer, and include sales training, dealer/agent meetings and surveys, outlet and product identification, point-of-sale display practices and special promotions. The most obvious merchandising tools are attractive containers and packaging. The precise method of displaying trademarks and logos on packaging, promotional literature, fancy goods or delivery fleets, is carefully controlled, as the company has too much to lose if copycats intervene. A product-orientated company, on the other hand, is one which makes a product or provides a service for a few special customers. It rarely has to advertise to the public and its important informational records are more difficult to identify. Since the function is more concerned with meeting price and product specifications, its records will form part of the negotiating procedures.

The records which are created in this area of commercial activity may be extremely valuable. Sales brochures, for example, glossy and transitory though they may appear, are often the only place where technical specifications of the products and services are easily available for reference. A number of good histories of advertising[9] exist, and they should be consulted for further information on the development of different forms of advertising. Present-day marketing departments rarely retain a complete record of their activities, and it is likely that the archivist will have to intervene to ensure the preservation of packaging, advertising, literature, and so on. If the business has used advertising agents, these should be identified and approached to discover whether they hold any material of interest. Similarly the master copies of audio-visual advertising records are often left in outside hands and should be located and preserved.

The types of advertising record which are worthy of permanent preservation include:

- Press advertisements, often kept in guardbooks.
- A selection of proof copies of advertisements.
- Samples of point-of-sale displays, such as mock-ups and photographs of the way the products should be displayed in retail outlets.
- Commissions to artists and designers to produce new shapes, labels, packaging, and the related artwork, photographs and illustrations.
- Manuals on house styles, logo-types and trademark displays.
- Advertising posters, photographs, films and sound recordings.
- Artefacts devoted to product advertising, e.g. ashtrays, T-shirts and other 'giveaways'.

This material is of value in current advertising and useful for displays and exhibitions.

Copyright in posters and showcards was secured by registration with the Stationers' Company in London under the Fine Arts Copyright Act 1862, and advertising agents, artists and photographers registered their work (usually under their name rather than the client's) to prevent others from using the artwork and slogans they had created in promotional campaigns.[10] Copyright was registered by completing a form giving a brief description of the work, the name and address of the owner of the copyright and the names and addresses of the 'authors' or artists. A copy of the work being registered was usually annexed to the form. The Imperial Copyright Act 1911 gave copyright protection without the need to register, and statutory registration at Stationers' Hall ceased on 1 July 1912. The register and entry forms are held in the Public Record Office, in the COPY class, which includes registers dealing with books, literary and commercial; paintings and drawings, general, artistic and commercial; and photographs. Under the Copyright, Design and Patent Act 1988 the copyright ownership of advertising and related design work belongs to the commissioned artist or advertising agency, not to the company. Separate additional payments usually have to be made if the commissioning company wishes to retain original artwork and photographic negatives in its own archives.

Personnel records

The Combination Acts of 1799 and 1800 effectively curbed all industrial organization for both workers and employers. After their repeal in 1824 and 1825, the new trades which industrialization had fostered (such as cotton spinners, railway engineers and foundry workers) tended to emulate the activities of craft associations, and started to combine into trade unions.

These newly reconstituted trade unions negotiated wage rates and campaigned for improvements in working conditions. Most employers throughout the nineteenth century remained paternalistic, even in large firms operating on several sites. However, gradually wage rates, and such things as demarcation agreements, began to be established, either locally or on an industry basis. These arrangements were formalized by employers' associations, pioneered in Glasgow with the establishment of the Engineers Employers' Association in 1897. Shortly thereafter a number of associations, both national and local, were established. They began to look at a whole range of issues, far beyond wage rates and demarcation, acting as arbitrators in disputes, fixing prices, collecting production statistics, distributing information about government grants and subsidies, and defending generic products in overseas markets.

As businesses grew in size and complexity, salaried managers began to replace owners/directors, changing the relationship between the employee and the employed. Increased investment in new techniques during the First World War, coupled with increasingly tight controls over government expenditure, demanded closer attention to cashflows and productivity. These pressures grew during the serious recession of the inter-war years and became acute during the Second World War, when the government was determined to ensure value for money. Increased productivity required the analysis of working methods and practices, and inevitably changed the character of industrial relations in large concerns, leading in the post-war period to plant bargaining and the advancement of nationally agreed rates.

Joint Industrial Councils, consisting of management and workers' representatives, were established by many big companies in less well organized sections of industry in the reconstruction period after the First World War, under the twin influences of the Ministry of Labour and the Industrial Society. These were an effective form of continual consultation and local collective bargaining until the early 1930s and survived in many companies until the 1950s.

Wage and salary records

Until the early part of the twentieth century wage and salary books were the only personnel records kept by many firms. They are technically financial records (see p. 151), sometimes showing the wage rate or grade of an employee and hours worked, but often only providing a list of staff in each department with little individual detail. These records rarely survive as a complete series, as they have changed format over time, from volumes to cards to machine-readable records. They can be very voluminous for large companies. When they survive as a complete series, they should be considered for permanent retention, especially if no other form of personnel record has survived.

Staff and employee lists and service records

Employee lists and service records, including record cards or registers, often provide not only details relating to individuals' jobs, such as job title, wages received and work location, but also information about their family and their home address. In recent times they sometimes include a photograph. Staff and managers' personal details were usually kept separately from those of the general employees, and senior management files are often held by the company secretary. From the 1920s personal files were created for individuals, and it is from this date that the largest companies in the United Kingdom established personnel departments, with directors formally in charge of personnel matters.

Nineteenth-century personnel records should be kept, as these can be used not only for the study of family history but also by economic and labour historians. With regard to twentieth-century records, archivists may often have to more selective because of the bulk of the material which survives. Personnel records for all individuals require to be kept for at least 30 years after an employee has left the company or retired. Thereafter these records should be sampled, by means of a statistically reliable method. Such records can be used by labour historians to reconstitute the social history of a factory, workplace or local community.[11]

Training and education records

From the early nineteenth century apprentices received formal training outside the company in mechanics' institutes and from professional bodies. In the 1870s there was considerable concern about the seeming inadequacy of British technical training as compared to that available in Germany, which resulted in the foundation of technical colleges and a greater awareness in certain industries (notably chemicals and precision and electrical engineering) of the need for formal training. This was reinforced by the experience of the First World War, and the establishment in the inter-war years of national curricula in certain trades, often supported by City & Guilds or equivalent examinations. Since the Second World War, training has become commonplace throughout industry and commerce. In 1958 trade associations, trade unions and government departments came together to form the Industrial Training Council to oversee training and qualifications at all levels. In 1964 the Industrial Training Act was passed, leading to the establishment of Industrial Training Boards for individual industries. As these boards are semi-official bodies, the records should find their way to the Public Record Office, but this may not have happened in all cases. More recently larger companies have developed their own schemes, with supporting courseware.

Apprenticeship indentures and papers concerned with details of training schemes and recruitment should be permanently retained, as they provide information on staff and craft training and education which is not usually available elsewhere. If an employee resigned he generally took his indenture with him to prove that he had served an apprenticeship; otherwise they tended to be left with the company. There is much interest in the development of training. Material from before the Second World War does not often survive and should be preserved; thereafter a selection should be made, taking care to retain all records relating to policy and examples of curricula and courseware.

Trade union records

Union records in the form of deputation books, minutes of local management/employee joint consultative and negotiating meetings, demarcation and new technology agreements may also exist within the records of a business. These records should be permanently preserved, as information about local union negotiations is rare.

Welfare records

From the 1880s a few firms also began to provide medical and dental facilities for their workers, initially for those who had been injured at work, and later for all their workers. Few medical records from the nineteenth century have survived as doctors tended to regard these as their personal property, but accident registers and individual claims for workmen's compensation have survived from about 1906 onwards. Accident and safety reports, details of medical schemes and reports of medical officers require to be kept for the lifetime of a business. Knowledge of past working conditions is becoming increasingly important. These records must be preserved because employees may claim damages before industrial tribunals for deafness and other latent medical conditions caused through working practices which would now be seen to have been inefficient or negligent. It has become just as important to establish where employees worked before they joined the company as where they worked during their working lives with the company. Indeed, as new carcinomas emerge (asbestosis is perhaps the best known example of this problem), it may be necessary to trace all the employees who worked in a particular section of a factory. Such records comprise medical notes, X-rays (especially where ionic radiation was present), environmental surveys, and the full working histories of individual employees.

Firms often subsidized sick and burial societies which had been established by employees. Any surviving records, such as minutes and financial records, should be permanently retained, as they provide an insight into the living conditions of employees which is not to be found elsewhere.

Pension and superannuation records

As employees extended their service with the same company, it was recognized that the firm's responsibility did not stop on the day that a worker retired. Widows of long-serving men, and workers who had to retire through ill-health or old age, were given special grants of money or small pensions. The National Insurance Act 1911 established the concept that while pensions should be paid by the state, workers should start to contribute towards health insurance and unemployment benefit while they were still in full employment. At first only a small section of the workforce was covered by the terms of the National Insurance Act, which was later extended during the inter-war years to cover the whole workforce. After the First World War large companies started to create their own pension and superannuation funds for staff and in a few cases workers. Such pensions and grants were unusual and entirely discretionary, that is, with no formal rules with rights for workers and claimants. Larger companies established new departments, while smaller ones used professional fund managers to administer this new feature of company welfare. New arrangements had to be made to ensure that contributions were effectively invested to yield a maximum return. The trustees generally comprised representatives of both employers and employees.

Pension and superannuation scheme trust deeds and rules, trustee meeting minute books, fund annual accounts, investment records, actuarial valuation reports and contribution reports require to be kept for the lifetime of the scheme. The records of pensioners require to be kept for 10 years after the cessation of benefit. The trust deeds and rules, trustee minute books and annual accounts of any such pension schemes should be permanently preserved, as they will be the only source of information on the schemes.

Recreation club records

Minutes of meetings, photographs, lists of members, newsletters, and papers and correspondence detailing the operation and activities of company-sponsored hobby, long-service and sports clubs should be permanently preserved. Many firms produce staff magazines, which should also be permanently retained, as they contain valuable information on staff promotions, events and personalities.

Management services records

During the twentieth century various administrative developments have produced management services sections within larger companies. The first of these was the increase in office automation (see Chapter 3) and the introduction of time and motion study practices, in the larger companies from the 1930s, to tighten up work methods, which were not keeping pace with productivity targets. Work study became an essential tool in managing production processes and setting rates of pay for piecework. Organization and Methods (O & M) was another tool to reorganize office systems. By the 1950s, when mechanical tabulating started to give way to the computer, management services were born.

Since the 1970s, corporate planning has become a prominent part of management services. Corporate planners are responsible for developing future strategies for the organization and its divisions. The documentation produced is usually highly confidential and is held by the senior executive, sometimes not even company secretaries having access to the whole plan. These records should be permanently retained. The records of management services in general tend to be comparatively sparse, but where files of correspondence, reports and other papers exist, they should be carefully appraised, because even though they contain information not readily available elsewhere, much of it is of transitory nature. This applies especially to work-study reports.

Production records

Production records vary greatly between service-providing businesses and those which manufacture products, and among different manufacturing concerns. The production records of retailing, mining, heavy engineering and financial-service companies, for example, are very different. The manufacturing, servicing, and technical activities dealt with in this chapter are, however, shared by many businesses and produce some common records. It is not, however, possible to describe in any detail all the records that may be found in each manufacturing and service industry.[12]

Production encompasses the various procedures which convert raw materials and semi-finished components into the final product, or the mechanisms and infrastructure required to provide a service. It comprises the making or assembly of the product and the inspection, packing and despatching of the finished article from the warehouse. Records dealing with manufacturing and distribution processes must be appraised in relation to the process itself, and should reflect the massive changes wrought by mechanization and new technologies during the last 150 years.[13]

Costing records

Costing records, detailing the cost of raw materials, fuel and labour are technically financial records (see p. 150). They are an invaluable source for the historian and should be permanently retained, not so much for the financial information they contain as to explain why particular functions, buildings, craftsmen and so on were added to costing structures.

Estimate and order books

Cost books are usually cross-referenced by job/order numbers with job/ order books and contracts. A large object assembled from many different parts, such as a steam engine, was usually built to a customer's specification, and the costing carefully estimated before an order was placed. Details were then transferred from the estimate book to the order book, and a copy of the order was sent to the works for the product to be made. These books may be arranged by contract number and contain a full specification of the product, showing when work started and when it was completed. Similarly, when an insurance company wrote a life policy, a copy was entered into a register along with details of the premium, personal information about the individual, and the date of maturity. These records, although often bulky, should be permanently preserved, as they provide information about production and services which is unavailable elsewhere.

Stock books

Many enterprises carry stock, e.g. manufacturers, wholesalers and shopkeepers. The management of stock is often critical to success or failure. Details of stock and its purchase/book value are recorded in stock books. They can be bulky, and selection for preservation must depend on the character and significance of the enterprise and the quality of the information recorded.

Photographs

Photographs of products were taken not only for advertising but also to show the customers how large-scale orders were progressing. They also visually record the production process and should be permanently preserved. Vast quantities of photographs of products can exist from after the Second World War. As a rough rule of thumb, all pre-1960 photographs (both prints and negatives) should be retained, and a selection only of those dating from 1960 if large accumulations survive. Appraisal should, however, be undertaken by someone familiar with the business to ensure recognition of significant features.

Quality assurance documentation

Quality assurance documentation has little historical value and can be destroyed. Care should, however, be taken over records which may be required as evidence in actions under the Latent Damage Act 1986.[14]

Machinery records

Operating handbooks and maintenance records concerning machinery used in production are not of historical value and should be destroyed unless the machinery is to be preserved, or was invented especially for the manufacturing process. In such a case these records should be considered for permanent retention. Drawings of machinery used in the production process should also be preserved for the life of the machinery.

Technical drawings[15]

In order to make a product, the drawing office prepares designs from the specifications produced by the design engineers and estimating departments, and works with the shop foremen who translate drawings into actual products. There are several kinds of drawings, i.e. general arrangements, major sub-assemblies and details. During the early nineteenth century engineering drawings were usually no more than sketches, and the exact dimensions of the finished products were left to shop-floor workers. Later fully dimensioned drawings were made, and they became more detailed as the subdivision of labour progressed and products became more complex. There are usually many views of each item, including plans, outer and sectional elevations, and 3-dimensional drawings. The aim is to portray the product and its components exactly, simply and completely, with all the necessary instructions for manufacture. Drawings may be accompanied by books of specifications. They often survive in large quantities, because their retention allowed the company to quote for spares and plant refurbishment. The variety of physical formats in which drawings may be found are listed below:

- Original drawings on high quality cartridge-paper.
- Tracings on paper or cloth.

- Copy press copies, reverse and identical, from 1780s.
- Blueprints from 1860s, i.e. paper coated in a light-sensitive compound which turns blue on exposure to daylight.
- Hectographs from 1870s (commonplace from 1900s), i.e. transfer of aniline ink from a master copy via a gelatin plate. This was replaced by spirit duplicating from the 1920s.
- Dyelines prepared from tracings from 1920s, i.e. paper treated with diazonium salts sensitive to ultra-violet light. Originally known as the ozalid process. Blueprints were used to make positive copies.
- Photographic negatives and prints, particularly from the Second World War.
- Microforms, usually aperture cards made up from 35mm film.
- Computer-assisted designs (CAD), i.e. drawings produced, stored and amended with the use of special computer-assisted design software, usually in the form of magnetic tapes or disks.

Drawings may be weeded down to general arrangements and sub-assemblies except where they relate to plants still in operation or to important products which would interest enthusiasts. They should not be judged by their attractiveness, as they are functional records and should be appraised as such. Expert advice should be taken where selection is difficult. Clients have a direct interest and should be asked whether they wish to take custody of drawings which would otherwise be destroyed. In any case a record should be kept of drawings which have not been retained. Duplicates of drawings and other records should be examined carefully, as each may be annotated uniquely. Drawings may also be affected by the copyright and official secrets legislation, and advice may need to be taken before access or reproduction is permitted. Drawings produced for government contracts may be public records. Conveniently most firms with large holdings of technical drawings kept a register of drawings, recording drawing numbers and providing a brief description of the contents. They should be retained

Research and development records

Many kinds of firm, ranging from pharmaceutical companies to food processors and large retailers, have departments consisting of scientists, engineers and specialist technologists who research and test new and existing products. Research laboratory ideas and experiments become field trials, which will be recorded in technical reports and laboratory notebooks. The latter are created by research scientists as a kind of diary of events during the period of experimentation in which observations are recorded. The result of the research is detailed in a technical report. The records of failed experiments are very often as important as those of successful work, because, as knowledge increases in a given area, the information they contain may be used again to produce successful results.

A successful patent may well hinge on the date of these experiments and trials. In the case of pharmaceuticals and food products marketed in the United States of America all records of development and trials must be kept under Food and Drugs Administration regulations for 20 years from the date trials ceased. Other countries have different requirements. There are various regulations throughout the world relating to a wide range of product types. Expert advice may need to be sought when considering which records are worthy of preservation.

A twentieth-century administrative development has been the creation of a series of technical committees, covering the whole range of a company's technical expertise, to co-ordinate the research and development effort. These committees produce progress reports and minutes of meetings which define future activity and control research costs, and their records should be permanently preserved.

Non-company records

Records that do not properly belong to a company may be found among its 'official' records. They may belong to the founding family or may reflect a company's role within an industry or geographical area.

Trade papers

Most companies belong to an employers' or trade association of one kind or another. In the nineteenth century these associations fixed prices, set production quotas, negotiated wage rates, played a part in training and research and development, and in many respects controlled the activities of individual companies. Their influence diminished after the Second World War, and such practices as price-fixing have been illegal since the Restrictive Trade Practices Act of 1956. The records comprise minutes of meetings at which prices and production quotas were set and issues of common concern discussed, printed publications, and correspondence; they tend to be fuller when the company's representative acted as chairman or secretary to the association. If the records are not annotated and they are duplicated elsewhere, e.g. the records of the association in question may be deposited in a local or national record repository (notably the Modern Records Centre at Warwick University), they can be destroyed.

In many areas employers created local trade associations (sometimes branches of national associations) which dealt with such local problems as the labour market and supply, railway rates, liaison with local authorities, district rates of pay, hours of work and so on. The records comprise minutes of meetings and supporting documentation which was used to provide the information the employers' associations needed. Again, if the company representative also served as the chairman or secretary, the documentation tends to be fuller and should be permanently preserved.

Private or family papers

From the eighteenth century until in some cases well into the twentieth century the firm's book-keeper often also looked after the affairs of the founding family. Since the company probably started as a one-man band or a partnership, it is often difficult to separate the early records of the owner's business interests and his private affairs. Family papers often consist of diaries; correspondence, usually in-letters; books of account; portraits; commissions (military and civil); real estate records; papers of executorships or trusteeships; wills; and, in this century much the most bulky, tax records. They reflect the family's external activities, which often increase as the company develops and becomes more important in the local community. Such records where they exist should be permanently preserved.

Conclusion

Unlike corporate and financial records, which at least share some common characteristics, the records described in this chapter are more disparate. It is impossible to provide hard and fast guidelines for retention policy, beyond prescriptive periods. Much will depend on the sector of activity, the existence of material elsewhere, and current management needs. When in doubt, seek expert advice internally and from historians, as many of these classes of records have been used extensively for histories, both nationally and locally.

Notes

1   A. A. Dibben, *Title Deeds 13th – 19th Centuries* (The Historical Association, London, 1971); and J. C. K. Cornwall, *How to Read Old Title Deeds XVI–XIX Centuries*, 2nd impression (Pinhorns, Isle of Wight, 1970). See also N. W. Alcock, *Old Title Deeds. A Guide for Local and Family Historians* (Phillimore, Chichester, 1986).
2   For further information see A. Mace, *Architectural Records in National and Local Collections: Guidance Notes for Archivists and Record Offices* (Royal Institute of British Architects/Royal Commission on the Historical Monuments of England, 1987).
3   See M. Beresford, 'Building history from fire insurance records', *Urban History Year Book* (1976); and S. D. Chapman, 'Business history from insurance policy registers', *Business Archives*, 32 (1970), pp. 10–16.

4 N. Davenport, *The United Kingdom Patent System. A Brief History with Bibliography* (Kenneth Mason, London, 1979).

5 Registers and indexes of patents are preserved at the Patent Office, Southampton Buildings, Chancery Lane, London, until they are 50 years old and then they are destroyed. The Science Reference Library in Southampton Row, Chancery Lane, London, a division of the British Library, holds printed copies of all patent specifications granted since 1617 and personal and subject indexes. The Patent Office has since 1854 published a weekly *Journal of Patents* (available in most large public libraries). The Patent Rolls are held in the Public Record Office, Chancery Lane, London, in class C 66. See also *Patent Holdings in British Public Libraries* (Sheffield City Libraries, Sheffield, 1973); B. Woodcroft, *Alphabetical Index of Patentees of Inventions* (London, 1854, republished 1969); and H. Harding, *Patent Office Centenary. A Story of 100 Years in the Life and Work of the Patent Office* (HMSO, London, 1953, reprinted 1975).

6 Representations of trademarks up to 1938 are held by the Public Record Office, Kew, in class BT 82. Later records remain with the Patent Office at the Trade Mark Office in State House, High Holborn, London. Trademarks were also published in the *Trade Mark Journal*, which is available in most large public libraries, but is not indexed. Current trademarks are indexed alphabetically by subject, with an indication of when they were first registered and details of ownership. Directly a trademark lapses, it is removed from the register and the documentation destroyed. See also *Designs and Trade Marks: Registers and Representations*, PRO Information Sheet No. 42; and Patent Office, *A Century of Trademarks* (Patent Office, London, 1976).

7 These are mainly located in classes BT 42–48 and BT 50–53 at the Public Record Office, Kew. More recent designs may be inspected at the Designs Registry, State House, High Holborn, London. See also S. Levitt, 'The uses of registered design samples in the Public Record Office, Kew, for the study of nineteenth century clothing manufacturers', *Business Archives, 50* (1984), pp. 45–53.

8 R. P. T. Davenport-Hines (editor), *Markets and Bagmen: Studies in Marketing and British Industrial Performance, 1830–1939* (Gower, Aldershot, 1986).

9 For example T. R. Nevett, *Advertising in Britain: A History* (Heinemann, London, 1982); B. Holme, *Advertising: Reflections of a Century* (Heinemann, London, 1982); and R. Opie, *Rule Britannia: Trading on the British Image* (Viking, Harmondsworth, 1985) and *The Art of the Label. Designs of the Times* (Quarto, London, 1987).

10 Further information is available in a Public Record Office handbook: M. Jubb, *Cocoa and Corsets. A Selection of Late Victorian and Edwardian Posters and Showcards in the Public Record Office* (HMSO, London, 1984).

11 For example, D. Drummond, 'Specifically designed? Employers' labour strategies and worker responses in British railway workshops, 1838–1914', *Business History, 31: 2* (1989), pp. 8–31.

12 Information on the production records of specific industries can be found in the following books: L. S. Presnell and J. Orbell, *A Guide to the Historical Records of British Banking* (Gower, Aldershot, 1985); H. A. L. Cockerell and E. Green, *The British Insurance Business 1547–1970* (Heinemann, London, 1976); M. S. Moss and J. R. Hume, *Workshop of the British Empire. Engineering and Shipbuilding in the West of Scotland* (Heinemann, London,

1977); and L. Richmond and A. Turton, *The Brewing Industry, A Guide to Historical Records* (Manchester University Press, Manchester, 1990). The papers produced by the Business Archives Council and Society of Archivists Joint Working Party on Business Records, 1987–89, comprise detailed discussion of the records in ten industrial and commercial areas. These are financial services; mining; mechanical engineering; building contractors and developers; railways; solicitors, estate agents and architects; electrical engineering; shipbuilding; publishing and retailing.

13   See M. S. Moss on the use and selection of technical records in M. S. Moss and J. R. Hume, *Workshop of the British Empire. Engineering and Shipbuilding in the West of Scotland* (Heinemann, London, 1977), pp. 155–82.

14   See A. Appleton, 'The selection of records for retention: statutory limitation periods in contract and tort', *Business Archives*, 57 (1989), p. 17.

15   This is based on information contributed by Alison Turton and published in the mechanical engineering section of the papers produced by the Business Archives Council and Society of Archivists Joint Working Party on Business Records, 1987–9.

Further reading

J. Armstrong and S Jones, *Business Documents. Their Origins, Sources and Uses in Historical Research* (Mansell, London, 1987).

G. S. Bain and G. B. Woolven, *A Bibliography of British Industrial Relations* (Cambidge University Press, Cambridge, 1979).

P. Meinhart, *Inventions, Patents and Trademarks* (Gower, London, 1971).

Modern Records Centre, *Trade Union and Related Records*, 3rd edition (Modern Records Centre, Coventry, 1983).

Business archive formats

Serena Kelly

Paper records

Paper has been the preferred medium for information storage since the fifteenth century and, despite such recent technological developments as electronic mail, word-processing and optical disk storage, approximately 95 per cent of all records are still held in paper form. This is not to suggest that the business archivist can afford to ignore non-paper records, or that the percentages will remain the same in the future, but to indicate that the vast majority of records managed by a business archivist will be in a paper format.

Physical characteristics

Paper is made by sieving an aqueous suspension of vegetable fibres which, before the nineteenth century, were obtained by hand-processing rags (see Chapter 3). With the advent of papermaking machines, the quality of paper declined. Processing and bleaching agents with inherent impurities were introduced, and wood pulp was substituted for rags. Paper made from wood pulp falls into two main types. Firstly, mechanical or ground-wood paper is made by debarking the tree and grinding the trunk up into splinter-like fragments. The resultant material, which needs to be mixed with about 40 per cent other fibre to make paper, contains resinous materials called lignins which bind the fibres together. Lignins are degraded by heat and/or light to produce complex organic acids which will destroy cellulose. Paper made in this way therefore tends to be impermanent. Alternatively, tree chippings may be treated chemically to dissolve the lignins and free the fibres. If the processing and subsequent washing is carried out thoroughly, this kind of paper may be capable of long-term survival. A more recent development is paper made from semi-chemical wood; this has sufficient of the lignins removed to free the individual fibres, but residual lignins remain and can cause permanence problems. Thus while most paper suffers from inherent instability, paper made before the beginning of the nineteenth century is likely to be in a better condition, and to last longer, than paper made during the twentieth century.

In recent years increased use has been made of recycled paper. Recycling usually has an adverse effect on paper quality, as each time paper passes through the manufacturing process the average length of the cellulose fibres is reduced. A high concentration of short fibres weakens the paper. Recycled paper is therefore not suitable for long-term storage. There are a number of papers that are manufactured to archival standards. These are based either on good quality chemical wood or on cotton linters, and can be manufactured with an alkaline reserve.

A contributory factor to the impermanence of paper records is the ink with which the information is written or printed. Before the mid-twentieth century the most widely used ink was ferrous sulphate or iron gall ink, a generic term which covers thousands of different recipes. While clear and legible if stored correctly, the ink fades on continuous exposure to light, and, if badly prepared, can be so acidic as to damage the paper. Its very variable composition renders its properties and permanence uncertain. From the mid-twentieth century iron gall inks have been superseded by dye-based inks. These fade with time and some are soluble in water. Coloured inks, which consist of a colour suspended in water and gum arabic, also fade and are liable to smudge. Very little is known about the permanence of ball-point pen ink or the inks used in fibre or felt-tipped pens. In general, black printing inks do not pose major permanence problems. The inks in fabric ribbons used in early typewriters consisted of dyes held in spirit or water and glycerin, and with time these inks fade and smudge, although carbon ribbons made of film produce type that is far more durable.

Paper records have been and are produced in all businesses – either as loose sheets, files and bound books, or such items as maps, posters and product wrappings. Ironically, the adoption by businesses of computer technology has frequently led to an explosion in the amount of paper generated. Large stacks of computer print-out will be found in almost every department of a modern company.

Appraisal

Appraisal of paper records can cause problems. Vast amounts are generated, but only a small proportion can or should be kept. As little as 5 per cent of the records created by a business are worthy of long-term preservation. Decisions over what should be kept and what might be disposed of must be based on a clear view of the company's statutory and administrative obligations and needs, as well as a sense of the historical significance and value of the material. These decisions must be incorporated into a strategic records management and archive policy and should not be based on the *ad hoc* decisions of different employees (for detailed discussion of appraisal and records retention policies see Chapter 10).

Storage

Environmental conditions

Paper records to be retained for long-term storage need to be protected from:

- *Handling*. This is a major cause of physical damage.
- *Pollution*. This can originate from the atmosphere or from poor storage materials and can cause staining and fading.
- *Unsuitable temperature and relative humidity*. The higher the temperature and relative humidity, the greater the rate of chemical deterioration, in particular the risk of mould growth. A low temperature and relative humidity causes paper to dry out and become brittle, and leather to become powdery.
- *Biological attack*. Fungi, insects and rodents feed on some of the constituents of paper.
- *Disasters*. Fire, flood, theft, vandalism.

Conditions inside the archive repository must be carefully controlled to achieve a consistent and clean environment. The temperature and relative humidity should be regulated by air conditioning to create a constant temperature between 13°C and 18°C, and a constant relative humidity between 55 per cent and 65 per cent. The system should be monitored daily. Rapid fluctuations in temperature and relative humidity are particularly damaging and should be avoided. Air should be filtered to eliminate dust and harmful chemicals. No gas, water or waste pipes should run through the archive repository, and all electrical fittings should be enclosed. If present, fluorescent tube lights should be fitted with diffusers and ultra-violet light filters. Appropriate security arrangements should also be made.

Packaging

Most paper records should be placed in boxes or other containers before being shelved. All boxes should be made of acid-free materials and designed to fit their contents. They should be robust and easy to handle. If the contents of the box are fragile, any spare space should be packed with acid-free paper to prevent damage when the box is moved. Outsize items, such as maps, plans, drawings and posters, should ideally be stored flat, unrolled and unfolded, in plan or map chests. Horizontal storage avoids the risk of strain and distortion which can be caused by vertical storage. This is particularly important if accurate measurements may need to be taken from the items stored. If rolled, outsize items should be wrapped around the outside of acid-free tubes, which should then be stored horizontally. Files should be placed in suitably sized boxes. Ideally all metal clips, pins, staples and pressure-sensitive tape should be removed.

If an extensive collection of volumes is to be shelved, it is a good idea to build the shelves to fit the size of the volumes, so that large and small volumes can be stored separately. If the cover or binding of a volume is in good condition and has no particular value, the volume may be stored on a shelf without additional packaging. If the binding is of unusual significance and is in good condition, the book should be wrapped in a renewable bookjacket made from acid-free paper. If it is in poor condition, the book should be wrapped and placed in a suitable box.

Retrieval

All items and containers should be labelled and retrieved through finding aids (see Chapter 11). Documents should be used by researchers in a searchroom which is environmentally suitable, supervised and secure.

Photographs[1]

Since the mid-nineteenth century photographers have been experimenting with a great variety of materials and techniques to produce an improved image or to create particular effects, and the archivist should be aware of the various stages in the evolution of the photograph.

The photographic image may be either positive or negative. A negative is a photographic image in which light and dark tones are recorded as opposites. Light is transmitted from the subject and causes the silver halides in the emulsion to alter. The stronger the light, the greater the effect it has on the halides and therefore the darker they turn. Areas from which little or no light is reflected leave clear areas on the emulsion. In colour negatives every colour in the original is represented by its complementary. A positive image is one where the tonal values correspond to the original subject. A positive is made from a negative by passing light through it to a second light-sensitive material. Positive images were first produced on metal by means of the Daguerreotype process, but this photographic base was superseded during the nineteenth century by the widespread use of glass and paper. Less common has been the use of ceramics, fabric, leather, stone and wood. Negative images are found on glass, paper and film. The proper care of photographs is dependent on a basic knowledge and awareness of photographic materials and processes.

Physical characteristics

Metal

The first widely used photographic process was the Daguerreotype process, introduced in 1839. Copper plates were prepared with a layer of silver sensitized with iodine vapour. They were then exposed in the camera and the image developed by mercury vapour. Each Daguerreotype was unique, and, if the image had to be reproduced, the plate had to be rephotographed. The image is normally laterally reversed, to give a mirror image of the subject. Daguerreotypes can be recognized by their metal backing and by the fact that if the plate reflects a light ground, the image appears to be negative. The chemical instability of the process required the image to be sealed beneath glass. The image is usually grey, although over-exposure in the camera can produce 'solarization', which makes the light areas appear darker. Many were hand-tinted. Daguerreotypes pose serious preservation problems, as the surface coating is very fragile and nineteenth-century glass is inherently unstable. The ferrotype, or tintype, process used black enamelled iron in place of copper plates. This produced a direct positive image which is greyish-black or brown.

Glass

Glass superseded metal as the common base for photographs once a suitable medium for stabilizing the silver salts had been developed. This was initially achieved by coating the glass with a layer of albumen, but after 1851 a thick layer of collodion became the favoured medium. This process created a negative image which was altered to form a positive by backing the glass with black paint, cloth or paper. In America a method of sealing the glass plate to a covering sheet of glass was patented, and such photographs became known as ambrotypes. Wet collodion glass plates are distinguished by an uneven covering of the glass at the edges and the corner held by the photographer was usually completely uncovered. The dark areas of the negatives are greyish-black and the light areas a characteristic creamy-white. The coating on the glass may shrink and crack over time.

Gelatin dry plates superseded the wet collodion process during the 1870s. As they were coated by machine, the covering on the plates was even and uniform. From 1888 gelatin emulsions were coated on to paper and from 1889 on to film. This process forms the basis of almost all modern photography. The image is dark to reflected light and is prone to tarnishing.

Paper

Early photographers experimented with coatings on paper to produce high-quality positive prints. The most successful coatings were albumen and gelatin. W. H. Fox Talbot used uncoated salted paper in the calotype process which he patented in 1841. This process used paper negatives as well as positives, and the prints are characterized by a mottling, which was created by paper fibres in the negative. The image in salt prints rests on or near the top layer of the paper and is very vulnerable to surface abrasion and atmospheric pollution, and they also have a tendency to fade.

Albumen-coated paper was considered to be an improvement on salted paper. The print is usually reddish when first produced, but, if not toned with a gold solution, the red fades and the white areas discolour to yellow. Depending on the thickness of the coating, the surface varies from a slight sheen to a thick gloss. Unmounted prints have a tendency to curl, crease and tear, but they are usually found mounted on card.

From the 1880s the use of silver-gelatin-based papers became widespread for both negative images and positive prints. The developed image was usually black and white, but chemical toners, the most popular of which was sepia, could be used to colour the image. The paper was made in a range of thicknesses and the texture varied from matt to glossy. A hardening agent was frequently used in the processing; an excess of this agent can result in brittle emulsions, and a deficiency can cause the gelatin to become sticky, especially if kept in a high relative humidity environment. Early photographs were produced on fibre-based paper, but from the 1960s resin-coated paper was introduced and is now widely used. The resin coating prevents the substance of the paper from becoming wet, and therefore greatly reduces the processing times. It is also cheaper than fibre-based paper because a lower grade of paper can be sandwiched between the outer layers. Resin coatings can, however, cause crazing of the emulsion and its breakdown can eventually cause the image to disappear. It is therefore essential to transfer images from resin-coated to fibre-based paper for long-term storage. Fibre-based paper is, however, expensive and difficult to obtain.

Film

Cellulose nitrate, or celluloid film, was introduced in 1888 as a transparent substitute for glass negatives. It is highly inflammable, with some samples becoming spontaneously combustible at temperatures as low as 50°C, and becomes increasingly volatile with age. On decomposition it emits oxides of nitrogen which are acidic and cause oxidization. These gases will cause most organic material such as paper, gelatin and leather to deteriorate. All negatives produced before 1952, when safety film based on cellulose acetate was introduced, are suspect. Polyester film, introduced in the mid-1960s, is considered to be much tougher than cellulose acetate and is available in film widths of 8mm, 9.5mm, 16mm and 35mm.

Appraisal

Before accessioning, it is important to check whether an image is indeed a photograph. If it is homogeneous in its half-tones, it is a photograph, but if it is broken up by lines or dots, it is a printed image. Identification is not always simple, and will be helped by the use of a good hand lens or a low-powered microscope.

In a business, photographs will be found in the greatest numbers in the public relations, marketing and sales departments. Important occasions or milestones in the company's development, such as the opening of a new factory or the retirement of a chairman, will usually be recorded by a photographer for the house journal or annual report. Indeed the editorial office of the house journal may hold large accumulations of photographs. Advertising departments and sales forces rely heavily on photographs to bring products to the attention of the public and retail outlets. Many will, however, be duplicates and can be discarded. Another prolific source of photographs will be the premises department, which may well hold project photographs recording the stages of work in the building or redevelopment of offices and factories. It is also important to remember that photographs may accompany reports and correspondence and be filed with them.

Photographs, like other records, must be appraised as they will not all be worthy of long-term storage. Appraisal decisions must be based on detailed knowledge of the personnel, events, activities and products that are, or have been, important to the company, and on an understanding of the various photographic processes. Accessioned photographs should be closely related to other material held in the archive. Photographs entirely unconnected with the company should be transferred to a more appropriate repository. It should be remembered, however, that the research value of photographs is frequently unrelated to the original reason for taking the picture. Historians of dress, for instance, will be interested not in who was at a particular celebration in the company's history, but in the clothes the participants were wearing. Even if photographs cannot be identified or dated, their subject matter may well suggest that they should be retained. Similarly, early photographs have an intrinsic value beyond their evidential value and nineteenth-century photographs should not be destroyed. In general the cost of storing and cataloguing photographs will mean that the larger the collection, the more selective the archivist will have to be. Badly composed, poorly processed or damaged photographs may have to be weeded out.

Most users of photographic collections assume that copies will be available on request. It is therefore important to establish the copyright ownership of photographs and decide upon what terms they may be reproduced.

Storage

Environmental conditions

For all photographs and film, the lower the temperature in which they are stored, the slower the rate of chemical decomposition. This is particularly true of colour film and prints, as all colours are based on dyes which will eventually fade even in the dark. Black and white photographs and film are best stored at a stable temperature between 10°C and 13°C, while colour requires a lower temperature, between 0°C and 2°C. The relative humidity should be constant between 30 per cent and 50 per cent, preferably below 40 per cent. A high temperature combined with a high relative humidity will cause gelatin emulsions to soften and stick to other surfaces, and will encourage mould growth. Such conditions will also speed up the deteriorative effect of any residual processing chemicals, causing the image to turn brownish-yellow. A low temperature and relative humidity will cause the emulsion layer to crack and peel or become brittle. Frequent fluctuations in temperature and relative humidity are most damaging as they cause the emulsion and base materials to expand and contract at different rates, eventually causing them to separate. Rapid transfer of photographic records from repository to searchroom should, therefore be avoided.

Pollution in the atmosphere can cause particular problems for photographic archives. Damaging pollutants, such as sulphuric acid, nitric acid, sulphur dioxide, hydrogen sulphide, oxides of nitrogen and ozone and any oxidising or reducing agents, can fade and stain the image. Dust and dirt can scratch the image and also deposit acidic compounds and moisture.

Light, particularly ultra-violet light, causes damage by its heating effect and by stimulating decay. The darker parts of the image absorb more heat than the lighter parts, causing dimensional stresses. It also fades colour prints and speeds up residual chemical reactions. Such damage is cumulative. It is essential therefore that all photographs are stored in the dark. Archived colour transparencies should never be projected, and unique, original prints never photographed after a working copy has been made. Recurrent photocopying will also speed up deterioration of photographs.

Packaging

As photographic records occur in many shapes and sizes, the packaging for long-term preservation must be tailor-made to suit particular items.

Paper prints

Paper prints may be loose, mounted, framed or stuck into albums or scrapbooks. An unmounted print can be protected inside a transparent, chemically inert envelope, or supported with conservation-quality board cut a little larger than the print and wrapped in polyester film. In neither case does the print have to be removed from its covering for use. The seams of envelopes should be narrow and located at the edges of the envelope. Protected in either of these ways, prints can be stored vertically or horizontally. The chemical inertness of the materials used is essential. In practice this means that they must have a pH between 6.5 and 7.5 and contain no alkaline buffers, iron or aluminium compounds, dyes, pigments, reducible sulphur or lignin.

Colour prints are inherently unstable but may be preserved for a certain length of time by being kept in dark, cold storage. If colour prints have to be kept permanently, three-colour separation master negatives have to be made on black and white film. This method preserves in silver the dye layers of the original colour image and allows its later reconstruction. This is, however, an exacting and expensive process. A more feasible method is to make black and white negatives from original colour photographs. The content of the image will therefore be preserved, but the colours will reproduce as shades of grey, resulting in a loss of contrast and possibly of information.

The frames and mounts of photographs should be removed if there is any doubt about their archival qualities. If either is integral to the image, it should be reassembled to archival standards. Any information written on the back of mounts or frames should be recorded and, if significant, should be kept or photocopied on to archivally stable paper.

Oversize prints should be kept flat in map or plan chests and interleaved with neutral paper, or rolled around the outside of large diameter tubes. The tubes should then be wrapped in acid-free paper and tied with unbleached tape. Oversize prints should not be placed inside tubes, as removal will damage them. Copy negatives and prints should be made to reduce handling of the original.

Scrapbooks and albums pose particular preservation problems, as the paper, glue and plastic sheets are usually unsuitable from an archival point of view. It used to be common practice to remove photographs from albums and scrapbooks, but they are now recognized as possessing great intrinsic historical value as well as allowing the photographs to be seen in the sequence in which they were taken or arranged. Each album or scrapbook should be assessed individually, and every effort made to preserve them intact. Damaged or heavily used albums should be copied by rephotographing, not photocopying. They should be individually wrapped in acid-free paper and stored flat in document boxes. If necessary, the pages should be interleaved with acid-free paper.

Glass plates

Glass plate negatives and positives should be individually wrapped in a chemically inert paper envelope. Wrap-around envelopes are preferable to bags, as the latter can scratch the negative or abrade flaking emulsion. The emulsion side should be placed away from glued seams. Plates with flaking emulsion should not be stored in plastic envelopes, because of the detrimental effect of static charge. The wrapped plates should be stored flat in acid-free boxes or placed upright in boxes that have been grooved to take them. If the former method is adopted, care must be taken not to place too much weight on the bottom plate. A disadvantage with the latter method is that, if enough room is left to allow easy removal of individual plates, a great deal of space is wasted. Broken or cracked glass plates should be packaged to provide maximum support. Such packaging is best left to professional conservators.

Film

As cellulose nitrate film is highly inflammable, it is crucial to identify it and make arrangements for copying on to safety film. The identification of nitrate film is usually straightforward. The highlights are often brownish in colour and the non-emulsion side has a dimpled surface in reflected light. A simple test to identify nitrate film involves burning a very small sample on the end of a needle. It will burn rapidly and form one or two curls of solid ash, depending on whether it has been coated on one or two sides with gelatin. This test must be carried out in a well ventilated room. An alternative, but less reliable, test is to drop a small piece of film into a test tube containing 43cc of trichloroethylene and 25cc of trichloroethane. Nitrate film will sink, acetate film will float and polyester film will settle at mid-level. Negatives and transparencies on polyester film should be stored in chemically inert paper or polyester sleeves. Ideally the sleeves should be transparent, so that the negatives and transparencies do not have to be removed for viewing. These sleeves can either be placed on binders or stored flat in acid-free boxes.

The complexity and variety of chemical components that have been used to produce photographs necessitate a very careful approach to their repair and conservation. Archivists should limit themselves to copying, physical stabilization and the provision of a suitable storage environment. The professional advice of an expert conservator should be sought if conservation work is required and the temptation to undertake emergency repairs should be resisted.

Retrieval

Photographs are difficult to arrange and describe not only because of the number of photographs that are usually involved, but also because the research value of individual items is likely to be unrelated to the original reason for taking the photograph. However, as the business archivist will be more conversant with the structure and activities of the business than with the contents of the photographs, the most sensible arrangement remains that according to provenance. The collection will then need to be indexed and cross-referenced by subject. The subject categories will be dictated largely by research demands, but the potential for varied and extensive cross-referencing will be greatly enhanced by the use of a computer in producing a finding aid.

Separate collections, e.g. those created by a particular photographer or taken systematically, should be left intact and not integrated with other photographs. Individual photographs can, however, be grouped together to form an artificial collection, or added to a general collection. Any action taken in this regard must, however, be documented. Any relationship that exists between photographs and written material should also be explained in the finding aid. Where a photograph occurs in a correspondence or report file, the relationship must be carefully analysed before a decision is taken to remove it. If left in the file, the photograph must be protected by an acid-free envelope. The accessions register should note the provenance of the photograph, its date, title or subject, and the name of the photographer. It should also clearly state whether a photograph was accessioned as part of a collection or as a discrete item.

If it is essential to mark the photograph, this must be done on the reverse with a soft lead pencil. Under no circumstances should ink be used, as it can stain the image on the other side and the pressure of writing can cause cracks and indentations in the emulsion. The surface of negatives or transparencies should not be marked in any way. If mounted in a paper or inert plastic frame, the frame only should be labelled. Where the photograph is mounted, it is always preferable to mark the mount rather than the photograph itself. The problem with marking the packaging only is that the photograph and packaging could easily become separated.

Films[2]

Business and industry began to make use of motion pictures soon after the commercial advent of the cinema in 1895. Early films were largely promotional company portraits, although some advertisements were made in the medium. Few films ran for longer than 15 minutes. From the 1920s, however, film became more widely used by businesses. Most films continued to be commissioned from firms that specialized in the production of advertising or industrial film, although a handful of large companies established their own film units. Technological progress increased the value of film to business particularly after the use of sound became widespread in the 1930s and colour production became the norm during the 1960s. Although all early film was black and white, it could be tinted, toned or coloured to produce a colour image. The use of film in many areas of business was commonplace by the 1950s, although within 20 years it had begun to be ousted, on grounds of cost, by video tape. The 1970s and 1980s saw the widespread use of videos for personnel training and communications, and for sales purposes. Videodisks were introduced in the 1980s.

Physical characteristics

Cinematic film consists of a transparent, flexible base coated with a photographic emulsion, and is moved through viewing equipment by perforations which engage with rotating sprockets on one or both sides of the film. It can be either positive or negative and is made with differing chemical constituents in a variety of sizes or gauges. The cinema industry adopted 35mm as the standard size for film in 1909. Other gauges manufactured are 9.5mm (from 1922), 16mm (from 1923), 8mm (from

1932), and Super 8 (from 1965). Of these 16mm has been the most widely used in industry since the 1940s.

Until 1952 almost all 35mm film was made with a cellulose nitrate base. Unfortunately this type of film is inherently unstable. Cellulose nitrate decomposes over time and makes the film highly inflammable, causing it to ignite easily and burn quickly. During the final stages of decomposition the film disintegrates into a powder. This is preceded by stages when the film begins to smell, becomes sticky and starts to congeal. These symptoms must be recognized promptly, as the nitrous gases formed during decomposition can detrimentally affect film stored nearby.

Most film manufacturers had ceased to make cellulose nitrate film by 1952, opting instead for safety film made of cellulose acetate. This does not, however, mean that all post-1952 films are safety-based, as film laboratories continued to use up old stock or attach nitrate leaders to safety film. On the other hand, smaller gauge film had almost always been produced on an acetate base. Early safety film was produced on cellulose acetate but today cellulose triacetate is considered to be the best safety base. Acetate film is not inflammable. It ignites with difficulty and smoulders rather than burns. Most problems associated with safety film are the result of incorrect storage and misuse rather than inherent chemical instability. Polyester tape is thought by many to have greater strength than even cellulose triacetate, and is widely used for the manufacture of videotape. Its recent introduction, however, means that long-term durability of videotape is uncertain.

Appraisal

When making films, businesses have tended to concentrate on industrial films promoting the company as a whole or on films advertising particular products, and there has been an enormous growth recently in the use of videos for training and promotional purposes. In most cases therefore both films and videos will be found in the marketing, sales and personnel departments. The 3 major considerations that must be borne in mind when appraising film records are the technical quality of the record, the equipment needed to access it and whether or not there is any material to identify the film or explain the circumstances surrounding its production.

Cellulose nitrate film clearly presents a technical problem, and tests should be made to identify it. The same identification test may be used as for cellulose nitrate photographic film (see p. 194). However, a single reel of film may be made of different types of base, and margin markings which say 'safety film' or 'nitrate film' should be treated with caution. As soon as cellulose nitrate film is identified, specialist advice should be sought from the National Film Archives or local repositories which hold filmed records.[3]

Colour film also poses particular preservation and appraisal problems. Coloured images are considerably less durable than black and white images and will eventually fade completely. Some colours fade faster than others, and, although this process can be slowed by storing film under correct conditions, it cannot be halted. The only certain way to preserve the colour in films is to make a black and white separation negative of each of the three basic colour images used in the film, which can be used to build up a print in the original colours. The costs of long-term colour preservation need to be balanced against the administrative, legal and research value of the film.

The aim of the appraisal process is to locate and identify the best possible preservation material – generally the original master. However, both original negatives or positives and intermediate printing materials are likely to make good preservation masters. Intermediate materials are often diversely labelled as duplicate or dupe negative, duplicating positive, fine grain master, interpos, interneg and colour reversal intermediary. Often a company will only hold show-prints, as the original printing materials were retained by the production company or processing laboratory. Reel and can labels may bear the names and addresses of these agencies.

Film should only be accessioned if technical equipment exists for it to be made available to researchers. If the long-term cost of maintaining this access is not supportable, the business archivist should consider donating the film to a specialist film archive.

The research value of filmed records is enhanced if accompanying documentation exists to illustrate the circumstances surrounding the production of the film. All production files should be accessioned with the film. If such material does not exist, the subject matter of the film should be assessed carefully to determine whether a decision to retain it is justified.

Storage

Environmental conditions

All film must be protected from unsuitable environmental conditions, atmospheric pollution, light and excessive handling. Unless all film is to be stored at a temperature low enough to slow down the colour-fading process, colour film should be stored separately from black and white film. Both must be kept where the temperature and relative humidity can be controlled and stabilized. If film dries, it becomes shrunk and brittle, and if conditions are too damp, the gelatin layer on the film becomes sticky, encouraging mould growth and ultimately destroying the emulsion layer completely. Over-humid conditions can also cause 'vinegar' syndrome, which affects safety film base and can destroy it. This problem is so-called because of the strong acetic acid smell characteristic of such decomposition.

International Standard 5466[4] recommends that when several film types are stored within the same area, the relative humidity should be constant at 30 per cent and the temperature should not exceed 20°C. It strongly recommends a storage temperature of 2°C or below for colour film. The National Film Archive in Britain, however, suggests that black and white safety film should be stored at no more than 13°C and at a relative humidity of about 50 per cent. Colour film should be stored at a maximum of 5°C and videotape at 18°C to 19°C and at a relative humidity of between 40 per cent and 60 per cent. Certain environmental recommendations have, however, been revised recently, and it is now thought that safety film and videotape should be stored at a relative humility of no more than 30 per cent to 35 per cent, and colour film should be stored at a temperature of 5°C to 10°C.

Packaging

All film is particularly vulnerable to damage caused by atmospheric pollution and excessive exposure to light. Reels should be stored horizontally in metal or, preferably, plastic cans. As even minute specks of dust or grit can cause serious damage, handling and projection should be kept to a minimum. A film should not be run through a projector unless it is known that a better preservation master exists. Video cassettes should be stored vertically in their protective jackets in a clean environment. Videotape is even more vulnerable to dust and dirt than film. It is too early to make categorical statements on the long-term storage properties of videotape, but the durability of both the magnetic coating on the tape and the crude, plastic mechanisms used in the manufacture of the cassettes are questionable. Early videotapes are also prone to print-through of the signal from one layer to another. The type of videotape most suitable for preservation purposes is broadcast standard tape.

Retrieval

Archived film records must be available for viewing. This requires not only specialized viewing equipment, but also a separate viewing room. The major problem with accessing material held on video is the great proliferation of machine formats and sizes. The archivist should work to reduce these to a minimum.

Ideally 3 copies of a film should be retained. The preservation copy should be used only to produce a duplicating copy and should be stored separately. Reference copies should be made from this duplicating copy, perhaps as videotapes. All reels and cassettes should be labelled as either preservation, duplicating or reference copies. Some abrasion of a film's surface occurs each time it is viewed, causing scratching of the base and emulsion. Films should always be shown on well-maintained equipment in environmentally controlled, clean conditions.

All film needs to be catalogued in sufficient detail to preclude the need to view it merely to determine whether or not it will be useful to the researcher. This will save time and prevent unnecessary usage of the film. Adequate cataloguing will include the title and synopsis of the film and, ideally, shotlists. The date and details of the film-maker should be included if known. Each reel or cassette should be listed and numbered separately, and its technical details noted.

Sound recordings[5]

Any business archivist, not just those working for a company that manufactures sound recordings as part of its product range, may be expected to preserve and make available archives held in the form of sound recordings. These could range in content from the recordings of chairmen's speeches and reminiscences of former employees to advertising jingles. Such recordings will be on disc or tape. If any sound recordings on wax cylinders or wax discs are discovered, advice should be sought from an expert conservator. Information on the care of all kinds of sound archives is also available from the National Sound Archive.[6]

Physical characteristics

Discs

Discs were first introduced around 1900. Originally coated with shellac or wax, the technology has progressed to acetate, to vinyl, and more recently to the compact disc (CD) made of plastic-coated metal. Shellac discs, which vary in core composition from cardboard to vulcanized rubber, are inherently stable but very brittle and liable to warp, characteristics that increase with age. Incorrect handling will cause surface damage and scratching, and the discs are prone to mould growth.

Acetate discs, which appeared in the 1930s, were made of metal, usually aluminium, or more rarely glass, coated with cellulose nitrate or occasionally a gelatin-based lacquer. Metal cores may be visible at the central hole, and there are often one or more additional holes close to the centre, although these may be obscured by the label. Acetate discs were also called 'instantaneous' discs, as they were designed to be directly cut on a recording machine. Each is therefore likely to be unique. The record industry still uses acetates to cut master discs, but tape is used for direct recordings. The size of acetates varies, but a diameter of 25cm or 30cm is most common. They resemble black vinyl discs but are stiffer. Acetates are unsuitable for permanent storage and should be copied on to tape.

Vinyl discs made of polyvinyl chloride were commercially available from 1945. They are not as brittle as shellac and are less unstable than acetates, but must be handled carefully as they are susceptible to warping and surface scratching.

Compact discs first appeared in 1983. They consist of a layer of aluminium sandwiched between, and bonded to, layers of plastic. When launched, the manufacturers made extravagant claims of 'lifetime' durability, which are already being treated with some degree of scepticism. The aluminium layer will corrode easily on contact with water vapour, the plastic is permeable and warping occurs in direct heat or sunlight.

Wire

Wire-recorders operated on the same principle as tape-recorders, and enjoyed some popularity in the United Kingdom and United States of America during the 1940s and 1950s. Recording wire is similar in appearance to light-gauge fuse wire, and is usually found on spools of 2 to 3 inches diameter. Wire is an obsolete format, and recordings should be copied for preservation on to modern tape.

Tapes

Tape-recording was developed in Germany in the 1930s and became increasingly common for all purposes in the 1940s and 1950s, gaining complete supremacy as a location recording medium in the 1960s. Until the advent of modern polyester-based tape in the 1960s, sound tape-recordings were made of cellulose acetate. This is not a good storage medium as it shrinks disproportionately on a reel, can snap and is prone to mould. Polyester-based standard play tape is the most appropriate medium for long-term storage of tape-recordings. It is robust and better able to withstand print-through (i.e. the transfer of magnetic information from one layer to the next in a reel).

Tapes are stored either on reels or in cassettes. One-quarter inch wide reel tape and one-eighth inch wide cassette tape are the most commonly encountered. Early reel tape was recorded with a single track. Two-track or stereo recording appeared in the 1950s and four-track was popular in the 1960s and early 1970s. The now universal form of compact cassette was introduced by Philips in 1964, and has been successfully adapted for stereo recording since the mid-1970s. Reel tapes should be used for archival purposes, as cassette tape is too thin and fragile for permanent preservation and the cassettes are easily affected by damp (causing tapes to stick) and mechanical failure. The size and compactness of cassettes make them ideal, however, for duplicate or reference copies.

The latest technological development in sound recording is digital audio tape (DAT). The quality of sound is higher than with more conventional analogue recordings, and recordings can be recopied without loss of quality. However, digital audio tape is still an unknown quantity in terms of durability and for the foreseeable future the expense of both the tape and the machines on which they must be played will limit their use.

Appraisal

If a company is manufacturing tapes and records as part of its product range, there will usually be a programme for archiving one copy of each disc or tape produced. In all other companies sound recordings will not generally be produced in large quantities. They will be found most often in the marketing and public relations departments, where recordings are made for television or radio advertising. The company secretary's office or the chairman's office may also have tapes of speeches or presentations made on notable occasions.

The basic principles of archival appraisal are still relevant in dealing with sound recordings. The archivist must have access to the necessary equipment to check, copy and conserve the recording and make it available to researchers. All sound recordings must be assessed to determine the quality of the recording, as inaudible tapes and scratched discs are of little use to researchers. While conservation techniques may improve recordings, they are costly, and this expense must be weighed against likely research use. Playback machines must be compatible with the form of the recording. If suitable expertise and equipment are not available in-house, advice should be sought from a local sound archive or the National Sound Archive.

A single sound recording may exist in alternative formats. The tape of a meeting may have been transcribed or a speech at an opening of a new factory may also have been filmed. The existence of such duplicates should influence appraisal decisions.

An assessment of the subject matter of the recording will need to be made. If it is likely to be of little interest to either internal or external researchers there is little point in accessioning the recording. If it is of particular significance, however, this may well outweigh other problems, e.g. in terms of the quality of the tapes or discs involved.

The archivist must have a clear idea of the circumstances surrounding the recording. The speaker, subject matter, occasion and date must be identifiable if the archivist is to be able to catalogue the recording and brief potential researchers. To ensure that this is possible all related documentation, such as cue sheets and photographs, should be accessioned with the recording. Archivists accessioning sound recordings must be aware of the implications of the copyright laws.

Storage

Environmental conditions

Both discs and tapes need to be stored under controlled environmental conditions, as the slightest damage will immediately result in a loss of information. In Britain vinyl discs are considered to be of archival quality, but in the United States of America a more cautious attitude prevails and polyester-based magnetic tape is used for all long-term preservation of sound recordings.

Discs should be stored at a constant temperature between 10°C and 21°C and a constant relative humidity between 40 per cent and 55 per cent. Fluctuations in both should be avoided. In order to protect them from dust and ultra-violet light, discs should be stored inside a polyethylene inner cover which should then be placed inside an outer cover made of card. The outer cover should have a flap that folds over the opening. Inside these covers discs, of the same size, should be stored vertically on shelves in metal cabinets divided by supports into sections of 150mm to 225mm. They should be packed sufficiently close together to prevent warping. The shelves and uprights should be free of protruding bolts and lugs, and the cabinets should have openings to allow for the easy circulation of air. Original covers and other associated material should be stored separately.

Acetate and cellulose tape will shrink and warp if conditions are too dry, so they should be kept at a constant temperature between 4°C and 16°C and a relative humidity between 40 per cent and 60 per cent, ideally around 40 per cent. A range of 35 per cent to 45 per cent is recommended for polyester tape. Tapes should be kept away from magnetic fields (field sources include magnetic locks, lightning conductors and speaker cones) in a fire-proof area. If fire does break out, carbon dioxide fire-extinguishers should be used on burning tapes, as powder and water extinguishers will cause irreversible damage. Audio tape is made of the same material as computer tape and requires the same standard of storage. Purpose-built computer tape storage areas may therefore be a logical place to store tape recordings.

Packaging

Each tape should be wound on plastic reels and kept in a container of non-corrosive metal, inert plastic or acid-free cardboard, which should be placed inside a soft, self-sealing polyethelene bag. Tape containers should always be stored vertically on metal racks. They should be checked regularly for sound quality and rewound every 12 months at playback speed to reverse the curvature of the tape and relieve sticking.

All recording formats are fragile and suffer a relatively high loss of quality through normal use. The master copies of discs and tapes should therefore be played once only to create a duplicate copy, ideally on standard play reel-to-reel tape. The duplicate copy can be used to produce further copies on either reel-to-reel tape or cassettes. All equipment must be kept dust-free and tape heads and guides regularly cleaned and demagnetized. Recordings should always be handled with care using cotton or plastic gloves.

Retrieval

Retrieval problems associated with sound recordings stem from the fact that they are inaccessible without technical equipment. To minimize the cost of this equipment, sound recordings, which can occur in a variety of sizes with different densities and playback speeds, may be reduced to a standard format.

As the contents of tapes and discs are not immediately obvious, particular reliance will be placed on finding aids. There is no one cataloguing system that is appropriate to every collection of sound recordings, but whichever system is adopted must be used consistently. On accessioning, the date, speaker/performer, occasion and brief subject matter of the recording must be noted and each disc or tape given a unique reference number. All copies of the recording, whatever the format, should be given this number. Recordings should be labelled with a reliable permanent, spirit-based marker, such as Indian ink, on both the disk label or tape spool and the outer container. Once accessioned in this way, a more complete catalogue entry should be compiled, particularly if the tape forms part of an oral history project. Although users may find transcriptions of sound recordings very convenient to browse through, it must be remembered that they are very time-consuming, and therefore expensive, to produce.

Microforms

Microforms are reduced-size film images of original documents. In the past photographic processing was required to transfer data from paper to film, but with the advent of computer output microfilm (COM), digital data can be transferred directly from a computer on to microfiche or, less commonly, microfilm.

Microforms have long been used by businesses to store large amounts of data cheaply, to allow simultaneous reference to data by several users and to safeguard original documents. A business archivist is therefore likely to encounter non-current records in microform and must be aware of the particular problems posed by this format.

The technology can also be used to great advantage by the business archivist in administering the archive. When deciding to microfilm documents that have been accessioned in a different format, the archivist will be prompted by one or more of the following considerations:

- To preserve documents that are fragile or likely to be damaged by excessive handling.
- To preserve documents that contain elements that are inherently self-destructive, e.g. dyeline drawings that will fade on exposure to light.

- To facilitate use by enabling copies of archival material to be sent through the post.
- To enable multiple access to archival material and allow central records to be used locally.
- To facilitate reference to large unwieldy items, such as maps and technical drawings.
- To save space by housing originals in cheaper accommodation out of head office.
- To create security copies of very important archival records.
- To enable the publication of archival material and finding aids.

Unless a microfilming unit exists within the company, the archivist will use a commercial bureau to produce microforms. When commissioning this work, several bureaux should be asked to quote for a specific job, and the archivist must feel confident that the security of the records, and of the data they contain, is safeguarded. The work should be carried out in accordance with the relevant British Standard recommendations.

Physical characteristics

The three types of micrographic film currently available are silver halide, diazo and vesicular. Silver halide film is the oldest of the three and has long been manufactured to rigorous standards of permanence. It is therefore generally used to store master copies. It must, however, be treated carefully. Unlike vesicular film, it is prone to fungus and can develop microscopic blemishes. It is also sensitive to water and humidity damage to a greater extent than other film materials. Duplication changes the polarity of the film, so that a negative master will produce a positive duplicate. Diazo film involves the use of ammonia as a developing agent, and is not considered to be of archival standard because of possible fading of the dyes and staining of the clear portions of the film. It is, however, the most widely used film for reference purposes and low-cost production of duplicates. There is no agreement on the length of time the image on diazo film will survive – estimates vary from under 10 years to over 100 years. Duplication does not alter the polarity of the film. Vesicular film may withstand adverse conditions of use better than silver halide film, but it is not as stable as diazo film. The film image consists of small bubbles within a plastic layer. As the permanence of the bubbles is unknown, vesicular film cannot be considered to be archival. Duplication alters the polarity of the film. Microfilm exists in a variety of formats – roll film (16mm, 35mm and more rarely 105mm), microfiche, jacketed microfilm, cartridges, cassettes, aperture cards and Computer Output Microfilm (COM).

Microfilm is notoriously difficult to date because the technology has changed very little over the past 40 years. Accompanying packaging provides the clearest indication of dating, although there are general rules, e.g. film on metal spools is likely to be earlier than film on plastic spools and black and white film with sprocket holes predates black and white film without sprocket holes.

Appraisal

Before microform records can be appraised they have to be identified. The nature of the format can lead to complications of identification of which the business archivist should be aware:

- Microfilming blurs the distinction between types of paper record and it is not immediately clear whether books, files or individual sheets have been microfilmed. The film or fiche will have to be checked frame by frame to identify the records, their covering dates, provenance and arrangement.
- Costs of microfilming will have been kept down by filling one film before beginning another. The division between rolls or fiche will not therefore necessarily reflect the divisions between different paper records. Again the archivist can only be confident of an accurate identification after checking frame by frame.
- If microfilming in the company as a whole or in particular departments was not managed, controlled and documented strategically, the content and purpose of the microfilmed records will have been obscured. This is a common problem, as many companies have, in the past, introduced a blanket policy of microfilming in the mistaken view that this alone would solve an existing and persistent space problem.

Once identified, microforms can be appraised in exactly the same way as paper records. The business archivist will need to make a judgement on the archival value of the records, based on an assessment of evidential and informational values. The assessment will, however, have to be made on the basis of the entire roll or fiche rather than on the merits of particular frames. Sampling decisions will also have to be made on this basis. The smaller format may, however, allow the archivist to keep a complete series of records rather than to sample.

Storage

Environmental conditions

The essential requirements for the storage of microfilm are:

- Filtered, purified air, circulated by means of forced draught.
- Temperature of between 15°C and 25°C (ideally not exceeding 20°C).
- Relative humidity of between 20 per cent and 40 per cent.

- Avoidance of rapid changes in both temperature and relative humidity.
- Protection against fire and water.

Microforms can be damaged in a number of ways. Low relative humidity causes them to become brittle; warm, damp conditions encourage mould growth; dust scratches the image; and chemical contamination causes the image to fade. They should be handled carefully and protected from malfunction of reading equipment. In many cases of damage the best course of action is to refilm, but if this is not possible, professional conservation advice should be sought. Damage can be minimized by keeping a reference copy on cheap, tough film, a duplicating copy for producing further copies, and a master copy on silver halide film for security. If the master film is processed and stored to archival standards, it should last a very long time. Microfilm that is in use should, however, be checked regularly and copied as necessary.

Packaging

In the correct environmental conditions, microform can be kept in closed, non-airtight containers made of non-corroding materials, such as inert plastic. As certain chemicals cause film to deteriorate and the image to fade, all containers must be free of bleaching agents, glues and varnishes. Roll film should be mounted on inert reels or cores, and supported by acid-free paper slips and ties and not by rubber bands or paper clips. Fiche should be stored in acid-free envelopes.

Ideally microforms should be inspected regularly. A sample of 20 per cent of each format should be inspected every 2 years. Two per cent of each sample should be from material included in a previous inspection. The frequency of inspection should be increased if deterioration is found, and the cause should be identified and remedied. New copies should be made of all material that has deteriorated. This is a very high standard of inspection and one which a business archive with large collections of microform and slender resources may find difficult to achieve.

Retrieval

Any retrieval system depends on adequate listing of information. This is particularly true of data held in microform as it cannot be read without a machine, the contents are not obvious from the format and it is difficult to browse through rolls of film or sheets of fiche. The user will therefore rely heavily on finding aids and labelling to access particular rolls or fiches and even particular frames of information. Essential information includes the title, covering dates and provenance of the data held, and the contents should be described in sufficient detail to remove the necessity of accessing the microfilm to determine its contents. The status of the microfilm, whether it is the security, duplicating or reference copy, should also be stated. Similarly each separate box containing roll film, cartridge, cassette or aperture card should be clearly marked. Microfiches are usually labelled across the top edge and there is space on aperture cards on which to write or print information. Data held in miniaturized form are far more likely to be lost if not comprehensively listed than data held in paper format.

Unless all the microfilming in a company was managed strategically, the business archivist could be confronted with not only film and fiche, but also different sizes of film held in either cartridges, cassettes, jackets or aperture cards. If intended for archival storage, they should all be converted to silver halide film, ideally to a single format and one film width. The business archivist must avoid the situation whereby a range of different, increasingly obsolete equipment is being kept simply to access archival records. This is expensive and grossly inefficient. As readers and printers are more readily available for 16mm film, it would make sense to convert all film to that size. On the other hand, fiche readers have a number of advantages over roll-film readers; they are cheaper, more reliable, smaller, much easier to use and service and are available in a far greater range of models than roll-film readers.

As there is a variety of equipment on the market the business archivist will need to determine how many readers are needed, whether reader-printers are necessary or whether readers alone will suffice, what degree of magnification is required, and the sort of service agreement that will have to be arranged, before placing an order. Contact should be made with a number of suppliers and the archivist should ascertain whether any unneeded machines exist within the company.

The researcher who does not have a clear idea of the information required will feel inhibited or reluctant to look at records held in microform. Their physical format makes browsing difficult, prolonged use can cause eyestrain (although this can be minimized by using negative rather than positive film), and, unless adequate space is made available, it can be difficult to take notes. Also, as one 100 foot roll of 16mm film can contain up to 20,000 frames, a single reader can monopolize large amounts of data. Where the level of use is high, microforms could be presented to the user as fiche even if the original is on roll film. Initial hesitancy can be overcome by keeping equipment as simple as possible and giving clear, concise instructions. In order to conserve the records, readers should be kept clean and users directed not to touch the image.

Microforms are sadly lacking in visual impact and are entirely inappropriate for such public relations purposes as exhibition and publication. If good visual material is held in microform, it would need to be reconverted into paper format to realize its potential. Microfilming has a considerable advantage over alternative means of information storage, in that its archival properties have been tried and tested. Silver halide film can last for longer than some types of modern paper and it will be some time before the life of optical discs can be predicted with certainty.

Computer-readable records

Data held in a computer-readable form consists of magnetic or electronic impulses on a base material which can only be directly accessed and read by a computer. Magnetic tape and discs are now commonplace in the business environment, and the technology is advancing rapidly with the advent of document image systems and optical disc storage.

Physical characteristics

Magnetic tape

Magnetic tape is still the commonest means of storing data recorded digitally by a computer. It consists of a continuous strip of plastic material coated with a binder and a layer of magnetic oxide. Tape is available in a variety of lengths and widths, but the standard is 2,400 feet long and half an inch wide. Data is stored sequentially by selective magnetization of the surface, and is measured in terms of the number of characters recorded on one linear inch of tape. This is referred to as bits per inch, or bpi. The tape is wound on a reel made of inert plastic, usually with a diameter of $10\frac{1}{2}$ inches. Magnetic tape is essentially unstable, and data held in this form needs to be protected.

Discs

If data are 'on-line', they are stored inside a computer on a hard disc. When not needed for immediate use, they can be removed from current storage to storage on either magnetic tape or on a disc. A disc is a flat circular piece of metal or plastic which has a magnetic coating similar to that on ordinary recording tape. Tracks are available on each surface and data in a digital form are written to or read from these tracks. Discs may be floppy or hard. Floppy discs are removable, flexible and of lower capacity than hard discs (also known as fixed discs), which are non-removable. Both discs and magnetic tape are re-usable, as they can be remagnetized any number of times.

Optical discs

A more recent development in mass data storage is optical disc technology. Essentially, a semiconductor laser reads and writes data on the sensitive recording layer of an optical disc made of glass or metal. During the write operation the laser burns pits into this layer, causing an alteration in its reflectivity. To read data, light is reflected or not, depending on the presence or absence of a pit. Reflected light is converted into binary format. The optical digital disc is the more common form of this technology found in a business context, but videodiscs and compact discs may also be encountered.

Optical digital discs are increasingly being used in business to replace both paper and microfilm. Data are either scanned or digitized by a computer and stored on a disc. Indexing fields, if required, are set up by the user and completed as the document is entered. The index is stored separately on the computer's hard disc, and related documents are retrieved automatically. Documents can be recalled to the computer screen or printed as hard copies. For documentation in current use, the great advantage of optical disc storage is the high density of data that can fit on to one disc. The available sizes of disc are 5¼ inches and 12 inches in diameter, and the manufacturers claim that approximately 8,000 A4 images can be stored on the small disc and up to 50,000 images on the large disc. This high capacity may soon be increased. The discs are inherently stable, requiring no special maintenance.

The optical systems in commercial use are based on WORM technology (Write Once Read Many times). Redundant items of information can be dropped from the indexing system and thereby become irretrievable, but the physical image is still held on the disc. Fully erasable discs which can be rewritten are likely to be the next stage in the development of this technology. Other systems include videodiscs which are used for storing pictorial images with sound, and CD-ROM or compact, Read-Only Memory, discs, which are commonly used to store music but can also be used to record textual information in a digital form.

Appraisal

Computer-readable records will be found throughout a business. Computers are commonly used to store and analyse large amounts of standardized data and to aid design. In addition, the spread of word-processing and electronic mail means that in many businesses these are the standard means of generation and communication of information.

It is no longer safe for the business archivist to assume that the important documents will be only those that are eventually converted to a paper format. In the context of increasing sophistication of computer systems the business archivist needs to be proactive, to find out what is being generated electronically, what is never converted to paper and what is simply erased for re-use of tapes or discs. The business archivist must intervene at the record creation stage to ensure that significant data are safeguarded for permanent preservation along with complete and relevant documentation. Many records held in computer-readable format are continually being updated. The business archivist has therefore to decide at which stage a record is appropriate for long-term storage – generally a choice between periodic 'snapshots' of the data as they change, or capturing the data only at the end of the project.

The business archivist cannot assume either that it is not worth keeping records in computer-readable form because of their hardware and software dependency, or that all data in this format can be kept because they take up so little storage space. As with records in any other format, the business archivist will have to exercise the skills of appraisal, beginning with an assessment of the informational and evidential value of the record. Those chosen for permanent preservation must:

- Have a high informational content.
- Not be preserved elsewhere in a more easily accessible format.
- Be susceptible to analysis for purposes other than those for which they were generated.
- Not be aggregated to any significant degree.
- Have adequate accompanying documentation.

Appraisal decisions must be set in the context of the particular format of the record and the problems this poses. It is necessary to check tapes and discs to ensure that all or part of the data has not been corrupted or destroyed since creation. If data are damaged, decisions must be made on the proportion of illegibility which renders the tape or disc inappropriate for long-term storage. Advice, and in some cases acceptance of data sets on deposit, can be obtained from data archives such as the Economic and Social Research Council Data Archive at Essex University.

The hardware and software dependency of computer-readable records will add considerably to the cost of keeping such material. Any destined for permanent preservation should be reduced to a standard format, and arrangements made for periodic copying to ensure that the records do not become dependent on obsolete technology. Storage costs are increased by the need to create back-up copies and to control the environment in which tapes are stored. An assessment of long-term costs will therefore play a far more important role in the appraisal of computer-readable records than textual records.

A further issue that arises with computer-readable records is the fact that many tapes or discs will contain confidential and sensitive data. An anonymized version of a computer tape can be created either by deleting the confidential and sensitive information on the tape that is made available to users or, in the case of coded data, not providing the user with appropriate identification. The Data Protection Act 1984 does not inhibit preservation of computer-readable data for historical purposes, but requires registration of the application if personal information is held, data subjects to be allowed access to their records, and controls on disclosure of information to third parties.

Storage

Magnetic tape

Magnetic tape and discs are not considered to be ideal for long-term storage of data, but the risk of corruption can be decreased by making two copies of the tape or disc in different disc drives and by storing them separately. Estimates of the life of a tape vary from 12 to 20 years. The electro-magnetic signals attached to the tape can fade with time, and can also print through it to corrupt signals elsewhere. The British government code of practice for archival magnetic tape recommends annual transcriptions of tapes and rewinding and retensioning every 6 months, regardless of physical appearance.[7] In the absence of magnetic tape manufactured to archival standards, the only alternative to a programme of transcription and rewinding is to convert the data into a more stable medium, such as silver halide COM.

Controlled environmental conditions are essential for the long-term storage of magnetic tapes. Storage areas must be air-conditioned and kept free of dust and dirt. The temperature must be kept at a constant rate between 18°C and 22°C and the relative humidity should be stable between 35 per cent and 40 per cent. Frequent or extreme fluctuations in temperature and relative humidity should be avoided, as they will accelerate the deterioration of tape. Tapes must also be protected from high density magnetic or electrical fields, which can corrupt the signal. A tape or disc that is to be used in conditions of temperature or relative humidity different from those in which it is stored should be allowed to acclimatize for at least 24 hours before it is removed from its container.

All tapes should be stored vertically in protective cases. The containers should be transparent, non-magnetic and resistant to heat, moisture and dirt. As tape can be damaged by use, it is important to keep equipment clean and dust-free. Handling should be kept to a minimum, and should only be attempted with the use of lint-free gloves. Once damaged, data on a tape cannot be retrieved. Back-up copies should therefore be kept, updated regularly and stored in a different location.

Optical discs

Optical discs are physically robust and require no special storage conditions. However, as the technology is so recent, it is impossible to substantiate the manufacturers' claims of a life expectancy between 10 and 40 years. Tests to assess the suitability of optical discs as an archival medium have been implemented by the Public Record Office. No definite recommendations have yet been forthcoming, although there docs appear to be agreement that data will last longer on optical discs than on magnetic tape. For the foreseeable future it would appear that archiving optical discs commits the archivist to a regular programme of checking and possibly copying.

Retrieval

All accessioned computer-readable records must be accompanied by documentation explaining the structure and content of the data set and the operating system on which it was compiled, as well as procedures (with samples of paperwork) for the collection of the original data and its conversion to computer-readable form. The documentation should be sufficiently comprehensive to obviate the need for the user to access the tape or disc to determine its appropriateness and should act as a basic guide to the data. Both the records and the accompanying documentation should be listed in the repository's finding aids.

Tapes and discs will frequently contain different, unrelated data files. These must be indexed and cross-referenced in finding aids to ensure that data are not lost. If it is intended to allow users access to a complete tape, its confidentiality or sensitivity must be carefully assessed. Thought must be given to how the user will access computer-readable records. Will they be given access to a complete tape, will particular data sets be compiled especially for the user and will information be copied for the user?

All computer-readable records should be reduced to a standardized format, so that varying hardware and software do not have to be kept merely to access archived records. The business archivist must be careful not to be overtaken by technology. Developments in computer technology will not stop at optical discs, and businesses will always be ready to apply appropriate new technology to their business operations. For these reasons it is vital for archivists to keep up to date with new technology and its applications and be prepared to play an active role in the choice, design and management of the computer system used by their organization. A business archivist must be able to influence and inform record creation and record-keeping whatever the format.

Notes

1 Tom Collings of Camberwell College of Arts kindly assisted in the drafting of this section.
2 Roger Whitney of the National Film Archive kindly assisted in the drafting of this section.
3 The National Film Archive is a division of the British Film Institute and is based at 21 Stephen Street, London W1P 1PL. Local collections of film archives are listed in E. Oliver (editor), *Researchers' Guide to British Film and Television Collections* (British Universities Film and Video Council, London, 1985).
4 International Organization for Standardization, *ISO 5466: Photography –*

Practice for the Storage of Processed Safety Photographic Film (International Organization for Standardization, Switzerland, 1980).

5 Alan Ward of the National Sound Archive kindly assisted in the drafting of this section.

6 The National Sound Archive is based at 29 Exhibition Road, London SW7 2AS. Local collections of sound archives are listed in L. Weersinghe (editor), *Directory of Recorded Sound Resources in the United Kingdom* (British Library, London, 1989).

7 Civil Service Department, 'Recommended procedures for the care and maintenance of magnetic tape', *Central Government Code of Practice 14* (London, 1976). There are no British or International Standards regarding the archival storage of magnetic tape.

Further reading

General

J. G. Bradsher (editor), *Managing Archives and Archival Institutions* (Mansell, London, 1988).

British Standards Institution, *BS 5454: Recommendations for the Storage and Exhibition of Archival Documents* (British Standards Institution, Milton Keynes, 1989).

M. Cook, *The Management of Information from Archives* (Gower, Aldershot, 1986).

M. Cook and M. Proctor, *Manual of Archival Description* (Gower, Aldershot, 1990).

P. Emmerson, *How to Manage your Records* (ICSA, Cambridge, 1989).

A. Pederson (editor), *Keeping Archives* (Australian Society of Archivists Inc., Sydney, 1987).

I. A. Penn, A. Mordell, G. Pennix, and K. Smith, *Records Management Handbook* (Gower, Aldershot, 1989).

M. Roper, 'Advanced technical media: the conservation and storage of audio-visual and machine-readable records', *Journal of the Society of Archivists*, 7:2 (1982), pp. 106–12.

Paper records

C. Couture and J-Y. Rousseau (translated by D. Homel), *The Life of a Document: A Global Approach to Archives and Records Management* (Véhicule Press, Montreal, 1987).

D. L. Thomas, *Survey on National Standards on Paper and Ink to be Used by the Administration for Records Creation: A RAMP Study with Guidelines* (UNESCO, Paris, 1987).

Photographs

British Standards Institution, *BS 5687: Recommendations for Storage Conditions for Silver Image Photographic Plates for Record Purposes* (British Standards Institution, London, 1979).

British Standards Institution, *BS 5699: Processed Photographic Film for Archival Records*: Part 1, *Specification for silver-gelatin type on cellulose ester base*; Part 2,

Specification for silver-gelatin type on poly(ethylene terephthalate) base (British Standards Institution, London, 1979).

B. Coe and M. Haworth-Booth, *A Guide to Early Photographic Processes* (Victoria & Albert Museum, London, 1983).

T. J. Collings, *Archival Care of Still Photographs* (Society of Archivists Information Leaflet, 1983).

A. T. Gill, *Photographic Processes. A Glossary and a Chart for Recognition* (Museums Association, London, 1978).

K. B. Hendricks, *The Preservation and Restoration of Photographic Materials in Archives and Libraries: A RAMP Study with Guidelines* (UNESCO, Paris, 1984).

International Organization for Standardization, *ISO 5466: Photography – Practice for the Storage of Processed Safety Photographic Film* (International Organization for Standardization, Switzerland, 1980).

W. H. Leary, *The Archival Appraisal of Photographs: A RAMP Study with Guidelines* (UNESCO, Paris, 1985).

J. M. Reilly, *Care and Identification of 19th Century Photographic Prints* (Eastman Kodak Co., New York, 1986).

M. L. Ritzenthaler, *Archives and Manuscripts : Administration of Photographic Collections* (Society of American Archivists, Chicago, 1984).

Films

J. McBain, 'The value of moving images in recording business history', *Proceedings of the Annual Conference 1987* (Business Archives Council, 1987), pp. 85–97.

H. Volkmann, *Film Preservation: A Report of the Preservation Committee of the International Federation of Film Archives* (National Film Archive, London, 1965).

R. Whitney, 'Films in business archives', *Business Archives*, 57 (1989), pp. 47–62.

Sound recordings

H. P. Harrison (editor), *Selection in Sound Archives* (International Association of Sound Archives, Milton Keynes, 1984).

K. Howarth, *The Preservation and Storage of Sound Recordings* (Society of Archivists Information Leaflet, 1987).

D. Lance (editor), *Sound Archives: A Guide to their Establishment and Development* (International Association of Sound Archives, Milton Keynes, 1983).

A. Ward, *A Manual of Sound Archive Administration* (Gower, Aldershot, 1990).

Microforms

P. A. Barnes, *Microfilming and the Archivist* (Public Record Office, London, 1973).

M. Bottomley, 'Microfilm : making it and keeping it', *Proceedings of the Annual Conference 1987* (Business Archives Council, 1987), pp. 35–51.

British Standards Institution, *BS 1153 : Recommendations for the Processing and Storage of Silver-gelatin-type Microfilm* (British Standards Institution, London, 1975).

British Standards Institution, *BS 6498 : Preparation of Microfilm and other Microforms that may be Required as Evidence* (British Standards Institution, Milton Keynes, 1984).

M. I. Burmova and J. S. Kraitcheva, 'Microforms as archival materials abstract', *The International Records Management Journal*, 4:5 (1989), pp. 3–5.

N. E. Gwinn (editor), *Preservation Microfilming. A Guide for Librarians and Archivists* (American Library Association, Chicago and London, 1987).

International Organization for Standardization, *ISO 2803 : Photography – Silver-gelatin-type Microfilms – Processing and Storage for Archival Purposes* (International Organization for Standardization, Switzerland, 1974).

I. Moore, 'Undertaking a microfilming project : A case study', *Business Archives*, 53, (1987), pp. 21–9.

H. S. Fletcher Rogers, *Microfilm, Some Legal Implications* (Business Equipment Trade Association, London, 1985).

A. D. Smith, *An Introduction to Microfilm* (Business Equipment Trade Association, London, 1978).

Computer-readable records

L. Bell, 'The archival implications of machine-readable records', *Archivum*, 26 (1979), pp. 85–92.

British Standards Institution, *BS 4783: Storage, Transportation and Maintenance of Magnetic Media in Data Processing and Information Storage*: Part 1, *Recommendations for disk packs, storage modules and disk cartridges;* Part 2, *Recommendations for magnetic tape on open spools;* Part 3, *Recommendations for flexible disk cartridges;* Part 4, *Recommendations for magnetic tape cartridges and cassettes* (British Standards Institution, Milton Keynes, 1988).

M. Cook, *Archives and the Computer*, 2nd edition (Butterworth, London, 1986).

M. Cook, 'Computer generated records', *Approaches to Problems in Records Management* (Society of Archivists, 1986).

P. Emmerson, 'Computer generated records : some legal aspects', *The International Records Management Journal*, 4:5 (1989), pp. 12–6.

C. L. Geda, E. W. Austin and F. Y. Blouin (editors), *Archivists and Machine-Readable Records* (Society of American Archivists, Chicago, 1980).

M. L. Hedstrom, *Archives and Manuscripts : Machine-Readable Records* (Society of American Archivists, Chicago, 1984).

M. F. Taylor, 'The challenge of computer files : archiving and cataloguing', *Proceedings of the Annual Conference 1987* (Business Archives Council, 1987), pp. 18–34.

9

The repository

Chris Cooper

The repository is the place in which the company's archive is stored. It will consist of a strongroom or strongrooms, and it may also incorporate rooms for processing accessions of records and for storing materials and appliances needed for its functioning. It may be a separate building or part of a larger building. Its objects are:

- To ensure the permanent preservation of the archive in the best possible condition, under the company's control. It should protect it against all potential threats – water, fire, light, unsuitable atmospheric conditions, dirt and dust, mould, vermin, insects, thieves, vandals, and unnecessary wear and tear.
- To facilitate the safe and efficient use of the archive. It should store and service it economically in such a way that records can be easily found, withdrawn, brought to users and replaced, without risk of damage.

The company will already have rules and procedures for the protection of its property and will have insured it against loss or damage. However, because its archive is unique and irreplaceable, and has been selected for permanent preservation, it merits an exceptional level of protection. The repository will therefore require rules and procedures more stringent than usual, and features and equipment rarely found in ordinary business premises, whether offices or storage areas. A good repository is a specialist unit which will almost certainly have to be purpose-built or purpose-converted.

This chapter aims to give the company the information it needs to evaluate the place in which it stores its archive and, if it is below standard, to draw up a brief either to improve it or to replace it. It focuses on design, equipment and technical features; the management of the repository is covered only when it relates to these matters. It sets out the highest standards, mostly derived from the British Standard on the subject, *BS 5454*[1], but tries to indicate their relative importance, since few companies will be able to achieve them all and many will have to spread improvements over several years. However, the British Standard recommendations should all be regarded as desirable objectives for inclusion in the company's archive policy.

Although the recommendations in this chapter relate to the repository, they should also be applied as far as possible to other places in which the records may be held from time to time, e.g. areas in which they are consulted, photocopied, conserved or exhibited.

The site of the repository

Company archives are usually allocated space in existing buildings. However, if a company is considering a site or sites for a new repository, whether separate or part of a larger building, it should avoid any which are:

- Liable to subsidence.
- At risk from flooding, whether from natural or man-made causes.
- Difficult of access, whether by staff and users or by vehicles used for emergency services or for delivering records.
- Near sources of atmospheric pollution, fire risks and other potential dangers, e.g. from industrial processes.
- Incapable of allowing future expansion, whether horizontal or vertical.
- At an inconvenient distance from the fire brigade or from other parts of the company to which the repository is functionally related: for example, the administrative buildings, records centre and reading room.
- Difficult to protect against thieves and vandals. For security, the ideal repository would be on an island site with a clear perimeter which could be illuminated at night, surrounded by a fence.

It is desirable that the archive is in one location, since split sites, and even separate areas within the same building, are likely to be functionally inefficient and to require the uneconomical duplication of costly features.

The repository building

Successful repositories have been established in all sorts of buildings – new and old, high and low, above ground and below, purpose-built and converted. All are acceptable, providing they can be made to meet the most important of the standards for accommodating the archive which are outlined in this chapter. The basic requirement is for a robust structure able to carry substantial loadings and providing large, open areas without too many vertical columns which might interrupt shelving layouts and workflows. However, the following general factors should be considered:

- New or purpose-built buildings are likely to be more functional, more capable of meeting requirements, and easier to prepare for possible future expansion, than old ones.
- The conversion of older buildings is likely to be more feasible for most companies, and will often be cheaper. However, experience has shown that the cost of bringing some buildings up to standard can exceed that

of building anew. No existing building should be used as a repository until its wiring and service pipework have been checked and, if necessary, replaced.

- Basements, while enabling economical site use and good thermal insulation, often present considerable problems in waterproofing, ventilation, and the disposal of water in the event of flooding.
- Buildings with large expanses of glass facing the sun will be difficult to keep adequately cool in the summer.
- Attics tend to be too hot in summer and too cold in winter.
- Locations near potential fire and flood risks – boiler rooms, water tanks, kitchens, etc. – should be avoided.

If the repository is part of a larger building, it should be a self-contained unit with regard to fire protection and security. Such a separation may anyway be dictated by other special features of the repository, such as the need for heavy floor loading and air-conditioning.

Control installations for services within the repository, such as air-conditioning, electricity and water supply – should be situated outside it, and not in a position which is accessible only through it. Ideally such services should be isolated. Pipes, ducts, electricity cables and such like should be sealed at the place where they enter the repository and at any openings in them outside the repository, so as to keep out insects and vermin.

The layout of the repository

The component parts of the repository and their layout should reflect its internal workflow patterns. The typical pattern for the movement of records is the following:

- *Loading bay or other delivery point*, for receiving accessions of records. The loading bay should give protection against wind and rain.
- *Reception area*, preferably linked to the loading bay, where accessions can be cleaned, if necessary, and inspected for mould or insect infestation and given appropriate treatment (see Chapter 12), before being allowed into the strongroom or other areas, where they might spread the infestation to records already held. The reception area should be well-ventilated and contain a table and racking sufficient to allow records to be opened out for cleaning and drying, if required. It should contain electric power points for fans and vacuum cleaners. It should be capable of being sealed off from other areas where records are stored or used, and should not share an air-conditioning or ventilation system with them.
- *Processing area*, desirable if accessions need checking, sorting, listing, labelling, boxing and such like before entering the strongroom. It

requires simple shelving, a table and chair and perhaps a lockable cupboard for storing materials. It may also be appropriate to have an additional storage room for empty boxes, spare shelves, and any other materials and appliances used in the functioning of the repository.

- *Strongroom*, for permanent storage.
- *Areas of use*: from the strongroom, records may be taken to places where they are used or processed, such as reading, photocopying or conservation rooms.

Communication routes

Ideally there should be easy and secure communication routes linking the above areas and leading to other parts of the building with which the repository is functionally related, such as the administration offices and records centre. Routes used for records should not be shared by members of the public or, ideally, by non-repository staff. If they are to be used by loaded trolleys, they should be level, without stairs, door sills or floor mats. Where a small change of level is unavoidable, a ramp should be provided. Large changes in level should be via a goods lift. Ideally communication routes should be at least 1.5m wide.

The strongroom

The strongroom is the part of the repository dedicated to the secure storage of the records, and, due to its requirements regarding security and the maintenance of a stable environment, it should not be used for other purposes. Ideally it should be big enough to hold the entire archive, with space to spare for future accessions. Dividing the records between a number of smaller strongrooms is likely to reduce operational efficiency, particularly if the rooms are widely separated. On the other hand, dividing up large spaces may be desirable in the interests of fire precautions, and if more than one environment is needed. For efficient and economical record storage, it is desirable that strongrooms are of regular shape and free of columns, buttresses and other features which may obstruct shelving layouts. If they are being newly constructed, their dimensions should be planned with reference to those of standard shelving units and recommended aisle widths.

Floors

Floors in strongrooms should be level, with nothing to obstruct the passage of trolleys. They should be hard-wearing and should not cause dust or be easily chipped. Concrete floors should be sealed. Floors should also be easy to clean, non-slippery and light in colour. As shelves loaded with records may be very heavy, floors need to be strong. The floor loading intensity will depend on the height of the shelving and on whether it is of fixed or mobile type. Evenly distributed loads exerting a force of $11KN/m^2$ are common, but when they are transferred via wheels to floor tracks, they create much higher line loads. Expert advice on floor loadings should always be sought.

Ceilings

Ceilings should be high enough to accommodate the shelves plus space for air circulation, air-conditioning ducts, light fittings and so on. *BS 5454* (section 4.8) recommends a minimum height of 2.6m.

Doors

Doors should be wide enough to allow the passage of loaded trolleys – at least 900mm – and should be without sills. They should be self-closing and lockable.

Cleaning

The strongroom should be cleaned regularly, since dust, as well as making records dirty, can carry potentially harmful mould spores and bacteria. There should therefore be sufficient electrical points for vacuum cleaners, whose nozzles should be fitted with a close mesh to prevent the suction of pieces of records. In any case such cleaners should not be operated near fragile records. Cleaning agents should not be of a kind that may cause damage to records and should not be stored in the strongroom. Cleaning staff should be trained not to carry out any activity which might harm the records, and should be supervised. The repository should be regularly inspected for signs of vermin or insects. If they are found, specialist advice should be taken on how to get rid of them.

Other strongroom features

It may be useful to provide tables or to reserve occasional empty shelves on which staff can rest records while they are identifying or consulting them. Accommodation for records location lists, which will usually be kept in the strongroom for security reasons, readers' tickets, a telephone and any other items used for the daily administration of the strongroom will also be desirable. However, work activity and traffic should be kept to a minimum in the interests of security and a stable environment. If the recommended environmental conditions are in force, the strongroom will anyway probably be too cool for staff to work in for long periods. The strongroom should be designed to provide for the rapid egress of water, in order to minimize damage from flooding, whether accidental or as a result of fire-fighting activities.

Strongroom equipment

Various types of equipment may be used for housing the records (shelving, boxes, envelopes, etc.) and for retrieving and transporting them (stools, steps, trolleys, etc.). Unsuitable equipment will increase wear and tear on the records, prolong retrieval time, and may be hazardous to staff.

Shelving

The most efficient and economical way of storing most records, whether free standing or in some form of container, is on shelving. A variety of shelving systems, capable of meeting almost all repository needs, is widely available from suppliers. In shelving systems the following terms are generally used: horizontal *shelves* are attached to vertical *uprights*; the unit of shelves between two uprights is a *bay*; a series of continuous bays forms a *run*, which can be *single* or *double sided*, depending on whether there are one or two lines of shelves between the uprights; and between runs *aisles* give access to the shelves and link up with *gangways*, which are the principal routes through strongrooms.

Shelf strength

A linear metre of records can be very heavy – up to 90kg – and the shelves and their supports and uprights must be able to bear such loads. *BS 5454* (section 9.2.1) recommends that each shelf should have a distributed safe loading exerting a force of not less than 1kN or 1.6kN/m^2.

Durability and non-combustibility

Ideally shelving should be made of sheet steel, although other non-combustible materials such as cast iron or slate are also acceptable. Wooden shelving should be avoided, because it is combustible and susceptible to insect attack. If its use is unavoidable, it should be treated to withstand fire and insects. Steel shelves, when they are used, should be covered by a stove enamelled, anti-corrosion, scratch-resistant paint.[2]

Convenience of use

Shelves should be easily adjustable at 25mm intervals, without mechanical aids, so that they can accommodate records of different sizes and be flexible for changing needs. The best systems tend to be those in which the shelves rest on brackets or clips attached to the uprights; nut and bolt systems are usually more difficult to adjust. Ideally the highest usable shelf should be no more than 1.8m above the floor, to allow easy access. In practice, however, the company will wish to make the most economical use of whatever vertical space is available, either with higher shelving, in which case safe means of access to the upper shelves will be needed, or with a two-tier shelving system. In order to allow the through storage of large documents on both sides of a double-sided bay, shelving systems which need back panels or cross-bracing, or which have raised edges at the backs of shelves, should be avoided.

Shelving runs should be no more than 10m in length before a gangway is reached. Shelving systems should have label-holders or other facilities so that every run, bay and/or shelf can be labelled. Each shelf should have a unique reference in a numerical or other logical sequence, so that a list of the locations of records can be maintained and they can easily be located, retrieved and replaced. The provision of table flaps at bay ends adjacent to gangways, on which staff can place records while they examine them, may also be desirable.

Protection for records

Shelving systems should facilitate the free circulation of air and thus prevent the formation of pockets of damp air which might lead to mould growth: top covering shelves and solid panels between or at the back of bays are undesirable; the bottom shelf should be about 150mm above the floor to allow air to circulate beneath, as well as to safeguard its contents from minor floods and to facilitate cleaning. Neither shelves nor uprights should have sharp edges or projections which may damage documents or staff (another disadvantage of most nut and bolt shelf-support systems). The distance between shelves should be the height of the tallest item plus about 20mm, to allow records to be removed and replaced without damage. Runs should be separated from outside walls by an aisle or gangway, in order to protect the records against possible damp penetration or local temperature variation; and should be at right-angles to any windows in order to minimize the risk of records being damaged by light.

The provision of economical storage on shelving

Shelving should be arranged so as to provide the maximum storage space, subject to fire regulations and convenience in withdrawing and replacing records. The standard, and usually the most efficient arrangement of shelving, is in series of parallel runs of double-sided shelves separated by aisles (see Figure 9.1a). In order to allow enough space for the removal and replacement of records, gangways should be at least 1.1m wide, and aisles at least 775mm. Aisles serving shelves containing deeper records should be 450mm plus the depth of the deepest shelf. Commercial suppliers of shelving are usually willing to draw up plans for optimal shelving layouts, if such specifications are given.

To ensure the efficient use of space in rooms with high ceilings, it may be necessary to have a two-tier shelving system, with stairs and galleries to give access to the upper levels. If so, the staircase should ideally have a straight flight and the gallery should be wide enough to allow the largest

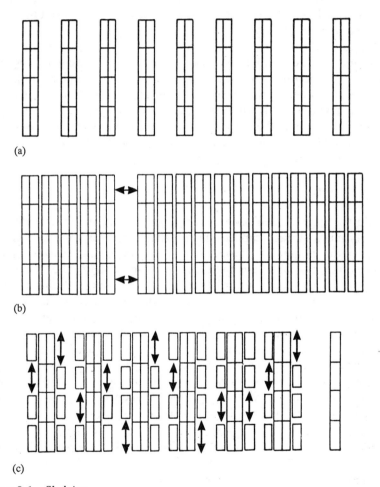

(a)

(b)

(c)

Figure 9.1 *Shelving.*
  (a) Room fitted out with traditional shelving.
  (b) Room fitted out with compact shelving, with transversal movement (compactus).
  (c) Room fitted out with compact shelving, with lateral movement.
Extracted from M. Duchein, Archive Buildings and Equipment *(K. G. Saur, 1988), with kind permission of the author.*

items stored to be removed and replaced without difficulty. The provision of a hoist to carry records between levels is very desirable.

Shelving systems of a variety of dimensions are available commercially; those based on a standard shelf length of one metre seem to be the most convenient and readily available for repository use. The more precisely the dimensions of shelves are matched to the records to be placed on them, the more economically the records will be stored; the placing of short or shallow records on high or deep shelving wastes space. The most economical storage method would be to place the records by size, that is, to sort them into size categories corresponding to standard shelf depths and standard arrangements of shelf heights, and to position them accordingly, regardless of their logical or archival sequence. This also has the advantage that the shelf intervals for runs can be set in advance and do not have to be adjusted individually to fit new accessions. However, this method requires the keeping of a detailed records location list. For the quick retrieval and replacement of records, it is probably better to arrange them in a logical or archival order according to the references they have been given, regardless of their size. Another principle of arrangement is to position records which are used most frequently, or which are difficult to move around because of their size or shape, in the places most convenient for delivery to users. The company will have to consider the advantages and disadvantages of each of these principles in relation to its own archive.

Mobile shelving

Mobile shelving is often used in repositories, since it can provide up to twice as much storage capacity in the same space as fixed shelving, by reducing the number of aisles needed to access the shelves. Several versions are available commercially, but they share the same basic principle. In closed-aisle systems (see Figure 9.1b) blocks of runs of shelves are mounted on metal tracks on the floor, with only one aisle space. When access is required, the runs are moved so that the aisle space becomes available in the required place. The movement can be effected either manually or mechanically, depending on the system used. In side-mobile systems (see Figure 9.1c) one or two runs of mobile bays, including a gap of one bay, are moved sideways in front of a static run in order to give access to the required inner bay. However, mobile shelving may not be suitable for all repositories for the following reasons:

- It creates a much higher loading in the same space and can therefore be installed only in rooms with very strong floors and supporting walls.
- It reduces the free circulation of air.
- It reduces speed and ease of access: an aisle usually has to be created and only one is accessible at a time. It is therefore not convenient for storing records to which frequent access is required.
- It cannot be used for storing documents which protrude over the edge of the shelf.

- It is unlikely to be feasible in rooms with uneven floors, of irregular shape or with many vertical support columns.
- It is more likely to malfunction than fixed shelving, and may require servicing, particularly if a mechanical propulsion system is installed.
- It is likely to be more expensive than static shelving for each shelf provided. However, some manufacturers can supply static shelving which is suitable for later conversion to mobile units, thus enabling the costs to be spread over a period of time.

In general, great care should be taken regarding the safety and stability of mobile shelving, and manufacturers' advice should be sought.

Storage

Containers

The best way of storing most types of records, particularly loose papers, files, small volumes and bundles, is in acid-free cardboard boxes designed for record use. Boxes can give protection in varying degrees against mechanical wear and tear, dust, light, fire, water, mould and rapid changes in temperature and humidity. The repository should have a range of different sized boxes, appropriate to the dimensions of the records it houses and also compatible with the types of shelving in the strongroom. However, they should not be so big that, when filled, they become too heavy or unwieldy for staff to handle. Records may also be given protection by being enclosed in sheets of acid-free paper, folders or envelopes designed for record use. Records on magnetic, photographic and other non-paper media may require different sorts of packaging (see Chapter 8). Further details and specifications for various types of storage container are given in *BS 5454* (sections 10 and 11 and appendix B).

Storing large records

Outsize volumes or files should be stored flat on shelves. Other large documents, such as maps, plans and posters, should be stored unfolded or unrolled, if possible, to avoid the risk of strain or distortion. They often therefore require special storage facilities, the most common being:

- Vertical storage cabinets. These are suitable for documents up to about 1.50×1.20m in size. They are mounted on suspension strips and hung from rods within the cabinet. However, the work of mounting the documents has first to be carried out, to a high standard (as recommended in *BS 4971*, part 2)[3]; and because of the risk of distortion to them, these cabinets should not be used for maps and drawings of accurate scale from which critical measurements may have to be taken.
- Horizontal plan cases. Documents are stored flat, preferably in

protective covers, in drawers about 40mm deep, either in conventional map-storage cabinets or in specially adapted shelving with solid sides, back and top, and fitted with a front dust cover. There should be a protective flap at the front of the drawer to prevent the records being caught against the upper surface when the drawer is opened.

- Very large documents usually have to be rolled around acid-free cardboard cylinders and stored across double-sided shelving, along more than one bay of cantilevered shelving, or on specially designed racks.[4] For protection, they can be wrapped in acid-free paper or placed in acid-free cardboard tubes.

Storing non-paper records

Records made of or incorporating materials other than paper are common in company archives and pose special storage problems. The commonest types are photographic materials, including microfilm and cinematograph film, and those on magnetic media, including computer, sound and video tapes and discs. The proportion of such records is likely to increase for the foreseeable future. Each of these types of record has its own requirements for proper storage, some of which differ from those recommended for paper records. In some cases they should be stored in different environments, and will therefore require their own rooms or compartments (see Chapter 8).

Trolleys

The repository should have an appropriate number of trolleys, with horizontal shelves, for moving records around. They should be strong, stable, readily manoeuvrable and not too large for ease of use in strongroom aisles and other confined spaces. They should be designed so that records cannot fall off them when properly loaded. Ideally their bearings should be of a type not requiring lubrication.

Stools and steps

For access to shelves higher than staff can safely reach, stools with non-slip surfaces, or mobile, self-locking, self-stabilizing steps should be supplied.

Fire precautions

Fire can destroy all types of record. Some methods of extinguishing fire can also cause damage. The repository must be designed and managed to minimize the risk of fire, and, if fire does occur, to prevent its spread, to ensure its rapid detection, and to secure its extinction in as safe a manner as possible. Because its archive is irreplaceable, the company should ensure that fire precautions for its repository are even more stringent than they would be for other buildings with a similar level of fire risk. Fire precautions are the subject of national legislation and local by-laws, and the company should consult the local fire authority and other appropriate fire experts about applying them to its repository.

Design aspects of fire precautions

Ideally the repository should be a detached building, well away from potential fire hazards. If not, it should be capable of being isolated from the rest of the building in which it is contained. In either case, the walls, floors and ceilings of the strongrooms should offer 4-hour fire resistance.[5] Doors, shutters, glazing, stairwells and lift shafts should be similarly fire-resistant. Finishing materials such as tiles, adhesives, paints and linings should be non-combustible.[6] It may be desirable to divide rooms with large floor areas (over about 200m^2) into fire compartments. Expert advice should be sought.

If the repository has an air-conditioning system, it should not communicate with air-conditioning ducts serving premises outside the repository, nor should ducts serving other premises pass through the repository. Further recommendations about air-conditioning plant are contained in *BS 5720*[7] and *BS 5588* (Part 9).[8] Doors, shutters, air-conditioning ducts and any other wall openings in the repository should close automatically in the event of a fire. Dampers in air-conditioning ducts should also prevent smoke from an external fire entering the repository. Doors and floors should not have grilles or other openings which would allow the passage of air.

Electrical plant and main switches should be located outside the strongroom. Main switches should control all electric currents, except those providing fire detection and protection. Electrical circuits should not pass through the repository unless they serve it. *BS 5454* (section 6.7.1) recommends that electrical installations in the repository should comply with the current edition of *Regulations for the Electrical Equipment of Buildings*, issued by the Institution of Electrical Engineers. They should be regularly maintained, and checked every 3 years.

Fire detection

The repository should be protected by an automatic fire-detection and alarm system.[9] Systems based on smoke or combustion gas detectors are preferable to heat- or flame-detectors, since volumes and boxes packed on to shelves are likely to smoulder and emit smoke for a period before bursting into flames. The chosen system should:

- Sound an alarm.
- Show the location of the fire on an indicator panel outside the repository.
- Transmit an alarm to the fire authority.
- Shut down the air-conditioning system and close fire shutters or doors and dampers in ducts.
- Open smoke vents.

Fire detection and fire extinction should be linked in a continuous system which detects the fire, sounds alarms, allows time for people to check if the alarm is genuine and to leave the repository, and then sets off automatic extinguishers.

Fire extinction

The repository should be protected by an automatic fire-extinction system. The common systems are:

- *Carbon dioxide.* This is effective and is unlikely to damage records. However, it is potentially lethal to staff, and requires the provision of large, heavy storage tanks. It is therefore generally considered unsuitable for repositories; it certainly should not be installed without the advice of the manufacturer and the Health and Safety authorities about preventing the system from discharging accidentally, or, if activated by a fire, when staff are still in the room.
- *Halon gas.* This is effective and does not damage records. However, it is expensive, difficult to service and potentially hazardous to the environment. It can also pose health risks to staff, about which advice should be taken. It is best suited for small areas housing valuable records. It is especially recommended for protecting records on magnetic media.
- *Water sprinklers.* This is effective and comparatively cheap, but it can damage records – not only in extinguishing a fire, but also if it leaks or is activated without cause. 'Dry pipe' systems minimize these risks. The best systems are activated only in the affected area and automatically switch off when the fire has been extinguished.
- *High expansion foam.* This is effective, but since the foam fills the entire storage area and can damage records, it is generally considered unsuitable for repositories.

In addition, portable fire-extinguishers should be installed at conspicuous points throughout the repository, preferably just inside each exit door.[10] They should be of the non-aqueous type.[11] Dry powder extinguishers should not be used on records on magnetic media; for these halon gas is recommended.[12] Fire-fighting equipment using water, both wall-mounted hoses and portable extinguishers, should be available outside the repository.

Management aspects of fire precautions

Whatever equipment is installed for the prevention, detection and extinction of fire, the repository staff should be trained to understand and to operate it. Ideally the repository should be regularly patrolled, night and day, in order that fire or fire risk is detected in good time. Smoking and the use of naked flames should be forbidden. Loose documents and other combustible materials should not be left out of their containers longer than is necessary. Film on cellulose nitrate base is highly inflammable and potentially explosive and toxic, and should not be stored in the repository; all films made before 1951 should be treated as suspect and specialist advice should be sought about their storage, copying and disposal. The fire authority should be made aware that the use of high pressure hoses and the complete soaking of records are likely to cause irreparable damage to them, and should be avoided if possible.

The environment of the repository

Records can be damaged by being stored in an atmosphere which is:

- Polluted by dust or other solid particles, or by harmful gases.
- Damp, particularly if there is also poor ventilation since this will allow the growth of mould.
- Too hot.
- Subject to large or repeated fluctuations in temperature or relative humidity.

The repository should therefore be designed to create and maintain an environment or environments favourable to the records. This is of the highest priority, since poor conditions may cause progressive, extensive, but difficult to detect damage to the whole archive over long periods.

Recommended levels of temperature and relative humidity

Optimal environmental conditions are not the same for all types of record. *BS 5454* recommends that the temperature and relative humidity (RH) for the different types should be maintained at constant levels within the following ranges:

- *Paper and parchment*: 13°C–18°C; 55 per cent to 65 per cent RH.
- *Magnetic tape (excluding computer tape)*: 4°C–16°C; 40 per cent to 60 per cent RH.
- *Magnetic media used in data-processing*: 18°C–22°C; 35 per cent to 45

per cent RH (except polyester tape, which should be 35 per cent to 45 per cent RH).

- *Gramophone records*: 10°C–21°C; 40 per cent to 55 per cent RH.
- *Still and cinematograph film, including microfilm*: this requires cool, dry conditions. *BS 5454* gives no specific recommendation but refers readers to specialist publications.[13]

BS 5454 (section 7.3.2) states that if the conditions recommended for materials other than paper and parchment cannot be met, the ranges 13°C–16°C and 50 per cent to 60 per cent RH are broadly acceptable. However, it also points out that some of the newer media require a colder and drier environment, and that specialist advice and the manufacturer's recommendations should be followed.

Companies often have safes or rooms with reinforced walls and doors and special locks, for storing records of exceptional value or confidentiality. However, the features which make them secure may also reduce the free flow of air, to the detriment of their environment. Particular care should therefore be taken in monitoring their conditions.

How to achieve the right environment

Thermal insulation

To facilitate the creation and subsequent control of a suitable environment, the repository building should give high thermal inertia. Ideally its entrances should have double doors enclosing air traps. Windows on external walls should be avoided or at least kept to a minimum. The repository should be constructed of materials which provide good thermal insulation. In some buildings environmental equilibrium may more easily be maintained if the strongroom area is divided into compartments whose doors are usually kept closed. These features will also help to reduce long-term running costs.

Protection against damp

The building should be constructed of materials which are impermeable to water. Waterproof foundations are advisable. There should be no trees or plants next to the walls. Roofs, channels, gutters, rainwater pipes and drains should be regularly inspected and maintained to prevent leakages. There should be no pipes carrying water or other fluids in the strongroom, nor passing above records within the building. If their presence is unavoidable, it is advisable to place trays underneath to carry away leaks, and to insulate any in the strongroom to prevent local temperature rises from hot pipes, or condensation drips from cold pipes. If the repository becomes damp, specialist advice should be sought about treating the dampness and preventing its recurrence.

The measurement and recording of temperature and relative humidity

The company should monitor the environment of its strongroom or strongrooms constantly. The best way of doing this is to install recording thermohydrographs, which provide a permanent record of both temperature and relative humidity, in each room of the repository, or, in large rooms, at different points within the room. Alternatively, thermometers and hygrometers should be installed, and readings recorded by staff several times a day. If regular night-time readings are not feasible, occasional sample readings should be taken, to check that there are no significant divergences from day-time conditions. Whatever measurement devices are installed, hand-held thermometers and hygrometers should also regularly be used to check conditions in other parts of the room, particularly where air circulation may be reduced, or near ceilings, where rising warm air may lead to higher temperatures. Instruments for measuring relative humidity need regular checking and calibration.

Air-conditioning

Buildings with good thermal insulation and protection against damp may allow acceptable conditions to be achieved, at least for paper records, simply by adjustments to the heating system, or by the occasional use of a humidifier, dehumidifier or fan (all of which can be hired as well as bought). However, in most cases, the installation of a mechanical air-conditioning system is likely to be necessary in order to achieve the required standards. Air-conditioning is particularly important if substantial records on photographic or magnetic media are to be stored, since these are likely to require rooms or compartments with separate environmental controls; smaller quantities can usually be accommodated in refrigerated cabinets designed for the purpose. Magnetic media also need special protection against dust, which air-conditioning can provide.

Air-conditioning systems should be able to heat or cool and humidify or dehumidify the air as required. They should also filter, clean and circulate it within the repository, as specified in *BS 5454* (section 7.4.3). They should be in continuous operation and should include an alarm to warn of breakdowns. The disadvantages of such systems are that they are expensive to install, run and service, cannot always be fitted into existing building structures, and seem to be vulnerable to malfunctioning. The company should consider the likely effect on the repository of periods of malfunctioning, and have a contingency plan to deal with them – such as opening doors and windows and using fans, heaters, humidifiers or dehumidifiers.

Electrostatic copiers should not be used in the repository. They give off potentially damaging ozone and nitrogen oxide gases.

Lighting in the repository

Good lighting is needed for the efficient use of the repository. When it is switched on, levels should not fall below 100 lux at floor level. In the strongroom, floor coverings and paintwork should be light in colour.[14] Fluorescent tubes and other lights should be placed centrally along aisles of shelving, except with mobile shelving, where they should be at right-angles. Ideally there should be a secondary lighting system, and a cache of torches, stored outside the repository, for use during power failures.

However, light also promotes the chemical degradation of all types of record, and can cause inks and pigments to fade. Ultra-violet light, present in daylight and the light from fluorescent lamps, is particularly harmful. The following precautions should be taken:

- Ideally there should be no windows in strongrooms and certainly none which admit direct sunlight. If windows are unavoidable, blinds, shutters or curtains should be used to reduce light penetration. Shelving should be placed at right-angles to walls containing windows.
- Within strongrooms, light levels should be kept as low as is compatible with safe and efficient use. Lights should be switched off when the strongroom is not in use. In a large strongroom the provision of local switches for individual gangways and aisles can allow access to them while the rest of the room remains dark. Fluorescent tubes should have ultra-violet light filters which cut off light of shorter wavelength than 400 nanometers.
- Records should be placed in boxes or other containers whenever possible.

Security

Although company records are rarely of such high financial value as to attract thieves to the repository, their irreplaceable nature merits a high degree of protection against theft and vandalism, and irresponsible use. The following measures are recommended.

Design aspects of security

- The repository should have an intruder alarm system.[15] Ideally it should be linked to a police station or security agency, providing 24-hour coverage.
- All possible means of access to the repository should be made intruder-proof. If windows are unavoidable, they should be small, barred, and

glazed with strengthened glass. Doors should be strongly constructed and equipped with thiefproof locks[16] of a type for which the issue of keys can be strictly controlled. Strongroom doors should not open into any part of the building to which the public have access. Doors of emergency exits should be designed to open only from the inside.

Management aspects of security

Proper security cannot be achieved unless it is established as a matter of company policy that the archive is a company resource which, by definition, is under the control not of those who created the records but of a single designated person – usually the company's archivist (or equivalent officer). Access to the strongroom and to its keys should be controlled by the company archivist, and should normally be restricted to repository staff. Necessary entry by others, e.g. for consultation or maintenance, should require specific authorization, and should be supervised by staff. Ideally strongrooms should not be used for anything other than storing records, and a separate room or rooms should be set aside for their consultation, whether by members of the company or by researchers from outside. Whenever records are taken out of the repository, say for use by readers or for photocopying, they should be under staff supervision and should be subject to a written control record of where they are and who is responsible for them.

Disaster-control planning

Most of this chapter is concerned with ways of preventing damage to records. Nevertheless, however carefully an archive is protected, it may still suffer a disaster which causes extensive damage. The most likely forms of disaster are flood and fire. After a flood the records are likely to be sodden, probably dirty, possibly contaminated, and very vulnerable to mould attack. After a fire the records will be fire- and smoke-damaged to varying degrees and will usually – if the fire has been extinguished by water – have suffered flooding too. If the fire has been severe or if high-pressure water hoses have been used, the records may be scattered and difficult to identify. Mould growth, leading to further damage, is likely to develop on sodden records after about 48 hours. Experience has shown that the proportion of damaged records which can be salvaged and conserved after a disaster depends on the speed and effectiveness with which it is met. It makes sense therefore for the company to protect the investment it has made in its archive by preparing a disaster-control plan, designed to mobilize human and material resources to carry out the necessary salvage and conservation procedures as quickly as possible. These procedures are described in Chapter 12. This section deals with the preliminary planning.

A disaster-control plan needs to take into account the fact that disasters:

- Tend to happen unexpectedly.
- May occur at the least convenient time – in the middle of the night, over a bank-holiday weekend, or when key members of staff are absent on leave.
- Can cause people who are overtaken by them or have to deal with their aftermath to act with less than their usual effectiveness, because of shock, panic or fatigue.

The plan should therefore try to allow for the worst possible circumstances, and should be as clear and as comprehensive as possible. It should be prepared in concert with the emergency services and with all relevant members of staff, including nightwatchmen and security guards. It should allocate specific responsibilities to staff and to deputies in the case of their absence. It should be prepared in writing, circulated to all those who need to know about it, and displayed at appropriate places in and around the repository.

The essential elements of a disaster-control plan concern the following.

People

It should include the names, work and home addresses and telephone numbers, and, where appropriate, disaster plan responsibilities of:

- Staff members and deputies.
- Plumbers, glaziers, electricians, builders, property managers, etc., whose expertise might prove useful, whether employees of the company or in business locally.
- Any others who may be able and willing to help and advise if a disaster occurs, whether on a professional, commercial or voluntary basis, such as archivists and conservators who live locally, specialist data-protection and archival damage-control companies and the local authority decontamination unit.
- The owners of the nearest deep freeze or freezer truck firm, and the nearest vacuum-drying facility capable of dealing with sodden records in bulk.

Priorities

The plan should include a location list of any salvage priorities, such as records of great value or significance, or those needed for the continuing operation of the business.

Equipment and materials

The company will need to acquire, store and record the location of equipment and materials which might be needed in a disaster, for example, water pumps, mops, buckets, polythene sheeting and bags to store sodden records, waterproof boots and clothing, crepe bandages to tie up volumes, paper and pencils, labels, blotting paper, extra trolleys, vehicles, dehumidifiers, fans, torches and portable emergency lighting systems. If it is not feasible for the company to acquire and store all such items, it should find out from whom they can be borrowed or hired at short notice. The plan should include a description of the location and means of operating any emergency electricity supply, and any stopcocks and gate valves for pipework which may affect the repository. The company will also need to ensure that there are sufficient containers and vehicles for taking damaged records quickly to specialist conservation facilities.

Space

The company needs to ensure that, in the event of a disaster, it can have access at short notice to accommodation for the following purposes:

- To allow damp records to be spread out for air-drying. This applies even if the bulk of such records are deep frozen and then taken out piecemeal for drying, since small numbers of records can occupy much space and it may take a month or more to air-dry some of them, e.g. volumes.
- If necessary, to store the records while the repository is being restored to use after the disaster.

Planning a repository

If a company is, planning a repository, whether new or converted, it will need to calculate (a) the size of the existing archive, and (b) the estimated size of additions to the archive over the desired life-span of the repository. Its calculations will need to take into account records which are to be stored in a separate compartment or room for environmental reasons, since they will affect the breakdown of strongroom space and will require separate specifications regarding air-conditioning and storage equipment. These factors are likely to increase the cost of the repository.

The size of the existing archive is probably best calculated in terms of the proposed standard shelf length in the new strongroom; if it is to be one metre, the figure required is the number of linear metre units of records which are held. The maximum height and depth of each linear metre unit will also have to be measured, since the former will govern the number of shelves per bay and the latter the depth of each bay, both of which factors will determine the floor area to be occupied by the shelving units. For shelving layouts and advice on storing records of varying heights and depths, see pp. 222–4). Separate calculations will be needed for records which will not be stored on standard shelving. The size of future additions to the archive will need to be estimated on the same principles by the company's records manager or equivalent officer, in consultation with the record-creating agencies within the company.

There is no generally applicable formula for calculating the floor area required. Much depends on the nature of the records, the shape and ceiling height of the strongroom, and the types of shelving or other storage units which are available or feasible. Careful and detailed calculations are indispensible in each case.

Ideally both the site and the structure of the planned repository building should allow further expansion at a later date, whether vertically or horizontally. It has been common for repository planners to allow for 20 to 30 years' growing space, but there has been a tendency for such space to fill up more quickly than expected, partly because its very existence can encourage those who create the records to accelerate the process by which they become archives, in order to relieve pressure on their own space. However, the increasing prevalence of records on more compact media (such as microfilm and magnetic tape) may counteract this tendency.

Drawing up an architectural brief

In briefing an architect or builder to design or convert its repository, the company will probably need to provide:

- An outline of the background to the proposed work and of its objective, with appropriate details of budget and timetable.
- A description of the purposes of the proposed repository, of the workflow patterns within it and of functional relationships with other buildings or parts of the same building.
- A description of the different rooms in the repository (if appropriate), with an indication of the space and the technical features and equipment required by each.
- A description of the services required by the repository as a whole, such as electricity, air-conditionining, etc.

In drawing up the brief, the company should take every opportunity to discuss problems and requirements with architects or builders, since they may be able to suggest methods and solutions unthought of by the company or its archivist. On the other hand, it is unlikely that they will be familiar with the special needs of archive storage, and the company should therefore ensure that they are guided by relevant publications.[17] It should also carefully scrutinize their plans and constantly supervize their work.

Notes

1 *BS 5454: Storage and Exhibition of Archival Documents* (British Standards Institution, 1989). An authoritative statement on standards. It includes reference to other British and international standards. Referred to throughout the chapter as *BS 5454*. All British Standards are available from British Standards Institution, Linford Wood, Milton Keynes MK14 6LE.

2 For the materials and finish of metal shelving see *BS 826: Specification for Steel Single Tier Bolted Shelving (Angle Upright Type)* (British Standards Institution, 1978).

3 *BS 4971: Recommendations for Repair and Allied Processes for the Conservation of Documents*. Part 2 *Archival binding* (British Standards Institution, 1980).

4 Detailed recommendations are given in *BS 5454* (Appendix A).

5 *BS 5454* (section 6.5.1) suggests consulting experts about 'appropriate' resistance. However, professional opinion in the United Kingdom generally favours a 4-hour resistance: see 'Guidelines for record repositories . . . issued by the Public Record Office, the Royal Commission on Historical Manuscripts and the Scottish Record Office' (1989), available on application to the issuing bodies.

6 *BS 476: Fire Tests on Building Materials and Structures*. Parts 3–8, 10–11, 13, 20–4, 31 (British Standards Institution, 1970–88), give further details relevant to this paragraph.

7 *BS 5720: Code of Practice for Mechanical Ventilation and Air Conditioning in Buildings* (British Standards Institution, 1979).

8 *BS 5588: Fire Precautions in the Design and Construction of Buildings*. Part 9 (British Standards Institution, 1989).

9 *BS 5839: Fire Detection and Alarm Systems in Buildings* Part 1 (British Standards Institution, 1988) gives guidance on installing and maintaining such systems.

10 See *BS 5306: Fire Extinguishing Installations and Equipment on Premises*. Part 3: *Code of practice for selection, installation and maintenance of portable fire extinguishers*. (British Standards Institution, 1985).

11 See *BS 5423: Specification for Portable Fire Extinguishers* (British Standards Institution, 1987).

12 *BS 6266: Code of Practice for Fire Protection for Electronic Data Processing Installations* (British Standards Institution, 1982).

13 Namely *BS 1153: Recommendations for the Processing and Storage of Silver Gelatin Type Microfilm* (British Standards Institution, 1975); *BS 5687: Recommendations for Storage Conditions for Silver Image Photographic Plates for Record Purposes* (British Standards Institution, 1979); *ISO 5466: Photography-Processed Safety Photographic Film-Storage Practices* (International Organization for Standardization, Switzerland, 1986); *ISO 6051: Photography-Silver Image Photographic Prints For Record Purposes-Storage Conditions* (International Organization for Standardization, Switzerland, 1986).

14 *BS 5454* (section 8.4) recommends that floor coverings should have a Munsell value of not less than 7.

15   *BS 4737: Intruder Alarm Systems in Buildings*. Part 1 (British Standards Institution, 1986).
16   *BS 3621: Specification for Thief Resistant Locks* (British Standards Institution, 1986).
17   Particularly *BS 5454* and M. Duchein, *Archive Buildings and Equipment*, 2nd edition (K. G. Saur, London, 1988). Duchein is of broader scope than *BS 5454* and particularly useful for its many diagrams and photographs showing practical solutions and applications. It also includes a model brief, designed for use in French provincial archives but nevertheless generally instructive regarding content and layout (see Chapter 2 and appendix 2).

Further reading

BS 5454: Storage and Exhibition of Archival Documents (British Standards Institution, 1989).
M. Duchein, *Archive Buildings and Equipment*, 2nd edition (K. G. Saur, London, 1988).
T. Padfield, 'Disaster planning', *Business Archives*, 55 (1988), pp. 39–47.

10

The corporate archivist and records management

Derek Charman

Records and archives management programmes

Records management has been defined as 'that area of general administrative management concerned with achieving economy and efficiency in the creation, maintenance, use, and disposal of records during their entire life-cycle'.[1] The life-cycle of a record extends from the time that it is created, whether it be on paper, microfilm, magnetic tape or disc, or in the form of a book, photograph, map, drawing, chart, or any other type of document, until the time comes for its disposal. It can be comprehended in three phases:

- *Active records* that are created and regularly used for the current business of a company, and are maintained in their place of origin or receipt.
- *Semi-active records* that are required so infrequently for current business that they should be transferred to an off-site store, preferably a managed records centre, pending their ultimate disposal.
- *Inactive records* that are no longer required for business purposes, and are due for disposal.

The records manager is primarily concerned with the management of records in the first two phases, and the archivist with the disposal of records in the third phase. They therefore look at disposal from different points of view; to a records manager it means the point at which records are no longer of any value for business purposes and can be destroyed or transferred to the archives; to an archivist it means the point at which records of long-term value to the business should be transferred to the archives for permanent preservation. Business archives can therefore be defined as inactive records preserved by the company which created and maintained them, or by their successors in title, or by an archives service, such as a local record office, in whose custody they have been placed because they are of permanent value.

The objective of a records management programme is therefore to ensure that the records of a company are managed efficiently and economically throughout their life-cycle; the objective of an archives management programme is to select and preserve records of continuing value to the company for administrative, legal, fiscal, operational, and historical purposes. These objectives are complementary, and they are best achieved as two facets of an integrated strategy.

Archives and records management strategy

The initiation of an integrated archives and records management strategy requires the full support of top management to be effective. It requires a systematic approach to all departments in order to survey the records that they create and maintain, to evaluate them for retention and disposal purposes, to develop improved and effective systems for the creation and maintenance of records throughout their life-cycle, and to select and preserve archives. It implies the existence within the company of functions responsible for archives and records management. Unfortunately many companies in the United Kingdom have neither function. Archives, if they are recognized at all, are relegated to accommodation which is useless for any purpose, let alone for the storage of archives, and they become of interest only when a significant anniversary, such as a centenary, comes round. The Business Archives Council and local archivists have done much to encourage the preservation of business archives, often by offering to take over responsibility for them, but much remains to be done to convince businesses that the preservation of historical records is justified on commercial grounds.

Records management has fared no better. Microfilming is still the first solution that springs to the managerial mind when an office is submerged under piles of paper, particularly where the computer has not only failed to stem the tide, but has served to increase the flow. Information technology is all too often employed without regard to the need for an holistic approach to the management of office records, which is impossible where control over electronic media is concentrated in one department, and control over paper, and microforms, is decentralized, perhaps even down to branch or section level. Best practice is therefore the only guide for companies that have yet to recognize the need for a strategic approach to archives and records management.

In large companies archives and records management are usually separate functions, but both should be the responsibility of a single manager to ensure proper co-ordination of the management of records within the organization throughout their life-cycle. In smaller companies the archives and records management functions usually operate as a single unit, the staff tending to specialize in either archives or records management activities. The manager immediately responsible for both functions should be a qualified archivist or records manager. In the United Kingdom formal training in records management is, at the moment, only available on university archive studies, diploma and master's degree courses, and qualified achivists are often appointed to take charge of both functions, either as corporate archivists or as corporate records managers; but it is not uncommon to find that unqualified and inexperienced individuals are appointed to fill such posts through ignorance, or in default of suitable candidates.

The position which these functions occupy within the company organization will vary according to the nature of the corporate structure. They can be assigned to the company secretary, who has a general responsibility for corporate records, but in larger companies they can be placed in the information department to support the company's general information strategy. In the latter case care must be taken to ensure that the nature of these functions is clearly understood and encouraged, because most information departments have developed out of computer departments, and their interests tend to be orientated towards a technological solution to records management problems. The right development of information technology is a matter of critical importance for all companies, but in the foreseeable future paper is likely to remain the medium in which the most important corporate records are maintained. The latest American estimates put this at between 94 per cent and 96 per cent at least until the end of the century.

The objectives of an integrated archives and records management strategy are therefore greater efficiency, cost effectiveness, and improved information retrieval. The main elements of such a strategy are:

- *Records surveys* to gather the basic information about the records created and maintained by the company.
- *Records schedules*, in which are incorporated retention periods for company records.
- *Records centres* to provide low-cost, high-density storage for semi-active and inactive records.
- *Vital records protection* to ensure the survival of records vital to the continuance of the company in the event of a disaster.
- *Archives management* to ensure the selection and preservation of the corporate archives.
- *Active records management* to improve systems for creating and maintaining active records by developing better files, correspondence, forms, reports, and directive management, and integrating information technologies into the general records management strategy.

The records survey

The objectives of a records survey are:

- To develop comprehensive records schedules in which all the recurring record series created and maintained by the company are described and retention periods specified for them, at the conclusion of which the records should be destroyed or transferred to the archives.
- To collect information which will make it possible to develop better

systems of managing records and information for the benefit of the company.

Where a records management function exists, the records survey should be carried out by specialist staff, consisting of one or more records analysts, whose job it is to compile inventories, appraise record series, and develop retention criteria for them. The job also calls for the analysis of existing systems for managing records, such as correspondence filing, in order to design and implement more efficient and cost-effective systems where appropriate. The success of a survey will depend on the degree of commitment by the company to a corporate records management strategy. The minimum commitment should be to the development of a corporate retention schedule, a corporate records centre, a corporate archive, and a vital records protection programme. A future commitment to the development of other necessary elements, such as the management of active records, should be incorporated in the general corporate strategy.

When the corporate strategy has been agreed, the head of the department in which the archives and records management functions are situated should circulate the heads of all other departments, reminding them of the objectives of the strategy, and indicating that a records survey is about to begin. It should be left to the records manager to arrange a programme of visits to departments to explain the mechanics of the survey, and to carry out a preliminary survey to determine the volume and type of records held by each department by means of a volume count. This is a simple count of the filing units (cabinets, lateral, shelving, etc.) in each room, and an estimate of the volume of records (files, print-outs, microfilm, magnetic tape, etc.) that they contain. The estimated total volume of records held by each department will enable the records manager to estimate the time required to complete the next stage of the survey, which is a detailed inventory of record series in each department, followed by appraisal, and the development of retention schedules.

The inventory

A records inventory is a complete listing of the record series created and maintained by a department, with sufficient supporting information to enable a proper appraisal and evaluation to be made of file formation and activity. A record series is a body of records arranged in a particular order – numerical, chronological, or alphabetical – such as purchase invoices or personnel record files; having the same physical form, such as maps and microfilm; or arising from a specific activity or purpose, and filed and used as a unit, such as correspondence files. Good inventory work is based on an understanding of the functions and history of the department concerned, and the records analyst should obtain as much information as possible, in the form of histories, organizational charts, and other documents bearing on the past and present activities of the department. The inventory should be conducted on the basis of a form, which should be designed to record information about a single series of records, but additional copies can be used as continuation sheets, if necessary. The form should have the following headings:

- The name of the department and the branch whose records are being inventoried.
- The name and telephone number of the person responsible for the records.
- The date that the inventory was taken.
- The title and description of the record series, including any alternative titles, and the earliest and the latest dates of the records in the series, noting any gaps.
- The type and physical description of the records, e.g. correspondence, or memoranda, book, photograph or microfilm, and arrangement.
- The nature of the equipment in which the records are stored, its location, and the volume of records in each location.
- The frequency of reference.
- The annual rate of accumulation.
- The existence of duplicates and related records.
- The purposes for which the records were accumulated and used, including any restrictions on access, e.g. confidential or secret.
- Any action taken within the department to retain or destroy records.

The order in which records should be inventoried will depend on the arrangements made with the department. It is, however, essential that every location in which active, semi-active, and inactive records are stored should be inventoried. In old-established departments it may be advantageous to start work in inactive and semi-active storage areas, where much useful information about the activities of the department can be gleaned. In most cases, however, it is better to start in the offices, where only active records should be stored. It is unlikely that many departments will be found in this happy situation, because few will have adequate off-floor storage for semi-active and inactive records, and fewer still the necessary staff to manage it. The service most often appreciated by departments is the removal of records from their office accommodation, either by destruction or storage elsewhere, which is one of the most important objectives of the inventory.

The compilation of a comprehensive inventory of the records in every department of a company is a time-consuming, and often a tedious, business, so much so that some records managers may be tempted to cut corners by relying on departmental staff to provide them with information about the record series that they hold. This can be done by means of a questionnaire, which is either filled in by the department direct or by a records analyst at a series of interviews with key departmental staff. This is not a practice to be recommended, firstly, because there can be no guarantee that the department will provide sufficient information to ensure a comprehensive coverage of the records that it holds; secondly, because a detailed inventory will pick up many small classes of records which can be easily overlooked during the compilation of a questionnaire; and, thirdly, because the analyst's progress round the department will provide a much better idea of the records management problems which are facing it than any number of interviews. Moreover departments are more likely to tolerate the analyst's presence in the department if he interferes as little as possible with its routine. Interviews should therefore be kept to the minimum necessary to identify and evaluate record series.

Appraisal

The next stage of the survey is to appraise the record series identified during the course of the inventory. Appraisal should be undertaken at two levels. At the first level a provisional evaluation and a recommended retention period for each record series should be submitted to the department concerned to determine how long it needs to retain each series for business purposes. Appraisal at this level is essentially a records management exercise. At the second level the archive function must determine which series have archival value, and thus should be considered for permanent preservation. It is, however, essential that an archivist should participate at the first level of appraisal, because retention decisions taken at this level on purely business grounds may jeopardize a decision on archival grounds. For example, a decision to destroy a series of files 5 years after they have been closed will effectively preclude archival review.

At the first level of appraisal the objective is to determine the administrative, legal, fiscal, and operational value and use of each record series, and to determine the length of time that these values and uses justify the cost of retaining them. Much of the information upon which these decisions are made will have been obtained in the course of the survey and recorded on the inventory forms, but questions which must be discussed with the department and with the archive function will inevitably arise, before disposal decisions can be finally agreed.

Administrative values

These values derive from the importance of records for determining the policy and procedures necessary to carry out the business of the company. These records will include articles of association, board and committee reports and minutes, budgets and budget estimates, registers of debenture-holders and members, annual returns, organizational reports and charts. Decisions about the retention of these documents must be taken in the light of the provisions of the Companies Act 1985 (c.6). In most cases administrative records can be stored at the discretion of the company. For example, the company registers of debenture-holders and members, which are always, by definition, in current use, may be held in the offices of a third party employed to maintain them on the company's behalf. There are, however, some exceptions. Under sections 288(1), and 401(1), and 407(1), the register of directors and secretaries, and the register of charges, must be kept in the registered office. The restrictions imposed by section 383 are of more significance, because they require a company to keep the minutes of the proceedings of any general meeting held on or after 1 November 1929 at its registered office. This section repeats the provisions of section 121(1) of the Companies Act 1929, which required that 'the books containing the minutes of proceedings of any general meeting of a company held after the commencement of this Act shall be kept at the registered office of the company, and shall during business hours be open to the inspection of any member, without charge'. The vesting date of the 1929 Act was 1 November 1929. The Act did not necessarily imply that minutes produced before 1929 could be destroyed, only that they need not be kept at the registered office of the company.

The minutes alone may not offer a satisfactory account of a decision taken at a general meeting, and the need to retain supporting documentation so long as the minutes themselves are retained is an inevitable consequence. Whether they need to be held in the registered office depends, to an extent, on whether they are likely to be of immediate interest to members. It seems unlikely that they would be required for more than a maximum of 15 years, which would cover most claims under the Limitations Act 1980 and the Latent Damage Act 1986, and it should therefore be a reasonable proposition to store the earlier records elsewhere. This is a matter of some importance, bearing in mind the cost of retaining records in office accommodation, particularly in London. Supporting documentation can be stored elsewhere, but, legally speaking, not the minutes of general meetings. The problem might be overcome if microfilm copies of the earlier minutes were held in the registered office and the originals stored by the company elsewhere, in safe custody. This might be permissible under Section 722 of the Companies Act 1985, permitting the recording of minutes in forms other than bound books, provided that there are safeguards against falsification. The cost of making such copies would, however, have to be considered.

Legal values

These values derive from the importance of records for defining the rights and obligations of the organization and its staff, and of the individuals and organizations with which it has dealings. Such records will include contracts, title deeds, leases, agreements, personnel records, and records relating to the health and welfare of employees. In general these records will be covered by the Limitations Act 1980, which lays down that, in respect of simple contracts, legal actions must be brought within 6 years of the last action in the matter. In the case of contracts under seal the Act lays down a period of 12 years within which actions can be brought. Except in the case of personal injuries, the provisions of this statute have been modified by the Latent Damage Act 1986, under which a plaintiff has an additional period of 3 years after becoming aware of any damage in which to bring an action, with an upper limit of 15 years from the date when the damage occurred, after which actions are barred. The list of records that could be required where a breach of contract in respect of either of these two Acts is possible could be extensive. The contract itself would be required, as well as papers relating to the negotiation of the contract and to the alleged breach. In addition, records relating to manufacture, quality control, dispatch, and receipt of goods, and other operational records could be essential. Care must therefore be taken to ensure that records in these categories are retained for as long as is necessary to ensure that the company is adequately protected.

Quality records are the subject of paragraph 4.16 of *BS 5750: Quality Systems*, Part 1 and *ISO 9001*,[2] which requires that a supplier should 'establish and maintain procedures for the identification, collection indexing, filing, storage, maintenance and disposition of quality records'. They must be legible and identifiable with the product involved, and they must be stored and maintained in such a way that they are readily retrievable in facilities that provide a suitable environment to minimize deterioration or damage and to prevent loss. Retention times must be established and recorded, and, where agreed contractually, must be made available for evaluation by the purchaser or his representative for an agreed period. The identification of quality records is one of critical importance to every business. The British Standard runs to seven parts, including Part 0 (*Principal concepts and applications*).

In the case of personal injury the Limitations Act bars actions after 3 years from the cause of the action, with the proviso that the period of time should run from the time that the individual could have been reasonably aware of the injury. This has considerable implications for the retention of such records as accident books and medical records, which can record ostensibly minor injuries that later led to more serious consequences. It is difficult to suggest a definite retention period for such records, but 50 years from the last date in an accident record book would not be unreasonable. Generally speaking, personnel records relating to the terms and conditions of service have a retention requirement equal to the length of service of an individual, and to any residual responsibilities that the company may owe to a person leaving their employ. In the case of long-serving employees this may extend for a period of 75 or more years after their engagement, particularly where superannuation rights are involved.[3]

Fiscal values

These values derive from the importance of records showing how money is obtained, allotted, controlled, expended and accounted for. Records include ledgers, account books, cash books, records of all purchases and sales, inventories, stock records, salary and superannuation records, the record of the assets and liabilities of the company, and the company's annual accounts. The period of retention for the accounting records of public companies, which must be kept at the registered office, or such other place as the directors shall see fit, is laid down in the Companies Act 1985 (section 222) as 6 years from the date on which they were made. However, the interpretation of this section is not always a simple matter, as the record of the assets and liabilities of the company, referred to in section 221 (3)(b), will include capital plant and equipment having a potential life of more than 6 years. In such cases the period of retention should begin when the asset is replaced or sold. Nor does this period of retention extend to the annual accounts prepared under section 227 of the Act, which include the balance sheet, the profit and loss account (or the income and expenditure account in the case of a company not trading for profit), and group accounts where appropriate. These accounts must be published, and as they are open to inspection by members, they fall into the same category as the administrative records referred to in section 383 of the Act, and should be retained for an indefinite period, but not necessarily in the registered office of the company.

PAYE records must be kept for at least 3 years after the end of the tax year to cover possible queries about employee's pay or tax and inspection requirements by Inland Revenue and DSS officers. It would, however, be a wise precaution to regard salary and superannuation payments records as being covered by section 221 of the Companies Act and to retain them for at least 6 years. In a business with a high risk of injury to employees the retention period can be extended to 10 years, to assist in the calculation of compensation.

Under section 222 of the Companies Act private companies are only required to retain routine accounting records for 3 years from the date on which they are made. However, the VAT (General) Regulations 1985 (Amendment) Regulations 1985, following a clause in the Finance Act 1985, direct that a taxable person must keep his trading account, profit and loss account, balance sheet, together with all related documents, orders, invoices, delivery notes, correspondence, etc. for 6 years, commencing with records 3 years old at 25 July 1985, under pain of a fine of £500. This effectively extends the period of retention for the accounting records of private companies to 6 years.

Operational values

These values derive from the importance of records bearing upon the productive activities of a company, in the broadest terms, whether they be manufacturing or financial. They include correspondence and memoranda, usually organized into subject or particular instance case files, such as customer files or order files relating to individual transactions. They also include records relating to manufacturing processes and quality control, records relating to scientific and technical research, engineering drawings, publications, and publicity material. As has already been noted, the retention of these records is conditioned by the Limitations Act 1980, and the period of 6 years must begin at the point at which a manufacturing process or a transaction has been completed. In the case of the records of research and development the period of retention will depend on the length of time that results are of commercial value to the firm. Where a process has been patented, retention will be conditioned by patent legislation which prescribes periods during which a patent remains in force, or can be renewed and amended.

The Consumer Protection Act 1987 places particular emphasis on the need to preserve records relating to manufacturing and quality control, to ensure adequate protection against claims in respect of damage suffered as a result of the supply of defective goods. Claims are restricted to cases where the goods were intended for private use, occupation or consumption, and a manufacturer may be party to a dispute, even if he had not supplied the goods direct to a consumer, but had supplied a defective product which has been incorporated in goods sold by another company. The time limit in such cases is 3 years from the time that the damage occurred, or that the plaintiff became aware of it, with an upper limit of 10 years after the product was supplied. *BS 5750*, referred to earlier in this chapter, should be used to identify the quality records which must be retained under this Act.

In general the volume of records and the length of time which they must be retained by a company have been increased by recent legislation, and European Economic Community legislation, which at present extends only to specific industries, such coal and steel, will become increasingly important after 1992. International standards, such as the one incorporated in *BS 5750*, will also have to be taken into account. The process of appraisal and selection of records must therefore ensure that the most important administrative, legal, fiscal, and operational records are retained for as long as, but no longer than, they are of value to the company. In principle, the aim should be to retain records containing the greatest detail about the activities of the company, occupying the smallest amount of storage space, because space costs money. Nevertheless the cost of storage space should not be an overriding factor where legal or other considerations are paramount; rather the aim should be to reduce storage costs to the optimum level. These principles apply, whatever the form in which records are created and maintained, but the increasing use of alternative forms of record which can only be read by means of a machine, such as microfilm, and magnetic and digital media, present particular retention problems.

Appraisal of machine-readable records

The Companies Act 1948, section 436, allowed companies for the first time to keep their registers, indexes, minute books, and books of account in forms other than bound books, provided that 'adequate precautions shall be taken for guarding against falsification and facilitating its discovery'. The company, and every officer of the company not taking adequate precautions, were liable to a fine not exceeding £50. This section was primarily designed to permit the use of loose-leaf binders for minutes and accounting records, but it was also extended to include the use of microforms, which were coming into vogue at that time. It was repeated in the Companies Act 1985, section 722, in broadly the same terms, but the term 'accounting records' was substituted for 'books of account', the amount of the fine for default was omitted, and an unspecified daily default fine was added. Section 436 of the 1948 Act does not cover the use of computers, as they were only at the design stage at the time. It was legitimized by section 723 of the Companies Act 1985, which states that any of the registers and other records mentioned in section 722 could be recorded in a non-legible form, provided that the recording was capable of being reproduced in a legible form.

The Companies (Registers and other Records) Regulations 1985 (Statutory Instrument 1985 No. 724) specifically extends the use of non-legible forms of record to virtually all the company registers mentioned in the Act, and enables a company to keep them wherever the work of registration is being carried out, not necessarily in the registered office (see Table 10.1). The effect of this measure has been far-reaching, for without the extended use of computers for share registration and the employment of banks and other financial institutions to undertake the work, the privatization of British Telecom, British Gas, British Steel, and the British water industry in under 4 years would have been impossible.

The use of microfilm or non-legible media for record series does not in any way alter or modify the retention periods considered appropriate for them, but because neither can be read without the use of a machine, the problem of ensuring that they comply with the law, and can therefore be used successfully in the event of legal proceedings, is a matter of greater importance. Under the 'best evidence' rule the original document must be produced in court, unless a satisfactory reason can be given for its unavailability. This requirement has been modified by two pieces of legislation, the Civil Evidence Act 1968 and the Police and Criminal Evidence Act 1984, both of which accept microforms and computer

Table 10.1 *Places for performance of duty to allow inspection of registers kept otherwise than in a legible form*[4]

Statutory provision	Register	Place
COMPANIES ACT 1985		
Section 211(8)	Register and any associated index of interests in voting shares.	*(a)* Where the register of directors' interests is kept otherwise than in a legible form, the place for inspection of that register. *(b)* Where the register of directors' interests is kept in a legible form, the place where it is so kept.
Section 222(1)	Accounting records.	The registered office of the company or such other place as the directors of the company think fit.
Section 288(1)	Register of directors and secretaries.	The registered office of the company.
Section 353(1)	Register of members.	The registered office of the company provided that: *(a)* if the work of ensuring that the requirements of the Act with regard to entries in the register are complied with is done at another office of the company, the place for inspection may be that other office, and *(b)* if the company arranges with some other person for the carrying out of the work referred to in *(a)* above to be undertaken on behalf of the company by that other person, the place for inspection may be the office of that other person at which the work is done; so however that the place for inspection shall not, in the case of a company registered in England and Wales, be at a place outside England and Wales and, in the case of a company registered in Scotland, be at a place outside Scotland.
Section 354(3)	Index of the register of members.	*(a)* Where the register of members is kept otherwise than in a legible form, the place for inspection of that register. *(b)* Where the register of members is kept in a legible form, the place where it is so kept.
Section 362(1)	Overseas branch register.	Any place where, but for these Regulations, the register would be permitted to be kept under section 362(1) of the Act.
Sections 407(1) and 422(1)	Register of charges.	The registered office of the company.

Statutory provision	Register	Place
Schedule 13, paragraph 25	Register of directors' interests.	*(a)* Where the register of members is kept otherwise than in a legible form:
		(i) if the place for inspection of that register is the registered office of the company, that office, and
		(ii) if not, the place for inspection of that register or the registered office of the company.
		(b) Where the register of members is kept in a legible form:
		(i) if that register is kept at the registered office of the company, that office, and
		(ii) if that register is not so kept, the place where that register is kept or the registered office of the company.
Schedule 13, paragraph 28	Index of the register of directors' interests.	*(a)* Where the register of directors' interests is kept otherwise than in a legible form, the place for inspection of that register.
		(b) Where the register of directors' interests is kept in a legible form, the place where it is so kept.
Schedule 14, paragraph 4(1)	Duplicate of overseas branch register.	*(a)* Where the register of members is kept otherwise than in a legible form, the place for inspection of that register.
		(b) Where the register of members is kept in a legible form, the place where it is so kept.

records as evidence, provided that they can be reproduced in a legible form and the reproductions authenticated. The requirements for the authentication of microforms and computer records are, however, different.

Microforms

Microform copies of paper documents in the form of reeled microfilm, jacketed microfilm, microfiche, and aperture cards, are regularly accepted in both civil and criminal proceedings, but some doubt still remains about their admissibility. If evidence based on an enlargement from a microform copy is challenged in court, proper authentication of the circumstances in which the microform was created will be required in both civil and criminal proceedings. The basic requirement is that the microform should have been produced in accordance with an established procedure. The outline of a satisfactory procedure will be found in *BS 6498: Guide to the Preparation of Microfilm and Other Microforms that may be Required as Evidence*

(1984). Quality standards, which are also important, are recommended in other British Standards.[5] It must, however, be emphasized that some documents, particularly poor quality or coloured originals, are not suitable for microfilming. Updatable microforms will not be accepted in the courts, because they cannot be relied upon as a true and accurate record. Computer Output Microforms (COM), which are made direct from electronic data as an alternative to paper, are acceptable in the courts, subject to the same requirements for authentication as other microforms.

A summary of the minimum requirements for a microform programme, recommended in the *BS 6498*, is given below:

- *Authorization of filming.* A form, signed by the person having custody of documents before they are filmed, should be filmed as the first document in the sequence of documents to which it refers or retained in its original form for the life of the film.
- *Camera operator's certificate.* A form recording the operator's name, and the date of filming, certifying that the microform is a complete record of the documents passed to him, should be filmed as the last document in the sequence of documents to which it refers.
- *Certificate of acceptance.* An authorized person should sign a form stating that the microforms of the documents have been checked and accepted.
- *Certificate of destruction.* Where documents are destroyed after microfilming, an authorized person should sign a form certifying that destruction has taken place, recording the date of destruction, the reference numbers, and dates of the documents, and the reference numbers of the microform copies of the documents.
- *Register.* A register should record the dates and reference numbers of the authorization, the 4 certificates relating to the filming and destruction of the documents, and the references and locations of the master microforms.

Computer records

Computer records are treated very differently by the courts, because, of their very nature, they are infinitely updatable, and therefore prone to error and to fraudulent and criminal misuse. The variety of computer crimes is too extensive to be dealt with in detail here, but they include 'hacking', i.e. external penetration and alteration of ostensibly secure computer programs; internal fraud and damage carried out by disgruntled employees; software 'viruses', such as the 'Friday 13th' virus, which corrupted programs and lost data, or rendered it inaccessible, and software errors, such as that which transferred £2 billion from a United Kingdom bank to United Kingdom and United States companies in the space of 30 minutes. Fraudulent activities are sufficiently common to lead to the suspicion that large companies fail to prosecute offenders for fear of loss of public confidence. Organizations which rely exclusively on on-line computer systems are particularly vulnerable to an increased risk of fraud. Office automation systems belong in this category, as deliberate falsification of documents created and transmitted across communications networks can be relatively easily accomplished.

Nevertheless the courts will accept computer records in evidence, provided that the circumstances in which they were produced can be satisfactorily authenticated. Section 69 of the Police and Criminal Evidence Act 1984 clearly indicates the problems of authentication:

'In any proceedings, a statement in a document produced by a computer shall not be admissable in evidence of any fact stated therein unless it is shown –

(a)   that there are no reasonable grounds for believing that the statement is inaccurate because of improper use of the computer;
(b)   that at all material times the computer was operating properly or if not, that any respect in which it was not operating properly, or was out of operation was not such as to affect the production of the document or the accuracy of its contents'.

The Data Protection Act 1984 (c.35), which deals exclusively with 'automatically processed information relating to individuals, and the provision of services in respect of such information', also has implications for the retention of computer data, particularly the requirement that 'Personal data held for any purpose shall not be kept for longer than is necessary for that purpose or those purposes'.

In order to comply with the minimum requirements of the law, it will in future be necessary for companies to ensure that housekeeping systems for their computer operations are as foolproof as possible. Daily logs of computer operations, including breakdowns and malfunctions, must be meticulously kept, and full details of the form and development of software programs, and the dates on which they are regularly run, must be available. Security measures, such as the form and allocation of passwords, and individual accessibility to data banks must be rigidly maintained, especially at work stations, where serious breaches of security can occur, such as an operator leaving a personal computer or a computer terminal running in his absence. An effective back-up and disaster-recovery programme is also indispensible. Nevertheless the risk of corruption and loss of data will remain, and the larger and more complex the system, the greater the risk.

The retention of electronic data which has been 'archived', i.e. stored off-line in magnetic or digital form for possible future reference, also presents problems. The retention period of 6 years implied by the Limitations Act 1980 raises questions both of storage costs and of data recovery. Magnetic tape, the cheapest medium, is costly to maintain, as it must be run regularly to ensure that there is no data transfer from one part of the tape to another. Storage conditions are also critical, calling for temperature and humidity control, and freedom from electrical fields. The compatiblity of hardware manufactured by different companies, and of different generations of hardware manufactured by the same company, also raises the question as to whether data recorded on tapes more than 2 or 3 years old can be easily recovered in case of need. With on-line systems, such as electronic offices, there is the additional problem of the regular deletion of documents that are no longer required for reference, to ensure that the system is not overloaded. This can lead to the establishment of arbitrary rules for the deletion of all documents, often as little as 2 years old, unless a good case can be made for retaining them. This places too much reliance on highly subjective decisions by the individuals creating documents in the system to regulate records retention. It also suggests that the system itself is suitable only for documents of a relatively ephemeral nature. Alternative methods of retaining electronic data are by conversion to microform by a COM process, or by transfer to an optical disc system, but both these processes are expensive, and can only be justified for data of long-term value.

The inevitable conclusion is that it would be unwise to hold any records on-line which require authentication by signature or by the company seal, except for reference purposes. It automatically excludes all primary documentation required by the Companies Act, such as minutes, balance sheets, and annual accounts. It also casts considerable doubt on the admissibility in evidence of significant documents forming part of an electronic office system, created and maintained on-line, which would in normal circumstances require authentication by signature. It suggests that original documents of primary evidential and informational value should be maintained in hard copy.

Archival appraisal

The participation of the corporate archivist in the process of appraisal at the first level has already been assumed as axiomatic. At the second level the corporate archivist must appraise records with a view to selecting them for permanent preservation as archives. It is impracticable, as well as unnecessary, to preserve all the records of a company, and at the most archives might represent between 5 and 10 per cent of the total documentation created and maintained by any organization. Such a percentage can, however, be no more than a useful guide, because the actual volume of records that should be preserved permanently will depend on the nature and activities of the company. It is impossible to lay down hard and fast rules for archival appraisal, as it is a field in which experience plays an important role. A knowledge of the history of a company is an indispensable pre-requisite of success, but there are some useful guidelines for the evaluation of records, which may be of some assistance.

Evidential values

Records have evidential value if they contain information bearing upon the origin, structure, procedures, and significant functions of a company. Those of archival value can be found in all the categories identified at the first level of appraisal. Careful study of the provisions of the Companies Act 1985 and other legislation will assist in their identification. Consider the following values:

- *Administrative values* derive from the importance of records for determining the policy and procedures necessary to carry out the business of a company.
- *Legal values* derive from the importance of records for defining the rights and obligations of the organization, its staff, and of individuals and organizations with which it has dealings.
- *Fiscal values* derive from the importance of records showing how money is obtained, allotted, controlled, expended and accounted for.
- *Operational values* derive from the importance of records bearing upon the productive activities of a company, in the broadest terms, whether they be manufacturing or financial.

The final decision about the preservation of particular series of records as archives will also depend on a number of other factors.

Duplication

This can exist in two forms. In the first form the information contained in one or more record series can be reproduced as an effective summary in another. In such cases the series containing the most information in the most convenient form should be retained in preference to the others. In the second form the records themselves may be duplicated in another organization. In such cases the organization in which the records originated should be responsible for preserving them, but care must be taken to ensure that the records are being retained elsewhere before important documentation is discarded.

Finding aids

If a series of records has effective finding aids, such as lists and indexes, these must be preserved with the records themselves.

Confidentiality

If records contain information of a highly confidential nature, especially in relation to individuals, the question as to whether permanent preservation is justified will arise. Where the information is of sufficient importance to justify retention, steps should be taken to ensure that the records are preserved under adequate safeguards, which will prevent disclosure until the appropriate time. This is particularly important where external restrictions are placed on access to the information, e.g. by the Data Protection Act.

Condition of the records

If records are in a poor state, the cost of preservation and conservation must be taken into consideration. Unless the importance of the records justifies the expense of restoration, a series may have to be abandoned.

Informational values

Records may also have informational value if they contain facts of interest not only to the company which created and maintained them but also to research workers in other fields. Archives selected on grounds of their evidential value will have informational value, but series of particular instance records, e.g. individual shipping files relating either to ships chartered for particular voyages or to ships regularly carrying cargoes to various parts of the world, can be of great value to those researching the export of goods to particular countries, or the shipping industry generally. Research interests, particularly at university level, should be consulted if there is any doubt about the informational value of a record series. If the informational value of records can be established objectively, the series should, wherever possible, be retained intact, but it may often be too costly to preserve the whole of a bulky series in its original form. Microfilming is a possible alternative, but it is likely to prove just as expensive. Sampling may therefore be the only reasonable alternative.

Sampling records for retention

Felix Hull has laid down some useful guidelines for sampling records. Sampling, he says 'should only take place . . . where there is some doubt about the validity of retaining the whole class or series of conventional paper or textual records, but when automatic destruction is regarded as too drastic a course of action . . . or when it is felt proper to retain some examples from an otherwise destructible category of records'.[6] For effective sampling, the series of files must be homogeneous, that is to say the contents of each file must contain the same or similar records. The size of sample will vary according to the documentation and to the circumstances in which it is made, but in principle the larger the sample, the more satisfactory it is likely to be. There are a number of different methods of sampling, each more or less satisfactory according to the nature of the record classification system:

1 *Qualitative or selective sampling* is where the archivist selects files which he believes to be of particular significance. This is a highly subjective process, and the files selected are unlikely to be representative of the whole series.

2 *Systematic sampling* is where the archivist selects files according to a particular pattern. There are a number of such patterns in common use:

- A representative topographical sample can be taken where the work of a number of area or regional offices is so similar that the records of one of them can be selected to represent them all. The disadvantage of this method is that area offices which ostensibly perform the same functions may differ substantially in the work that they actually do, e.g. according to ethnic or economic circumstances.
- An alphabetical sample can be taken by preserving the records filed under one or more letters in an alphabetical series to represent the whole. Care must, however, be taken to choose an appropriate letter. For example, the letter 'M' in Scotland would produce a disproportionately large number of files.
- A numerical or serial sample can, for example, be taken by selecting every tenth file or box of records in a series arranged in numerical order, or those files with a particular terminal digit, say '5'. This method should not be adopted if records are arranged alphabetically, topographically or chronologically.
- A chronological sample can be taken by selecting all the records for particular years according to a regular pattern, e.g. the records for every fifth or tenth year in a chronological sequence. The problem here is that the years chosen may miss significant events, such as an economic boom or recession.

3 *Random sampling* is a statistically sound method of selection, with no element of bias, based on the use of computer techniques to develop random number tables, and appropriate samples for each series.

Random sampling is clearly the most representative method of those listed above, as it provides the most accurate picture of a series as a whole; but it is a sophisticated technique, which cannot be effectively employed in the absence of specialized computer applications. Most corporate archivists must be content to use the method of sampling which suits the particular series to be sampled.

The transfer of company archives to an archive organization

Where the corporate archivist is unable to find storage space for archives, either because they are excluded by the acquisition policy adopted by the company, or because they would have to be sampled, or destroyed if no alternative home can be found for them, it is desirable that, as a matter of policy, the possibility of placing them in the custody of another archive organization should be considered. In some cases specialist repositories may be appropriate – say universities prepared to accept archives bearing on the research projects in which their academic staff are engaged. The company may indeed be in regular touch with universities specializing in its chosen field of operations. The disadvantage of this approach is that a particular university may at any time decide to change its field of research. Non-specialist archives, such as local record offices, are a more reliable alternative, as they will be interested in accepting company archives originating in, or relating to, their area, provided that they have sufficient space in their repositories.[7]

In the past local archives and universities were accustomed to accept collections on very liberal terms of deposit, which allowed depositors to withdraw them at relatively short notice, solely with a view to realizing their capital value. A company transferring its archives to another organization should therefore expect to find that certain safeguards against premature withdrawal are required. In some cases an outright gift will be requested, but where a deposit is accepted, due notice of withdrawal and compensation sufficient to cover any expenses incurred by the archive organization while the archives were in its custody, will be required.[8]

Scheduling

When the appraisal of the record series of each department has been completed, details of each series, and the recommended retention period should be agreed (by the records manager and the corporate archivist if the two functions run in parallel, or by the records manager or corporate archivist alone if both functions are the responsibility of a single manager) and submitted in the form of a records retention authorization for approval by the department and any other functions whose approval is considered necessary by the company. The company secretary, the internal auditor, and the head of the legal department are most frequently consulted. The information included in the authorization should be sufficient to enable the series to be identified and to make decisions about retention as simple as possible. The information should be tabulated in the following columns:

- The title and reference number of the record series, and the covering dates and the volume of records in the series taken from the inventory sheets.
- The period that the series is active, and must therefore remain in the originating office. This is usually indicated by means of a symbol. For example:

C Current year is appropriate for financial records.
T Termination is appropriate for files series where papers are added to a file until the subject or case is teminated.
+ A plus sign followed by a number placed after the symbol, e.g. C+ 1, indicates the number of years or months which the records should remain in the office for reference purposes, before they are transferred to high-density, low-cost storage in a records centre.

- The length of time that semi-active records should remain in the records centre for reference before disposal. This is indicated by a second figure in a separate column representing the number of years.
- The total retention period for the records in the series, calculated by adding the figures in columns 2 and 3.
- The ultimate disposal of the records by destruction, review or transfer to archives, which is also represented by a symbol, for example:

D Destruction.
A Archives.
R Review.

The review symbol is appropriate for subject and other similar files, where a once-for-all retention period for the series cannot be established, because individual files differ in importance, and therefore require greater or lesser periods of retention. A file-by-file review is appropriate in such cases, the first review to be carried out 7 years after a file is closed. This should ensure that only the minimum number of files need be retained for a further period as potential archives.

The records retention authorization should also include, in a remarks column, appropriate recommendations and information on the following subjects:

- Sampling.
- Duplicate series.
- Alternative formats for particular series, e.g. microfilming or computerization, if appropriate.
- Vital records identified during the course of the inventory, which should be protected by the storage of duplicates in alternative accommodation from which they can be recovered in the event of a disaster which destroys the originals.

When the necessary approvals have been obtained, the following action can be taken:

- Records that are already time-expired should be destroyed by departments, under the supervision of the records manager.
- Semi-active records held in office accomodation should be transferred to the records centre in accordance with established procedures.
- Records identified as archives should be transferred to the custody of the corporate archivist, in accordance with approved retention criteria.
- Continuing record series should be incorporated in a records retention schedule issued by, and on the authority of, the records manager.

Cost savings and schedule audit

The cost savings, in terms of office space recovered, which can be expected from the development of systematic records retention schedules should be considerable. Where no schedules previously existed, a records manager might expect that up to one-third of the records inventoried should be destroyed, one-third transferred to low-cost storage in a records centre, and only one-third should remain active in the offices.[9] These savings are directly related to the floor space previously occupied by the records, which will become available for more efficient alternative use. It is, however, essential that the application of the schedules should be regularly audited to ensure that semi-active records do not again accumulate in expensive office accommodation. The records manager should therefore be responsible for ensuring that departments review their records retention schedules annually to take account of changes in departmental organization, legal and other retention criteria, and record keeping practices, such as the introduction of new computer systems or microforms, and the creation and cessation of record series.

Vital records and disaster planning

The opportunity afforded by the compilation of a detailed inventory of the records of a company should be taken to identify and protect vital records essential for the reconstruction of the organization, and the resumption of normal business activities, within 24 hours of a disaster. There are 5 main categories of disaster:

- *Human factors*, such as terrorism, civil commotion, and wars.
- *Contamination*, by such agents as chemicals, asbestos, and radioactive fall-out, which is, unfortunately becoming increasingly common.
- *Fire*, which will destroy records completely. Even after a fire has been

extinguished, enough heat may remain in enclosed areas to cause secondary fires to develop, e.g. in papers stored in filing cabinets, or in magnetic tape, up to 3 days after the fire has apparently been put out.

- *Water*, which will damage records in whatever medium they are held. As water is the usual method of extinguishing fires, water damage following a fire can cause as much, if not more, damage than the fire itself.
- *Natural disasters*, such as floods, which can occur in low-lying areas, earthquakes, and volcanic action which are essentially regional hazards.

A vital records programme

A prudent company will establish a programme designed to protect records and information vital to its survival. The programme's elements are:

- The identification and selection of the records and information to be protected.
- The determination of appropriate methods of protection.
- The establishment of administrative policies and procedures to implement the programme.
- The establishment of auditing procedures to maintain the programme after it has been implemented.

The programme should be co-ordinated by the records manager, who should have responsibility for company records in their active, semi-active, and inactive phases, and the necessary expertise in handling records in bulk.

Selecting vital records

Storing vital records costs money. Only those records essential to the survival of the company should be selected for protection. Among the most important categories are those which enable the company to collect income due to it, protect the company against possible fraud or overpayment of claims, and provide adequate information about assets.

Record series falling within these categories are:

- *Financial records*: accounts receivable, loans and other financial transactions, general ledgers, registers and other records proving payment.
- *Employee records*: payroll and pensions.
- *Manufacturing records*: production specifications, engineering drawings, plant and other inventories, research and development information.
- *Negotiable instruments*: stocks, shares, loans, cheques.
- *Insurance policies*.

- *Property records*: deeds, leases, patents, trademarks, licences, franchises, capital investments, and capital assets.
- *Major contracts and agreements, with amendments.*
- *The vital records protection plan.*

Methods of protection

- *On-site storage* in fire-resistant equipment; this is suitable only for the short-term storage of uniquely important records, such as deeds and agreements, while they are in active use.
- *Off-site storage* in a vital records centre, properly protected against anticipated hazards. This can be a facility owned by the company, a commercial facility, or a facility shared with another company. A part of the company records centre can be used for this purpose.
- *Dispersal* through the normal routine distribution of vital information to various locations for use and reference (so long as records are maintained at 2 or more different locations, additional protection may not be necessary), or through the planned distribution of copies specifically created for the purpose, which should be held in the vital records centre.
- *Duplication* in cases where no extra copies are available, such as deeds and other legal documents; paper copies are to be preferred, but microforms can be used, provided that steps are taken to ensure that microform readers will be available in the event of an emergency. These should also be held in the vital records centre.

Administrative policies and procedures

Details of records identified as vital should be incorporated in a vital records schedule, together with information about the location of both the originals and the copies, and the frequency with which they will be rotated, i.e. superseded by copies of later documents in the same series. Vital record copies are active for only a relatively short period, commensurate with the activity of the originals. For example, payrolls will be superseded on a weekly or monthly basis, but it may be necessary to rotate them on a 12-monthly basis for full protection. Steps must also be taken to establish efficient systems for packing, and recording transfers of vital record copies to the vital records centre; and for implementing the rotation programme, which must be regularly monitored to ensure that it is functioning efficiently.

Records centre storage

The cost savings resulting from the development and implementation of records retention schedules cannot be fully realized unless low-cost, high density accommodation is available for the storage of semi-active and inactive records until they are due for destruction or transfer to archives. This storage facility, or records centre, should be properly staffed, and managed by the records manager. Unless the company is very large, only one records centre should be necessary, and it should replace all other record storage areas previously used by departments, apart from a small number required for the storage of semi-active records, retained by departments under the terms of their retention schedule. The chief benefits to be obtained from establishing a records centre are security; reduction in the cost of storing semi-active and inactive records; regular transfers of records to ensure that semi-active and inactive records are not unnecessarily retained in office accommodation; rapid retrieval of information; and regular, systematic destruction of records when their useful life is over.

The following system should be instituted:

- *Security.* The centre should be protected against fire, flood, and unauthorized access. Access to the storage area should be restricted to the staff of the centre.
- *Cost benefits.* Storage ratios should be at least 3 cubic feet of records to one square foot of floor space in the record centre, as compared with one cubic foot of records to one square foot of floor space in office accommodation.
- *Transfer of records.* Records should be transferred by departments in standard containers supplied by the centre, accompanied by lists of the contents compiled by the department on standard forms.
- *Retrieval of records.* Requests for records are normally made by departments on the telephone or by fax, but they can also be made in writing. Records are returned to the department within 24 hours of a request being received in the centre. A searchroom should be available at the centre for use by departmental staff wishing to consult records in person.
- *Destruction or transfer of records to archives.* The staff of the centre should monitor the retention periods of records transferred to the centre, and advise departments when they are time-expired. Records should be destroyed by the centre in accordance with the retention schedule, under secure conditions. Records scheduled for preservation as archives are transferred to the custody of the corporate archivist when they are time-expired.

Records centre and archive accommodation

The areas used for storing departmental records before the records-management strategy is implemented are unlikely to be suitable for re-use either as a records centre or as a vital records centre, on grounds both of security and lack of storage space, unless they are situated in a suitable building remote from the company offices. The centres should therefore be created by adapting suitable existing premises, by building new premises specially designed for the purpose, or by leasing space in a commercial records centre. The decision will depend on which of the alternatives is the most cost-effective in terms of accommodation and running costs, and, to an extent, on the location of the premises.

In the long run a purpose-built centre or a building converted for the purpose will prove to be the most effective solution, as either can combine the functions of a records centre, a vital records centre, and an archive repository (if the problem with regard to statutory company records can be overcome), since the accommodation requirements for all three differ only in degrees.

The corporate archives programme

In the event the corporate archivist may have no responsibility for records management, and there may be no corporate records manager to carry out the records survey that is the essential preliminary for an efficient archives and records management strategy. In such cases the corporate archivist must at least seek to persuade management to agree to a survey designed to identify archival material throughout the departments of the company, starting with the departmental semi-active and inactive records stores, but extending to records held in office accommodation to ensure full coverage. The objective of such a survey is to identify record series of archival value and to ensure that they are regularly transferred to the archives when they can be released by departments. If, at the same time, the company can be persuaded to appoint a records analyst to the staff of the corporate archives, then the corporate archivist can offer to carry out a full inventory and scheduling operation of the kind outlined earlier in this chapter.

Notes

1   P. Walne (editor), *Dictionary of Archival Terminology*, ICA Handbook Series, 7 (K. G. Saur, Munich, 1988).
2   British Standards Institution, incorportating ISO (International Standards Organization) 9001, 1987.
3   Other Acts having implications for a company's relations with its employees which must be taken into account in determining retention criteria for records are: the Disabled Persons (Employment) Act 1944, the Rehabilitation of Offenders Act 1974, the Health and Safety at Work Act 1974, the Employment Protection and Sex Discrimination Acts 1975, and the Race Relations and Fatal Accidents Acts 1975.
4   S.I.1985 No.724, Schedule 1.
5   British Standards Institution, *BS 4187: Microfiche* (British Standards Institution, Milton Keynes, 1985, 1988), Part 1:1981(1988) and Part 3:1978(1985) for

specifications for microfiche formats; *BS 4210: Specification for 35mm Micro-copying of Technical Drawings* (British Standards Institution, Milton Keynes, 1989), Part 1:1977(1989), *Operating procedures*; Part 2:1977(1989), *Photographic requirements for silver film*; Part 3:1977(1989), *Unitized microfilm carriers (aperture cards etc.)*; *BS:5623:1978(1985): Specification for microfilm jackets, A6 size* (British Standards Institution, Milton Keynes, 1985).

6 F. Hull, *The Use of Sampling Techniques in the Retention of Records: A RAMP Study with Guidelines* (UNESCO, Paris, 1981), p. 48, para. 6.8.

7 J. Foster and J. Sheppard, *British Archives: A Guide to Archive Resources in the United Kingdom*, 2nd edition (Macmillan, London, 1989) is an invaluable source of information about specialist as well as local and national repositories.

8 For further guidance see p. 404 on the deposit of private papers, which discusses terms of deposit from the point of view of the company archivist as recipient.

9 P. M. Lybarger, *Records Retention Scheduling* (ARMA, Kansas City, 1980), p. 34.

Further reading

A. Appleton, 'The selection of records for retention: statutory limitation periods in contract and tort', *Business Archives*, 57 (1989), pp. 11–18.

ARMA, *Vital Records Guidelines* (ARMA Standards Program, Kansas City, 1984).

K. Aschner (editor), *Taking Control of your Office Records: A Manager's Guide* (Knowledge Industry Publications, New York, 1983).

W. Benedon, *Records Management* (The Trident Shop, California State University, Los Angeles, 1969).

D. Charman, *Records Survey and Schedules: A RAMP Study with Guidelines* (UNESCO, Paris, 1984).

M. Cook, *Archives Administration. A Manual for Intermediate and Smaller Organisations and for Local Government* (Dawson, Folkstone, 1977).

P. Emmerson (editor), *How to Manage Your Records: A Guide to Effective Practice* (ICSA Publishing, Cambridge, 1989).

F. Hull, *The Use of Sampling Techniques in the Retention of Records: A RAMP Study with Guidelines* (UNESCO, Paris, 1981).

W. O. Maedke, M. F. Robek and G. F. Brown, *Information and Records Management*, 3rd edition (Glencoe Publishing Company, Encino, California, 1987).

A. Pederson (editor), *Keeping Archives* (Australian Society of Archivists Inc., Sydney, 1987).

I. Penn, A. Morddel, G. Pennix and K. Smith, *Records Management Handbook* (Gower, Aldershot, 1989).

11

Finding aids

Stephen Freeth

The finding-aid system

'Finding aids' is an imprecise and general term for the whole range of devices by which archivists keep track of the archives in their care. There are in fact various kinds of finding aid, compiled for different purposes, the main ones being the accessions register, or brief chronological record of accessions received; the rough list, or transfer list, of the records in each accession; the archive list, popularly known on the analogy of library cataloguing as the catalogue, which contains the full descriptive information about the records; the indexes; and the shelf-list, which gives the physical location within the storage area of each entry in the catalogue. Between them these should provide, firstly, administrative control of the records (by showing where any given record came from, and when, and under what terms), and secondly, and usually much later, intellectual control, i.e. a detailed and accurate understanding of the records, the reasons for their compilation in the first place, their dates, contents and interrelationships, and usefulness for research.

Administrative control, achieved through the accessions register and the rough/transfer list, is much easier to achieve than intellectual control, and is merely the archival equivalent of stock control in a commercial context. Intellectual control is essentially the role of the archive list or catalogue, which requires careful composition and editing and, to be carried out successfully, must conform to established archival principles. These will be discussed in more detail below. The catalogue, especially if it runs to more than just a few pages, should be supported in turn by indexes, of names, places and subjects, which will bring together scattered references within the text of the catalogue itself. These indexes may in turn be supplemented by other separate indexes, which analyse the contents of particular original records, for example a subject index to a set of minute books or series of house journals, or a name index of the correspondents in a series of letters. The different types of indexes, and their merits, are discussed in greater detail on pp. 303–11.

Not only do these finding aids have different purposes, but together they should form a finding-aid *system*: the accession register should serve as a guide to the rough/transfer lists; the rough lists should be seen as a preliminary version of the catalogue; the catalogue should be supported by the accessions register for administrative purposes, and by the indexes for intellectual/research purposes; while the indexes could not exist without the text of the catalogue, and its system of references, and would be useless if the shelf-list did not show the location in the storage area of any given item.

In some repositories it may be useful or necessary to introduce further levels of finding aid:

- *A general guide* to the archives, to make the shape of the holdings of the repository clear to visitors. This is particularly desirable where the collections have grown too large and amorphous to be comprehended easily.
- *Handlists* (abstracts) of the descriptions of particular popular records, drawn together from different parts of the catalogue.
- *Calendars* (comprehensive analyses) of individual key records, whereby all the information in the original, such as its purpose or message, its date, and all proper names and their context, is extracted and summarized so that there is generally no further need to consult the original.
- *Transcripts*, whereby the entire text of a document is copied out word for word.
- *Editions*, whereby a transcript of a document or group of documents is accompanied by a detailed introduction, giving the historical background and importance of the record(s), and by copious explanatory footnotes.

All these finding aids have their uses. For example, a general guide may provide a labour-saving leaflet for people visiting the repository for the first time; handlists may help to publicize particular aspects of the archives to relevant groups of users or potential users (for example, in a business repository, staff records to family historians, or old photographs to the public relations department); while calendars, transcripts and editions can be used to prevent repeated requests for the same items, thereby saving time and trouble, reducing wear and tear on fragile originals, avoiding repetitive questions, and improving security.[1] However, valuable though they are, they are not central to the finding-aid system, which should be the archivist's main priority.

Finding aids and computers

The following pages describe the manual preparation of finding aids. However, computers will nowadays almost certainly offer a more efficient means to the same end, and indeed some of the advantages of computers over a manual system are stressed in what follows. Computers will also allow for the production of tailor-made finding aids for particular purposes, by combining elements from different finding aids in a manner that would be impossible without great effort within a manual system. Nevertheless, not everyone will have access to computers, or to the relevant technical expertise and support, while the basic principles and approaches underlying archival finding aids remain the same whether or not computers are employed. In addition, the purposes of the different finding aids can perhaps be explained more clearly in a manual context, where each element in the system of finding aids can be clearly distinguished. (For a full discussion of computers and their usefulness in managing business archives, see Chapter 13.)

Are finding aids really necessary?

There is always a temptation, especially in an archive unit with a small staff, to rely on memory to answer questions about the contents of the archives, and to see the preparation of finding aids, and in particular the compilation of detailed catalogues of the records, as slow and relatively unimportant when set against more specific and short-term tasks. However, these activities are at the very core of archives work, as well as among the most complex and demanding that the archivist has to perform. There should therefore always be a long-term central programme to explain and present the archives through finding aids that are as detailed, helpful and comprehensive as necessary.

The main benefits of well-designed and carefully prepared finding aids are as follows:

- They tell the archivist about the archives. Without finding aids, the archivist cannot possibly remember the full range of the records, their different types and dates, or the different information they contain, but only those items that are, for example, of direct personal interest, or have been looked at recently. In addition, in the absence of adequate finding aids, succeeding archivists will be placed in a near-impossible position of ignorance about the contents of the archives.
- The process of compiling detailed catalogues helps to correct myths and misconceptions about the records, and to reveal what is *not* known about them. It is very easy to make assumptions about records on the basis of their physical appearance, or a cursory glance at a few items. Only proper examination, including a formal attempt to describe archives, and to relate them to other contemporary records with which they were originally intended to be used, will reveal their full contents.
- Finding aids tell other people about the records, and export the archivist's knowledge to immediate colleagues, to other departments of the same organization, and to researchers. Security considerations should prevent anyone but the staff of the archive unit from having direct access to the storage areas. Finding aids therefore allow both staff and outsiders to understand the collections quickly and efficiently, and to research their chosen topics with the minimum of personal assistance.
- Detailed catalogues set out the arrangement of the archives on paper, and make it possible to apply unique reference numbers to them. While all archives contain a few items that are readily identifiable, such as bound volumes of board of directors' minutes with gold-blocked titles

and dates, most records consist of comparatively anonymous papers, volumes or files. It will be both undesirable and impractical to write a full description on the outside of each one of these items, especially if they are to be stored several at a time in boxes or containers; a referencing system is therefore essential. Such a system has the added advantage of allowing records to be stored at random, since they can each be identified by their unique reference, and located through a shelf-list. This is better than simply keeping all the archives of an organization side by side on a shelf or shelves. It allows records to be stored by shape and size, where this is desirable for conservation reasons or to save space, and enables additional material to be added later without shunting existing records along the shelves.

- Finding aids are a defence against theft or misplacement. They help to show when an item has gone missing, and provide a description to help find it.

The main types of finding aid

The accessions register

The accessions register is a running record of archival material received into the archive unit, and is designed to impose immediate administrative control over it. Each new consignment of records should be regarded as an 'accession', and entered in the register.

The register should include the following: date of accession; accession number (the first accession being numbered 1, and so on); source; and very brief details of the accession itself. There should also be columns to show whether or not the archivist has power to destroy any unwanted material, and whether access should be restricted on the grounds of confidentiality, and further columns to help keep track of the accession as it changes from uncatalogued to catalogued – perhaps one column for the reference numbers of any records from the accession that have been catalogued, and another to be marked with a tick when cataloguing of the entire accession has been completed. Finally, there should be space for remarks, e.g. if any records are in particularly bad condition, or are subsequently returned or destroyed. A suggested layout for an accessions register is shown in Table 11.1.

The register can be on cards, in a loose-leaf format, or entered in a volume. Some archivists deliberately keep it in a large and heavy volume as a safeguard against loss or damage, because of its importance as a central point of reference for all accessions. If there are a lot of accessions, it may be necessary in addition to index them by source and by subject, and to keep these indexes with the accessions register. On the other hand, if the accessions register is held on a computer system, it may be possible to generate indexes automatically, both in hard copy and for on-line

Table 11.1 *ABC plc archive unit accessions register*

Accession number	Date received	Source	Description	Power to destroy?	Restricted access?	Reference nos. of catalogued items	Tick here when cataloguing complete	Remarks
1	1/1/92	Finance dept. (Mr Smith, Finance Director, ext. 1234)	300 files re investments in other companies, 1900–30 (5 shelves)	Yes	No	See separate inventory		Inventory in accession file. Many files v. mouldered and need repair before can be used. ?Destroy or return.
2	2/1/92	Co. Secretary	First minute book of HIJ Trust Co., 1864–9 (1 vol.)	No	No	HIJ/1/7/1	√	
3	10/1/92	Albert Smith (co. pensioner) 123 High Street, London N32	Air raid warden's diaries re co.'s London HQ, 1940–5 (2 vols.)	No	No			Gift to company. See accession file.

A possible layout for an accessions register in a business archive unit. This layout, intended for a volume, can easily be adapted to a loose-leaf or card format, or used to create a computer database. Other columns might also be useful in some repositories, e.g. terms of transfer (loan, gift, purchase, deposit, etc.); fumigation; physical condition; and progress of cataloguing (listed; list typed; list sent to transferrer/depositor, NRA, etc.).

reference. It should also be easier to produce security copies of the entire register.

In addition to the accessions register, there should be a series of accessions files. These can be arranged so that there is one file for each accession, numbered to correspond with the entries in the register, and containing all the correspondence, rough lists, receipts and so forth relating to that accession; alternatively, and especially where the archives unit receives records from a comparatively small range of sources, perhaps as part of a records management programme, there can be just a few files in alphabetical order of transferrers, or a single accumulating file cross-referenced by date. However, there will almost certainly be some accessions which for various reasons have no written record other than the entry in the register.

The actual records forming any one accession, if not catalogued immediately, should be appropriately boxed, placed in the storage area as a distinct group, and clearly labelled with their accession number. Their location should also be recorded in the shelf-list, which should contain a separate section, arranged in accession number order, for uncatalogued material. The records should not normally be merged or mixed with other uncatalogued accessions, even from the same source, or with catalogued material, as this may lead to confusion in the future. It would seem useful to allocate a particular part of the storage area to uncatalogued as distinct from catalogued material.

As soon as any items from an accession are catalogued, they should be transferred to that part of the storage area reserved for catalogued material, and re-entered in the shelf-list. Their new, permanent reference numbers should also be entered in the accessions register and/or accession file.

The rough list (transfer list)

As its name suggests, the rough list, or transfer list, is simply a checklist of the contents of an accession of records into the archive unit. Its purpose, like that of the accessions register, is to impose administrative control over new arrivals of records, and it should give enough information to show the approximate size and nature of each accession; to allow one accession to be distinguished from another; and to enable stray items to be identified. It is compiled quickly, at the time records are transferred to the archives unit, and can equally well be compiled by the person transferring the records as by the archivist. Indeed it may be useful for the archivist to equip potential transferrers in advance with pre-printed forms, to try and ensure that each transfer of records is accompanied by the necessary information.

The entries in the rough list will almost always be unstructured, simply appearing one after another, like an inventory or auction sale catalogue. They may also be inaccurate in some degree, or lacking in detail. The entries for volumes will probably be more reliable than those for loose papers, for obvious reasons: volumes often have titles and dates on the outside (though these should never be taken at face value), while their contents, bound together in order, can identify themselves in a way that a jumble of papers cannot. Loose papers, on the other hand, may appear in the rough list with little more than a physical, rather than an intellectual, description. Typical examples might be 'audit papers, c.1960, 1 box', 'legal papers, 20th century, 1 tin trunk', 'photographs, undated, one bundle', and so on.

The rough list should form the receipt from the archivist for an accession of records, and should include the following:

1 A space for the accession number to be added.
2 The source of the records and date of transfer.
3 A checklist or inventory of the records.
4 Space at the side in which to enter the full reference numbers of items from the checklist as they are catalogued.
5 Space at the bottom for a signed receipt from the archivist to the transferrer.

It may also be useful to leave a space for brief details of any special conditions, such as power to destroy, no access without special permission, and so on. The full details of these extra conditions will be given in the correspondence and other papers in the accession file. Figure 11.1 shows an example of a rough list on a printed form.

The rough list should be checked for general accuracy at the time the records are received, to ensure that the ranges of dates, and the numbers of volumes or boxes, tally with what has been transferred. One copy of the rough list should then be signed and given to the transferrer as a receipt, and another kept in the relevant accession file. As records from the accession are catalogued, their reference numbers can be entered in the margin of the rough list, next to the relevant entries, as well as in the accessions register.

It may be helpful for the archivist to keep third copies of the rough lists of all uncatalogued material, for the use of members of staff. This can be especially useful if the catalogue is not very far advanced. There may be requests for information from the transferring department, or from senior staff, and in such circumstances it will be convenient to survey the rough lists as a batch, and not accession by accession or department by department. However, this should be no more than a practical expedient, and does not render the detailed catalogue unnecessary. The rough list may have been compiled under difficult circumstances, or at great speed, and may lack any true understanding of the records. It will not have involved any detailed arrangement of the records, and will not therefore allow for the imposition of permanent reference numbers or any serious attempt at indexing. In addition, any one rough list will relate only to one particular accession of records, and will not be integrated into other relevant parts of the archive. Figure 11.2 shows the differences there might

```
┌─────────────────────────────────────────────────────────────────┐
│                          ABC plc                                   │
│           FORM FOR TRANSFER OF RECORDS TO ARCHIVE UNIT             │
│                                                                    │
│  Please receive the following for the company archives:           │
│  Transferrer's name, position, department, extension ............ │
│  .................................................................  │
│  Signature ....................................... Date .........  │
│  Items for transfer and existing references (if any):             │
│                                                                    │
│  ABC & Co. records                                                 │
│  1  Directors attendance books. 1910–30. 2 vol.                    │
│  2  Annual reports and accounts. Printed. 1860–1945. 1 box.        │
│  3  Directors' minutes. 1860–1930. 6 volumes.                      │
│  4  Accounts ledgers. 1860–1910. 12 vol.                           │
│                                                                    │
│  Power to destroy: Yes/No                                          │
│  Restricted Access: Yes/No                                         │
│      If yes, please give details of restriction                   │
│  .................................................................  │
│                                                                    │
│  For Archive unit use:                                             │
│  Received the above: Signature of archivist..................... │
│                      Date ...........................              │
│  Accession number ...............................                  │
│                                                                    │
│  Top copy: to be signed and returned to transferrer as a receipt.  │
│  2nd/3rd copies: to be retained by archives unit                   │
└─────────────────────────────────────────────────────────────────┘
```

Figure 11.1   *An example of a rough list on a printed form.*

be between the rough-list entries and the catalogue entires for a small group of records.

It is probably not a good idea to show rough lists to outside researchers as a matter of course. They may be misled by inadequate entries, confidentiality may be breached, or they may take an unwelcome interest in material which the archivist may subsequently wish to reject or destroy. However, if time elapses and it is not possible to prepare a full catalogue, the rough list will have to be used, whatever its faults. It should therefore always be competent, and able to stand up to scrutiny.

Survey lists of records held elsewhere

Archivists are often asked to survey accumulations of old records held in other buildings or departments, and to prepare rough lists of them, perhaps as a preliminary to transferring them to the archive unit. Such surveys often need to be carried out in difficult conditions, e.g. in cramped and dirty attics or basements. In such circumstances it is important for the archivist to work quickly, and to compile a competent picture of the records without getting bogged down by details. The main task will be to identify the records of different companies, or of different branches or

---

ABC and Co. Ltd
a Board of directors' minute books. Include minutes of shareholders' meetings,
    1872–93, 1912–14. 1860–1930.
    6 vol.
    1   1860–72   4   1912–22
    2   1872–93   5   1922–6
    3   1893–1912   6   1926–30

b Directors' annual reports and accounts. 1860–1954 (1924–7 missing).
    92 booklets in 3 bundles. Printed.
    1   1860–1900
    2   1901–20
    3   1921–54

c General ledgers. 1860–86, 1899–1910.
    3 vol.
    1   1860–75   3   1899–1910
    2   1876–86

d Cash books. 1860–80.
    4 vol.
    1   1860–66   3   1871–6
    2   1867–70   4   1876–80

XYZ and Co. Ltd (estd. 1875; acquired by ABC and Co. Ltd in 1892)
e Directors' annual reports and accounts. 1875–92.
    17 booklets in 1 bundle.

f General ledgers. 1875–92.
    2 vol.
    1   1875–87   2   1887–92 latter part blank

g Cash books. 1875–92.
    3 vol.
    1   1875–82   2   1882–9   3   1889–92 latter part blank

Note in particular the following differences between the descriptions in Figures 11.1 and 11.2:

Rough list no. 1 (no catalogue entry). These directors' attendance books have been rejected by
    the archivist as worthless, despite their acceptance initially, and have therefore been
    omitted from the catalogue.
*Rough list no. 2 (**b** and **e** in catalogue).* These printed reports have proved to relate not only to
    ABC and Co. Ltd but also to an early acquisition, XYZ and Co. Ltd. Note also that the
    stop date in the rough list (1945) has proved to be a clerical error for 1954; and that the
    reports for ABC and Co. Ltd for 1924–7 are missing. A good deal of sorting/disposal of
    duplicate reports has also taken place, though the catalogue does not mention this.
*Rough list no. 3 (**a** in catalogue).* The rough-list entry was essentially accurate, but was too
    brief. Note the presence of shareholders' minutes for some years, and the increased
    business of the board after 1922, revealed by shorter date ranges per volume.
*Rough list no. 4 (**c, d, f, g** in catalogue).* The rough-list entry was imprecise and comparatively
    useless. Again, the records of companies ABC and XYZ were mixed up. There appears to
    be a full set of account books for XYZ and Co. Ltd, whereas what there is for ABC and Co.
    Ltd is much less complete than was suggested by the rough list.

Figure 11.2   *The final catalogue entries for the records in the rough list in Figure
11.1, illustrating typical weaknesses and faults in rough lists.*

departments of the same company, and to identify the main sequences of corporate records of each organization, such as the minute books, or general ledgers. (For further details of archival sequences see p. 280). The following points may also be useful:

- It is important to discover who is in charge of the place where the records are kept, to obtain agreement to the archivist carrying out a survey, and to ensure that any labelling or rearrangement that may be carried out by the archivist will be kept safe until such time as the records are transferred. The person in charge will not necessarily be the same as the person who brings the records to the attention of the archivist.
- Permission should also be sought to rearrange the records if necessary. This will make survey listing much easier, since sequences of records can then be dealt with collectively (for example, 'share registers, 1850–1960. 98 volumes'), and not in a number of random scattered locations.
- Any records which are *not* to be listed should be clearly understood in advance. For example, there may be material which is still considered current, or the archivist may be asked to ignore any material later than a certain date. There will be no point in adding anything of this nature to the survey list, though it may be worth noting elsewhere for future reference. Such material should, if possible, be relocated or otherwise distinguished from the records included in the survey list.
- Before survey listing can begin, the archivist should carry out a brief reconnaissance of the entire storage area, to discover the size of the problem, any special areas of concern, any spare space which might be used for sorting purposes, and so on; and should work out a plan by which the whole of the storage area can be examined systematically, without exception. It can be useful, especially with a storage area of irregular shape or layout, to divide it into sections which can then be examined one by one.
- All the records in the storage area that appear on the survey list should be clearly marked with labels. This will remind the archivist where they are, should it take a while for them to be transferred; it will enable the archivist's colleagues to take over the task at a later stage, if necessary; and it will make it clear to others that the records are being worked on and should not be disturbed. Paper of different colours is a good method of indicating the records of different companies, or of different branches or departments of the same company. All labels should be large, prominent and clear.
- Notices should be placed in prominent positions within the storage area, and at the entrances to it, stating that the records have been examined by the archivist and should not be disturbed. They should also give the date of the survey, and details of where the archivist and the person in charge of the storage area can be contacted. A typical notice might read as follows:

WARNING
RECORDS LABELLED BY COMPANY ARCHIVIST [date]
DO NOT DISTURB

Contact: office manager [name; location within the building; extension number]; or archivist [name; location; telephone number].

The catalogue

The catalogue is the most important finding aid for the user, in that it captures and sets out in a clear and coherent form the archivist's knowledge of the collection. It should describe the archives accurately and in detail, make clear the relations between them, and explain the history of the organization that produced them. However, it is only a *representation* of the records, not a substitute for them. It indicates what is available, why it was compiled, its completeness, its physical nature, and the kind of information it contains. As soon as the researcher has identified what he needs to look at, the catalogue's task is done. The archivist should not therefore be tempted to consider the catalogue a work of art in its own right, or the next best thing to publishing an article about the records in a learned journal. It is merely a set of signposts, and should always be concise, clear, and shorn of unnecessary material.

The catalogue is prepared in two stages. First comes the arrangement of the records into order, according to established archival principles, and then follows the description of the records. The correct terminology for the process of cataloguing is therefore 'arrangement and description', or more simply 'listing', though in common parlance archivists talk about 'cataloguing' in the same way as they refer to the 'catalogue'. Arrangement, except in the case of certain computer applications (see p. 285), should always precede detailed listing.

Listing priorities

The archivist must decide which archives will be catalogued first, as a priority, and in what detail, and which will be left unlisted until later, which may mean for the indefinite future. There will almost certainly never be enough time and money to catalogue all the records to the highest standards. Choices will have to be made. Some records will have to be dealt with in a relatively cursory fashion to make time for more detailed work elsewhere. The difficulties will come in choosing just which records are to be treated in this way.

It may be useful, in attempting to solve this problem, to analyse the use made of the archives, and gear the finding aids accordingly. This cannot of course be the whole answer – such usage may not fall into obvious or unchanging patterns, nor should the archivist encourage one particular user or group of users to dictate the treatment of a collection of records. In addition, the process of listing a collection in detail almost always teaches the archivist a great deal about it; listing for its own sake, independent of current research trends, can thus widen horizons, as well as avoiding the dangers of favouritism. Nevertheless responses to user demand can please researchers, prevent confrontation and reduce the danger of professional arrogance and prejudice, and are therefore valuable so long as less popular areas of the archives are not completely ignored as a result. After all, enquirers and users are often the chief justification for there being an archive unit at all. It need hardly be added that it is also the archivist's responsibility to destroy or otherwise dispose of any material that is unworthy of permanent preservation on legal, administrative or historical grounds, rather than waste time in cataloguing it, and that the permission of the owner of the records must always be obtained first.

Archival arrangement

The archives of any organization need to be 'arranged' because they do not consist of single items on their own, as do most printed books, but are closely related to each other. The board minutes, for example, of a limited company will provide a basic chronological framework of the progress of the business; the correspondence files will give additional details about the various initiatives and projects undertaken, and a better picture of the personalities involved; the accounts will give the financial picture; and the memorandum and articles of association will provide the legal frame-work within which the whole enterprise was conducted. There will also be links within each category of records. For example, entries in the board minutes may cross-refer to earlier entries, or to the minutes of committees and sub-committees; while on the accounts side, the cash books and journals will contain entries corresponding to the individual invoices, receipts and so on in the annual bundles of vouchers to account; the ledgers will be derived from the cash books and journals; and the balance sheets will be prepared from the ledgers.

In addition, individual archival records were rarely intended to be read in isolation, or indeed by third parties, and do not usually have clear and informative titles, like those of published works. Instead they usually have administrative names, such as 'board minutes' and 'share registers'. This is because archives are produced as by-products of administration, to provide officials with a record of their decisions and dealings with others. Some records may no longer have even an administrative title, and the archivist will therefore have to provide an alternative, such as 'unidentified account book, 1870–4'. It would be meaningless to try and catalogue the records of a business individually and separately.

From the user's point of view also the best way of unlocking the information in a business archive is to use those items which the firm's record-keeping practices, and known history, suggest will be most profitable. Here again the catalogue helps the user by showing what records are available, and how they relate to each other.

The principle of provenance

The first important principle of archival arrangement is therefore that of provenance: records must be listed according to their provenance, by which is meant the organization, or part of a larger organization, that created them. The records of different organizations should not be mixed, nor should the records of different departments or branches of the same organization be confused. Any attempt to group by record type all the minutes, say, or ledgers, or share registers for a number of independent organizations will confuse the relations between the different types of record of the same organization. Even worse problems will arise if this treatment is applied to such records as correspondence files; here the ability to understand clearly who assembled a file, and why, is an essential part of comprehending its contents, whether original letters received, carbon copies of letters sent, original memoranda, notes of telephone conversations and so on. Failure to observe provenance will therefore seriously compromise the evidential value of this sort of material to the historian.

Any attempt to mix and merge separate collections of archives in one single large catalogue by *subject* (another superficially attractive option) rather than by provenance must also be avoided. Archives almost always contain information on a whole host of subjects, irrespective of the original purpose for which they were compiled. The records of a mining company, for example, will not be restricted to mining alone, but will probably contain information on such topics as the history, geology, topography and politics of the countries where the company operated, market conditions over the period of the company's active life, shipping, insurance, and labour relations, to name but a few. Furthermore the majority of individual records within the archives of the company will offer information on many of these topics simultaneously, and will not fall neatly into subject categories. An arrangement by provenance, however, should make subject-indexing easier. If the records of, say, the mining company already referred to are kept together, the major themes from the *entire* archive can be indexed in relation to the collection as a whole, rather than record by record. General index entries can thus refer users simply to 'ABC Mining Company Ltd' for such subjects as 'mining', 'gold', 'South Africa' or whatever; these general entries can then be supplemented by further entries picking up noteworthy aspects of individual records.

The principle of provenance also requires that records of subsidiary companies be distinguished from those of the parent company, because the subsidiaries are separate legal entities. Similarly, in the case of take-overs, the records of the acquired company should be listed separately, because up to the time of the take-over it was an independent concern. They should remain discrete if the company is kept in existence after the take-over as a new subsidiary of the purchaser. In the case of amalgamations, where companies merge on an equal basis, the archivist can either treat the new, merged company as a new entity, and its archives as a new collection, or more likely, if one company is the major party to the merger, treat the archives of that company both before and after the merger as one single collection, and keep the records of the lesser company distinct. In such circumstances the main sequences of archives of the major party often continue unaffected by the merger, and if the archivist treats the records as one single collection, he is merely continuing the treatment of the administrators who created them. This approach is equally valid where mergers take place between different departments or branches of the same organization.

A common problem with businesses is changes of name. Companies or their component departments can easily change their name, sometimes more than once, but this does not mean that the archives of each different name should be kept separate. The company/department is still essentially the same, and the principle of provenance therefore requires that the records be described together. Changes of name do, however, present a problem when compiling the catalogue, perhaps best solved by taking the latest, or current, name of the organization and listing all the records under that one name. The existence of the archives of the organization under its earlier name or names should be indicated to researchers through the indexes, which should cross-refer to the current name, e.g. 'Jones and Smith Mining Co. *see* ABC Mining Co. Ltd'. The chronological framework of changes of name down the years should also be brought out in a brief historical note at the start of the catalogue. Future changes of name, which of course cannot be predicted, can perhaps best be dealt with as they arise by additions to this historical note, and by further cross-references from the new name(s) to the standard form used in the catalogue.

In a computer application, the usual means of ensuring that such records are catalogued under a single name is to use an on-line authority file of approved names, with cross-references from former names, later names and variants. As well as helping the researcher, such an authority file can be designed so as actually to prevent the archivist from cataloguing under non-standard names. There is always a danger of this happening, and thus of archives being inadvertently split, wherever an organization's name has changed out of all recognition over the years.

The principle of the sanctity of original order

The other important principle of archival arrangement is that of the sanctity of original order: the archives of an organization should be arranged in the order that they had when last in active administrative use. The principle of original order can indeed be seen as the application of the principle of provenance at a lower level; provenance ensures that the records of an organization are kept distinct, to preserve their evidential value as a group, while original order ensures that nothing is done within the records of the one organization to damage their original arrangement, or the relationships between them.

Perhaps the most important application of the principle of original order is in relation to sequences of records. Administrators tend to compile and use records in sequences, which archivists call *classes* (internationally known as *series*). In these sequences each item contains the same sort of information as its fellows in the sequence, but for a different time period, say, or person, or place, or letter(s) of the alphabet, or subject. Examples of sequences are a set of minute books, each book continuing the contents of its predecessor; or a set of customer ledgers, where all the ledgers cover the same time period, but are divided up by letters of the alphabet, the first ledger containing customers with names beginning with A and B, the second containing C and D, and so on. A set of annual bundles of financial vouchers also forms a sequence, and so does one single bundle of, say, completed copies of the same printed form. The principle of original order demands that these original sequences should be kept intact, and not be split up. The records arranged in sequences can indeed often form the majority of the archives of an organization, and the archivist's ability to recognize, preserve or recreate original sequences of records as necessary is therefore a major weapon in arranging and describing collections.

In the case of sequences of volumes, even of two volumes only, there will be obvious economies of description in keeping and describing them together, and little reason to split them up. Problems can, however, arise with sequences of loose papers, where the temptation to rearrange the papers in a different way can be very strong. A classic example arises from the common practice in the past of arranging letters received from outside correspondents in annual bundles, with the contents of each bundle in date order; it can seem highly desirable to abandon these bundles, and instead to place the letters in an alphabetical arrangement by correspondent. However, this should be resisted. If the arrangement, however perverse, is original, it should be preserved. To do otherwise will obscure the original order, and make it more difficult for researchers to follow in the footsteps of the original administrators. It will render useless any contemporary finding aids, such as wrappers or inventories, and destroy any cross-references, themes or common denominators within the original arrangement. These themes may reflect particular preoccupations or emphases at the time the records were created, and be an important part of the value of the records as historical evidence. Historians and researchers may indeed be equally interested in what the records do *not* contain as in what is actually included.

An arrangement by original sequences or series will also help to reveal any gaps in the surviving records. A gap in a date sequence, a numbered sequence or an alphabetical arrangement will make it clear that something is missing; the existence of a few bundles arranged on a common principle, say one bundle per year, will raise the question of whether other bundles for other years have not survived. It is therefore important for the archivist to notice, and display through the catalogue, any less obvious evidence of gaps in the records, e.g. where the contemporary reference numbers of a sequence reveal a gap at the *start* of that sequence.

Any bundle of loose papers which does not form part of a sequence should also be kept together if it is an 'original' bundle, which displays the arrangement in which the records were originally used. The principle of the sanctity of original order still applies. The original administrators kept the documents together as a bundle, and the archivist should do so too.

Many archives will also contain a rump of jumbled material, usually loose papers, which have lost their original arrangement. The first priority here, clearly, is to reconstruct the original order of these papers as far as possible, using such evidence as similarity of content and format, endorsements, old wrappers, and folds and creases. The existence of other similar papers within the archive which have retained their original order in perfect condition will clearly be useful. However, if there is any doubt as to what the original order actually was, it will be better to impose an obviously artificial order rather than a phoney 'original' order. A small number of such items can be lumped together as 'miscellaneous papers'; but if there are too many for this to be helpful, the papers should be divided up on the basis of their content, for example by date, person, place or subject. Any such artificial order is of course only a last resort, when the original order cannot be discovered, and should be clearly indicated as such in the finding aid.

When it comes to the structure of the catalogue, however, the principle of original order is often compromised. In theory the structure of the catalogue should follow the structure of the organization at the time it created the records; but this structure may not be discoverable, or may have changed over time, so that the catalogue would have to be split into several sections, each differently arranged, in order to conform to the structure of the organization at any given period. This clearly would be impractical, and so archivists tend instead to invent for each archive a clear but neutral structure, based upon a classification scheme. A classification scheme sets out the records of an organization according to the functions that it performed (for example, share records, staff records, records of premises and property), and helps the user find his way around the catalogue in an unbiased manner. A sample classification scheme for business records, arranged by function, is set out below. The scheme attempts to be comprehensive enough to cover the various legal structures possible for a business (such as partnership, deed of settlement company, statutory company, or limited liability company), and also to take in the infinite number of functions, aims and objects that different businesses might have. Few but the largest and most varied business archives will therefore contain more than a fraction of the types of record covered by this particular scheme, while parts of the scheme, such as section 3.3, may be inadequate for the needs of some business repositories. The scheme is therefore no more than a starting point, and should be adapted to suit local circumstances. The scheme also suggests how catalogues might be divided by sub-headings to make their layout easier for the reader to use. Two versions of a short sample catalogue using the scheme and its sub-headings can be found on pp. 299–300.

The scheme itself is as follows:

1 Corporate records
1 Royal charters/Acts of parliament.
2 Deeds of settlement.
3 Memorandum and articles of association.
4 Certificates of incorporation.
5 Partnership agreements.
6 Amalgamation/liquidation papers.
7 Minutes of meetings of managing body, e.g. board of directors, partners.
8 Records relating to these meetings, e.g. agenda, presented papers, attendance books.
9 Minutes of annual, extraordinary and other meetings of shareholders and debenture-holders.
10 Records relating to these meetings, e.g. agenda, proxy forms, circulars.
11 Directors' annual reports and accounts to shareholders.
12 Committee minutes and related papers.
13 Registers of directors and secretaries, and of shareholdings and interests of directors.
14 Seal books.
15 Miscellaneous.

2 Share records
1 Prospectuses.
2 Registers of shareholders.
3 Application and allotment records.
4 Registers of debentures and debenture-holders.
5 Transfer registers and forms.
6 Share and debenture certificates.
7 Probate registers.
8 Dividend books.
9 Annual returns to Registrar of Companies.
10 Amalgamation/liquidation records, e.g. notices to shareholders, allotment books.
11 Miscellaneous.

3 Internal administration
1 General letterbooks and correspondence (concerning internal administration, not conduct of business).
2 Memoranda books.
3 Departmental administrative records.
4 Miscellaneous.

4 Accounting and financial records
1 Balance sheets and profit and loss accounts (not for shareholders).

2   Trial balances and balance books.
3   Audit papers.
4   Private, general, impersonal and personal ledgers.
5   Sales and purchase ledgers and other specialized ledgers.
6   Journals.
7   Waste books, day books, cash books.
8   Invoices.
9   Bill books.
10   Bank pass books/cheque books.
11   Bad and doubtful debt records.
12   Investment records (except where investment is the business of the company).
13   Tax and excise records.
14   Management accounts.
15   Miscellaneous.

5   Legal (other than property/premises)
1   Records of patents and trademarks.
2   Agreements and licences.
3   Records of litigation, including opinions of counsel.
4   Miscellaneous.

6   Operation
1   Manufacturing records (vary according to business).
2   Estimate and order books.
3   Day books.
4   Distribution records.
5   Letterbooks/correspondence (concerning conduct of business).
6   Other records concerning operation of business (vary according to business).
7   Technical drawings.
8   Research and development records.
9   Miscellaneous.

7   Marketing and public relations
1   Stock catalogues.
2   Leaflets.
3   Advertisements.
4   Photographs and videos.
5   Press releases.
6   Company magazines.
7   Miscellaneous.

8   Staff and employment records
1   Wages and salaries books.
2   Personnel registers and records.
3   Pension records.

4   Training and apprenticeship records.
5   Health and safety records.
6   Industrial relations records.
7   Recreation clubs and societies records.
8   House journals.
9   Miscellaneous.

9   Premises and property records (except where property is the business of the company)
1   Property records, e.g. registers, rentals, surveys.
2   Premises records, e.g. building agreements and plans, plant registers, inventories, valuations, architectural drawings.
3   Repairs records.
4   Insurance records.
5   Title deeds, etc.
6   Miscellaneous.

10 Other
Unpublished histories, photographs (not used for advertising), trade association papers, etc.

11 Branch/agency records (where these are distinct from head office)

12 Family papers

The categories in this classification scheme should not be interpreted too rigidly. For example, section 2.4, registers of debentures and debenture-holders, can be used for other related material, such as minutes of the trustees of a debenture issue, and not merely for the formal registers.

Conflicts between provenance and original order

Sooner or later the archivist will encounter a straightforward conflict between the principle of provenance and the principle of original order.[2] A classic example of such a conflict in the business context is the archive of a solicitor's practice which includes various records of a business, or of a number of businesses, for which the practice acted in the past as legal adviser or even as secretary. Should these records, which may include major sequences such as minute books, be catalogued among the records of the practice, or separately, as records of the businesses concerned? The dilemma can be all the greater if the businesses still exist, and have their own collections of archives.

   Another example of a conflict between provenance and original order is where the company secretary of a limited company with a number of subsidiaries keeps all the minute books, say, or all the share records of the various companies together, and perhaps even applies a working numeration to them. Should the archivist list the records of the various subsidiaries separately, following their provenance, because they are separate legal entities, or together, following their original order, because that will reflect the order in which they were used?

There are no easy answers to such conflicts. In instances such as those above some archivists will follow provenance and some original order. Whichever solution is adopted, it should of course be supported by all necessary cross-references, so that the user can see clearly what has been done, and so that the relationships between the different records are not obscured.

The effect of computers on archival arrangement

Computerized catalogues have numerous advantages over manual systems. In particular, they can provide powerful searching and sorting facilities to enable catalogue entries to be retrieved and ordered according to, for example, provenance, subject matter, reference numbers, and date ranges, as required, and can thereby dispense with the need for separate indexes. Order of input is immaterial because of the sorting facilities of computers, and because information is stored randomly. Further details of the use of computers in the compilation and use of finding aids are given in Chapter 13.

It might therefore seem that computers remove the need for the archivist to observe the principles of provenance and original order: if records can be catalogued in any order, and still retrieved, there will be no need for the records of the same organization to be listed together, or for arrangement to precede description; and classification schemes, in the traditional sense, may be rendered unnecessary.[3] There is indeed some truth in this, and a few business repositories do input catalogue entries randomly as a matter of practical convenience.

However, many of the database software packages in common use among archivists still require records to be arranged before being catalogued, so that the appropriate level of descriptive detail can be chosen in each case. In addition, no matter how well the computer can sort catalogue entries in response to specific requests, there will still be a need, as there is under a manual system, to produce lists of the *entire* records of individual organizations, so that researchers can survey and comprehend all the available material of an organization together. Such a list will be arranged most appropriately by the function, and then by the form, of the records. In order to achieve this, the provenance and nature of particular records will have to be considered and an appropriate identification device incorporated into the database structure. Thus the archivist will still need to ensure that all descriptions of records are clear and distinct, and will still need to acquire a detailed familiarity with the archives before they can be described successfully. It is only by sorting and arranging an archive collectively, and understanding it thoroughly before any catalogue entries are finalized, that an archivist can successfully compile a clear and consistent catalogue. This process will also allow original sequences to be catalogued and presented to the user together far more elegantly and comprehensibly than if the individual components of each sequence were to appear as random and separate catalogue entries. Arrangement therefore should still be carried out wherever possible, even when computers are employed.

Therefore, although computers store information randomly, they do not dispense with the principles of provenance and original order, which must still be observed in the formatting of both input and output. They can also make such operations as additions to an existing catalogue much easier.

The physical arrangement of the catalogue

The catalogue will almost certainly contain lists of the records of more than one company or organization. The business archivist may work for a company that has subsidiary or associated companies; it may also have taken over other companies and their records at some point in the past. The company will also, almost certainly, itself be divided into different departments, and may have a number of remote branches. Following the principle of original order, the archives of all these companies, departments and branches should be kept distinct. The front of the catalogue should therefore contain contents pages, listing these different archives and their individual, subsidiary catalogues in the order in which they appear. It does not greatly matter whether this order is alphabetical, or gives major companies and then minor companies or whatever, so long as it is clear. Both the contents pages and the rest of the catalogue should also, wherever possible, be word-processed. This will make it easier to alter or add to the catalogue whenever necessary, and will also generate automatic revisions of the pagination. At the same time it may still be useful to mark the divisions between the different sections of the catalogue with tags or coloured card, for ease of access. A fully computerized catalogue will be even better, and remove the need for much of the deliberate 'signposting' necessary with a manual system.

The subsidiary catalogues, of the records of each company, department or branch, should be made up of a number of standard elements. Each should start on a separate page, with a preliminary statement containing the following: the name of the organization; where the records were transferred from and when; the terms of transfer and accession number(s); the date(s) and author(s) of the catalogue; any other general instructions, such as the opening hours, address, telephone number and access arrangements of the repository; and whether or not there are any restrictions on access to specific items. A typical preliminary statement might read:

ABC MINING COMPANY LTD: COMPANY SECRETARY'S
DEPARTMENT
Records transferred from the Company Secretary, 15 June 1994
(accession number 25).

Catalogued by J. Jones, July 1994.

Subject to any special restrictions below, these records are available at the ABC Mining Co. Ltd archive unit, [address], 9am–5pm Mondays to Friday. A prior appointment is essential.

NOTE: NO ACCESS TO BOARD MINUTES WITHOUT PER-MISSION OF COMPANY SECRETARY.

With a larger collection, transferred in stages, a briefer form may be more appropriate:

ABC MINING COMPANY LTD: COMPANY SECRETARY'S DEPARTMENT
Records transferred by the Company Secretary, various dates, 1993–4 (accession numbers 13, 25 and 45).

Catalogued by J. Jones, July 1994.

Refs. . . . [i.e. various additional items, accession numbers . . .] added by S. Smith, September 1994.

Subject to . . . [as above]

NOTE: . . . [as above]

In such instances the precise details of the transfers will be discoverable if necessary from the accessions register.

The preliminary statement thus makes clear whether or not a catalogue is still being added to, and allows the researcher to identify new entries. The details of the address of the repository and its opening hours will be useful if copies of the catalogue are to be supplied outside the repository, for example to the departments which transferred the records, to members of the public, or to outside bodies, such as the Royal Commission on Historical Manuscripts for inclusion in the National Register of Archives.

After the preliminary statement should come a brief administrative history of the organization that created the archives, again on a separate page. In the case of a company this should include its origins, objects and founders; brief details of its legal structure (for example, the date of incorporation as a limited liability company and whether public or private, or, if a partnership, dates and details of the successive partners); details of any take-overs or changes of name; the various addresses from which it conducted its business; any major changes during its history in its business activities (for example, from rubber planting to timber distribution, from trading to merchant banking, from trade in SE Asia to trade in Brazil); and some indication of the existence and business of any subsidiary companies, cross-referenced if appropriate to the catalogues of their archives. In the case of a department or branch of a company, the brief history should give details of its creation, purpose within the company, relationship with other departments or branches, and location; it might also be useful to repeat the brief history of the parent company in some form, for clarity. The brief administrative history should also include a bibliography of any useful books and articles about the organization and its history, and details of any records known to be held elsewhere, such as by the controlling family, the company, department or branch, or the local record office. An appendix, giving a list of chairmen/directors/partners/senior managers, branches and the like, as appropriate, may also be helpful.

The catalogue of the actual records should now follow. The records should already have been arranged by provenance into their original order, as far as possible, in the manner discussed above. If the catalogue is substantial, it should be preceded by a contents page, indicating its principal subdivisions. It will also be helpful to provide a key to any abbreviations used.

The following is a checklist of the standard elements of a catalogue:

- Title of collection, i.e. the name of the organization that created the records.
- Date(s) and source(s) of transfer(s) of records to repository; terms of transfer; accession number(s).
- Date(s) and author(s) of catalogue/addition(s) to catalogue.
- Name, address, telephone number of repository; opening hours; normal policy on access.
- Special restrictions on access, if any.
- Brief administrative history of the creating organization (including some details of the parent organization if the catalogue is of the records of a department or branch); a bibliography of useful books, articles etc.; and information about records held elsewhere, e.g. family papers, records deposited in the local record office, or material still held by the company, branch or department. If appropriate, a list of chairmen/directors/partners/senior managers, branches and the like can be added as an appendix.
- Contents page (if catalogue substantial).
- Key to abbreviations used in the catalogue.
- Catalogue entries for the records, reflecting their original order and giving reference numbers by which items can be ordered from the storage area.
- Index (if catalogue substantial). However, it may be better to dispense with specific indexes of this nature in favour of a union index to all the catalogues, especially under a manual system, where the two versions of the same index will probably have to be compiled separately. Computerized indexing will make it a relatively simple matter to produce indexes in both forms as a result of one indexing effort.

Archival description

It is not possible in a general chapter like this to give more than a brief and basic introduction to the compilation of individual catalogue entries; however, a good deal of theoretical work on archival description, its structure and data elements, has recently been published by a team from the University of Liverpool.[4] These publications analyse the different levels at which archives may be described, from that of the entire archive of an organization down to individual pieces of paper within a bundle of material, and attempt to suggest and define a body of relevant technical terms. They also discuss many examples of different styles and levels of catalogue descriptions, gathered from a variety of repositories. They should be studied for further guidance on cataloguing, together with the additional works listed in Further reading, p. 314.

Records should be catalogued by their original administrative titles, if possible, or, failing that, in terms which approximate to them as nearly as possible. Thus for example board of directors' minute books, cash books, or journals, should be described as such.[5] Further descriptive information about the contents of some records, or about their relationships with other records, may be desirable, but should be subordinated to the administrative title, which should appear at the start of the catalogue entry. In the case of directors' minute books, or of cash books and journals, it is probably unnecessary to add any further detail as to the contents, since these are standard types of record; however, a more obscure contemporary title might be explained as follows:

ABC MINING COMPANY LTD: GENERAL MANAGER'S DEPARTMENT
'Black book', summarizing annual output from the bauxite mines in British Guiana, together with statistics of annual capital investment at each mine; number of workers and output per worker per mine; and notes on labour conditions and industrial relations. 1960–5.
   1 volume.

In this example the contemporary term 'Black book' is meaningless to the researcher, and needs explanation. It also needs to be placed in quotes, to make clear that it is the original name of the item.

It is not necessary for the archivist to describe every physically distinct item, i.e. every book, or piece of paper, in the archive one by one. If the contents of a file, or bundle, or folder of material were used *together*, they should be listed together, for example:

Company Secretary's in-letters concerning share registration. 1903.
   1 bundle of 300 items.

An itemized catalogue of each item in the bundle may indeed be useful in certain cases, but should not be the first priority. Such a catalogue will not reflect the way in which the records were originally used, while the effort and expense of producing it may well not be justified by the value of the additional information produced.[6]

In the case of some bundles, the catalogue entry may suggest the actual subject matter of the documents more closely, for example:

> Company Secretary's in-letters from Mrs Jane Bloggs, Blackheath, asking for a new share certificate to replace the one eaten by her dog. 1903.
>   4 items in envelope.

It would perhaps be wrong simply to describe the contents of this envelope as 'Company Secretary's in-letters concerning share registration. 1903. 4 items in envelope', because it would fail to explain why the smaller bundle had been kept distinct. Even if we cannot see why Mrs Bloggs' letters were kept separate, the fact remains that they were, and the catalogue should reflect this. She may turn out to have been the wife of the chairman of the company!

It is also important for the archivist to describe records impartially, and to avoid highlighting subjects of personal interest, or of interest to others, if they would have been unimportant at the time the records were created. Such highlights will affect the clarity of the catalogue as a description of the content and purpose of the records, and introduce a modern bias. There is of course nothing wrong in adding extra detail to a catalogue entry, but it should always be relevant to the aim of explaining the administrative purpose and function of the records. The catalogue should be an austere document: if any points of interest seem so valuable that they must be included, they should appear as footnotes to the main entries, and be regarded as exceptional.

The catalogue should also be concise, and consistently laid out, each entry following a set pattern. Catalogue entries are much easier to compile and use if each of their various components has an allotted place and format. For example, it may be useful to put the dates of each entry at the end of the description, after a full stop, and the physical details of the records on the next line, indented slightly from the margin. This pattern was followed in the examples above, and allows the inclusion of extra information, and extra dates, while leaving the important dates clear, for example:

> Deeds of the company head office at 1, Acacia Avenue, London W1; include an inventory of office fixtures and fittings, 1874. 1801–1963.
>   1 bundle of 40 items.

Here the use of the semicolon shows that the entry is not yet complete, and that subsidiary information is about to be given, while the comma before

1874 shows that this particular date is part of the subsidiary information, and that the outside dates of the deeds as a whole have still to be given.

Some indication of the sizes of volumes can also be helpful, and can make it easier to locate missing items. One simple method is to decide on a 'normal' size, say a range of heights, which will be described simply as '1 volume', and to describe all volumes larger or smaller than the range of 'normal' sizes as 'large' or 'small' volumes respectively.

The physical details can also be expanded to give details of available indexes or schedules of those specific records. Though not strictly part of the physical description of the records, such information will stand out better than in the middle of the main description or as an appendage to the whole entry. To make it still clearer it can also be underlined. To take the last example again:

> Deeds . . . . 1801–1963.
>   1 bundle of 40 items. For schedule see register of deeds, ref. [and the reference number of the register].

Any access restrictions on a specific item, bundle or sequence can conveniently be placed right at the end of the entry, on a new line, and in capitals, where they will stand out. Thus the same entry would read:

> Deeds . . .
>   1 bundle of 40 items . . .
>
> NOTE: ACCESS RESTRICTED.

The actual form of words of the restriction can be varied to suit local circumstances.

The dates given at the end of a catalogue entry should be the dates of creation of the actual records being described. If the date of creation of a record is not stated in the record itself, but is discoverable for certain from other sources, it should be given in square brackets []. Care is also necessary with later copies of earlier texts. A catalogue entry should not say:

> Deed of settlement. 1824.
>   Paper, 1 booklet. Printed.

if it really means the following:

> Printed copy of the deed of settlement, 1824. 1956.
>   Paper, 1 booklet. Privately printed by the company.

The second entry is superior to the first in that it states clearly that the item is a copy of an earlier original, and carefully distinguishes between the two. The same approach should be adopted for contemporary copies:

Certified copy of the Royal charter of the company, 1846. Compiled
c.1846.
1 volume.

Once again, the details of the original have been carefully distinguished
from those of the copy. It would not be correct to describe this record
simply as 'the Royal charter of the company'.

There is of course an infinite variety of possible patterns of catalogue
entry. For example, some archivists place the dates of the records in a
separate column, to one side of the descriptive entries, where they can be
scanned all together; others underline all proper names in the descriptions.
It does not really matter which pattern is followed, provided the same
pattern is used all the time. It is therefore a good idea for the archivist to
adopt and enforce a standard 'house style', to ensure consistency of
presentation. For further comments on 'house style' see pp. 302–3.

The archive may also include such non-paper records as photographs,
microforms and cinematographic film. Here again, these should be
described in such a way as to indicate their contents, relationship with
other records, and usefulness for research. The format of the actual
catalogue entries should follow that of the rest of the catalogue as far as
possible. For further information on cataloguing non-paper records see
Chapter 8.

Printed material

Published works which form part of an archive should also be described by
means of a standard format. Essential features for printed books and
pamphlets will be: name(s) of author(s) or editor(s), if possible; title of
work, underlined; name of publisher and date of publication, in round
brackets; and a brief physical description, for example:

A. C. Pointon, The Bombay Burmah Trading Corporation Limited
1863–1963 (privately printed, 1964).
1 volume. Printed.

The physical description, which would not necessarily appear in this form
in a standard bibliographic description, should imitate the format of the
manuscript catalogue entries, but at the same time show clearly that the
items are printed.

Note, however, that administrative records in printed form, such as
circulars to shareholders, directors' annual reports and accounts, and the
like, should be described in the same way as other manuscript archives,
and not in a bibliographical format:

Directors' annual reports and accounts. 1920–65.
46 items in one bundle. Printed.

Notice of extraordinary general meeting. 1947.
1 item. Printed.

Sequences of records

It was noted above that most archival records are compiled and used in sequences, which archivists call *classes*, or *series*. A set of directors' minute books for a company is an obvious example. The contents of these sequences should not be described individually, book by book, at the level of the individual item, but all together, at the level of the entire class, as follows, with the individual volumes identified only by their distinctive details:

> Board of directors' minute books. 1824–1955.
> 72 volumes.
> > 1   1824–6
> > 2   1826–8
> > 3   1828–31 . . .
> > 72   1954–5

Here the description of the records has been given for the whole sequence of minute books together, at class level. All that is given for each volume is its *distinctive* details, that is to say its covering dates. A description of the class book by book would look something like this:

> 1   Board of directors' minute book. 1824–6. 1 volume
> 2   ”   ”   ”   ”   ”   1826–8. 1 volume.
> 3   ”   ”   ”   ”   ”   1828–31. 1 volume.
> . . . etc.

A more extreme example might look like this:

> XXX AND CO. LTD
> Board of directors' minute book. 1824–6.
> 1 volume.
>
> XXX AND CO. LTD
> Board of directors' minute book. 1826–8.
> 1 volume. . . . etc.

These latter examples, though less elegant than the first version and wasteful of effort and paper, would be perfectly usable; they would, however, have been much less successful if the descriptive information about the records had been longer than just five words. A catalogue entry with a much fuller introductory description might be:

> Registers of overseas staff. Up to 1901 these include European staff only; from that year foreign salaried staff are also included. Some details

of foreign staff before 1901 can, however, be traced from the overseas salary books, refs. [reference numbers]. 1854–1958.
  25 volumes. Volumes 1–22 indexed by personal names; volumes 1–8 and 15–25 also indexed by place.
  1   1854–63
  2   1863–74 . . . etc.

This example brings out the advantages of a description at class level rather than at item level. Archival sequences can remain in use for a very long time – in extreme cases from the Middle Ages to the present day – and are often adapted over time to meet changing circumstances. The example also shows how important it is for the archivist to analyse records thoroughly, and bring out the ways in which they relate to one another.

Some sequences will be incomplete. In such cases the description should make clear that there are gaps, while the tabulation of the individual items should show what is missing. One possible approach is as follows:

Board of directors' minute books. 1824–1955. Incomplete.
  5 volumes.
  1   1824–6
  2   1826–8
  3   1920–2
  4   1922–6
  5   1954–5

In this example the outside dates of the sequence have been given, with a statement that the sequence is incomplete. An alternative approach would be:

Board of directors' minute books. 1824–8, 1920–6, 1954–5.
  5 volumes.
  1   1824–6
  2   1826–8 . . . etc.

To add Incomplete to this second entry would imply that the minutes were fragmentary even for these specific years, which would not be correct.

Some sequences have no clear chronological progression. If there is no other means of ordering the entries, they should be arranged in date order by opening date, thus:

1   1824–38
2   1833–7
3   1838–52
4   1839–53

However, additional detail can often be added to make matters clear to the reader, for example:

Scrapbooks of company engineer's drawings of mines administered by the company. 1865–1960.
> 4 volumes.
>> 1 British Guiana. 1900–60 ('no. 1')
>> 2 Java. 1890–1950 ('no. 2')
>> 3 South Africa. 1865–1910, with one item of 1938 ('no. 3')
>> 4 South Africa. 1911–48 ('no. 4')

Here the sequence is essentially topographical rather than chronological, and also contains a 'mini-sequence' for South Africa. Enough detail has been given to make this clear, and also to show that the 1938 plan of a South African mine is an exception to the pattern.

'Rogue' dates

'Rogue' dates, as in volume 3 in the last example above, can be a problem. If most of a group of papers fall within a limited date range, say 1865–1910, but there is other material of 1938, it is misleading to give the dates in the catalogue entry as '1865–1938'. The solution will vary, however, according to the relative significance of the material for the 'rogue' year. If there are just a few 'rogue' items, this should be stated explicitly, as in the example above, so that they are minimized relative to the other records. Another example might be:

> 1870–7, with 5 items of 1893.
>> 1 bundle.

A 'rogue' year with significant material should be expressed in a more neutral fashion, by the use of 'and':

> 1865–1910 and 1938
> 1870–7 and 1893.

Brackets, as in '1865–1910 (1938)', are sometimes used, but their meaning is not immediately clear to the user, and they should therefore be avoided.

'Particular instance' papers

'Particular instance' papers (PIPS) also present problems for the archivist. These represent individual examples or cases of one general kind of business, for example insurance claim files, where each file contains the papers relating to one single claim against an insurance company. Such papers effectively form a sequence like any other, and if not too large, can be treated in much the same fashion as other sequences, the main information being given at the level of the whole sequence, and only the distinguishing details being given for each file, bundle or whatever. For the claim files referred to above, a suitable catalogue entry might therefore be as follows:

House structure insurance claim files. 1890–1960.
  250 files.
    1   36 High Street, Borchester. 1890
    2   Cosy cot, Ambridge. 1893 . . . etc.

However, for the majority of PIPS, this approach will be ruled out by the very size of the sequence. It is not uncommon for the number of files, bundles or whatever in a series of PIPS to run into the thousands, if not tens of thousands, and some different cataloguing method is therefore necessary. The simplest, and probably best solution, often available as a result of the sheer size and importance of the sequence to its original compilers, is to use the contemporary finding aids, perhaps a register or series of registers, and by doing so to keep the description of the sequence of PIPS very brief:

Registers of house structure insurance claims. 1890–1960.
  15 volumes. Indexed. On shelves in reading room.
    1   1890–1900 . . . etc.

House structure insurance claim files. 1890–1960.
  Approximately 15,000 files in 150 boxes. For schedules and indexes of these files, giving contemporary reference numbers, see the contemporary claims registers, [refs.]
    Box 1.   Files 1890/1 to 1893/42
    Box 2.   Files 1893/43 to 1897/2 . . . etc.

In these examples the contemporary registers of claims are presented in the catalogue as the lists and indexes of the claim files, and are stored in the reading room for immediate use. The catalogue entry for the files consequently presents no more than a general picture of the sequence, together with a breakdown of where any given file is to be found. The files themselves have simply been boxed in their original order. No effort has been made to give any meaning to the contents of each box.

Much greater difficulties occur with large sequences of PIPS where the contemporary finding aids are missing or incomplete. In such circumstances it is still desirable, for obvious reasons, that the catalogue entry should be brief, but it is unlikely that time will be found to recreate the original finding aids. With luck, the original order of the papers will allow some sort of arrangement by date or by letters of the alphabet, which will go some way towards helping the user to understand the series. The claim files already referred to might be catalogued under such circumstances as follows:

House structure insurance claim files. 1890–1960.
Approximately 15,000 files in 200 boxes.

        1   1890
        2   1891
        3   1892 . . .
. . . 198   1960 Jan. – Apr.
     199   1960 May – Aug.
     200   1960 Sept – Dec.

The files have now been reboxed, and can be requested by year. The more recent files, being more bulky, have required more than one box per year, and are in blocks of 4 months at a time. Users of the catalogue are still left ignorant as to the precise contents of the claim files, but can make some limited use of the material. A disadvantage for the archivist is that the records now occupy a lot more boxes!

The original order of a sequence of PIPS should always be retained if possible. The size of the sequence, the very reason that PIPS present problems at all, will make it highly unlikely that an artificial order can successfully be imposed.

Old reference numbers

Reference numbers allocated during the active use of the records by the organization that created them should normally be recorded in the catalogue entry, if they are known, in inverted commas, since they may be referred to in other contemporary records, and may also help to make clear the original order. In the case of single items, these earlier references can appear either at the end of the catalogue entry or within the entry itself. Thus the same item might be described as, for example,

General ledger. 1864–9.
  1 volume. 'no. 1'.

or

General ledger 'no. 1'. 1864–9.
  1 volume.

With sequences of records, the earlier references should appear next to the relevant item:

General ledgers. 1860–1938.
  20 volumes.
    1 missing
    2 missing
    3 1860–5 ('no. 3')
    4 1865–74 ('no. 4')

    5   1875–83 ('no. 5') . . .
   22   1929–38 ('no. 22')

Partners' out-letter books. 1865–1923. <u>Incomplete.</u>
   25 volumes.
    1   1865–6 ('no. 1')
    2   1866–8 ('no. 2')
    3   missing
    4   1870–2 ('no. 4') . . . etc.

Registers of life-insurance policies. 1865–1910.
   5 volumes.
    1   1865–77 (nos. 1–250)
    2   1877–90 (nos. 251–500) . . . etc.

In the first two examples there are additional refinements. Volumes have been listed as 'missing'. The old reference numbers show how many volumes have been lost, and the catalogue can therefore allocate dummy numbers to them, in case they should ever reappear. This is particularly useful in the first example, where the gaps come at the start of the sequence and would otherwise be concealed from the user. Note, however, that the dates and the total number of volumes should refer to the surviving records, and not to the series as originally compiled.

In the last example the serial numbers of the life policies have been quoted beside the dates of each volume, since the compilers of these volumes appear to have thought of them in terms of the policies that they contained, and not in terms of their date spans.

Catalogue reference numbers

As part of the process of description, records are assigned reference numbers. There are of course a great many different numbering systems in use among archivists;[7] the important thing is that the system, whatever it is, should be consistent, universal, and also expandable, to allow for later additions and interpolations. It is also a good idea to keep the numbering system as simple as possible. Archivists have always tended to produce complex, perhaps over-complex, schemes of numeration, no doubt as a result of their training in hierarchical classification. However, researchers often find complex numbering schemes baffling to use, and they should therefore be avoided if possible.

One possible numbering system, based upon the suggested classification scheme shown on pp. 282–4, incorporates the numbers of the main sections of the classification scheme (corporate records, share records, etc.), and of the different types of record within each section, into the catalogue reference. Re-using and adding to some of the earlier examples, this gives the following:

ABC MINING COMPANY LTD

1 Corporate records

1/3/1 Memorandum and articles of association. 1863.
   1 volume. <u>Printed</u>.

1/7/1–72 Board of directors' minute books. 1824–1955.
   72 volumes.
      1/7/1 1824–6
      1/7/2 1826–8
      1/7/3 1828–31 . . . etc.

2 Share records

2/5/1 Share transfer register 'no. 1'. 1824–7.
   1 volume.

  . . .

9 Premises and property records

9/1/1 Register of company title deeds. Compiled 1965, and containing schedules of the deeds of all real property held by the company at that date.
   1 volume.

9/5/1 Deeds of the company head office at 1, Acacia Avenue, London W1; include an inventory of office fixtures and fittings, 1874. 1801–1963.
   1 bundle of 40 items. <u>For schedule see register of deeds, ref. ABC 9/1/1.</u>

NOTE: ACCESS RESTRICTED.

The advantages of this system are that it is fairly easy to apply; it gives a number to every item that has been described, while making it a simple matter to add accruals of records, such as a directors' minute book from 1955 onwards (ABC 1/7/73) or a second bundle of company deeds (ABC 9/5/2); and it is easily expanded, so that if, for instance, it was necessary to number the individual deeds within ABC 9/5/1, they could become ABC 9/5/1/1–40. Omissions can also be rectified fairly easily: should for example a memorandum and articles of association earlier than 1863 be found, it would become 1/3/1, and the present 1/3/1 would become 1/3/2. If on the other hand we wished to insert the new discovery when we already had existing items numbered as 1/3/1–10, we could renumber the former 1/3/1 as 1/3/1A, and leave the other numbers unaltered. Such a system also allows those familiar with it to identify records from reference numbers alone.

The disadvantage of such a system is that it is somewhat cumbersome, and therefore prone to error and miscopying. As an alternative, reference numbers can be kept much simpler, perhaps just plain numbers, with sub-numbers for the individual items in sequences of records. Indeed all the records in the repository can receive references from the same rising number sequence, and without any mnemonics to identify each archive collection. The same catalogue entries as above might appear under such a system as follows, the first number (205) being no more than the next available catalogue reference number:

ABC MINING COMPANY LTD
Corporate records
205   Memorandum and articles of association. 1863.
   1 volume. Printed.
206/1–72   Board of directors' minute books. 1824–1955.
   72 volumes.
      1   1824–6
      2   1826–8
      3   1828–31 . . . etc.

Share records
207   Share transfer register 'no. 1'. 1824–7.
   1 volume.

Premises and property records
208   Register of company title deeds. Compiled 1965, and containing schedules of the deeds of all real property held by the company at that date.
   1 volume.
209   Deeds of the company head office at . . . etc.

Additions to the catalogue, if they are not to be added to existing references, can simply be allocated the next unused reference numbers in the rising number sequence, and written into the catalogue at the appropriate point.

Such a system is certainly easier in many ways. On the other hand, it will be difficult if not impossible for either staff or visiting researchers to identify the record that goes with any particular reference number unless the entire catalogue is maintained in a duplicate series of entries in reference-number order. This second version of the catalogue will of course omit the catalogue sub-headings, and each entry will be laid out slightly differently, so as to state the name of the archive collection to which it belongs:

205
ABC MINING COMPANY LTD
Memorandum and articles of association . . .

206/1–72
ABC MINING COMPANY LTD
Board of directors' minute books . . .

207
ABC MINING COMPANY LTD
Share transfer register . . .

A computerized system would avoid the need to maintain two versions of the catalogue, since the computer would be able to treat the same entries in different ways. It would avoid the need for constant cross-checking between the two versions to make sure that they were still the same, and it would be able to cope with accruals and additions without retyping.

Numbering and labelling

In theory every record, i.e. every volume, sheet of paper or whatever forms a separate physical object, should be marked with its permanent reference number as soon as it is catalogued. Thus, ideally, if a catalogue entry reads 'Vouchers. 1870. 1 bundle', every piece of paper in that bundle should be numbered. This will help guard against theft, and allow stray material to be replaced easily. In practice, however, this approach is normally too time-consuming, except for particularly noteworthy or valuable records. A more common approach is therefore to number the records at the level at which reference numbers have been allocated in the catalogue. Thus, if the catalogue allocates a reference number to '1 volume', that volume should be numbered. If the catalogue allocates a reference number to '1 bundle', that bundle should be numbered on the outside, so that it is clearly identifiable with the description in the catalogue. The contents of the bundle, however, should be left blank, because the catalogue has not allocated any sub-numbers to them, and thus offers no means of ordering one item from the bundle as opposed to another.

In the case of a more complex example, such as:

Papers relating to the Private Act of Parliament. 1886.
Five booklets, 3 rolled plans and 4 bundles, in box.

the outside of the box alone should be numbered, because the catalogue entry has again failed to describe, or allocate numbers to, the individual items or bundles in the box so that they can be called for separately. It therefore follows that if at any stage a catalogue entry is rewritten in greater detail, so that the contents of a bundle, say, are listed with sub-numbers, then the numbering of the actual records will need to be altered to match.

Volumes should be numbered inside the front cover, on the earliest available page, avoiding marbled endpapers and the like. They should also be numbered on the outside, so that the number is visible as the book rests on the shelf. One possibility is to use glued labels, and to stick them low down the spines of hardbound volumes, if the thickness of the volume allows, and if the spine itself has not come off. However, if the spine is unsatisfactory, the label can be fixed to the bottom left corner of the front cover. An alternative method is to use strips of card, one inch wide and at least 6 inches long, which can be placed between the pages of the volume so as to project above the covers. Both methods have their disadvantages: labels fall off and get lost, while strips of card, however long, tend to fall down inside their volumes or on to the floor. If the archivist is ever fortunate enough to have any volumes recased or rebound, he or she should take the opportunity to have the reference numbers blocked permanently on to the new spines by the binder.

Single records other than volumes, e.g. single sheets of paper, sheafs physically joined together and the like, where they are individually numbered in the catalogue, should be numbered directly on to the record itself. The numbering should be carried out in a manner which is prominent and clear, avoids the text of the original as much as possible, and defaces it no more than is necessary.

Bundles of loose material should be numbered on a label attached to the tape that holds the bundle together, or, if the records are held in a wrapper, folder or other container, on the outside of that container. The archivist should be cautious of using the same tape or container for more than one reference number in the catalogue. If this is necessary, it should be clearly indicated in the catalogue, to warn both archivist and user that a request for one particular item will necessitate the production of others as well. Examples might be as follows:

Cash books. 1910–15. Each volume covers alternate days of the week.
2 volumes, tied together.
   1   1910–15 Mondays, Wednesdays, Fridays
   2   1910–15 Tuesdays, Thursdays, Saturdays

Patent for the xyz process. 1933.
1 item, bundled with the other patents [refs. . . .]

The catalogue entry or entries for the other patents will of course need to convey a similar message to that in the second example.

The same approach will be necessary where the importance of a particular batch of papers has caused the archivist to abandon a catalogue entry that lists them simply as a batch, and to sub-number them instead.

Layout and 'house style'

The catalogue should have wide margins, at least 1½ inches on the left and one inch on the other 3 sides, and be double-spaced. The left-hand margin will make binding easier; the other margins and the double spacing will make it possible to insert additions and corrections to the text. The catalogue should also be laid out consistently, and make use of spacing, and of different styles of lettering, to indicate the relative importance of different headings. The following lettering styles, numbered here in order of importance, should be more than enough, and should be available on a word-processor:

1	**ABCDE**	4	**Abcde**
2	<u>ABCDE</u>	5	<u>Abcde</u>
3	ABCDE	6	Abcde

Thus in the sample catalogue on p. 299 the main heading is **ABC MINING COMPANY LTD**, in bold capitals; the three main divisions of the catalogue, **Corporate records**, **Share records** and **Property and premises records**, are all in bold type, in a mixture of capitals and lower case; while the entries themselves are in normal type, in a mixture of capitals and lower case. Within the individual catalogue entries, the hierarchy is shown by indenting. Three levels of indenting are normally considered the maximum comprehensible in any one catalogue entry.

It is also helpful to users if a catalogue follows a consistent 'house style'. The use of capitals, punctuation and hyphenation, the forms of dates, and the use of standard abbreviations for words of frequent occurrence, are all cases where consistent presentation will improve appearance and clarity, as well as saving effort and space. Typical choices might be:

Use of capitals:	Company Secretary/Company secretary/company secretary
Punctuation	Directors' minute books/Directors minute books
Exact dates	25 December 1945/25th December 1945/1945, 25 December/25.12.1945/ 12.25.1945
Spans of years	1840–1850/1840–50

Once again, it does not matter what style is adopted, provided it is used consistently, and all the time. A few useful cataloguing conventions and abbreviations are shown in Table 11.2.

The indexes

Indexing, like cataloguing, is a complex subject with a specialist literature of its own. It is not possible here to give more than a few hints and suggestions about indexing in an archival context, and for detailed technical advice readers are referred as a starting point to the works listed in Further reading, p. 314. However, it is also true that technical defects matter less in small indexes than in large ones, and that few business archive repositories can expect to generate indexes large enough for these problems to assume significant proportions. Archivists should therefore be encouraged to produce indexes of their holdings without worrying overmuch about the finer points of indexing theory.

Indexes exist to bring together scattered references, and to guide the

Table 11.2 *Some useful conventions and abbreviations for catalogue entries*

1 Jan. 1750/1	This convention, indicating 1 January 1751, *not* 1750, resolves the ambiguity that arises with dates from 1 January to 24 March for years earlier than 1752. Until 1 January 1752 the year ended on 24 March, not the previous 31 December. Dates from 1 January to 24 March therefore appear in contemporary records as belonging to the previous year, 1 January 1751 in modern parlance appearing as '1 January 1750'. Confusion even at the time means that many contemporary records say '1 January 1750/1' in such circumstances.
7/20 Sept. 1906	A second convention, to show a date both 'New Style' and 'Old Style'. The modern Gregorian calendar was not adopted by some countries, notably Greece and Russia, until the twentieth century, by which time it was 13 days ahead of the older Julian calendar. The archivist is quite likely to find overseas correspondence dated in this manner. In this example the date in, say, Russia was 7 September, while in England and other countries using the Gregorian calendar it was 20 September.
1840–50	From 1840 to 1850.
1840 × 50	Some time between these dates.
1840 and 1850	1840, 1850 only.
[1840]	Date not give in the document but inferred/identified using other sources.
*c.*1840	*Circa* (around) 1840.
n.d. or nd	No date, undated.
temp.	'In the time of', as in '*temp.* George III' (from the Latin, *tempore*), useful for assigning a rough date to an item.
w.m. or wm	Watermark, also useful in assigning a rough date, as in 'N.d., w.m. 1843'.

reader to specific information without the need to read an entire body of text. They can also be 'read' on their own, in a deliberate attempt to discover the range of contents of the indexed original. In the archival context indexes normally fall into two groups – those which relate to the text of the catalogue, and those which relate directly to the contents of various individual records, such as an index to a minute book, or to the accounts in a ledger, or to the correspondents in a letterbook. The indexes to the catalogue will be produced by the archivists, and should normally be designed to be comprehensive; the indexes to various individual records will be little more than a ragbag of specific indexing projects at various dates. Some of them will be contemporary with the creation of the records; others will have been compiled later. However many there are, they will each be highly individual, created more or less to their own rules, and even in aggregate will cover no more than a tiny percentage of the archives in the repository.

A two-pronged indexing strategy is therefore recommended, by which the indexing effort of the repository can be directed where it is most needed, and avoid unnecessary work. Firstly, there should be indexes to the whole of the catalogue, arranged in three parts, by names (of people, companies, brands, etc.); by places (of factories, offices, branches, projects, etc.); and by subjects (including products, services, processes, etc.). These should be kept up to date, and stored in the reading room, to give researchers a good overview of the archives and to lead them to relevant parts of the catalogue. Secondly, and quite separate, there will be the indexes to specific records. Those that already exist should be clearly advertised in the catalogue, as described on p. 291 above; if necessary, they can be made available in the reading room either in the original or as photocopies. Others should then be compiled whenever it is clear that repeated reference is being made to the same record or records. This will save time in the long run, and also avoid wear and tear on fragile original material. Apart from this, however, such indexes should be avoided. No attempt should be made to produce a comprehensive series of indexes to the contents of all original records, or to integrate indexes of original records either with each other or with the indexes to the catalogue: the information in the archives will be too vast, while the different styles of these individual indexes will make it pointless to try to unify them to any significant extent.

Indexing the catalogue

The indexes to the catalogue should aim to include all names, places and subjects that are referred to in catalogue entries. However, the introductory texts to the archives of each separate organization, giving brief histories of the firms concerned, should not be indexed as such. Instead their key points should be picked out and indexed in relation to the archives of that organization as a whole. Thus, for example, the introduction to the catalogue of the records of the ABC Mining Co. Ltd might describe its creation and development as a gold-mining company in Java, 1824–1950, with one major figure, John Bloggs, founder of the firm, as chairman during the first half century, 1824–72. These elements should be indexed as follows, without reference to the introductory text:

Bloggs, John. For records of John Bloggs, founder of ABC Mining Co. Ltd, and also chairman, 1824–72, see archive catalogue of ABC Mining Co. Ltd.

Java. For records of ABC Mining Co. Ltd, relating to gold-mining in Java, 1824–1950, see . . . [as above].

Mining. For records of ABC Mining Co. Ltd, gold-miners in Java, 1824–1950, . . . [as above].

Once this has been done there will of course be no need to index these same topics all over again in relation to individual catalogue entries in which they specifically appear.

It will be clear from the above that introductory texts to the archives of specific organizations need to be carefully compiled with indexing in mind, so as to bring out the key elements in the history of the firm concerned. By the same token, the archivist should not be tempted to index interesting material within individual records unless it is specifically referred to in the relevant catalogue entries. Instead the catalogue entries themselves should be reworked (provided this does not conflict with the requirements of their original order), so as to make explicit reference to the material that is of interest, and then indexed.

The arrangement of the entries

With a manual system, the index entries may be prepared on cards in the first instance. They may subsequently be transferred to a word-processor, to allow regular updating, and presented to the user in the form of pages at the back of the catalogue. Alternatively, if the archivist obtains the appropriate indexing software, it should be possible to input entries direct into a computer, as the need arises, and to allow the computer to do the sorting. The index thus created can either be interrogated on-line, or printed out for use in the form of hard copy.

Each index entry should consist of a heading and a reference. Except in the case of general references, such as those discussed above, these references will indicate specific catalogue entries. Where the same heading has several references, they should be arranged in an order that is clear to the user, and be separated from each other by punctuation. Simple examples from the index of names might therefore be:

Doe, John, WXY 1/1/1.

Roe, Richard, WXY 1/1/1, 1/2/1, 1/2/2; XYZ 1/1/1, 1/1/2.

Smith, Arthur, WXY 1/1/1.
    John, PQR 1/3/1.
    Robert, HIJ 1/3/1.

Thus there is a reference to John Doe in the catalogue entry for one record of the WXY archive; there are references to Richard Roe in three WXY records and in two more from the XYZ archive; and so on. Note also how in each entry the surname, the principal element, has been placed first, followed by the forename; and also how the several different people called

'Smith' have been presented as sub-headings, in alphabetical order of forename, for clarity.

Where there are more than, say, 6 references to a heading, they should be broken down into sub-entries, for example:

Roe, Richard: agent of ABC Mining Co. Ltd in Brazil, ABC . . .
               baker, XYZ . . .
               surveyor, XYZ . . . etc.

The entries might alternatively be broken down by the archives to which they refer:

Roe, Richard: ABC . . .
              WXY . . .
              XYZ . . . etc.

Index entries should be arranged in alphabetical order, counting as far as the first comma or other mark of punctuation, and then starting again. There are two standard methods of arranging entries in alphabetical order, viz. letter-by-letter, as in:

Rioja Importing Co. Ltd.
Rio Tinto Zinc Co. Ltd.
Riverside Restaurant.
Rivers Steam Navigation Co. Ltd.

or word-by-word, whereby shorter words precede longer words with the same initial letters:

Rio Tinto Zinc Co. Ltd.
Rioja Importing Co. Ltd.
Rivers Steam Navigation Co. Ltd.
Riverside Restaurant

As can be seen, the two methods produce different results. Whichever method is used must be used all the time.

In the index of names, it will be necessary to decide on a standard order in which to present entries which begin with the same word but which relate to different things, such as persons or companies, as in:

Smith, John
Smith, John, and Co.

Entries will also need to be presented in a standard spelling or form, with appropriate cross-references from possible variants. In the case of names of people, examples might be as follows:

Hill (Hylle), Robert, WXY . . .
Hylle *see* Hill.

and

Joanes *see* Jones.
Jones, Albert, WXY . . .
        (Joanes), George, ABC . . .
        William, HIJ . . .

In the first example, the catalogue actually refers to someone called 'Robert Hylle', but the entry is indexed under the standard form, 'Hill', with the variant in brackets; the second, more elaborate, example shows the variant as one of a number of Joneses, all the others of which appear in the catalogue in the standard form.

If there are a number of references to George Jones, some in the variant form and some in the standard form, the index can show this too:

Jones (Joanes, Jones), George, [references].

Variant names in the index of places can be cross-referred thus:

Siam *see* Thailand.
Thailand (Siam), . . .

Here again, the non-standard form should appear in brackets beside the standard form, for clarity.

Some indexing problems

Problems with the index of names will include the treatment of company names. In the case of, for example, 'J. & R. Pulpit Ltd', the following is suggested:

Pulpit, J. & R., Ltd . . .

The major word, 'Pulpit', has been placed first, so that the company name appears in the index of names under 'P', not 'J', with the other portions of the company name immediately after. The word 'Ltd' is therefore left at the end. The same treatment is suggested for partnerships:

Pulpit, J. & R., and Co. . . .

In the case of partnerships where the partners have different surnames, it may be valuable to index each name in the title, for example:

Allan, Wrenn and Co., . . .
Wrenn, *see* Allan, Wrenn and Co.

Here again, care is needed. 'Wrenn, Allan, and Co.' would be hard to interpret as the entry under 'W', since it could easily be taken as an actual trading name of the partnership.

Other problems with the index of names will include the treatment of double-barrelled surnames; of names beginning with M'-, Mc-, Mac-, etc.; and of the names of the nobility. In the case of double-barrelled surnames, a recognized approach is to cross-refer from the first element to the second, thus:

Bannerman, Campbell-, Sir Henry . . .
Campbell-Bannerman *see* Bannerman.

In the case of names beginning with M'-, Mc-, Mac-, etc., it is best to index them as though they all began with Mac-, with cross-references from the variants, thus:

Mackenzie (McKenzie), John, . . .
McKenzie *see* Mackenzie.

In the case of names of members of the nobility, it is best to index under the family name, and to cross-refer from the title. This gets round the problem of individuals who bear different titles at different stages in their lives. For example:

Hardup, Dukes of, *see* Spendthrift.
Spendthrift, Albert, 1st Duke of Hardup . . .
    William, 2nd Duke of Hardup . . .

Full details of noble titles are available in such works as Cokayne's *Complete Peerage.*[8]

The index of places will also present problems, particularly over foreign places. The names of all places in foreign countries, of all foreign countries, and of all continents that appear in catalogue entries should be indexed, and foreign places identified with their countries for clarity, thus:

Berlin, Germany . . .
Cologne, Germany . . .
Europe . . .
France . . .

However, without further entries, the researcher interested in entries for Germany will not find 'Berlin' or 'Cologne' without reading through the index, and may miss an equally useful record indexed under 'Europe' alone. This problem can be reduced by indexing all foreign places automatically under both the place and the country, thus:

Berlin, Germany . . .
Cologne, Germany . . .

Europe . . .
France . . .
Germany (Berlin) . . .
        (Cologne) . . .

This will mean that the researcher interested in Germany will find all the entries for 'Germany' or for places within Germany grouped together, which will clearly be an advantage. Unfortunately, little can be done to make the 'Europe' entry more noticeable; the constituent countries should not all be indexed every time the name of a continent appears in a catalogue entry.

The index of subjects

These few simple rules should make it possible to construct workable, if crude, indexes to names and places mentioned in the catalogue. The index of subjects will be more complex, because it will not be taking actual words from the catalogue, but drawing 'subjects' from it, and indexing them under a set of approved terms. The problem then will be whether to construct a set of terms (a thesaurus) first, with cross-references from non-standard words with similar meanings, or to invent terms as they are needed.

There is no doubt that for large indexes this problem is crucial. Without a standard vocabulary, the subject index can rapidly get out of control. A standard vocabulary prevents the multiplication of different terms for the same subject, and thus makes sure that vital information is grouped together. In addition, a standard vocabulary can indicate to the indexer whether a given subject is worth indexing at all. Despite this, it may be better in the first instance to carry out subject indexing on an *ad hoc* basis, and to devise subject terms piecemeal. The subject index will almost certainly be small enough for synonyms among the indexing terms to be identified and eliminated afterwards, because the arrangement of the catalogue by provenance will ensure that much of the subject content of the records is conveyed to the researcher automatically, by virtue of the classification scheme.

Computerized indexing

Computers can make indexing much less labour-intensive. Perhaps the most useful methods of computerized indexing are:

- Free text information retrieval, which concords words in the text to create machine-held indexes to them, either by a 'go' list, which indexes only specified words, or by a 'stop' list, which indexes all words except common ones such as 'the', 'a', 'and', etc.
- The creation of machine-held indexes to keyword fields separate from the main text.

The need for the archivist to design the indexes, and to make sure that they produce exactly what is wanted is much the same as under a manual system; but the actual labour of indexing can thereafter be largely an automatic function. This will be much more efficient than a manual system, where indexing is a second and separate operation after cataloguing. The computer should also be able to produce relevant catalogue entries in their entirety, but highlighting the index term, in response to index searches, rather than just a list of catalogue references. This again will be a great improvement over a manual system. It should also be possible to print out answers to index searches in hard copy if required, and to carry out combined searches outside the range of a manual system, such as a request for 'all the catalogue entries which contain place A *and* name B'.

Indexing individual records

Indexes of individual records can be compiled in whatever form seems best. If, as has been suggested above, such indexes are prepared only in response to high user demand, there may well be an existing model to follow. User demand is likely to be heaviest for records which have always been seen as holding key information, and the archivist is therefore more likely to be plugging gaps in existing indexes than creating indexes entirely from scratch.

The shelf-list

The shelf-list indicates the shelf on which a specific record is to be found. Each shelf should have a reference number, and a good method of achieving this is if each bay of shelving (each set of shelves between 2 uprights) is allocated a number, and each shelf in the bay is then sub-numbered, starting from the top. Thus if bay 20 contains 6 shelves, they can be referred to as shelves 20.1 to 20.6. This method will enable the archivist to add/remove shelves to/from any particular bay without affecting the numbering of the shelves within any other bay.

The numbering of the bays and shelves should proceed around the storage area in a clear and regular fashion. However, there may well be parts of the storage area where the numbering of the bays is somewhat random. It is useful therefore to display a plan of the store, showing the bay numbers, in a conspicuous place.

The shelf-list will be in 2 sections, one for uncatalogued material and the other for catalogued. This will reflect the rough division of the store itself into 2 areas, one for uncatalogued material and the other for catalogued. Uncatalogued material will appear in the shelf-list in accession number order, and catalogued material in catalogue reference number order. Typical entries for each section might be as follows. Note the restriction on access to ABC 9/5/1:

Accession 25	shelves 20.1–6, 21.1–6
Accession 43	shelves 31.1–4
ABC 1/3/1	shelf 51.1
ABC 1/7/1–10	shelf 56.1
ABC 1/7/11–20	shelf 56.2
ABC 9/5/1	shelf 94.3 RESTRICTED

In practice, the words 'shelf' and 'shelves' can be dispensed with. In addition, 'ABC', indicating the collection in question, could be omitted from individual entries and replaced by a general heading.

The use of a shelf-list for catalogued material allows the archivist to store material by its physical shape and size, and thus to pack more material on to the shelves than if the records were stored in reference number order. For example, if all the catalogued volumes, from whatever source, that are 10 inches high are placed on shelves set at intervals of 11 inches, they will make good use of the available space. The same principle applied across all the collections in the repository will probably achieve savings of 50 per cent or more compared with records shelved in reference number order, because under the latter system, if records are stored vertically, the shelves need to be positioned at a sufficient interval to accommodate the *tallest* item on the shelf. Such savings can be of vital importance, especially if the storage area is located within high-cost office space. The disadvantage of random storage for catalogued material is of course that it usually scatters the records of any one organization throughout the storage area, rather than keeping them together. It is therefore less convenient for the archivist to make a general examination of any given collection, or to produce a quantity of records from the same collection for a researcher. Despite this, the advantages of random storage are considerable. They eliminate the problem of 'outsize' material, which must of necessity be stored separately, even when the rest of the collection is kept together, and prevent the accidents that can occur if records of different shapes and sizes are stored together on the same shelf.

For security reasons the shelf-list should be kept distinct from the catalogue, and not available for use by the public or by the staff of other departments. However, it will almost certainly need frequent revision and updating, as material is catalogued and reshelved, as records are stored afresh to save space or to make access to them more convenient, or as they change their format as a result of conservation treatment. In addition, it may be useful to maintain the shelf-list in duplicate, one copy in the reading room and the other in the storage area. Here again, therefore, there would seem to be scope for word-processing, to produce regular 'clean' versions of the whole list. Still better will be a computerized shelf-list, which can be incorporated into the computerized accession register and catalogue. This should make it possible to permute the shelf-list from reference number order into shelf order, to facilitate stocktaking, and should also enable the archivist to print out, for example, all the restricted material on request. Unauthorized access to the shelf-list can be prevented by means of a password known only to the staff of the archives unit.

Conclusion

This chapter has attempted to describe and discuss various general principles which the archivist should follow in preparing finding aids. However, it does not follow that every repository should apply these principles in an identical fashion; local circumstances can give rise to local solutions. The precise details of the various examples of accessions registers, catalogue entries and so on should not therefore be followed too literally.

Despite the advice given in this chapter, intractable problems are bound to appear. In such cases the archivist should take advice, perhaps from a number of different repositories, so that suggested solutions can be compared and contrasted. The repositories themselves may be visited, so that the background and reasoning behind the proffered advice can be understood more fully. It is very important that archivists should not operate in isolation.

The archivist who visits another repository for the first time is reminded of how it feels for the user entering a strange reading room and attempting to make sense of the finding aids. Archive units exist not only to preserve archives but also to make them available to users, and if the archivist can keep the needs of users at the forefront at all times, things should never go very badly wrong.

Notes

1 Where the original is legible, the benefits of a transcript, and perhaps of a calendar also, can be achieved with far less effort by the use of a microfilm/ microfiche copy, or even a photocopy, kept in the reading room for the convenience of researchers and staff.

2 For a recent description of conflicts between provenance and original order, see S. Healy, 'The classification of modern government records in England and Australia', *Journal of the Society of Archivists*, 11: 1 and 2 (1990), pp. 21–6.

3 See J. Pepler, 'The impact of computers on classification theory', *Journal of the Society of Archivists*, 11: 1 and 2 (1990), pp. 27–31.

4 See M. Cook and M. Procter, *A MAD User Guide* (Gower, Aldershot, 1989); and *Manual of Archival Description*, 2nd edition (Gower, Aldershot, 1990).

5 The archivist should of course ensure that the contemporary titles are correct, and be aware of the danger of companies using up stocks of blank books, especially account books, more or less at random, whatever the title printed on the spine.

6 If the contents of a bundle of, say, correspondence prove to be so important as

to require listing one by one, this should perhaps be done in an appendix to the main catalogue, cross-referred from the catalogue entry.

7 G. H. Williams, 'The construction and allocation of reference codes: a starting point for discussion', *Journal of the Society of Archivists*, 11:3 (1990), pp. 85–94.

8 See G. E. Cokayne, *Complete Peerage* (Alan Sutton, Gloucester, 1982).

Further reading

Cataloguing and indexing
British Standards Institution, *BS 3700. Preparation of Indexes* (British Standards Institution, 1964).
J. Butcher, *Copy-Editing* (Cambridge University Press, Cambridge, 1977), Chapter 8.
M. Cook, *Archives Administration. A Manual for Intermediate and Smaller Organisations and for Local Government* (Dawson, Folkestone, 1977), especially Chapters 6 and 7.
M. Cook, *The Management of Information from Archives* (Gower, Aldershot, 1986), especially Chapters 5 to 8.
M. Cook and M. Procter, *A MAD User Guide. How to Set About Listing Archives: A Short Explanatory Guide to the Rules and Recommendations of the Manual of Archival Description* (Gower, Aldershot, 1989).
M. Cook and M. Procter, *A Manual of Archival Description*, 2nd edition (Gower, Aldershot, 1990).
S. Healy, 'The classification of modern government records in England and Australia', *Journal of the Society of Archivists*, 11: 1 and 2 (1990), pp. 21–6.
R. F. Hunnisett, *Indexing for Editors* (British Records Association, London, 1972).
D. R. Jones, 'Archival cataloguing. A select bibliography', *Business Archives*, 61 (1991), pp. 55–9.
A. Pederson (editor), *Keeping Archives* (Australian Society of Archivists, Sydney, 1987), especially Chapters 5 and 6.
J. Pepler, 'The impact of computers on classification theory', *Journal of the Society of Archivists*, 11: 1 and 2 (1990), pp. 27–31.
D. Robinson (editor), *The Listing of Archival Records* (Society of Archivists Training Committee, 1986).

Business history and surveys of business records
H. A. L. Cockerell and E. Green, *The British Insurance Business 1547–1970. An Introduction and Guide to Historical Records in the United Kingdom* (Heinemann, London, 1976; 2nd edition in active preparation).
F. Goodall, *Bibliography of British Business Histories* (Gower, Aldershot, 1987).
D. J. Jeremy (editor), *Dictionary of Business Biography. A Biographical Dictionary of Business Leaders Active in Britain in the Period 1860–1980*, Volumes: 1 A–C; 2 D–G; 3 H–L; 4 Mc–R; 5 S–Z (Butterworth, London, 1984–6).
P. Mathias and A. W. H. Pearsall, *Shipping: a Survey of Historical Records* (David and Charles, Newton Abbot, 1971).
J. Orbell, *A Guide to Tracing the History of a Business* (Gower, Aldershot, 1987).
L. S. Pressnell and J. Orbell, *Guide to the Historical Records of British Banking* (Gower, Aldershot, 1985).

L. Richmond and B. Stockford, *Company Archives. The Survey of the Records of 1000 of the First Registered Companies in England and Wales* (Gower, Aldershot, 1986).

L. Richmond and A. Turton, *The Brewing Industry. A Guide to Historical Records* (Manchester University Press, Manchester, 1990).

L. A. Ritchie, *Modern British Shipbuilding: A Guide to Historical Records* (National Maritime Museum, London, 1980).

Royal Commission on Historical Manuscripts, *Surveys of Historical Manuscripts in the United Kingdom: A Select Bibliography* (HMSO, London, 1989); includes a section on business records.

Royal Commission on Historical Manuscripts, *Records of British Business and Industry 1760–1914. Volume 1. Textiles and Leather* (HMSO, London, 1990).

A. Slaven and S. G. Checkland (editors), *Dictionary of Scottish Business Biography, 1860–1960. Volume 1. The Staple Industries. Volume 2. Processing, Distribution, Services* (Aberdeen University Press, Aberdeen, 1986–90).

S. Zarach, *Debrett's Bibliography of Business History* (Macmillan, London, 1987).

Local and business directories

P. J. Atkins, *The Directories of London, 1677–1977* (Mansell, London, 1990).

Bankers' Almanac and Year Book (first published 1845, annual thereafter; originally published as *Banking Almanac*).

British House Journals (British Association of Industrial Editors, London, 1956).

Burdett's Official Intelligence (first published 1882; annual thereafter; title changed in 1899 to *Stock Exchange Official Intelligence*; from 1934 incorporated into *Stock Exchange Official Year-book*, for which see below).

Current British Directories. A Guide to Directories Published in the British Isles, 11th edition (CBD Research Ltd, Beckenham, Kent, 1988; first published in 1953).

Directory of British Associations, 8th edition (CBD Research Ltd, Beckenham, 1986; first published 1965).

Directory of Directors (first published 1880; annual thereafter).

C. W. F. Goss, *The London Directories 1677–1855. A Bibliography with Notes on their Origin and Development* (Archer, London, 1932). Now largely superseded by P. J. Atkins, *Directories of London*, as above, but still useful.

The Insurance Directory and Year Book (first published 1842).

Kelly's Post Office Directory of London (first published 1800 as *New Annual Directory*; from 1837 published by Kelly and Co., London. Annual throughout).

Guide to Key British Enterprises (Dun and Bradstreet Ltd, London. First published 1963; biannual till 1975, thereafter annual in two volumes. From 1975 incorporates *British Middle Market Directory*).

Kompass Register of British Industry and Commerce (first published 1962; annual thereafter).

P. Millard (editor), *Trade Associations and Professional Bodies of the United Kingdom* (1st edition, 1962; 7th edition, 1985).

Newspaper Press Directory (first published 1849).

J. E. Norton, *Guide to National and Provincial Directories of England and Wales, excluding London, Published Before 1856* (Royal Historical Society, London, 1950).

Red Book of Commerce or Who's Who in Business (published 1906–39); includes partners as well as directors.

Register of Defunct and Other Companies removed from the Stock Exchange

Official Year-book (Macmillan, London, 1990; previous editions to 1980 published by Thomas Skinner and Co., East Grinstead).

G. Shaw and A. Tipper, *British Directories: A Bibliography and Guide to Directories published in England and Wales (1850–1950) and Scotland (1773–1950)* (Leicester University Press, London, 1989).

Stock Exchange Official Year-book (first published 1876 as *Stock Exchange Year-book*; annual thereafter. From 1934 incorporates *Stock Exchange Official Intelligence*, formerly *Burdett's Official Intelligence*, and name therefore changed to *Stock Exchange Official Year-book*).

The Times 1000 Leading Companies in Britain and Overseas (first published 1965 as *The Times 300*; title changed in 1968 to *The Times 500*, and again in 1971).

Who Owns Whom. United Kingdom and Republic of Ireland (first published 1958; annual thereafter).

Willings Press Guide (first published 1874; annual thereafter).

Record office directories and other useful reference works

J. G. Bartholomew, *Gazetteer of the British Isles*, 9th edition (John Bartholomew and Son Ltd, Edinburgh, 1972). Identifies villages, counties and other places, and provides standard forms of their names.

C. R. Cheney, *Handbook of Dates for Students of English History* (reprinted with corrections, Royal Historical Society, London, 1981). Provides regnal years, and calendars of each year from the Middle Ages onwards (may be useful in cataloguing deeds of real property), and describes in detail the changes in the calendar in 1751–2.

G. E. Cokayne (editor), *Complete Peerage of England, Scotland, Ireland, Great Britain and the United Kingdom, Extant, Extinct or Dormant* (2nd edition, in 13 volumes, 1910–59; reprinted in reduced facsimile by Alan Sutton, Gloucester, 1982). Gives accurate information about the peerage from the Middle Ages to the present day.

J. C. K. Cornwall, *How to Read Old Title Deeds, XVI–XIX Centuries*, 2nd impression (Pinhorns, Isle of Wight, 1970).

A. A. Dibben, *Title Deeds: 13th–19th Centuries* (Historical Association, London, 1968).

J. Foster and J. Sheppard, *British Archives. A Guide to Archive Resources in the United Kingdom*, 2nd edition (Macmillan, London, 1989). Much more comprehensive than the Royal Commission on Historical Manuscripts' *Record Repositories*, listed below, but still specifically excludes in-house business archive units.

E. B. Fryde, D. E. Greenway, S. Porter and I. Roy (editors), *Handbook of British Chronology*, 3rd edition (Royal Historical Society, London, 1986). Lists kings and queens; English, Scottish and Irish officers of state; and archbishops and bishops of England, Wales, Scotland and Ireland.

H. Hart, *Hart's Rules for Compositors and Readers at the University Press, Oxford*, 39th edition (Oxford University Press, Oxford, 1983). An excellent guide to good editorial practice and house style.

Public Record Office, *Guide to the Contents of the Public Record Office*, 3 volumes (HMSO, London, 1963–8; parts 2 and 3 of a revised edition were published on microfiche in 1983).

L. Richmond and A. Turton, *Directory of Corporate Archives*, 3rd edition (Business Archives Council, 1991).

F. Rodgers, *A Guide to British Government Publications* (New York, 1980).

Royal Commission on Historical Manuscripts, *Record Repositories in Great Britain. A Geographical Directory*, 8th edition (HMSO, London, 1987). Lists record offices in the United Kingdom 'whose objectives include the systematic collection and preservation of written records other than those of their own administration', and therefore excludes most in-house archives units.

12

Conservation

Helen Forde

A well-organized business archive is one in which due attention is paid to the proper preservation and conservation of the records; if that is ignored, there is hardly much point in having an archive. An understanding of conservation practice and the choices available is essential for business archivists if they are to help their employers to make intelligent decisions which are both cost-effective and in the best interests of the archives.

The British Standards Institution's published recommendations, *BS 4971: Repair and Allied Processes for the Conservation of Documents*, Part 1 (revised 1988), is essential for the archivist who needs to know something about conservation. It is not, however, a textbook, and should be used only for reference purposes and to explain specialist terms rather than as a practical manual.

Definitions

Archive and book conservation has well-defined limits. The meaning of the words preservation, conservation and restoration have been honed down to a point at which three distinct but complementary operations are involved and very separate techniques are used.

Preservation

This is the global term, one which can encompass conservation and, to some extent, restoration. It does not, *per se*, require specialist techniques, but it does call for knowledge about suitable environmental conditions and storage, and it requires good sense. While it is sometimes described as passive conservation, it includes all the managerial and financial considerations necessary to ensure that the conditions in which archives are stored are not hostile and that good housekeeping and sound handling practices are followed by all those using and caring for the archives. All aspects of preservation are very much part of the job of an archivist (see Chapters 8 and 9).

Conservation

This is the technical side of preservation, and requires the additional, interventionist, skills of trained conservators for all but the simplest tasks.

It is directed to the maintenance of the *status quo*: in other words to ensuring that further deterioration is arrested and that potential hazards such as tears, ragged edges or holes are repaired with suitable and compatible materials to prevent further damage.

Restoration

This carries the conservation process further and also requires the work of a specialist, though one trained in a slightly different way. It rarely plays a part in the archive world, but it is as well to understand its difference from conservation, in that it restores the item as near to its original condition as possible, using suitable materials and filling in missing parts.

Both preservation and conservation properly fall within the field of the archivist and conservator; restoration does not. The archivist has an obligation towards the preservation of the material in his or her custody, just as the main duty of the conservator is to maintain the existing physical condition of the archives.

Ethics

Ethical considerations underlie many of the responses and actions of the conservator and should form a basis from which the archivist might work:

- The format and content of the archive must remain inviolate in order to preserve evidence. The legal and historical value of the original will thereby be maintained for the future.
- The interests of the documents must prevail over those of the users.
- The preservation of the archive as a whole must outweigh the needs of the individual documents; political or commercial pressure to concentrate on the conservation of one at the expense of another must be resisted.

The principles which govern conservation for any archive are the same for business archives, and comprise the following:

- The integrity of the document is of the highest importance to both archivist and conservator, and the retention of all evidence, however insignificant, is one of the main principles adhered to by conservators. Under no circumstances must any mark on the paper or any line on a drawing or map be covered over; no figures, even if scratched through, obliterated by repair material; and no processes used cause any fading.
- Conservation materials must tolerate the same conditions and react in the same way as the original. Thus the paper used for repairing an account book should be of the same weight as that used when the book was made up in order to prevent strain where the old and the new are

joined. Substitutes should only be used where it has been clearly demonstrated that they are suitable. For instance, the use of Japanese paper for conservation has become increasingly common despite the different characteristics between it and traditional western papers; but its advantages, stemming from its long fibres and light weight, together with a tradition of purity of materials, make it acceptable.

- Materials must be clearly distinct from the original in order to demonstrate that work has been undertaken. This requires a fine judgement between using repair material which is neither so similar as to make it indistinguishable, nor so dis-similar that the aesthetic quality of the conserved document is unacceptable. The stark contrast offered by many earlier repairs to their originals would now be regarded as unnecessary, but every conservator has to consider how best to indicate the presence of his or her work.

- No materials or processes should be employed if they cannot be removed or reversed if required. This has become an obvious need as the chemical understanding of conservation has increased. No longer are new processes hailed as the answer to all conservation problems. There is no palliative which will arrest deterioration in all cases, and every development must be rigorously tested to ensure that, in case of unexpected long-term chemical reactions, it can be reversed without harm to the original. An early example of failure to appreciate the consequences of an apparently innocuous material was the use of gall to enhance faded ink, when, in the long term, the gall made the original unreadable; more recently the use of soluble nylon as a consolidant has become suspect, as it can cause yellowing of the original and, after some years, cannot be readily reversed. The result has been a return to traditional materials demonstrably capable of withstanding deterioration and producing no ill effects.

- Minimal repair imposes a discipline against excessive and unnecessary work on documents or volumes. The art of conserving an item includes the ability to retain the character of the original as nearly as possible. Thus the feel and weight of the paper is as important as the texture of an old leather binding or the creases worn on to the surface of a well-used map. It is no part of the conservator's job to alter these, but it is part of his or her skill to retain such characteristics while preventing further deterioration. It can require considerable determination to advise that no action at all should be taken, but it is advice that both archivists and conservators have to be prepared to give and accept if necessary.

- No process which causes damage to, or in any way weakens, the material of which the document is made should be used.

Prevention

Handling the records

Much of the archivist's work will comprise passive conservation or preservation, and one of the most basic areas of these is good handling practice. Whether archival materials are being handled in the repository, the searchroom or at the photocopier it is possible to encourage care and respect for materials. In the repository separate storage for oversize items, rolled maps and plans, volumes and files is desirable. Trolleys used to transport materials to readers or staff should be carefully packed and not overloaded. Fragile items should be handed out in containers and with warnings about their state; some items should not be produced at all. Large or damaged volumes should be supported at the spine, preferably on some soft cover or cushion. Documents should be photocopied with extreme care, particularly in the case of volumes whose spine and sewing are at risk if forced down on the platen.[1] Fragile paper, oversize maps and all parchment should be copied by some other means, such as photography or microfilming, though the latter is also hazardous unless extreme care is taken.

Monitoring storage

Another essential task is the monitoring of the storage area for signs of mould, insect or rodent infestation. Mould occurs locally in spots when the item has become damp and been stored without being dried out first. General mould is more frequently due to poor storage conditions, leaking roofs, windows or pipes. Growth is stimulated by the relative humidity rising to a level within the growing range of fungi; it will continue until storage conditions are improved. Insect infestation also occurs in areas of high relative humidity, silverfish and some beetles being attracted by damp conditions. The presence of cellulose and other foodstuffs also attracts them, as well as being a prime cause of rodent infestation. Strict rules should be observed to prevent the presence of food and drink in the archive repository. In most cases it is more important to recognize the cause of the problem than to identify the particular spores or type of insect; if more precise information is needed expert help should be sought.

The conservator

There comes the moment when some practical work has to be done, and a clear appreciation of the complexities of full conservation techniques will help determine the safe limits. It is an unhappy truth that in some cases ill-considered conservation work has resulted in further damage or the need for re-repair at a later date.

The options are basically three: setting up a conservation workshop, employing a freelance conservator for specific work or the archivist undertaking some basic conservation work. In the end the result is likely to be a combination of some or all of these options, together with some very hard thinking about preservation practices to reduce future demands for conservation. Such thinking should be based upon an understanding of the relationship between archivists and conservators.

The archivist and the conservator

The current relation is largely due to historical accident. The archive profession, commonly one which is only entered at postgraduate level, has gradually changed from being predominantly academic to being pre-dominantly managerial. Managing conservation programmes has become an important aspect of this role. By contrast, the academic role of the conservator has expanded as the basis of the profession has widened. The craft skills on which the profession was founded are now no longer sufficient. Today student conservators are trained not only in the technical and aesthetic skills which form a large part of their work, but also in an understanding of the chemical characteristics of the materials with which they are working. Conservators are taught to make choices and take informed decisions. They are in a position to offer advice to archivists and to use academic tools to discover more about their subject. Archivists who, in the past, have been accustomed to take decisions on such matters have new-found allies of considerable standing.

Training

Qualifications are important in an emerging discipline which is shedding its craft image and gaining scientific respectability. Conservation training is offered at a number of further, or higher educational, colleges, of which the best known is Camberwell College of Arts. Binding courses which include an element of conservation are held at Guildford Technical College and at the London College of Printing. All afford an opportunity to learn a variety of techniques which develop not only craft skills but also a knowledge of chemistry and the ability to observe and analyse different aspects of conservation practice.

Some of the major national archive and library institutions offer on-the-job training for their employees; although this does not lead to a paper qualification, many of the senior conservators in this country were thus trained. Their experience and ability are substantial, and at this stage in the development of conservation as a profession their contribution is crucial. Eventually all conservators will be qualified but not for some years yet.

Training for conservators in smaller offices, whether local authority, business archives or any other organization, can be a problem if the post is an isolated one. To meet this need the Society of Archivists runs a training programme designed to give on-the-job training to such recruits, using a network of instructors from different record offices.

Finding a conservator

To complement academic training a conservator needs considerable hands-on experience. Judgement can only be based on such experience. It is important therefore to take experience into account when considering employing a conservator, whether as a consultant or as a permanent addition to the staff of the archive department. For most business archives consultancy will be the only option. How can a suitable conservator be found?

The first enquiry should be to the nearest record office or business archive for information about local conservators. More widely, the National Preservation Office at the British Library[2] maintains a list of conservators who may be consulted. The Conservation Unit, Museums and Galleries Commission,[3] maintains a register which includes some archive and book conservators, and in Scotland a directory of conservators is available from the Scottish Conservation Bureau.[4] There is, however, no system for licensing conservators in the United Kingdom, and no universally applied accreditation scheme.

Commissioning a conservator

Choosing the right conservator for a particular job is important, as the wrong choice could be detrimental to the monetary or archival value of an item. It may be necessary to choose between several conservators, and it is important to investigate the options fully:

- Provide a clear, written explanation of the work required, and explain the future use of the item needing conservation. Be ready to discuss different conservation techniques to ensure that the method chosen is suitable.
- Visit the conservator's workshop to see if it is well-organized and shows evidence of careful handling of items undergoing conservation.
- Take up references and look at some examples of work undertaken elsewhere.
- Get an estimate for the work. The cost is likely to be high, given that the work is professional, labour-intensive, and carried out by specialized

equipment and with quality materials. It will nevertheless be cheaper than employing a conservator as a member of staff.

- Establish a time-scale.
- Check the security of the temporary place of deposit, and take out insurance cover for items removed from the archive premises.
- Check arrangements for the transportation of the items, particularly if they are in a badly damaged state.
- Ensure that a record of conservation work undertaken is kept. Most conservators will do this automatically; indeed careful records of work carried out imply a professional attitude.
- Test the work with one document before handing over a whole batch.

Employing a conservator

Employment of conservators on a permanent basis is a much greater undertaking. Anyone considering setting up a conservation unit needs to employ a conservator first to plan and commission a workshop before any conservation work is done. The vacancy could be advertised in the professional literature circulated to archivists and conservators, and at any of the conservation training establishments. Advice about the appropriate status of a conservator in the company, the educational expectations for certain grades, and the likely salary levels, can be obtained from the professional organizations.

The archivist as conservation manager

Whether or not a conservator is employed permanently, there are various management tasks which can raise conservation and preservation awareness at all levels of the organization. A conservation strategy should be adopted.

Conservation survey

A proper assessment of conservation needs is essential. Without such an assessment it will be impossible to forecast the future conservation requirements, justify budget allocations and prioritize expenditure wisely. In an existing repository a survey can be done at any time (preferably before decisions are taken about conservation needs) and can form part of the basic accessioning process for new records. In an archive which is being established it can be incorporated into the initial listing procedures.

Surveys of series of records or complete repositories can be carried out quite simply, provided that the personnel concerned are aware of what they are looking for. The following aims should be defined before survey operations begin:

- To provide an assessment of the condition of the archive, based on sampling techniques.
- To collect and analyse data on particular types of record which are at risk on account of their age, previous storage conditions or the materials originally used.

The findings of the surveys should form the basis for a preservation and conservation strategy.

Archival knowledge of the records is a great help here, since it should be possible to categorize the different groups of records. Categories worth looking out for will include:

- Important administrative or legal documents, such as minute books and accounts, which are likely to have been created on good quality paper.
- Ephemera which may nevertheless have historical value.
- Early paper made out of rag (which should be in reasonable condition) and later papers made out of mechanical wood pulp (which is likely to be in much worse condition).
- Records which are known to have been stored in dry, stable conditions.
- Records known to have come from poor storage or on which there is evidence of mould or infestation.

Comparison between these various categories, added to the criteria for determining priorities (see below) will clarify conservation decisions.

The forms on which the information required is recorded must be simple but comprehensive. The layout in Figure 12.1 is suitable.

It is as well to test such forms before embarking on the full survey, particularly if using non-professional help. It is also worth experimenting to see how quickly the survey can be done. Limited resources may determine how large a sample can be taken – whether, for example, it is possible to sample as many as every tenth record or whether it is only going to be possible to look at every one in a 100. Surveyors need only assess the condition of the documents; the appropriate treatment should be a decision for the conservator in consultation with the archivist.

Conservation priorities

Once a survey has been carried out, individual priorities still have to be decided in order to work within a budget. The following should be considered when drawing up plans for future work:

- The intrinsic value of the document to the organization, which can include the administrative value, the historical value, the public relations value and the monetary value.

```
┌─────────────────────────────────────────────────────────────────┐
│ Date of survey: .........................................  Name of surveyor: ...............................
│ Document reference: ............................  Document date: ...............................
│ Priority for treatment – high/medium/low
│ Type of document – file/volume/loose documents/map/plan/photographs
│ Type of protection – boxed/unboxed/file cover/folder/envelope/wrapping
│ Condition of documents – bad/fair/good
│ Type of damage – torn paper/loose paper/paper deterioration
│                   dirty/faded inks/faded image/foxing
│                   damp/previous or current mould infestation/
│                   previous or current insect infestation
└─────────────────────────────────────────────────────────────────┘
```

Figure 12.1   *Conservation survey form.*

- The likely reference demand for the document.
- The conservation needs of the document.
- The most cost-effective method of conserving the document.

Balanced judgement is one of the prime requirements of a successful conservation manager, but decision-making can be simplified by devising a scoring system (see Figure, 12.2). Within the range 1 to 3, a value is assigned to each of a number of relevant considerations, the highest number representing the most important. Those documents with a lower total will have lower priority in the conservation programme than those with the higher numbers. It may be necessary to give a double weighting to some categories, such as conservation requirements, which are more important than others.

Conservation budget

Conservation is expensive. The resources available will be limited – they must be used to the best advantage and be seen to be cost-effective. The scale of the conservation operation will depend upon the results of a survey, and might range from the employment of a full-time member of staff to a basic programme of preservation copying or boxing. A budget will, however, be required for any conservation programme, and arguments

```
┌─────────────────────────────────────────────────────────────────┐
│ Document reference: ............................  Decision: high/medium/low priority
│
│ Reference value               [ ]
│ Historic value                [ ]
│ Public relations value        [ ]
│ User demand                   [ ]
│ Conservation requirements     [ ]
│                              ─────
│              Total      [    ]
└─────────────────────────────────────────────────────────────────┘
```

Figure 12.2   *Priority assessment form.*

will have to be prepared to convince the company that expenditure is justified. In addition to monetary resources, premises dedicated to conservation, together with the provision of minimum basic equipment, are also likely to be necessary.

Establishment of a workshop

Even without expert assistance the archivist can create a rudimentary workshop. In any archive it is important to have a space, away from the storage area and the office, where material can be laid out and inspected for mould or damage. Ideally this should be close to the point of entry into the building to avoid any contamination of existing holdings. It should be accessible by trolleys and have tables large enough to unroll substantial maps and plans if necessary. Racking should be provided to allow damp items to be dried out, and fans and dehumidifiers should be available to assist the process if there is a large amount of wet material (see also Disaster-control planning, pp. 233–5).

Basic equipment for a workshop includes:

Polythene sheeting.	Scissors.
Japanese paper for basic repair.	Soft brushes.
Small paste brushes.	Powdered adhesive.
Powdered rubber pads.	Cottonwool.
Blotting or absorbent paper.	Wooden spatulas.
Covered weights.	Sponges.
Leather dressing mixture.	Acid-free envelopes.
Acid-free manilla paper for making covers.	Record cards.
Acid-free boxes for storage.	Polyester envelopes.
Acid-free cardboard tubes.	Board cutter.
Silver-safe interleaving paper.	Hand press.

This basic equipment should allow some simple conservation work to be done, if absolutely necessary, by non-specialists, and will also provide a good basis for a professional. As in the repository, it is essential to monitor and adjust the temperature and relative humidity appropriately (see Chapter 9). Protective clothing, including overalls, rubber or polythene gloves and face masks should also be available.

Health and safety

Health and safety risks must be considered very carefully. Providing the necessary safeguards will involve expenditure in order to comply with the statutory health and safety regulations (Health and Safety at Work Act 1975). Details can be found in official safety literature and, in the case of substances, on manufacturers' labels. In addition, there are strict rules about the provision of guards on machinery.

From 1990 the Control of Substances Hazardous to Health (COSHH) regulations make it mandatory for all substances used in conservation practices to be assessed for risk; all assessments must be noted and updated as necessary. This is something with which every conservation workshop, however small, has to comply. Manufacturers are obliged to provide detailed descriptions of the components of their products, and any visitors to the archive premises must be warned of potential hazards. Current regulations should be discussed with the company's health and safety officer.

Irrespective of the legislation there are certain sensible precautions which should be adopted:

- Avoid contamination of staff, the premises or other archives, by ensuring that there are suitable workplaces to dry and clean dirty or infected documents before accessioning.
- Prevent exposure to excessive dust by the use of face masks.
- Avoid handling irritants without proper gloves.
- Wear protective clothing to ensure that neither clothing nor hair catches in machinery.
- Plan the workspace so that liquids and other substances can be used, carried and stored without danger.
- Ensure that electrical appliances are installed correctly, and avoid trailing flexes.

Conservation treatments

A range of conservation options exist, and all conservators have their favourites. Decisions will be based on a variety of factors, but it is helpful for the archivist to understand what might be possible.

Mould infestation is best eradicated by ensuring that documents are replaced in suitable storage conditions when they are dry and have been wiped or brushed down in safe conditions outside the storage area; fumigation is not advised, since none of the chemicals currently used have anything other than a temporary effect. No protection is afforded to documents returned to incorrect storage conditions. Deep freezing down to $-30°C$ for 36 hours is recommended for the eradication of infestation by insects.

Paper

De-acidification is frequently undertaken when paper has a low pH value (below 5.5); this neutralizes the acid and builds in an alkaline buffer. It is not always necessary and care should be taken not to subject the document to treatment if it appears to be stable. Aqueous de-acidification is the most common method, but it should never be undertaken unless the inks or pigments have been tested for fastness. Sometimes mere washing in pure water will be sufficient, but immersion in a solution of calcium or magnesium bicarbonate is more common. Spray de-acidification can be used for bound materials where it is not intended to take the volumes apart; the alkaline solution is suspended in a solvent which dries quickly, but it does only allow for surface treatment. Mass de-acidification of books is practised in some countries, but this is still a developing science, and there are no facilities available in the United Kingdom at present.

Traditional paper conservation may be carried out by any of a number of techniques, although it is usually carried out by means of damp materials. Where the text covers both sides, the repair material can be supported by a thin tissue; small holes may be infilled but substantial edge repairs may need to be strengthened with a frame of new paper. It is important that the old and new papers blend into each other smoothly, avoiding thickening at the join or a weak area which might be at risk. Resizing, if necessary, at the end of the operation will return some strength to the paper.

Lamination is used as a cheap alternative which can be carried out much more quickly. Once de-acidified and dried, the document is sandwiched between two layers of coated tissue. The adhesive bonds to the paper under heat and pressure, forming a skin through which the document can be read. Although reversible, it is not ideal, since it subjects the document to heat which may age it, and interferes with the ability to produce a satisfactory standard of resolution in any subsequent microfilming operation. It is most frequently used for documents which are made of inherently unstable materials and at risk through high use.

Leaf-casting is a method of paper repair which uses cotton or flax fibres in solution. A pulp suspension is drawn through the holes by vacuum to form a new paper where the old is missing. It is particularly useful for leaves of books which are of the same type of paper and with uniform damage but can also be used very successfully on documents, especially those for exhibition. Special equipment is required and skill is necessary to prevent pulp being spread over the surface. Precise calculation of the quantity required is important. The subsequent appearance and feel of the document is usually good, and there is no added bulk for storage.

Encapsulation is increasingly used as an alternative to lamination to protect documents where there is a need for support but no real requirement for active conservation techniques. De-acidified documents, dried and pressed lightly, are sandwiched between two layers of polyester, the edges of which are joined together by ultra-sonic welding, heat or sewing. The main disadvantages of the technique are that the original material is physically inaccessible, although perfectly legible on both sides, and more bulky to store.

Parchment conservation is similar to traditional paper work, but uses parchment for the repair material, supported as necessary by collagen or gold beater's skin. Although this is also undertaken with damp materials, great care must be taken not to saturate or over press the parchment, or it will become irreversibly translucent.

Binding

Book conservation is a specialized form of binding. It may be required either for papers which were bound up to ensure survival or for fine bindings of material originally created in that format. Different styles are adopted according to the intended use of the volume. Archival bindings must be carefully disbound, the contents and the original case conserved and replaced in a style as near to the original as possible. Each stage should be carefully documented, using photographs as well as written reports, to ensure that details are not overlooked. The archivist should read these as a basis for discussion about progress and intentions. The conserved volume should be boxed to prevent subsequent damage; box construction represents a comparatively small part of the total cost and is generally justified. The cost of the conservation of bindings will, however, be high, and should only be contemplated where it is really important to retain the original for archival or aesthetic reasons. Bound material which has come apart, whether or not originally intended for binding, need not be rebound if the cost will not warrant it. In such cases the spine has frequently become detached from the boards and there is no need to replace it if the whole can be boxed; the book cover is after all, only another form of protection.

Guarding and filing is a modern method of achieving the security offered by a binding for separate sheets or encapsulated documents. Paper guards, or polyester for encapsulated material, are attached to conserved documents and then filed in post binders or sewn between boards. In either case the contents are easy to extract for reproduction or exhibition and the process is relatively quick, easy and cheap.

Seals

Seals on documents are frequently friable or flaking. Consolidation is achieved with a mixture of beeswax and resin, to which dyes can be added to achieve an aesthetically acceptable appearance. If the thread of a pendant seal needs conservation, a textile conservator should be consulted.

Textiles

Textiles, whether in the form of samples, articles of clothing or upholstery, should be cleaned and sewn on to support backing where necessary. Aqueous cleaning can only be undertaken where the material and the dyes are suitable; they must be tested thoroughly first. Dry-cleaning with a handheld suction cleaner improves appearance and removes harmful particles of dirt.

Film and tape

Black and white photographic prints are usually treated by storage in inert containers, in a stable, cool, and dark environment. Little work has been done as yet on the complex problems of conserving the emulsion which holds the image. In any case identification of the nature of the photograph concerned is necessary before any treatment can be applied (see Chapter 8). Microfilm, microfiche, film, tapes, magnetic media and optical discs also require clean, stable conditions for storage. Copying is the only form of conservation possible.

Alternatives to conservation

Conservation is the most expensive of the options available to the archivist. Other options include substitution programmes and protective boxing strategies.

Substitution copying

Substitution copying can be a final solution in cases where original material – as opposed to information – is disintegrating. In the last resort it is the information which has to be preserved. Great care is needed in handling deteriorating archives, however, as the act of copying may destroy them entirely. The following copying methods are available:

- Microfilm or microfiche can be used for copying series of records, but the equipment is expensive and trained personnel are needed to ensure that the result is of an archival standard. In a business archive it is likely that such an undertaking could only be carried out with the co-operation of a commercial or academic publisher of microforms. It is one of the cheapest ways of preserving information.
- Electrostatic copying is particularly suitable for documents which exist only in copies made by earlier methods. Many of these older methods used processes and materials which were impermanent, with the result that the image is subject to fading. Any preservation copying should use permanent paper and machines which are well maintained and operated.
- Black and white photography can be used for copying, but it is expensive and should only be undertaken if the documents concerned are of the greatest importance. It is usually a means of allowing access to material frequently used or on exhibition; prints can be substituted for the original, while the negative is kept in appropriate storage. It is also a method which can be used to preserve the image of colour

photographs, which are themselves particularly prone to fading and discoloration.

Boxing

Boxing archives is probably the cheapest method of preservation. It is an option open to every repository for nothing more than the cost of the boxes and careful handling of the documents.

The following points should be borne in mind when purchasing boxes:

- They should be strongly made, with no extruding metal edges.
- They should be acid-free. Checks should be kept on this, as manufacturers sometimes change specifications without warning.
- The documents should fit in easily, without being forced or bent. Too much material will cause damage to the items inside when attempts are made to remove something; too few may damage each other while the box is carried. In the latter case it is wise to include pads of folded, acid-free, corrugated or similar paper to protect the contents.
- Different sizes should be purchased. A survey will suggest the most commonly required sizes, and boxes can then be bought more economically in bulk.

Opinion varies about the preservation aspects of methods of storage. Shelving boxes upright is likely to be more cost-effective in shelving and has the advantage of easy removal. However, there is the danger that loosely packed documents will sag if they are not packed out within the box. Horizontal shelving is limited by the awkwardness of retrieving the bottom boxes, which can result in clumsy handling and damage to the contents. In practice many repositories adopt both methods, depending on the size of the items in question and the frequency of use.

Volumes can also be placed in boxes or stored upright on shelves. If they are unprotected, it is important that careful shelving practices are observed:

- Ensure that the volumes stand upright.
- Support large volumes.
- Avoid gaps in rows.
- Avoid mixing small and large volumes.
- Avoid shelving too tightly.
- Protect books on either side of those which have clasps or bosses.

Maps, plans or architectural or technical drawings which are too large to box can be rolled, or placed between sheets of acid-free, heavy manilla paper. They should be rolled around acid-free tubes (never put them inside the tubes, as they will be damaged on extraction) or they can be protected with a covering of acid-free paper, secured with tape and shelved with an identification tag attached to the roll. Manilla folders can be cut to size and the map or plan placed inside before being put into map drawers. The latter should never be filled too full, because of the difficulty of removing individual items.

All labels and inks used to identify items in storage should be of archival quality. The paper used for labels should be of good quality, and if stuck to the boxes, should be coated with water soluble adhesive. Marking ink should be ineradicable by solvent or bleaches, non-bleeding and non-migratory, non-fading and non-destructive to paper.

Exhibitions

Displaying archive material in temporary exhibitions or permanent museum cases has very considerable implications for conservation. The guidelines issued in *BS 5454: Storage and Exhibition of Archival Documents* should be followed, and the archivist should be rigorous in checking that suitable environmental conditions and light levels are maintained. Professional conservators can be employed to mount archival materials for display; the designer of any such exhibition should be able to recommend one.

The archivist as a practical conservator

Practical work undertaken by the archivist should be limited, given the inevitable lack of specialist knowledge about conservation techniques and the current health and safety legislation. There may be occasions when something *has* to be done, but it is unwise to be lured by the promise of quick solutions in a situation where it is so easy to make matters very much worse.

If limited conservation work, such as is described below, is undertaken, it is essential that a record is kept of what is done. This can be achieved very easily be devising a simple record card filled out as necessary (see Figure 12.3). Much of the information may already be available from the survey form but it is important to make out a separate record card, either manually or on a computer. This will be sufficient to inform a conservator about the original condition of the document and what has already been done.

Paper

Paper deteriorates for many reason. The main problem is the breakdown of the cellulose, which comes from wood pulp and which, together with the

---

Name of archivist: .... *Date of treatment*: ....
Reference/title of document: .... *Date of document*: ....

More than one category in each section may be indicated:

Original make-up of document and materials used – written documents/maps/
plans/drawings/photographs/textiles;
paper/carbon copy/photostat/computer paper/negative/positive;
ink/typewritten/hand-coloured/printed;
file/bound volume/loose papers.

Condition – torn/folded/tightly rolled;
damaged by insects/mould/water/fire/dirt/exposure to light;
includes metal tags/clips/pressure sensitive tape.

Treatment including materials used – dry/flatten/dryclean/encapsulate/conser-
vation/rebox;
pressing papers/powdered rubber/inert polyester/Japanese tissue/adhesive/
acid-free box.

Additional notes: ....
....

Figure 12.3 *Conservation record card.*

alum-rosin used as a size, provides a high level of acidity. Exposure to light
causes such paper to become brown and brittle, and ultimately to break
down. Mechanical ground-wood paper, such as that used in newspapers, is
particularly unstable. Older and higher quality papers, where the main
cellulose came from rag or cotton fibre, are less vulnerable.

Ink can also affect the paper, particularly if it is made from iron-gall.
Other problems can include flaking, due to the failure of the gum
incorporated into the solution; fugitive tendencies due to the use of
modern vegetable dyes which are unstable (as in felt-tip pens); and fading
of modern inks made to flow easily in steel nibs or mixed with oil or wax for
use in ball-point pens.

Basic treatment can do little to reverse any of these faults but it can
prevent further damage until proper conservation treatment can be carried
out. All pins, clips, metal binders and plastic covers should be removed.
Tears and splits can be held together by means of acid-free coated tissue
and a tacking iron or spatula, thermostatically controlled. Papers should be
lightly cleaned with a powdered rubber pad or loose rubber powder, and
pressed lightly in a press, or under boards and weights. Cut a strip of tissue
to size and place over one side of the tear adhesive side down; then run a
warm tacking iron over the tissue. Turn the document over carefully and
apply the same treatment to the other side. Press flat under weights. This
simple treatment is a much better solution than any of the proprietary
pressure-sensitive tapes, of which the adhesive is likely to spread and
ultimately break down. It can be used for all types of paper, and paper-
based maps and drawings.

Volumes

Torn leaves can be treated in the same way as single sheets. Pages torn right out can be tipped back in to prevent them being lost, using ordinary repair paper and a safe adhesive. A hinge of the same length as the original should be cut from Japanese paper, creased down the centre and lightly pasted with a small amount of refined starch powder made into cold-water paste. A tin of such powder will last a long time and there is no danger of it going off, unlike ready mixed varieties. The strip should be placed half on the detached page and half on the facing page immediately next to the gutter, pressed well down with a spatula or similar tool and left open to dry after any excess paste has been carefully wiped away.

Leather spines on volumes which are suffering from red rot, the result of using leather which has not been manufactured to an archival standard, cannot be restored to their previous condition, but, providing that the deterioration is only slight, they can be improved by using a leather dressing. It should be applied very sparingly with a cloth and then polished off after being left to dry. Apply this very thinly; too much, and sticky leather, almost impossible to clean, results. Even leather bindings which are not visibly rotting will benefit from this treatment, but it must never be used on rough calf.

If the boards are falling off the text block, it is better to tie them up firmly with unbleached linen tape than to attempt to refix them to the endpapers. The latter will not be strong enough to support the boards and will tear, making the volume even more difficult to repair later. If the spine is falling off, it, too, can be kept in place with a tape tied round the whole book, or, better still, the whole item can be boxed. The latter ensures that all the pieces remain together and provides the best support and protection.

Photographs

Photographs are found in every modern archive, often uncatalogued and in difficult formats for storage, loose or bound in albums glued with dubious adhesive to highly acidic mounts. Identification of the type of negatives or prints is a job for the specialist, and conservation work should not be attempted. It is, however, possible to store both in individual, protective envelopes if they are loose, or to interleave the pages of an album if there is danger of one print coming into contact with another. Inert polyester envelopes can be obtained from specialist firms. It is important to check that they are not made from pvc, which contains plasticizers that will ultimately cause degradation. It is preferable to label the envelopes rather than the prints themselves, although pencil can be used to put a reference number on the back. Stamping ink should not be used, as it is likely to bleed. Inter-leaving paper can be obtained from specialist suppliers and should be used for albums; no attempt should be made to remove the prints from any backing material.

Glass negatives should be stored in acid-free bags or folders with no central join, as the adhesive can cause damage to the image. They should be stored in boxes, specially made for the purpose, which should not be too large, as a quantity of such negatives is very heavy, and the plates should fit in neatly to avoid any danger of damage. They should be clearly marked as glass and stored on a shelf within easy reach.

Textiles

Textile conservation is another specialist area where the only options available to the archivist are protective measures. Individual items of clothing or large cloth samples can be wrapped in acid-free tissue and stored unfolded. Textile sample books pose the same problems as photographic albums with unsuitable adhesives and unstable mounts. These can be interleaved with acid-free tissue to avoid the worst effects of off-setting from one type of material to another and to prevent dyes interacting. Small individual pieces of material can be put in polyester envelopes. Textile conservators at the Victoria and Albert Museum[5] or at the Textile Conservation Workshop at Hampton Court[6] should be asked for further advice.

Post-disaster treatment

Part of an archivist's essential duties must be the formulation of a disaster control plan to deal with the aftermath of a flood, fire or other catastrophe (see Chapter 9). The services of a conservator will be essential in treating records which have been severely damaged. If, however, no professional advice is available, the following basic treatment must be carried out to avoid damage caused by mould growth which may well occur if the archives are left wet.

Paper which is merely damp can most easily be air-dried; individual papers can be hung on lines to dry, volumes can be stood on tables with the leaves carefully fanned open, or laid flat with the pages interleaved with absorbent paper. If fans are available, a wind tunnel can be created to maximize air-flow. Dehumidifiers can be used to assist the drying of not only the archival material but also of the premises.

Photographs and microforms must be treated differently; they should both be put in buckets filled with clean cold water. Photographs, or negatives, should be washed with running water and then air-dried. This must be done within 24 hours to avoid damage. Microforms and magnetic tape should, however, be taken, in water, for specialist treatment. The commercial suppliers of the materials will be able to advise, and should be contacted as part of the disaster-planning process.

Soaked documents should be placed in freezer bags, labelled and put in a deep freeze. Commercial deep-freezing companies will provide facilities and the necessary blast-freezing. Subsequent vacuum-drying will remove the moisture in a vapourized state without causing further harm to the record; conservation work can then be carried out when facilities are available. Prior to freezing, soaked volumes should also be placed in bags before being packed into containers, spine downwards for support. Expert advice should be sought about the freezing of parchment or photographs, as there is professional disagreement about the safety of the practice.

Suppliers of materials and equipment

The materials and equipment required for simple conservation work are very basic, and many of the items can be obtained from non-specialist shops. It is worth checking several suppliers before buying any of the items, as prices vary, as do the quantities in which materials can be bought. It is often more economical to buy small amounts than to make an apparent saving by buying in quantity; conservation items can in some cases deteriorate, and long-term storage can be a problem. It may also be worth considering making a joint purchase with another local archive repository.

Conclusion

It is more important for an archivist to take an intelligent and enquiring interest in conservation than to try to undertake it. However, the pre-liminary and preventative work of preservation is very much within the remit of every archivist, and should be regarded as an essential part of the job; nor should it stop there. Preservation is a concern of users and owners of archives alike and the archivist has the obligation to ensure that this is well-publicized. It is no less important than conservation, and good preservation practice can prevent the need for expensive conservation work in the future.

Notes

1   See *BS 5454: Storage and Exhibition of Archival Documents* (British Standards Institution, 1989), pp. 13, 16.
2   The National Preservation Office, The British Library, Great Russell Street, London WC1B 3DG.

3   Conservation Unit, Museums and Galleries Commission, 16 Queen Anne's Gate, London SW1H 9AA.
4   Scottish Conservation Bureau, *Scottish Conservation Directory 1985/6* (Scottish Conservation Bureau, Edinburgh, 1985). Available from Scottish Conservation Bureau, Scottish Development Agency, Rosebery House, Haymarket Terrace, Edinburgh EH12 5EZ.
5   Textile Conservation Department, Victoria and Albert Museum, Cromwell Road, London SW7 2RL.
6   Textile Conservation Centre, Apt. 22, Hampton Court Palace, East Molesey KT8 9AV.

Further reading

H. Anderson and J. McIntyre, *Planning Manual for Disaster Control* (National Library of Scotland, Edinburgh, 1985).

A. D. Baynes Cope, *Caring for Books and Documents*, 2nd edition (British Library, London, 1988).

BS 4971: Repair and Allied Processes for the Conservation of Documents: Part 1, *Treatment of sheets, membranes and seals* (British Standards Institution, 1988); *Part 2 Archival binding* (British Standards Institution, 1980).

BS 5454: Storage and Exhibition of Archival Documents (British Standards Institution, 1989).

S. A. Buchanan, *Disaster Planning, Preparedness and Recovery for Libraries and Archives: A RAMP Study with Guidelines* (UNESCO, Paris, 1988).

A. Calmes, R. Schofer and K. R. Eberhardt, 'Theory and practice of paper preservation for archives', *Restaurator*, 9 (1988), pp. 96-110.

P. Chapman, 'The National Preservation Office', *Archives*, 81 (1989), pp. 26-30.

A. Clydesdale, *Chemicals in Conservation* (Scottish Society for Conservation and Restoration, 1982).

G. M. and D. G. Cunha, *The Conservation of Library Materials*, 2nd edition (The Scarecrow Press Inc., New Jersey, 1983).

R. H. Ellis, *The Principles of Document Repair* (London School of Printing and Graphic Arts, London, 1951).

N. E. Gwinn (editor), *Preservation Microfilming. A Guide for Librarians and Archivists* (American Library Association, Chicago and London, 1987).

C. B. Hendriks and A. Whitehurst, *Conservation of Photographic Materials: A Basic Reading List* (National Archives of Canada, Ottawa, 1988).

J. McLeary, *Vacuum Freeze-drying, a Method Used to Salvage Water Damaged Archival and Library Materials: A RAMP Study with Guidelines* (UNESCO, Paris, 1987).

C. C. Noguiera, 'The use of microfilm as a means of archival preservation', *ICA CCR-CRA Bulletin*, I (1982–3), pp. 47–53.

J. M. Reilly, *Care and Identification of Nineteenth Century Photographs* (Eastman Kodak, Rochester, 1986).

S. Rempel, *The Care of Photographs* (Nick Lyons Books, New York, 1987).

M. L. Ritzenhalter, *Archives and Manuscripts: Conservation* (Society of American Archivists, Basic Manual Series, Chicago, 1983).

R. E. Seton, *The Preservation and Administration of Private Archives: A RAMP Study* (UNESCO, Paris, 1984).

Trades Union Congress, *Hazards at work* (TUC, London, 1988).

D. G. Vaisey, 'The archivist as conservator', *Journal of the Society of Archivists*, 6: 2 (1978), pp. 67-75.

D. G. Vaisey, 'Archivists, conservators and scientists; the preservation of the nation's heritage', *Archives*, 79 (1988), pp. 131-43.

A number of journals include useful articles about particular aspects of conservation: *Abbey Newsletter*, *CAN* (Conservation Administration News), *Designer Bookbinder*, *Journal of the American Institute for Conservation*, *Library Conservation News*, *Paper Conservation News*, *Paper Conservator*, *Restaurator*, and *Studies in Conservation*.

13

The use of computers

Michael Cook

Since archives and records management services exist in order to store and retrieve information media, they are in theory especially appropriate for adaptation to computer methodology. If they are attached to organizations which are using computer systems for general management, then the case for controlling the archives by computers is strengthened. Computers can be used both for the internal control of the archives service itself, and as a means of communication and linkage with the rest of the company, its branches and departments.

This starting point laid down, it must be admitted that practical difficulties often prevent rapid and easy transition to computer management. Business archive and records management today have examples of trial projects towards automation, or initial limited computer systems, but broader or more comprehensive aspects of automation have not yet been explored. British companies have, in general, not yet assimilated all the consequences of automated management and communication; and, in most cases, managements are still introducing automated systems piecemeal and experimentally.

The rate of change in the computer world is high. Each month sees the introduction of a new development in software or hardware, generally accompanied by reductions in initial cost. Constant innovation among the products leads to instability in standards, and makes forward or co-operative planning difficult. In these conditions specific recommendations for current computer systems are likely to become obsolete quite soon. In describing computer applications, an attempt has been made to concentrate on underlying principles, and to indicate broad lines of development, but at the same time to give a simple and practical explanation of what is possible at the present time.

Basic knowledge about computers and their terminology

'Should I computerize my archive service?' It is hardly possible to avoid putting this question today. Every information service must use the tools of information storage and exchange, and these are what computers are. Consequently some knowledge about computing must necessarily form part of the archivist's essential skills. If archivists cannot receive basic training, then they must consider self-education.

In fact no previous training is needed for anyone to take up computing, or to take on responsibility for computerizing an archive service. This work does not need a training in science, mathematics or electronics. What is needed is the time and will to master the principles of any system, and to learn the specific command language required to run it; most of those who have succeeded in this process would add that opportunities for 'hands-on' experience and for personal experiment with actual machines are also highly desirable. During the learning period the would-be archival computer manager may often be helped very considerably by colleagues or trainers, and should therefore seek out training facilities wherever they exist; but essentially this is an area in which knowledge can only be acquired individually.

Successful managers are those who can delegate. It is of course possible to delegate the business of computerization. There are two reasons why archivists who decide to do this should nevertheless still take trouble to acquire at least basic technical knowledge, and keep closely in touch with the progress of their own application. One is that managers should not lose control over such a vital and fast-developing area. The other is that many of the standards and methods of professional work in archives and records are strongly informed by computer work. Computing terminology partly illuminates and partly obscures the important concepts which it uses. By learning and using the terminology of computer management, archivists are rediscovering concepts and practices which have always been the tools of their trade. One of the aims of this chapter is to make familiar the terminology which will be most useful.

Beginners should acquire a broad understanding of the public face of the computer world: sufficient perhaps to allow them to read and enjoy the computer page of a national newspaper. To get this amount of knowledge, archivists should read a popular introduction to computing. New books are published constantly, and one need only go to the computer section of a high-street bookseller to see what is available and attractive. From this knowledge base it is possible to learn useful new skills and get information on new developments from one of the popular computing magazines – choose one which relates to the make of computer used at work or at home, or to the small business user.[1]

A broad understanding should allow archivists to arrive at an appreciation of some of the choices which will be facing them at work. Some of these choices will determine the shape and function of their service for years to come. They may have to be made quickly, in the light of current developments, and to make them wisely, it is necessary to have some idea of the implications of each choice.

Aims and strategies

The ultimate aim of a computerized archive service must be the same as that of a manually operated one: to manage the archives, within the context of the overall information management system, to the best advantage of the company. The computerization side of it may be applied to any of the tasks and processes within this. Looking at the broadest picture, it should be the aim of the computerized service to provide rapid and co-ordinated control of all the data held in the archives. This can be a very complex programme.

To undertake any task with a computer, hardware and software must be chosen, bought, installed and maintained. Armed with basic knowledge, and a growing sense of personal involvement, archive managers can attack the problems of choice by considering the management implications, and by beginning to think about the actual tasks which might be done by computers. From this a plan, either for the immediate future or for a longer term, should emerge.

Planning, management and cost

From the point of view of planning, the main questions to be borne in mind concern the overall development of technical services in the company, which must be assured that technological developments within departments are compatible with each other, and conform to a broad development plan. Whether these developments are centrally controlled, or whether they are driven by departmental initiatives, is of course a separate question, but overall compatibility is desirable in either case.

This is especially true in the case of the archive and records management systems, because these are aspects of the central knowledge base of the organization. From the point of view of the archivist, this aspect of automation presents interesting opportunities for establishing close contacts with new sectors of the parent organization. It would certainly be unwise to embark on technological development without discussing the matter with, and perhaps ensuring the personal interest of, the technical personnel and departments. Hardware and software will have to be maintained, but there is also a need for a less formal kind of support (day-to-day problem-solving) which can usually only be given by individuals in the firm's technical departments. In any case the interest of such people will also be needed to solve problems of long-term database maintenance.

Problems of cost are not always the most dominant. Computer systems tend to become cheaper. Senior management today recognizes the need to make provision for automation, and will be watching for indications that an actively innovative approach has been accepted by their line departments. It may be more important to participate in the discussions which are part of the planning of an information management system (of which the archive and records management systems will be a part) than to be overly conscious of the specific capital or installation costs of a computer system for the archive department itself. However, there is a general professional requirement that archive managers should know the costs and the benefits of their service, and should be able to present a sound argument for their budget.

Making a case on cost

The case for investment in automation in the archive service is of course the case for investment in the archives themselves. If it is worth it to the company to maintain an archive service, then *a fortiori,* it is worth it to have a service at maximum efficiency. An information service which has no information technology is an inefficient service.

Automation affects and improves many of the professional processes carried on in the service. However, the most central of all these is the administrative and intellectual control of the materials: keeping and using them. To do this, archivists construct a database of information about the archives and their content, so that any item can be retrieved and put to use. By means of a computer, a single input of data can be used to create a range of different outputs, and the transcription and manipulation of the data in these will be more accurate than if the outputs were produced manually; so there will be less need to spend time on cross-referencing and checking. The case for computerization is therefore not that it directly cheapens the running of the service, but that it makes it possible for a small staff to create and manage a relatively complex administrative system.

The cost elements in setting up a computer system are divided into capital and recurrent costs. Capital costs include:

- Purchase of hardware (computer – or terminals and connecting line – and peripherals. Peripherals may include equipment for preparing input, and will certainly include output machines, at least a printer; and equipment for making back-up copies).
- Purchase of software (this may take the form of buying in expertise and material from an outside agency).
- Adaptation of premises.
- Initial staff training.
- Initial conversion of data or systems.

Recurrent costs include:

- Maintenance of hardware and software.
- Consumables (diskettes, printer ribbons, continuous stationery).
- Data preparation and input.
- Provision for replacement of hardware and software. There is a convention that personal computers have a lifetime of 5 years; central computers also have to be replaced.
- Continued staff training.

Making a case on efficiency

Complex corporate structures and operations can create extremely complicated accumulations of archives. It is difficult to imagine a manual archive management programme which can really give adequate and quick control over such materials. A computer database, or integrated pattern of databases, is the best hope of achieving effective control and retrieval.

The archive service which has its material described in a computer database can expect to be able to amend and update information very rapidly, and provide rapid, accurate and complete information in response to queries. Staff time is saved in this process, as there is much less searching for and physical handling of materials (which also helps to conserve the archives themselves).

Having a searchable database helps with all aspects of management, since the information needed for the generation of reports on responses to enquiries, loans, and so on, for audit, stocktaking and management reporting, can be rapidly produced. Appraisal is facilitated because duplicate holdings can be recognized by the system. Control generally is improved, including that over archives held in remote centres or departments.

Other management considerations

There are problems of inserting radically new systems into existing ones. It is difficult to assess the impact of new automation on the working practices of the department and its staff, and the degree to which new methods will cause old ones to break down. Similarly it is not easy to establish a real comparison between the costs of an old, manual system and the new one. Certainly a successful computer system will change working practices and the use of staff time in nearly every aspect of office life.

Experience has made some things reasonably clear. It is very unlikely that a new system will make it possible to reduce the existing staff establishment. It should be possible to improve output so that the creation of new posts may be avoided. To put this another way, the real benefit of bringing in computers is improvement in the quality, range and exchangeability of output, and in speed of response, rather than in the reduction of the labour of managing archives and records.

Management decisions on the broad aims and strategies of a future computer operation ought to be the result of a continuing debate within the department. Everyone's working life will be affected, and many will have valuable contributions to make. However, while the debate proceeds, it is possible to clarify current ideas about what equipment to use, and to consider what hardware will be chosen.

Hardware: mainframe or personal computer?

At the outset the most fundamental choice is the one between mainframe and personal computer (or micro-computer) systems. Most organizations of any size own and operate mainframe computers, which are used to drive the central administrative operations, particularly those connected with accounting. They have specialist staff and installations. Since they are already there, why should the archive manager not make use of them? On the other hand, personal computers are now widely available and cheap. In fact a stand-alone system acceptable to business is now available for the same kind of investment as would be needed for some good office type-writers. Either type of installation can be used effectively in an archival context. The choice between them must be made in the light of local circumstances, and particularly in the light of company policy.

Table 13.1 summarizes the advantages and disadvantages of mainframe and personal computer systems.

Some compromises are possible. Personal computers may be used as terminals to a mainframe, and this option might give some of the advantages of both approaches. They can also be linked together as a network, thus bringing their capacity and communication power closer to those of a central mainframe. Alternatively, mini-computers give many of the facilities of a mainframe, with some of its central support services, but with much less cost in capital expenditure and in physical installation. Since the distinction between mainframes and mini-computers is becoming much less clear, it is likely that in future ambitious systems for archival management will use networked personal computers, perhaps backed by one or more mini-computers. It is possible to extend a system piecemeal by adding some of these components later; however, such extensions are likely to need support by technically trained staff.

Figure 13.1 shows some of the most desirable features in a personal computer.

The capacity of a computer

Apart from the linked question of cost, it is the sizes of a computer's memory and storage capacity that are likely to be the most significant

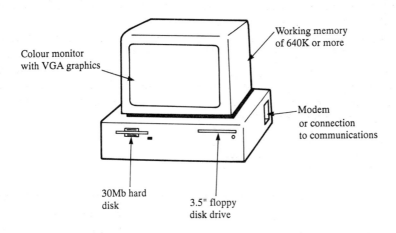

Colour monitor with VGA graphics

Working memory of 640K or more

Modem or connection to communications

30Mb hard disk

3.5" floppy disk drive

Figure 13.1 *Desirable features in a personal computer.*

Table 13.1 *Advantages and disadvantages of mainframe and personal computer systems.*

Mainframe	Personal computer
Advantages ● Links the archive management system to the central information and control systems of the company, affording the archives the potential to share in their development and in any information service department strategy. ● Allows access to large data storage and to software systems which emanate from the manufacturer or supplier of the mainframe: normally this means access to the software systems of a major manufacturer, such as IBM or DEC. Particularly important is the operating system supplied with every computer, which is likely to be a standard one, widely used in the industry. ● Provides centralized back-up of data and system maintenance, probably including automatic uprating of software systems as improved versions come out. ● Avoids many problems of training and experience as it is possible to rely on the expertise of others, and to call on them for advice. *Disadvantages* ● Requires the archive manager always to rely on others for back-up, advice and maintenance. Development of or changes in the system, or charges for the use of it, might be made without consultation. ● Restricts the archive manager to the use of software and other services provided. Back-up services are not always up to scratch. ● The involvement of archive staff would be less easy to stimulate, and training would be correspondingly more difficult, because the actual computer operation would be remote from most of them. ● May constrain by arbitrary limitations on the disc-storage space allowed to any one service. This disadvantage can be very serious, as more users come to depend on the system. Overloaded systems have slow response times, and the likelihood of breakdown increases.	*Advantages* ● Allows the archive manager to develop systems which really deal with the work in hand; there would be no need to assimilate and adapt systems initially devised for other purposes. ● Facilitates staff training and involvement by allowing archives staff to follow a plan specific to their department. This plan could set out a gradual approach to automation, analysing and taking on one group of tasks after another, with each stage involving full consultation between members of the team. ● Likely to reduce the initial capital outlay, although this depends on the firm's accounting system. *Disadvantages* ● Severe limitations of data storage or processing power. ● The development of systems within the archive service may occur in isolation from parallel developments in the rest of the company, which will bring great disadvantages later. ● Relatively difficult and expensive to get full backup and maintenance, which will probably be supplied by an outside agency.

factors in considering its suitability for archive work. This capacity may be measured in three contexts:

- The capacity to hold information in the computer's current memory, which must contain both the working information in hand at any moment, and also the set of programs or system instructions ('the software') which it has to use. This capacity is measured in kilobytes, abbreviated as K. For mainframes or mini-computers limitations in the size of this memory are not likely to be a constraint. For personal computers, the standard current at the time of writing, and one which represents the capacity to run most moderately priced software packages, is 640K. Larger memory sizes are becoming common. The larger this memory, the easier it will be to run complex software packages in the future. At present 640K is quite adequate, but if buying a new machine a memory of 1 megabyte (1Mb = 1,024K) would be a sensible minimum.
- The capacity to store and recall the whole set of data which is to be worked on in any operation. In archives the largest conceivable dataset would presumably be the descriptions of the entire archive, in which items can be searched for and retrieved: this would often be a large or very large database. Most company mainframes could cope with this, but only by adding appropriate storage devices, which could be costly not only in themselves but also in consequential additions to the central processor. Mini-computers similarly would need sufficient file-store space, which would have to be planned for at the time of installation. Where personal computers are concerned, this limitation is a major consideration. An essential would be a hard disc resident in the machine, possibly helped by an attached file-store device. The hard disc should have a capacity of at least 30 megabytes (30Mb). The earlier practice of keeping data on sets of diskettes, which have to be separately inserted into the machine to be read, is now impractical, but there should still be a drive for a floppy disc. The current standard for these (one much to be preferred) is 3.5-inch diskettes in hard protective covers, though many PCs still use 5.25-inch diskettes. New technology is constantly changing the standard.
- The way in which back-up data, or data not immediately being used, is stored. Back-up storage is necessary for every system. Mainframe services normally include an 'archiving' facility, which uses magnetic tapes or disks held in the central site. With personal computers, back-up data is usually held on spare sets of floppy diskettes, but other media, such as tape streamers, are becoming common. For an archival application, a tape streamer may be regarded as a necessity, since it should be possible to back up all working data in one single operation.

The capacity of personal computers in all these respects is increasing rapidly, and provided the right equipment is specified, archive managers should always be able to find computing equipment which can hold enough information.

Note that it is worthwhile raising the specification from the minimum and asking for a personal computer with a colour monitor. Although not strictly necessary if it is to be used solely for textual work, many text and database management software packages use colour as a channel of information. Taking advantage of this is to be recommended.

Standard software

Archival data may be bulky, but archivists do not need to do anything very complicated with it. The ability to enter data, amend it, sort it into different lists, and select relevant items from the main mass, is the essential task in archival computing. There are some problems of data structure which have to be solved, but none of the operations mentioned are particularly difficult or uncommon from the technical point of view. As a result of this, archivists are usually able to make use of standard software packages for at least some of the tasks they wish to carry out.

The most basic kind of software is the operating system (OS). This is a set of programs which every computer system (both mainframe and personal) must have; it allows the computer to carry out housekeeping jobs on the data it holds and to assist the user. Operating systems are almost invisible to the non-expert user, but are important because they may allow or prevent the importation of new software packages. There are a few operating systems which are widespread throughout the industry; it is important wherever possible to choose equipment which uses these, and to avoid non-standard packages. For this reason, some information about operating systems is needed even by inexpert users.

At the present time there is rapid development in the operating systems of both mainframes and personal computers. In the former case expert advice should be taken, as certain operating systems may limit the choice of manufacturer annoyingly. In the latter case systems such as MS-DOS or PC-DOS (often referred to just as DOS – Disk Operating System) have become very general, and are still standard. New operating systems which will support complex linkages between personal computers (local area networks) are becoming available, and archive managers would probably be well advised to consider acquiring equipment which will be capable of using them. Computing journals can be consulted for performance reports on such systems as UNIX or OS/2.

Software packages designed to do specific kinds of work are additional to the operating system, and themselves use it: this is the main reason why archivists should have some knowledge of their own computer's operating system. The packages usually include a word-processor and a database. (A third package, the spreadsheet, is often added by suppliers, to provide accounting facilities). The two should be linked, so that data can be transferred from one to the other without much formality.

The word-processor is a software package which allows relatively inexpert users to write textual information into the computer file-store, and to change and shape it in various ways. No particular data structure is required, so that word-processors can be used to write archival descriptions, letters or articles; to check and retrieve any part of the text; add graphic material such as tables or graphs, and to set up suitable output formats. Text produced by a word-processor on a near-letter quality (NLQ) printer should be good enough to use as camera-ready copy for internal printing. Table 13.2 summarizes the merits of some of the various printers available. It should be possible to produce any output from an archive service's system by this means: lists and inventories, publicity material, responses to enquiries, or selective or specific dissemination of information.

Table 13.2 *Features of some popular types of printer.*

Type	Quality	Typeface	Price range
Dot matrix	9-pin	Typeface	£125–200
	24-pin	Typeface	£200–300
Ink-jet		Typeface	£500–1500
Laser		Typeface	£1000–3000

Points to check
1 Compatability with database software.
2 Speed of operation: draft quality,
                        letter quality.
3 Noise.
4 Type of paper feed: continuous/single sheet.
5 Broad or narrow platen (80/136 characters).
6 Range of fonts available.

Specific information on makes of printer may be found in *The Computer User's Year Book 1990: Equipment, Services, Installations, Suppliers* (VNU Business Publications, London, 1990).

Nowadays word-processors can also be used to produce documents which are of equal standard to some published material (provided that a laser printer is available). It is normal to use word-processing simply as a means of producing typescript, but in its most elaborate form (probably with special software) it is termed desk-top publishing (DTP). There is great value in DTP for all kinds of marketing and publicity work. It offers sophistication of page design and layout, a variety of fonts and the ability to bring in graphics and images scanned from other sources. The boundary between DTP and the best word-processors is not easy to define, but special DTP software may be quite costly and elaborate. A warning should perhaps be given; the problems and possibilities of DTP software are quite different from those of database systems, and can divert staff from more important computer-based projects of a less glamorous kind.

A good modern word-processor should also be able (if requested) to produce output in a form which can be read by other software. This

Table 13.3   *Features of some popular database packages*

Package name	File, record and field characteristics	Main features
dBase III+ (Ashton-Tate)	Fixed-length fields, but easy to modify.	Easy to develop and adapt. Has applications generator. Input screens. On-screen help and tutor. World-wide standard.
dBase IV (Ashton-Tate)	Fixed-length fields, but easy to modify.	As above, plus powerful reports generator. Pulldown menus. Password security.
Fox Base Fox Pro (Fox Software International)		Emulates dBase III+ and dBase IV, but runs faster.
Data Ease (Sapphire International plc)	Large capacity.	Menu-driven. Relational data entry and report forms. Networking possible. Password security.
Superfile (Southdata Ltd)	Unlimited, takes large text fields. Variable length fields.	Good for 'large messy databases'. Word-processor interface. Data validation. Relational.
Cardbox Plus (Business Simulations Ltd)	Variable length fields.	Emulates card index. Powerful search and sort. Add on thesaurus and reports generator.
R:Base (Microrim (UK) Ltd)	Large capacity.	User-defined menus. dBase compatibility. Windows. Templates.
CDS/ISIS (UNESCO)	Variable length fields. Large text.	Multi-language international. User-defined input forms and reports. Power search and index with thesaurus. Archive specific application.
MicroCairs (Leatherhead Food Research Association)	Variable length fields. Large capacity.	Adaptable reports generator. Thesaurus. Networking possible. Password security. Input screens. Word-processor interface. Sort capability. Data validation.
Assassin (Associated Knowledge Systems)	Variable length fields. Large capacity.	Menu-driven. Password security. User-defined input screens. On-screen help and tutor. Word-processor interface. Thesaurus. Reports generator. Networking possible. Easy to develop and adapt.
Status (Harwell Computer Power)	Copes with large textbases with very little structure.	Powerful search facilities now being further developed. Free text input marked by tags. Thesaurus. Micro version available.

Package name	File, record and field characteristics	Main features
BRS/Search (BRS Software Products)	Variable length fields. Large capacity.	Text file compression. Thesaurus add on available. Sort capability. Password security. Adaptable printed output. Input screens. Word-processor and windows interfaces. Data validation.

All the above packages are easy to use, well-supported by suppliers or user-groups, and flexible in use.
Note: specific information on all software is available in R. Jones (editor), *The Good Software Guide* (Absolute Research, Watford, 1989, and revisions); and P. Hearn and J. McGee (editors), *The International Software Guide*, 5th edition (International Software Ltd, Brentford, 1989).

generally means that it must be able to produce an ASCII file (ASCII, pronounced 'Askey', refers to an international general standard for the interpretation of characters in electronic form).

The database management system (DBMS) is a software package which helps users to lay down a structure for the data they wish to store, and then allows them to manipulate the data they put into this structure. The result is an organized bank of data, where the information is distributed into appropriate categories, and where the relation between different bits of information is displayed. Many modern database systems are relational: they allow different files of information to be held, with the ability to relate one file to another. A system like this gives the user a useful power to retrieve different but logically connected bits of information. The success of such a system, though, depends on the aptness of the original design for the structure of the database, and the way in which the component files fit together.

The records which are held in files of data in databases[2] are structured into fields, which are designed to contain specific data elements. It is important that each field should be big enough to hold all the data which must be entered into it. Some database systems do this by fixing the size of the field at the maximum likely to be needed ('fixed-length fields'), but some allow fields of variable length. Archival databases tend to be very big, and it is probably crucially necessary to choose a database system which has variable-length fields. For this reason many of the most popular databases, such as dBase III plus or dBase IV, are not suitable for archival work; a system such as CDS/ISIS or Advanced Revelation would be much more acceptable on this ground.

Most commercially sold database systems really assume that much of the data they are to hold is numerical. These systems are usually good at doing arithmetic on this, and creating reports which give the results. There are also database systems which allow users to input large and variable amounts of free text. Such systems usually allow some structuring of the data: they do recognize distinct fields and specific types of data (such as dates), but allow the treatment of these to be flexible. Fields are variable in length, may not have to be predefined, and may be repeatable. These are the free text retrieval systems.

There are always some drawbacks to adapting standard software packages to archive management. Enthusiasts may attempt their own programming, and those with access to rich sources of finance or expertise may commission purpose-designed software. However, the compatibility and communicability of data held in industry-standard systems is of great value, and the successful archive manager is the one who can make best use of these factors.

Communications

Computers not only receive and store information, they can transmit and exchange it. Many firms are now installing communication systems which serve their departments and branches. The system ought to be able not only to transfer formal information, such as accounting data, but also unstructured text. The transfer of textual material is commonly called electronic mail (or Email). Organizations based upon mainframe systems can use territorial or specialist networks to provide links between their users. These networks now cover most of the planet. Personal computer users, or the partners who have joined in personal computer local networks, may also join communication systems through the telephone system, or through a combination of telephones and television broadcasting. There is in principle no reason why any computer-users should not be able to adapt their equipment to transfer data or to send and receive messages. Many personal computers can be fitted with the necessary equipment ('modems') to transmit and receive data through telephone lines, as a standard accessory.

The professional processes in archival management

An archival computer system ultimately has to provide a service which replaces or parallels the main professional work processes, and it does this by setting up a set of processes of its own. Each of these processes presents problems which have to be solved at the planning stage.

Standards of description

There are two infrastructural standards which are needed to work with technologies: standards for archival description and standards for the interchange of data between systems.

Archival description standards are set out in the *Manual of Archival Description* (MAD2).[3] Alternative standards are applicable in the USA and Canada.[4] The MAD2 standard operates within archive services in both public and private sectors. It includes a system for marking levels of arrangement and description so that they can be compared from one repository to another. The 5 main levels are numbered, extra levels being inserted between them if necessary:

1	Management levels
2	Group descriptions
(2.5)	(followed by subgroups).
3	Class descriptions.
4	Item descriptions.
5	Piece descriptions.

Descriptions at each level follow appropriate models. These models are made up by selecting data elements from a table, and setting them out in an appropriate pattern on the page or on the computer screen. The data elements are themselves arranged in logical groupings called areas and sub-areas. In most cases there are alternative patterns for the descriptions in their final form – these are the paragraph and list modes of description. MAD2 contains full rules and recommendations for using these standards, which should be flexible enough to be adaptable to any case. Modes of listing are illustrated in Figure 13.2.

The standard levels of arrangement and description should be built into an archival computer system, because they provide a standard which will underlie any co-operative or national scheme for the exchange of information or for reference. MAD2 data elements and the models they build up into (often called 'templates' in the context of computerized databases) can be written into software for use with archival management systems. Where this is done, specially formatted screens for the input and output of data are shown on the terminal or personal computer screens.

Most computer database systems have one important difficulty in relation to archival description – they are essentially flat files, sets of single-level descriptions. Systems like Cardbox illustrate this by their very name. Since, as we have seen, archival descriptions must allow for multiple levels, some manipulation of databases is often needed. The rapid development of hypertext may help to overcome this problem.[5]

The input form illustrated in Figure 13.3 is single-level in form, but closer examination shows that it can be used in several ways. There is an assumption that it is to be used for group level descriptions (branches or departments), but in fact it could be used, at class or even item level. If this is done, the entries for branch/department name and provenance can be used to link it to its context, which can also be set out in narrative text in the main description. Since in any output, unused or irrelevant fields can be omitted, this input seems flexible enough to allow multi-level descriptions without too much constraint. The same effect could be

(a) a file consisting mostly of text (paragraph mode):

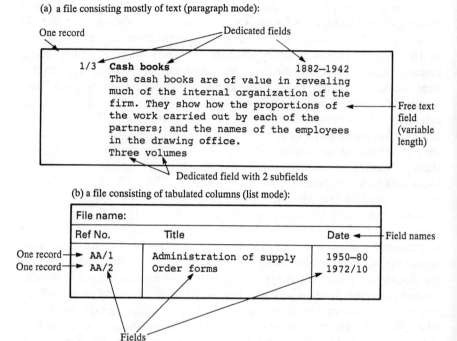

Dedicated field with 2 subfields

(b) a file consisting of tabulated columns (list mode):

Figure 13.2 *The structure of records and fields, using examples from list and paragraph modes.*

achieved by using a text retrieval system, which allows a much looser structure in the data.

Fields for sorting

Data which are to be used for sorting must be entered appropriately. This means that the principal term on which sorting is to be done must appear first. Either the text must be entered in an inverted form, or some form of tag must be used to instruct the system to ignore words (for example 'the'), or to perform the inversion.

Dates present special difficulties. If they are inverted, as International Standards Organization (ISO) standard dates are, they tend to be difficult for users to read. Thus, 19750215 is the ISO standard form for 15 Feb 1975. It is possible to get software which will translate one form to another. More simply, it may be necessary to include both forms of date in the input form. If there is any intention to search between ranges of dates, then there will have to be two date fields, the first and the last, in computer-readable form. If this kind of planning is applied to the data structure, the computer can be used to sort documents into date order and to carry out searches on ranges of dates, but at the same time print out dates that can be readily understood by lay users.

Standards for data exchange

In future, exchanging information is likely to be mainly by electronic means. This requires standards for the structure and presentation of data held within systems. This standard, internationally, is the Machine-Readable Catalogue (MARC). MARC was developed in the library world, originally by the Library of Congress in the United States of America, and was adopted as long ago as 1968. Since then MARC has come to be used all over the world in controlling the transfer of bibliographic data. Because there are different needs and conventions in each country, slightly different variations of the original US/MARC have developed in different parts of the world. There is a UK MARC for use in Britain, and a UNIMARC which sets out to provide a universally exchangeable version. Innovations in North America led to the production of a variant designed to accommodate archival descriptions, which was launched in 1984. This variant is known as the Archives and Manuscripts Control (AMC) format, and is fully endorsed by the Society of American Archivists. It is compatible with US/MARC. A version for UK MARC was made available experimentally in 1989.[6]

Computer systems for archival management, which include the possibility of exchanging data through electronic networks, should consider basing themselves on MARC AMC. Several large public access databases already use this format, and there are several software packages designed for archival use which incorporate it, using the structure of tagged fields to provide input screens and preplanned outputs.

These standards provide one important area of the final specification for an archival system. How they are applied in any particular case depends on the needs, character and aims of the archival management system in question.

Data capture

The first problems often prove to be the most difficult. How are the data to be collected in order that they should be fed into the computer system? The solution to this may affect the whole relationship between different categories of staff in the service, and between the archivists and their material.

In a big office data capture can be arranged by systematizing the relation between the sections which carry out different operations. The system developed by the Public Record Office to operate its first computer system, PROSPEC, illustrates this. Each operation was carried out by a different section, which was responsible for writing in its results to a common form. The form passed from one section to another with the archival materials: from accessioning to arrangement, shelving and boxing, description, microfilming (if this was done), and so forth. When the materials were finally put away in store, the completed form was passed to the data-processing section.

A smaller archive service will probably not find this a good model. It is customary in these to give the responsibility for all the processes carried out on a particular set of archives to one person, who then becomes expert on the subject area covered by that set. In these circumstances it would be natural for the archivist responsible for the professional tasks to be the one who deals with capturing the data for the computer. How this might be done depends greatly on the system selected, the hardware available and the attitudes of the archivists concerned.

Traditionally minded archivists, or those whose computer system is based at a physically remote centre, may content themselves with writing out longhand notes which then have to be interpreted by clerical staff. There is no doubt, though, that the logic of computer development is towards bringing the archivist directly into contact with computer input equipment. Bench-top terminals close to the work, or small ('lap-top') personal computers which can be used directly by the archivists during their daily work are likely to become the norm. This has implications for the deployment of clerical and paraprofessional staff resources in the long run.

At the present time, though, most services are still in the situation where data is captured by being written on paper. This still means that there may be a need to use a data-capture form which forces the archivists to structure the data and present it in a way which will help the clerical support staff.

Figure 13.3 gives an example of a simple data-input form.

The design of the data-input form should follow the design of the computer database, but it should be laid out in a way which makes it convenient for both the archivist who writes in the data, and the keyboard operator who translates it. It is useful if these processes are controlled by in-house rules (in extension of those provided in MAD2) for style and treatment of text, punctuation, an authority list for names of people and places, and so forth.

Data input

Information written out on paper has to be translated into forms which the computer can read. Someone must key the data, using a terminal or a personal computer which communicates directly with the central processor. This means that the typist should, if possible, be able to see the data being entered into the appropriate boxes, which represent records and fields, and can make corrections while going along. This method of working is termed interactive. Checking the result still remains a burden, as someone will have to read a proof of the input data, but the burden can be reduced by using the right software.

There are two aspects to checking input: validation and verification. Validation is checking that the right kind of data are being entered. In

```
┌──────────────────────────────────────────────────────────────────────┐
│                   United Manufacturers Plc                             │
│                          Archives                                      │
├──────────────────────────────────────────────────────────────────────┤
│                          Data input form                               │
│                                                                        │
│  01 Accession No. └─┴─┴─┴─┘              00 Level └─┴─┘                 │
│  02 Reference code └────────┘                                          │
│  03 Title      └──────────────────────────────────────────┘           │
│  04 Earliest date └────────┘         05 Latest date └────────┘         │
│  06 Description _____            │
│                 _____            │
│                 _____            │
│                 _____            │
│                                                                        │
│  07 Index terms   ──────────────────                                   │
│                   ──────────────────                                   │
│                   ──────────────────                                   │
│  08 Location    └──────────┘          09 Bulk └──────────┘             │
│  10 Security level  └──┘                                               │
│  11 Access control  └────────┘                                         │
└──────────────────────────────────────────────────────────────────────┘
```

Figure 13.3 *A simple data-input form.*

some cases validation can be done by the computer. For example, fields which are dedicated to specific data elements can be given machine-enforceable rules. Thus if there is a field for dates, any attempt to enter non-date information would produce a warning beep. It must be admitted that scope for this kind of validation is limited when an archives system is being used, because archival information tends so often to be non-standard. Date fields can be controlled when the entry is something like '07/03/1789', but not when it is 'a fortnight after Easter'. Nevertheless it is an important facility, especially now that standard word-processors contain automatic spelling checkers and dictionaries.

Even if all data can be validated, it still has to be verified. Verification is checking that the information entered is correct, which generally has to be done by humans spending time proof-reading. Word-processors reduce this burden, because entering amendments does not make it necessary to retype (and then proof-read again) the whole document.

An easy way for entering amendments as well as original data must be found. Experience shows that this is a vital matter. If it is slow and difficult to get amendments entered, and secure a correct text, staff will lose confidence in the system quite quickly. This fact, demonstrated by the failure of many early experiments in computerization, constitutes one of the main arguments for using a system which employs interactive relationships between the users and the machine – but they must be relationships which the users find comfortable and effective.

The process of inputting data makes some demands on the design and layout of the archive office. Where the terminal or personal computer is sited in relation to the work on the archives makes a difference. Ease of communication within the service is very important. However, although terminals and personal computers nowadays do not need a specially protected environment, they ought to be somewhere away from major sources of dust, and arranged conveniently for the person sitting at the keyboard. Direct light on the screen is troublesome. The terminal should also be available for use by all staff members who want to use it, which means that it should be on an accessible desk. There are health and safety restrictions on the periods over which one person may work at a terminal screen.

Output

The problem with designing computer systems is that there should be a clear idea of what output is desired even before there has been any input. The system cannot really be tested until it is run, and by that time there has already been a commitment of resources. This logical difficulty cannot be avoided. Output remains the whole point of the computer system. Good output is the result of good planning.

In an archival context there are essentially two kinds of output: finding aids and on-line databases. Finding aids are still the norm. This means that the computer system aims to produce information which is like the traditional typescript paper carrying the archival descriptions. The finding aids can be read directly from the screen, which speeds up production and reference use. If hard copy is required, computers are much faster at producing printed paper than typewriters were, and so to use them in this way should be an improvement: a better result should be possible using fewer resources. Nevertheless it is important to understand that if the computer is used in this way, the underlying traditional structure of the service must remain in place, essentially as a process for translating handwritten notes into neatly presented and distributable finding aids. Computers are capable of doing far more than this.

On-line databases show some of the potential for future change offered by computers. In this approach the data remain in the computer's file-store, and users retrieve it interactively, by asking questions, to which the computer can make reply. Software for interactive searching which has considerable subtlety and complexity has now been developed (although so far mainly on mainframes); it can be used to retrieve information very quickly from very large databases, and it can be used on various data-storage media.

The problem is that no one can use this method effectively without first mastering the technique of selecting combinations of keywords to make a search, and without first being fairly clear about what they are searching for. Interactive searching of a computerized database may well be more successful in the context of a single firm, where the users may be expected to be relatively expert. It would be a good way of letting users have access to the database from a remote branch.

Access to lay users can be improved by making the approaches to the database less complex. A system which uses a series of menu screens, each of which asks the user to make a choice, can be quite easy for newcomers to cope with. This is also a system which can be set up by an archivist who has acquired a taste for tinkering with operating systems. The technical knowledge required is not great. A more advanced approach, and one which needs both special software and advanced skills, is to set up an expert system. These systems are an application of Artificial Intelligence (AI), which will be an increasingly important feature of software packages in the future. In an expert system the computer can ask successive questions which narrow down the range of information required to answer a particular research enquiry. In a true expert system the computer can learn from outcomes of previous enquiries, and can take into account quite subtle distinctions between different kinds of enquiry. The questions and the responses to them are of course based upon preliminary programming supplied by the archivists. A simple sequence of questions might look something like this:

Computer: Which database do you wish to use? We have the following databases . . .
   (type 'help' for assistance)
   Patents
   Deeds to property
   Personnel . . .
User: Personnel
Computer: Personnel information is protected. What is your password and security level?

   [After this has been cleared] . . .

Computer: What department are you interested in? We have the following departments . . .
User: Accounting
Computer: What is the name of the person?
   etc.

If all searches could be directed in this way, much of the problem of user-education could be solved. The software required for setting up simple menu-led systems is now easily available, and has simplified much of the preliminary work. Designing a more complex expert system would take much preparation. Most of the work consists of working out professional (rather than technological) problems, and it should be reasonably easy.

There are other ways of making access to information easier. The database (and also word-processors) can be used to produce indexes in hard-copy format. To do this, there must be a way of marking the terms which are to be used as index entries. This can be done in one or both of two ways:

1   Marking the keywords which appear in the text with tags. The system will identify them, and print them out with the page or section number automatically attached.
2   Allocating a number of fields in which index terms can be entered. This method has the advantage that the actual term suitable for indexing is the one which appears, in its alphabetical place. Since the words in a narrative text do not always occur in the right way, it is probably best to have both possibilities in an indexing facility.

Both indexes and interactive searches are improved by using a structured vocabulary or thesaurus. Control of the language used in retrieval systems is always necessary. Some text retrieval software systems include ready-made thesauri, which can be put to use. In other cases the system itself can be made to help construct a thesaurus, or to create inverted files which help searches and index construction. (Inverted files are lists of terms inverted so that the index entry comes first, as with 'Smith, John'). The most user-friendly information retrieval facilities belong to systems which allow the user to call up and refer to lists of terms which appear in the text of archival descriptions. These terms can then be used to carry out a search.

Steps in setting up an archival information system

The system chosen, and the output visualized for it, should be seen as part of the firm's information system, and should be based on the general planning assumptions laid down for it. These may include guidelines which determine the choice of hardware, software, provision of support services and a development plan. On the other hand, many firms provide virtually no guidance. In both situations the archivist's main task is to determine goals, and analyse the work processes required for reaching them. This analysis can then be used to decide on the nature and scope of an automated system which can be brought in.

A simple sequence of development might look like this:

Stage 1   Scrap the typewriter and begin to use a word-processor for most writing tasks; devise a method for filing the resulting records.
Stage 2   Plan and introduce a single-purpose database to carry out a peripheral task.
Stage 3   Plan and introduce a multi-purpose database system for use within the archive service.
Stage 4   Develop the system to include participation in the firm's communication and information system, and develop the possibilities of running a network or giving remote access to computerized information.

Stage 1   Word-processing

All writing jobs should be included: letters, internal memos, rough listing and final archival descriptions, publicity materials, circulars, and so on. The record should still be created by making a hard copy of every document and filing it, but archival descriptions and formal documents (reports, published material, etc.) should also be kept on disc, where they can be most easily retrieved and put to use. An important objective is to get experience, so staff training is important, and should continue beyond the basic learning stage.

Stage 2   A simple one-purpose system

Systems for archival management may be divided into those that do a single task or a connected group of tasks, which can be isolated from the other work of the service, and those that attempt to set up a complex system to provide some kind of central control for the main work.

The following are examples of single-purpose databases:

- Accessions register (see Figure 13.4).
- Location index.
- Mailing/distribution list.
- Register of enquiries (see Table 13.4).
- A list of anniversary dates – foundation of branches, constituent firms, etc. (see Table 13.5).
- A catalogue of artefacts or art objects[7].

Any of these would provide experience of designing and working with a database, while carrying out a useful function within the archive service.

Accession no	Title		Dates
Provenance Originator Date received Brief description			
Bulk: extent		Type	

Figure 13.4   *An accessions register.*

Table 13.4 *A register of enquiries*

Field	Content	Size
Number	Serial number for filing	4 numerical
Date in	Date of enquiry received	Date format
Date out	Date enquiry dealt with	Date format
Name	Name of person enquiring	30 alphabetical
Department	Department of enquirer	May be coded
Subject	Topic enquired about	Large
Refs	Document references used	May be coded

Even simple databases require careful planning if they are to serve their intended purpose. In the case of the register of enquiries (Table 13.4) the structure is almost certainly too simple for real use. Are the date fields to be sorted into chronological order? If so, they should be in the form year–month–day. It should be easy to use the database to produce an alphabetical listing of the persons or departments that have asked questions. But to do this, the enquirers' names will have to be sortable. This means that they will either have to be inverted (surname before forename), which is unsatisfactory if they are to be used to output mailing lists; or they will have to be divided up into separate surname, forename and title fields.

But what about the principal field, the one which holds the subject of the enquiry? This must inevitably be filled in in plain language by the person who writes the register. If it is in plain language, it cannot be used to provide an alphabetical listing. If it contains all the necessary keywords, it can be used for interactive searching. Alternatively, some systems allow keywords in the text to be marked, so that they can be indexed automatically. If free text has to be retained, a Keyword in Context (KWIC) index could be made from the subject field.[8] An alternative might be to divide this subject field up into a number of short sub-fields, each

Table 13.5 *A simple database to list anniversaries.*

Field name	Content	Size/Type
Action date	Sortable date of event	ISO code
Date2	User-readable date	Date
Occasion	Event commemorated	Free text
Department	Parts of firm affected	Free text
Location	Note of relevant places	Text/code
Sources	Note of relevant archives	Codes
Pictures	Note of usable illustrations	Codes
Notes	Any additional information	Free text

starting with a keyword which could be put into an index. As always with keywords and index terms, there is generally a need for some form of vocabulary control or authority file to make it work properly.

Even such a simple database thus raises some fundamental problems:

- *The problem of field structure.* There is often a conflict between the need to sort or retrieve data in a field (which demands the inversion of data elements), and the need to display the contents of a field as output (which demands that data be in natural word order).
- *Indexing.* This technique requires ways in which the system can identify index entries, and the way in which keywords relate to each other. If the index is to be of any size, or if it is to be used in conjunction with other indexes, then there has to be a controlled vocabulary. At its most developed, this means that a thesaurus has to be constructed. A thesaurus is a list of words which sets out semantic relationships between them. Thesauri can be incorporated into computer systems so that the vocabulary can be automatically checked.
- *On-line searching.* Here, too, there is scope for the use of thesauri. The main problem is matching the user's idea of what he or she is looking for in a database with the wording actually contained within it. Unskilled users can often get a falsely negative result from a search, simply because they have not asked the 'right' question.

Designing a database is clearly a matter of wisely and consistently dealing with a constant stream of small difficulties. If this is so complicated with such a simple database with few possible uses, it can be imagined how relatively difficult it is to design a complex system which contains several large and relationally interlinked databases or files.

Stage 3: A complex database

Moving on to another stage of complexity, a central relational database management system might be considered, one which would control the main processes of the archives service. These systems may be summarized in their simplest form, as follows:

- Accessions register.
- Location register.
- Conservation control.
- Finding-aid system.
- Issue and return control.

The way in which these files interrelate will pose a series of problems similar to those posed by the design of a single database. For example, any particular record will appear in several of these files, in each case in a slightly different form:

- In the accessions register, which records its transfer from creator to archival storage.
- In the location register, which records the place given to it on the shelves.
- As descriptions at various levels in the finding aids.
- In the issue/return control record if it has been produced for use in the searchroom.

If a record appears in more than one file of this database system, it should be possible to enter and amend all the entries in one single operation. However, this is not always as easy as it might appear. Each file has a different function, and consequently the way any record in it is used and displayed is different from the way the same record is used and displayed in any other file. For example, a record which has been amended may be deleted from the location register and issue/return control, but

- it must not be deleted from the accessions record;
- the group or subgroup descriptions need not be altered where class or item description has been changed (and *vice versa*);[9]
- it may be desirable to update the location register to note the consequences of a change.

Like the example of the enquiry register, this case is presented in a simplified way. Relating two different files carries with it great potential for combining different bits of information, but at the same time it has great potential for misinformation and confusion. All these possibilities need to be examined at the planning stage. Extensive experiment is therefore absolutely necessary. The database planners have to be able to play with the system until they are sure that they understand the significance of every linkage.

At the end of the planning stage it is possible to go on to the immediately practical question of deciding on the broad outlines of a software system, and planning ways of setting it up and maintaining it.

Stage 4: Moving to a fully developed system

The ultimate goal for a business archive service, doubtless, is that it should be part of the overall information system of the firm. Archives are a common resource, and should be easily available for the firm's purposes wherever retrospective information is needed. The way in which this is done obviously depends on the way communication and information systems are developed in the company, and there are obvious links with the record management operation. It is important that the archive manager should have the expertise to join in planning consultations, and should be accustomed to discuss these matters with the technical staff of the company.

After the preliminary experiments and limited applications comes the task of defining the requirements for a fully integrated system. Traditionally it is said that at this point one needs to write out a specification. Writing this is indeed one of the most demanding and satisfying tasks in professional archive management, but it is very laborious and full of pitfalls. Doubtless in some circumstances it is something that must be attempted: for example, when it is intended to install a major hardware/software system that will serve a large organization for a number of years.

A simpler approach is possible where archive management is to be bolted on to an existing database system, where a limited in-house system is to be bought, or where a specified task is to be dealt with. In these cases the specification is something that could be retained in the mind of the archivist responsible, or at least, the written specification could be restricted to setting out certain of the basic facts: the size of the database, the size and structure of the files within it, the nature of the output expected, and the number and siting of input terminals. With this information clear, archivists can reasonably expect to be able to discuss their needs with the company's computing experts, and through them with computer suppliers, from whom they can obtain costings. The complete package is then in a condition in which it can be discussed with the funding authority, at which point the broad issues of compatibility and the long-term aims of the organization can be raised.

The plan itself and the specification which embodies it in practical terms should certainly envisage a limited pilot scheme, and an evaluation both of the pilot scheme and of the main scheme itself, after suitable intervals. All staff concerned should ideally take part in the evaluation.

Practicalities

A computer system has to work, both in technical and in management terms. A feasibility study should seek to satisfy all interested parties on the first, and then proceed to tackle the second.

Training and consent

There are many interested parties. In some ways the most important ones are the staff of the archive service itself. It is important that all grades of staff should be involved in the discussion and testing of any innovation. Introducing any computer-based system changes the work style and conditions of everyone in the service, and provides an opportunity of thinking out afresh the aims and objectives of every part of it. It is likely that some training will be needed – some of it formal, some of it incidental. Formal training may be needed at some stage for all staff, but in the first instance may be restricted to sending clerical staff on conversion courses.

Informal or incidental training comes from exposure to the working of systems and learning about their background and potential.

Technical feasibility

There is a real possibility that a computer system may not work; or, at least, that it may not work in the way expected. Experiment, followed by a limited pilot scheme, are necessary parts of the operation, and it is essential that the old manual system and its records should not be taken out until this stage is over.

Maintenance and forward planning

It is important not to overlook the questions of maintenance and replacement. Every computer system must be maintained. This means that both the hardware and the software should have support from specialists, and that precautions should be built in against the loss or corruption of data. The need to maintain the hardware, which probably includes electro-mechanical equipment such as disc drives and printers, is usually better recognized than the other aspects. There should be a maintenance contract, and this should include the right to call in expert help at short notice. Software maintenance ought to include 'hot-line' assistance and automatic access to free, or very cheap, improvements to the system. Smart operators may be able to identify the local source of 'shareware' packages which may be very useful as enhancements to the main system or to help with housekeeping tasks.

Back-up arrangements to ensure the safety of the data in the system should include both automatic background measures and office routine. Background measures may include systems which automatically make back-up copies and transfer them to alternative storage media at regular intervals, a type of operation specially characteristic of mainframe systems. If there is no automatic system for this, then a firm office routine is doubly necessary. Measures should be laid down clearly in the office rules, and should include such practices as the following:

- Every file to be copied to a separate medium (for example another diskette) on completion of the work.
- All data should be copied on a regular cycle, either at time intervals (twice a day, say), or at the completion of programme elements (whenever an operation is finished).
- Every file which contains an altered version or update should be date-stamped (this can be done automatically by many systems).
- Software-system diskettes should be copied before installation and kept in a separate store.

- Back-up diskettes should be tested from time to time, and recopied if necessary.
- Hard disks should be 'parked' at the end of the day's work.
- Machines should be regularly cleaned and protected from dust.

Some of these minor tasks can become tedious extras for clerical staff, and responsible professionals should never forget to see that they are actually done.

The greatest single danger of failure is the loss of substantial amounts of data as a result of misuse or accident. Computer users are at the mercy of chance a good deal of the time. Fortunately the computer's own powers can be used to provide a safety net which can preserve all or most of the data at risk. It is for this reason that the question of backing up data at regular or short intervals should be taken so seriously.

Replacement should also have a place in the system plan, preferably from the beginning. The life of a personal computer is usually reckoned as 5 years, and there may be a tendency for this period to shorten. Most personal computers are perfectly fit for continued work at the age of 5, but by then they will have been bypassed by new equipment so often that they will look incurably antique, and there may be problems of maintenance.

By contrast, mainframe systems may be more durable. In addition, the replacement of a central mainframe is obviously (in its technical aspects anyway) the problem of the specialist department which maintains it. That department would no doubt consult its users on the requirements for a replacement system, and would take measures for transferring active systems from the old to the new. The transferability of an old database to a new computer, with its new battery of software, is generally less of a problem technically than might be expected. The natural limitations of the old database remain of course, but the data can be retrieved and manipulated by using the new facilities.

Likely developments in information technology

The following brief survey of technologies and developments which are likely for the near future is limited to those relevant to work with archives.

Hypertext

The capabilities of database systems are now being greatly expanded by the development of hypertext – systems in which records entered in one database can be linked by keywords. Users can move the cursor to a keyword which appears on their screen (generally using a mouse to control the cursor), and, by pressing a select key, can call up related records in other databases. In advanced applications they can also call up related records in other media, such as video: these are called hypermedia systems. This development is likely to be very important in archive work, as it helps to overcome the problems posed by having different kinds of description at different levels.

Optical disc systems

Most computer records up to the present have been held on magnetic tape. Archivists have never been happy with this medium, which is essentially unstable, and the data on it expensive to maintain. There are problems of hardware and software if it is desired (as it must be in archives) to keep the data far into the future. The emergence of optical disk systems has therefore been of great interest. Three variants of this technology are relevant: video disk, optical digital disk and CD-ROM. These media are developing fast, and archivists should be aware of the possibility of using them in association with systems they are using or planning to buy.

Optical character recognition

Data capture and input tend to be very labour-intensive. Retrospective data input (converting the backlog) often presents impossible problems because additional staff would be necessary simply to rekey descriptions inherited from the past. It would be a help if the computer could be taught to read existing documents directly. Optical character recognition (OCR) is now becoming available more cheaply, and can be used for inputting typescript through a scanner. Software is also needed to provide a usable data structure for the (unstructured) data captured in this way. This type of OCR system has quite a high accuracy rate – probably over 90 per cent – but still needs to be checked manually as it proceeds. The success rate depends primarily on how good the original typescript is.

An example of a successful use of this technique is the conversion of manual catalogues at the Bank of England to a STATUS database.[10] STATUS is a system for managing textual databases, and is particularly apt for OCR, because it bases its data structure on tags which can be written into the typescript.

Artificial intelligence

Artificial intelligence (AI) aims to replicate human methods of thought and learning. Some early applications of AI, which are available, are of interest to archivists, the most obvious being expert systems. Another AI development is natural language systems to interrogate databases. On-line searching is rapid and flexible, but depends greatly on the ability of the searcher to translate queries into the language form needed by the software, and on the effectiveness of the thesaurus or vocabulary control built into the system. Query languages developed on traditional lines, such as those provided with such database systems as STATUS, or CAIRS, or the more generalized Structured Query Language (SQL), use queries which approximate to natural language but which fail if they do not conform to strictly defined patterns. Natural language systems enable searchers genuinely to use words and word order which occur in daily life, such as 'What do you have on the operation of patent law and licensing?' Systems of this kind exist at present, but require expensive infrastructure. They are likely to become much more readily available, and may help to overcome the comprehension gap between the managers and users of a computer information system.

High-speed text retrieval systems should assist this process. Archival databases are usually large, and searching them uses a great deal of storage space in the computer. New types of computer use parallel processing, pointing the way to systems which do not need expensive special facilities, but which may become standard in the information world.

Conclusion

This brief survey of archival computing in a business context highlights a few very important principles, which may be summarized as follows:

- Archive managers should consult their company's technical experts, and should participate wherever possible in the company's information planning. Their systems should be compatible with the company's other technology, and ultimately should be part of the company's information system.
- The most important factors are the archivist's own expertise and enthusiasm. It is possible for the requisite levels of expertise to be acquired without enormous effort, and there are no special pre-conditions.
- Experience may be gained by introducing technology gradually, starting at once with word-processing, and proceeding to single-purpose systems.
- When major installation becomes possible, the main professional skills needed by an archivist are the ability to analyse the aims and processes, to draw up an accurate specification and to evaluate results.

Notes

1 *What Micro?* (published monthly by VNU Business Publications, 32/4 Broadwick Street, London W1A 2HG) is a popular computing magazine with

a small business orientation which usually contains useful practical information and explanation for the lay person.

2 There is an overlap of meaning between the terms 'file' and 'database'. Normally, 'file' means a set of connected data with a common structure, and 'database' is a more complex assembly of data, often including more than one file. However, a database may also consist simply of one file, and in this case the term would be used to indicate that the data was used for a management purpose.

3 M. Cook and M. Procter, *Manual of Archival Description*, 2nd edition (Gower, Aldershot, 1990). A simple *MAD User Guide* (Gower, Aldershot, 1989) is helpful for inexpert readers.

4 These are, respectively, S. Hensen, *Archives, Personal Papers and Manuscripts*, 2nd edition (Society of American Archivists, Chicago, 1989); Bureau of Canadian Archivists, *Standard for the Description of Archival Fonds* (Bureau of Canadian Archivists, Ottawa, 1989).

5 R. Rada, *Hypertext* (McGraw-Hill, New York, 1990).

6 Available from the Archival Description Project, University of Liverpool.

7 The Museum Documentation Association, Building O, 347 Cherry Hinton Road, Cambridge, provides a cheap and well-supported package (MODES) for the task of cataloguing and documenting small museum collections, together with short training courses.

8 Details of this method of creating a machine-generated index appear in M. Cook, *Archives and the Computer*, 2nd edition (Butterworth, London, 1986).

9 The meaning is better expressed in MAD2 terminology: macro descriptions need not necessarily be altered where micro descriptions have been changed, and *vice versa* (see Cook and Procter, *op. cit.*, section 5).

10 H. Gillett, 'Computerising the Bank of England archives', *Journal of the Society of Archivists*, 9: 1 (1988), pp. 23–5.

Further reading

L. R. Carter and E. Huzan, *Teach Yourself Computers and their Uses* (Hodder & Stoughton, London, 1989).

M. Cook, *Archives and the Computer*, 2nd edition (Butterworth, London, 1986).

M. Dolphin, 'BRS/Search at the National Audit Office, *Business Archives*, 61 (1991), pp. 39–53.

A. J. Gilliland (editor), 'Automating intellectual access to archives', *Library Trends* (Winter, 1988), pp. 495–623.

J. O. Hick, *Information Systems in Business: An Introduction* (West Publishing, Minneapolis, 1986).

J. Orbell, 'The introduction of a computer-based modern records control system at Barings merchant bank', *Business Archives*, 55 (1988), pp. 29–38.

D. Roberts, 'Using computers and micrographics', in A. Pederson (editor) *Keeping Archives* (Australian Society of Archivists Inc., Sydney, 1987), pp. 253–80.

C. Smith, 'Using dBaseIII plus at the archives of Westpac Banking Corporation', *Business Archives*, 57 (1989), pp. 19–46.

D. Vernon, 'The application of CAIRS in an archival environment', *Business Archives*, 59 (1990), pp. 19–35.

T. E. Weir, 'New automation techniques for archivists', in J. G. Bradsher (editor), *Managing Archives and Archival Institutions* (Mansell, London, 1988), pp. 134–47.

P. Winterbottom, 'Using ASSASSIN at the archives of Imperial Chemical Industries plc', *Business Archives*, 59 (1990), pp. 47–63.

14

Access policy

John Booker

Most companies which maintain archives have also accepted the need to allow access to those archives for historical purposes. For the archivist, however, remains the difficult task of bridging between the extremes of simple acquiescence by the employer and precise questioning on the part of the researcher. What matters is the extent of co-operation which can be given and this must be established at the outset by an access policy professionally acceptable to the archivist and satisfactory in principle to the employer.

How this policy is arrived at will greatly depend on the archivist's status. If the post is a managerial position, the archivist may be expected to establish policy as well as implement it and bear responsibility for any consequences. If the post is more junior, and particularly if it is part-time, the archivist may be implementing the policy of the officer to whom he or she is immediately accountable, or of the partners, executive or board of the business as a whole.

The archivist and the employer

Whatever the seniority of the post, it is in the archivist's interest that a written access policy is discussed with, or at least presented to, the employer. It may be that the business archivist with professional freedom will submit the policy more as a note for information than as a document for discussion. Any archivist who fails to acquire written approval of access policy stands unnecessarily exposed to the consequences of a decision to grant access which results in embarrassment to the business, and lacks a useful defence against researchers who try to circumvent the archivist to gain access via, for example, members of the board.

In formulating policy the archivist must understand the conflicting pressures on the employer's judgement. Many businessmen will be reluctant to release information to outsiders, owing to the confidentiality and discretions of their job. On the other hand, some larger and older companies recognize a social obligation to make their records available. Although few might openly admit that this is their position, it is difficult to see how many archive services would survive, outside the normal realms of cost-effective return, if this were not the case. In another sense the attitude of companies reflects greater national tolerance in the supply and availability of information. Increasingly the question is changing from 'why should we . . .?' to 'why should we *not* . . .?' Publicity from North America and elsewhere on 'freedom of information' legislation tends to encourage this state of mind.

The archivist's professional stance should always be to encourage the employer towards a regularized and responsible liberality. Although many business archivists would not subscribe to a recommendation that standards should 'include service to research transcending the immediate interests of the firm . . .',[1] they will nevertheless feel a moral and social obligation to be helpful to historical enquirers.

If the business is a limited company, the facility, statutory since 1948,[2] for inspection of minute books of general meetings held on or after 1 November 1929 and of certain registers (mainly in relation to directors and shareholders) may help to remind the employer that access to its records is not an irrelevancy. The calibre of material statutorily retained is generally of limited historical use but legislation at least ensures that records are kept and can be made available, in theory at the company's registered office and often under the ultimate control of the company secretary.

Allowing access

The main issues which must be considered in formulating an access policy are:

- Which records are potentially available?
- At what date can records be released?
- To whom may records be shown?
- In what circumstances should the archivist refer back?

These are not, of course, the only issues which arise but others, such as policy on loans or reproduction, will come within the competence and discretion of the archivist.

Which records are potentially available?

Before making recommendations the archivist must have a clear idea of the evolution and structure of the organization. It is impossible to predicate an absolute strategy, given the infinite variety of companies and firms which fall within the loose definition of 'business'. Some organizations will already have a diagram of their historical growth, and most can supply the archivist with function charts of more or less recent origin. In industries with retail outlets (whether branch, office, shop, or public house) there should be a perception of the difference between the centre (strategy, co-ordination, and control) and the periphery (public interface).

In any business there is likely to be a distinction between records dealing purely with internal matters as opposed to those of the consumer or supplier, but it is unsafe to generalize as to their respective suitability for production. For instance, in the media industries the end-product is, by definition, public, but the stages in reaching it may be most sensitive; in high-profile service industries, particularly in the financial sector, the reverse is almost the case, in that dealings with the consumer are confidential, but policy decisions are often well-publicised; and in manufacturing industries there may be no 'safe' classes of record beyond advertising literature.

If the organization has well-known competitors, it could be argued that access policy need not be more restrictive than that of the competition, if the archivist believes rules adopted by colleagues to be soundly based. Indeed there are advantages for archivists in these circumstances to work together towards a common access policy; if such a policy is achieved, there are obvious benefits, too, for the research lobby.

At what date can records be released?

The national 30-year rule for public records is undoubtedly too rigid and generous a guideline for most companies to adopt, except for the blandest of records. Again, in such a broad context as 'business', it is impossible to make precise recommendations as to release dates, but the policy should be not so inflexible that the archivist has no room to manoeuvre and yet not so vague that the archive is effectively run without one. For instance, a policy of availability by date would be sensible, but this date may vary from one class of record to another. Questions of libel, breach of confidence, and the Official Secrets Act will affect the archivist's judgement.

The type of access policy to be avoided is one geared to a national milestone, such as the outbreak or end of the Second World War. Whatever impact such events might be felt to have had on the company's history, they leave the archivist at some stage with the task of renegotiating the position, usually with no similar milestone available. A rolling date is more satisfactory for archivist and researcher alike and can be incorporated in a computerized finding aid to allow automatic access to newly released records each year. Alternatively, there is a case for block release (for example, 5 years at a time) if the nature of the archive suggests it.

To whom may records be shown?

Obviously they may be shown to officers of the organization about their lawful business. Care must be taken to ensure that these officers are of a grade compatible with the release of the material. In large organizations the archivist must not be afraid to seek proof of rank, perhaps by asking the enquirer to sign a *pro forma* declaration that he or she is of the seniority demanded by the status of the records. Even more care must be exercised in companies where the work of one department alone is considered sensitive (perhaps because it is a contractor for government business) or there are records whose unauthorized release between departments might offend statutory or City regulations.

Sometimes the right of access to records is determined not by rank but by 'the need to know', especially where work is governed by the Official Secrets Act. As records mature the importance of such considerations diminishes, and the archivist will wish to establish with his or her employer the ground rules for an easing of restrictions.

As far as outsiders are concerned, any *bona fide* historical enquiry should be treated by the archivist sympathetically, regardless of its source, and without prejudice as to calibre or content. The definition of an historical enquiry is not a matter for business archivists in isolation, and part of professional expertise in general is to recognize a legitimate question. There is nevertheless a requirement for the archivist of a more sensitive business to spot the enquiry cloaked in historical garb but inspired by more dubious motives. Industrial spies and some investigative journalists are not renowned for their openness. There is no textbook solution for spotting the impostor, but the more experienced the archivist, the less likely he or she is to be duped.

In discussions with the employer the archivist should make it clear that access policy towards external enquiries must be even-handed. There should not be one rule on production for those who approach via a director and another for those who approach the archivist direct. An exception, however, can be made for the company historian, in which case the archivist should ask for written authority to produce records not otherwise available.

Some organizations will expect their archivist to be cost-effective, or at least not wholly without income, and may suggest a research charge. The archivist may wish to resist this, not only in principle as custodian of a fund of knowledge, but also because serious research students seldom have much money and revenue rarely compensates for lack of goodwill and accounting time. Charging also introduces practical problems as the archivist is in a weaker position for refusing lengthy research on behalf of an enquirer if this person is readily able to pay. This difficulty, however, can be minimized by charging postal enquiries at a higher rate than attendance by the researcher in person.

In what circumstances should the archivist refer back?

Enquiries which are not historical, or where the historical element has a wider significance, are those on which the business archivist should consult. Such enquiries are likely to emanate from the legal profession, news media or entertainment media. Added to these of course are enquiries which are reckoned by the archivist to be unlawful or malicious, or in any other way against the employer's interest. The referee might not necessarily be the officer to whom the archivist is accountable. For instance, an investigative journalist should be discussed with the press office, a lawyer with the legal department, and a television producer with the public relations manager. That is not to say that the archivist should never deal with the enquiry – the lawyer might simply want the exact date of incorporation of the company, and the television producer might just want a studio prop. But as all non-historical enquiries (and indeed certain historical enquiries of real importance) have the potential adversely or beneficially to affect the organization's reputation or even profitability, the archivist should inform appropriate departments of any significant activity in these areas, for information or advice. It is important that levels of contact should be high enough to take account of the widest implications for the company which access might entail. With a really difficult question from the legal profession or the press, it is reasonable for the archivist to direct the enquirer to approach via a more competent unit of the organization before making any significant response.

It might also be advisable to refer back with certain enquiries about company personnel. Most research in this area is about family history, and the archivist will generally have no trouble in releasing career dates, and similar basic information, if he or she is satisfied that nothing more than genealogy has motivated the enquiry. But in the event of the archivist holding records of a less bland nature, such as records of internal disciplinary hearings at whatever date, nothing should be shown without the advice of the personnel department.

Business sensitivity

The precise extent to which archivists in the private sector can make available material in their care is one of the main concerns to exercise professional competence and training. An essential pre-requisite for this task is an understanding of the sensitivities which underpin business and professional relationships.

Confidentiality

The existence of confidentiality is, at the very least, implicit in everyday business, and may be legally enforceable in the relation between client and professional adviser. The extent to which confidentiality is offered and demanded differs of course with the nature of the profession, and can be affected by changes in social values. In the nineteenth century, for instance, some architects refused to allow periodicals to publish building plans, because they considered it would betray the confidentiality owed to the client.

Two professions, banking and medicine, are associated with secrecy to an exceptional degree. In banking the obligation is now rooted in statute law,[3] and in medicine a breach of confidentiality is a form of 'serious professional misconduct', punishable by the General Medical Council, whose disciplinary powers are statutory.[4] But relationships in all major professions are attended by confidentiality, and in each case the controlling body is empowered to bring members to book for alleged infringement of acceptable practice.

Where these aspects of confidentiality are of particular concern to archivists and historians is not so much in the question of relationships between living people (who can be consulted), but in how far the obligation to secrecy survives after death. A recent American textbook notes that 'the death of the person who is the subject of the information removes nearly all of its private character. The only remaining concern is for other living individuals whose privacy may be affected'.[5] In Britain, however, it may be too pragmatic to consider confidentiality after death only in terms of survivors' interests. In the case of the medical profession, for instance, an obligation to confidentiality expressly continues after the patient's death. Bank archivists will take little comfort from case law, where one outcome of *Tournier v. National Provincial & Union Bank of England Ltd, 1924*[6] (still the leading case) was to establish that bank accounts remain confidential even when they are closed. There is nothing in this ruling to suggest that they become less confidential when the account-holder dies. The significance of death is that it removes exposure to libel, and therefore to one potential source of litigation, but it should not be taken as an automatic threshold for the release of information in any business or profession.

Constitutional distinctions between firms and companies, and resulting differences in scale of operation, can influence the perception of where confidentiality begins and ends. The partners of a firm, or directors of a small company, may feel able to take immediate and important decisions on the release of information, while in a large company questions of access or disclosure arising at the periphery may need to be referred to the centre, with consequent delay. Type and size of business, however, are not themselves indications of attitudes of mind in questions of access.

Commercial secrecy

Confidentiality may sometimes be a synonym for secrecy, but the latter is more often the legal term with a special significance for archivists in businesses which operate as some agency of government. All employees in these areas are subject to the Official Secrets Act, whether or not they have signed to that effect. However, any manufacturing industry, particularly in the high technology sector and especially in areas of design and development, will be wary of public scrutiny and have its own secrecy requirements. Companies which specialize in research and development, in the pharmaceutical or chemical industries, may have separate arrangements for the management of current records, but this does not mean that formulae and data already in the archives relating to past products are necessarily open to inspection. For instance, a drug might be in use for many years before it is suddenly prohibited, perhaps on the grounds that its side-effects are no longer acceptable. The manufacture and testing of this drug could then become aspects of a lawsuit, and the premature release of files to unauthorized persons might prejudice the company's position.

No less sensitive than the companies which invest millions of pounds in research for the future are those whose business rests squarely on the formulae of the past. For example, old recipes for condiments, soft drinks and dairy products may be jealously guarded by manufacturers, and an archivist who releases a dusty sheet of ingredients might still do catastrophic damage to the reputation and profitability of the business. Equally important to the company will be its brand name(s), protected by trademark. The defence and continuation of the trademark will be a matter for lawyers, but the archivist should be aware of basic trademark legislation, which has become significantly tighter as a result of the Copyright, Designs and Patents Act 1988. Under the Trades Description Act of 1968 the offence of forging a trademark, introduced back in 1887 by the Merchandise Marks Act, was removed. Under the 1988 Act, however, it has been reintroduced, by way of clauses to be inserted in the Trades Marks Act 1938, which remains in force. As it is now an offence not only to copy a registered trademark but also to use one only 'nearly resembling' it, the archivist will obviously be wary of showing files which might prove the company's official lack of interest in draft or discarded trademarks uncomfortably similar to those in force.

Similarly, the archivist should be aware of patent law regulations, at least in outline, to prevent basic errors of disclosure within the protected term (normally 20 years, since the Patents Act 1977). As a general rule, however, no archivist should have anything to do with external enquiries about trademarks or patents, however innocently packaged, without advice and authority from competent areas of the company.

The problems of industrial espionage, or unlawful 'leaking', are more for the records manager than the archivist, although both posts will need trustworthy support staff and a constant awareness of executive anxiety. In fact it is unlikely that an access policy in these circumstances will be anything more than a duty of referral to a higher echelon of management. If the organization is more governed by security than secrecy, e.g. safe-manufacturing as opposed to missile-building, then restrictions are a matter for the company itself without overtones of governmental control. In this case obsolescence of the product might well encourage its historical exploitation: for instance, a woodcut engraving of an old-fashioned safe will not jeopardize modern development, and management might see commercial advantage in demonstrating the longevity of the business.

Restricted records

If the business archivist needs to be unusually aware of sensitivities it will generally be apparent from his or her contract of employment. In companies contracting to government it may be a condition of employment that the archivist subscribes to the Official Secrets Act; in other companies, e.g. in the financial sector, it may be necessary to sign an in-house declaration of secrecy, itself enjoined by the company's articles of association. In fact, there are unlikely to be many businesses where the archivist is not sometimes legally constrained to act in a way contrary to the professional instinct to be helpful.

The most famous disincentive to disclose has always been section 2 of the Official Secrets Act 1911, which many people considered impossibly broad. This made it an offence to communicate information of state to any person not authorized to receive it, or for the benefit of any foreign power, or in any way prejudicial to the national interest. It was also an offence under the same section unlawfully to retain such information, fail to take reasonable care of it, or conduct oneself so as to endanger it.

The Act has now been superseded by the Official Secrets Act 1989, which replaces section 2 'by provisions protecting more limited classes of official information'. In effect this limits sensitivity to defence, international relations, and crime and special investigations, and makes it an offence for any person 'who is or has been a Crown servant or Government contractor' to make an unlawful and damaging disclosure within those areas. (The Act also of course relates to disclosure by former members of the security and intelligence services.) Archivists will particularly wish to note section 8 of the new Act, by which a Crown servant or government contractor commits an offence by unlawfully retaining a document, or neglecting to return it, or dispose of it, when requested, or failing 'to take such care to prevent the unauthorized disclosure of [it] as a person in his position may reasonably be expected to take'. In short, the situation for the archivist is scarcely any different under the new legislation.

It might well be argued of course that whatever statutory restraints exist against disclosure, it has never been the intention of Parliament to legislate against *bona fide* research. This has not always been a problem restricted to official secrets. A parallel comes to mind with the Rehabilitation of Offenders Act 1974, which appeared to prohibit archivists from releasing details of a spent conviction at any date in history. Similarly the research lobby might suggest that the obligation to secrecy in section 19 of the Banking Act 1979 did not mean to bar historians from records of banking, despite their omission from the exceptions to the rule of non-disclosure. But any archivist who fails to keep rigidly to the law, in any context, must be aware of the gravity of the risk.

Living within the law

If the business archivist with sensitive records can accept that there is some difference between the spirit and the letter of legislation, it is possible, with caution and common sense, to arrive at a *modus vivendi* with historians which is not too far removed from the position of archivists elsewhere. But the fact that these problems exist at all is why it is so essential for the archivist's own protection that access policy is agreed with the employer.

A more general way forward in the service industries is indicated by the legislation of banking. One of the rare occasions when disclosures of information can be allowed by the Banking Act is when it is 'with the consent of the person to whom the information relates'.[7] This is useful, because if the 'person' is a company, then it is sufficient to ask current management or successor interests for permission. If the company was or is a customer, it is generally better for the archivist, rather than the researcher, to approach the company: this makes it clear that the latter is not trying to avoid or pre-empt the bank's own position, and if the question is put without recommendation, there is no weakening of the archivist's professional neutrality. It also avoids annoying customers with continued and unco-ordinated approaches from individual researchers. In any other businesses which have a clear client relationship such a procedure could well be adopted.

As a general rule, however, in any business where sensitive records affecting other people's interests are kept, 100 years from the creation of the document may provide a useful guideline for safe disclosure when no other dispensation exists. It may well be possible, as has been suggested above, to come within that period on particular occasions, but the date of 100 years allowed by government for the release of census information can be argued as the yardstick for the release of personal information as a whole.

The initial enquiry

It is now appropriate to examine how requests for information or access are received and should be handled.

The prospective researcher

Business archivists can expect the same avenues of contact with researchers as their colleagues in the public sector, but are entitled to make more formal procedures for access. It is reasonable, for instance, not to see casual, off-the-street enquirers but to insist on visits by appointment. Enquiries by telephone are sometimes acceptable, if the information requested is to hand, or uncomplicated, and it is obviously sensible for researchers to telephone simply to establish whether their line of enquiry is worth pursuing. But researchers should be asked to write a letter if their interest goes any deeper. Few archivists normally ask for referees or sponsors, but a letter is an earnest or serious intention on the part of the enquirer and a starting point for the archivist, who can consider calmly the appropriate level of response.

Unfortunately it must be said that few letters which are received in business archive repositories are well written and ironically academics are some of the worst offenders, failing to give the range of information which the archivist requires. There is often no precise statement on the course of study and requirements are woolly or all-embracing. Given that the precise direction of a thesis may alter with the availability of material, it is nevertheless important for an archivist to know not only *what* a person wishes to see, but *why* he or she wishes to see it; also archivists must from time to time account to their superiors for the running of the archive, and communication by telephone does not leave evidence to justify time spent answering some enquiries.

It is also sensible for the prospective researcher to state the source of his or her knowledge (if any) of the business archive. Has it, for instance, been gleaned from published sources, such as Pressnell and Orbell[8] or Richmond and Stockford,[9] or has the enquirer been to the Royal Commission on Historical Manuscripts in Chancery Lane and found references in the National Register of Archives? Good tactics in any serious enquiry must always be to give too much rather than too little information: no-one minds receiving a long letter if it is to the point, comprehensive and explanatory.

The archivist's response

In reply, if the enquiry is legitimate, the archivist should indicate what kind of material is available and state the general conditions under which access is granted. If there is no relevant material, it would be helpful to give broad advice on where to try next. Assuming, however, that information exists, the best arrangement is for enquirers to be invited to visit, to conduct their own research.

There are advantages in this for both sides:

- The researcher knows best what he or she really wants.
- The archivist has more time to deal with proper professional duties (assuming support staff to invigilate at the visit).
- The archivist is not put in danger of offering a written opinion which might be used against the company's interests in an enquiry which, despite an historical presentation, proved to be a legal issue.
- Personal contact with academics adds stimulus and motivation to more humdrum duties and perhaps earns an element of respect from the

employer (who might have seen the archive service as essentially an in-house function).

- Personal contact also helps build a bond of trust between archivist and researcher.
- The archivist is often able to help more than the original enquiry suggested after discussion of the enquirer's research interests.
- The essence of history is the process of personal research and discovery and answers should not come gift-wrapped.

Preparation of material

How far research is undertaken by the archivist, in anticipation of the visit, to narrow down the field of evidence is of course a problem for the profession as a whole. If the researcher will be coming from some distance and seems likely to be pressed for time, it will be helpful to eliminate sources which prove, on examination, to have no bearing on the enquiry. In addition, pages in, for example, a minute book could be flagged, particularly if the archivist is not keen on the whole book being rummaged, perhaps because the index (if any) is known to be defective or the book is in poor condition. It might also be necessary for the archivist to vet letter files before their production, in case any of the subject matter is confidential. On the other hand, some researchers feel that preselection deprives them of the satisfaction of establishing dead ends at first hand; others may feel that material is being withheld for ulterior motives or may not trust the archivist to have grasped the real thrust of the enquiry. Another factor of course is the distance between searchroom and repository, and the size of the object. There is little point in hauling a 20 kilogram ledger between five floors or two buildings simply to establish its irrelevance.

The point at which a document is barred from production on grounds of its physical condition will depend to a large extent on whether the archivist has a conservation budget. If there is a prospect of repair work, it is reasonable to embargo production until the book is in better condition. If no conservation is possible, the archivist has a dilemma: there is little point in keeping documents which are too damaged to produce, but the use of damaged documents will lead eventually to their total disintegration. An answer sometimes lies in closer assessment of the nature of damage. Loose documents which are fragile, perhaps through previous dampness, should obviously not be handled, but could be viewed through a transparent folder; books which have lost their covers, but are still sewn and intact, could be produced with a label reading 'Handle with the greatest care'. Books which have sound covers, but pages which are badly flaking at the corners or sides, should probably not be produced at all.

The internal enquiry

At least half and generally most of the enquiries to a business archivist are likely to be internal, and it should not be forgotten that there is a greater obligation to be of service to the employer than to the public. By the same token, the archivist will be expected to give help and advice to the organization to an extent not countenanced for the public. He or she may well be expected to research and report back, and give an opinion in a matter not wholly historical. Legal questions are, however, likely to go no further than the production of records, as those who create them are usually best placed to interpret them.

At times it might be advisable to invite an internal enquirer to visit. For instance, the question being posed may be very technical and an irrelevant answer from the archivist would waste company time. However, management can reasonably expect the archivist to be responsive to all questions concerning the corporate memory and the fact that research may make inordinate inroads into the archivist's daily routine is not an argument in the company's eyes against the wider cost-effective deployment of their personnel. On the other hand, staff conducting research for private reasons should be treated no differently from members of the public.

Searchroom management

Searchroom may be too grand a name for the place where researchers are invited to attend. Often the visitor will share a room with the archivist, working at a desk or a table cleared for the duration of the stay. This can be unsatisfactory for the archivist, who may perhaps wish to discuss private aspects of company business by telephone, but at least it ensures a high level of supervision.

Establishing bona fides

Once a researcher has arrived, it is customary to require his or her signature on a declaration which summarizes the conditions of access. This document might form part of a more general application form to see company material. An example of a declaration form is given in Figure 14.1. The second clause is important, because when access is given to a multi-faceted record like a minute book, there might be a temptation to extract material unrelated to the enquiry. The idea behind the third clause is that the archivist, or more senior officer, will have the opportunity to correct errors of fact and expunge references which are deemed, for one reason or another, to be undesirable. There should be no need to read the whole work – just references based on the organisation's own archive.

Form of Declaration

In consideration of my being allowed access to the archives of [company name], I undertake:

1 To furnish proof of my identity.
2 Not to make notes about, nor subsequently to disclose to anyone, any information relating to any business of the company outside the agreed subject of my enquiry.
3 To submit to the archivist, [company name], the final draft of any text which I propose to publish, or include in a thesis, which is based on the records of the company.

Signed ....

Date ....

Figure 14.1   *Researcher's declaration form.*

Customary as these declarations are, it must be admitted that the legal protection which they afford rests more on hope than on reality. If the researcher ignores the undertaking, and publishes a mildly embarrassing paper, it is unlikely that litigation would produce a penalty remotely worth the cost and publicity of the action. In addition, in giving its approval to the text, a company could seem to be agreeing with the wider views of the author, whereas it might be better to remain neutral. Perhaps the best that can be said for the signed undertaking is that it should remind the researcher that the company sees access to its archives as more than a matter of course. Failure to comply would lead to the researcher being barred from further access, and this is perhaps the ultimate sanction.

The spin-off value of an honoured declaration is that the archivist gains, at least in draft, a copy of work produced in whole or in part from the corporate archive. This might well be useful in dealing with subsequent enquiries of the same nature, although care must be taken to protect the copyright and privacy of the researcher. There could be very embarrassing consequences, for instance, from the release to a new enquirer of the draft thesis of a previous researcher before its submission to the relevant university, or of a draft article before its publication.

At the preliminary interview, archivist and researcher should establish the ground rules which are mutually acceptable: in other words, the archivist should explain the implications of clause 3 in the declaration, and the researcher should reveal personal sensitivities to the disclosure of his or her work. If the researcher insists on the privacy of study, then the archivist will not mention it, even to another potential researcher proposing to cover similar ground. The archivist, however, could well be under an instruction to report, at agreed intervals, to higher management the names and topics of users, and this duty transcends the obligation to the researcher. If this instruction exists, the archivist will make it clear at the time of the interview.

Rules and registers

An alternative to the declaration, or in some offices an addition to it, is a sheet of searchroom regulations. The sample regulations reproduced here (Figure 14.2) could be used when no declaration form is intended, as clauses 3 and 10 cover the main points of the latter. Alternatively, these clauses could be omitted when the declaration form is in use. Regulations can be attached to the search register in such a way that the signatory is aware that the act of signing constitutes an undertaking to observe them.

It is probably worth keeping a search register, however few the number of personal visits. The register should record date, name, address or institutional connection, topic of research, and perhaps the exact course of study (if any). It is important to note not only initial but also all subsequent visits and a signature is better than a name in block capitals. In no sense is the register just a visitors' book, but its use could be extended to include those who call perhaps more informally but nevertheless on legitimate business. The main benefit of a search register is that it enables the archivist to report accurate statistics to his or her employer of the identity and purpose of those who are given access to company records. A useful secondary benefit, if a sustained increase in the number of visits can be established, is that the archivist is in a position to counter moves within the organization to limit office space or threaten unfavourable relocation, and may even have a case to argue for larger premises.

As well as a search register, the archivist should keep a separate register of every request for information from both inside and outside the company, and covering every medium of enquiry. A typical register has columns for date of request, name and address (or department) of originator, topic, medium (e.g. letter, telephone, oral instruction), and date of answer. A further column for cross-referencing to a correspondence file might also be considered. The fact that enquiries range from a simple request for an old photograph or catalogue to an invitation to contribute an article to a professional journal does not matter: the extremes cancel out and in the aggregate emerges a reasonably balanced picture of one aspect of the archivist's workload. Again, the statistics are useful for professional accountability, allowing the archivist to submit quarterly or half-yearly reports.

Once a certain threshold of activity has been reached, there may be an argument for extra staff, a personal computer, photocopier, or some other medium for processing enquiries more efficiently. Many public repositories use *pro-forma* cards, filed by subject, to keep track of enquiries and direct staff to answers already provided on a given topic. While these cards will probably be unnecessary in a business archive, given the lower level of use, it will certainly be convenient to have standard answers on file for stock questions, such as the blazonry of company arms.

With regard to rules, it may be the case that the archivist wishes to avoid over-formality. Certain prohibitions are, of course, always to be enforced, e.g. no eating, drinking or smoking. In other ways, however, practice need not be rigid: a small repository with relatively few visitors might wish to keep public hours flexible, particularly if a researcher has come a long way and hopes to complete his or her work in one visit. Likewise, if the

---

[COMPANY NAME]
REGULATIONS FOR READERS

- Access to the archives is by appointment only and at the discretion of the archivist. The company reserves the right at any time to restrict or prohibit access without notice.
- Access is granted on the understanding that the reader is engaged in *bona fide* historical research, and that information obtained will in no way be used against the interests of the company.
- No information may be extracted from documents beyond the agreed subject of research.
- Times of access are a matter for discussion between archivist and reader and may be subject to variation at short notice.
- Every reader must sign the search register on each day of attendance. Signing implies that these regulations will be observed. Proof of identity may be requested at the first signing.
- Smoking, eating and drinking in the searchroom are prohibited.
- Readers may write only in pencil. The use of tape-recorders, portable typewriters or word-processors is at the discretion of the archivist.
- No mark shall be made on any document and no person shall lean upon any document or place on it the paper on which he is writing. Generally the greatest care must be taken in handling documents, and they must never be removed by the reader from the searchroom.
- Documents may be photocopied or photographed at the discretion of the archivist, who reserves the right to charge a fee for this service.
- The final draft of any text which concerns the business of the company, insofar as information has been gathered from the company's records, must be submitted to the archivist for approval before publication. In this connection an academic thesis is regarded as publication.

[Name and position]

[Date]

Figure 14.2 *Searchroom rules.*

archivist is not single-handed, it might be kind to stagger lunch hours to give the visitor, if not an opportunity to work right through, at least a closure period shorter than an hour. But the researcher must never be left unattended, and the timetable of the day must always be established at the start of the visit.

Most archivists will wish to restrict researchers to writing in pencil, a requirement which has become universal in public repositories over the last 20 years to protect records from wilful or accidental marking. Unfortunately pencilled notes are liable to fade, and no objection need be raised to small typewriters, portable word-processors or tape-recorders, provided the noise is not disruptive.

Constructive preparation

Even the smallest business repository should keep catalogues or lists of the records, and classes of records, which it contains. These should be given to the researcher on arrival, both as an *aide-memoire* of what he or she is looking at, in the context of the documentation as a whole, and to encourage the correct quotation of catalogue marks (if any) in references. If the range of finding aids extends to a manual index – of persons, places and subjects, say – this could also be made available, along with any published histories of the business. Many archives are now making computer finding aids directly available to researchers as a means of improving access and reducing space and personnel commitments. Computer databases can be made user-friendly by the construction of simple menus and most systems suitable for archive applications have integral facilities for the creation of different levels of security. In-house researchers in particular may find computer finding aids extremely helpful.

It is an obvious courtesy to the researcher to have agreed records on the table in advance of the appointment, but the amount of material to be produced at any one time is a more difficult problem. The archivist will find it hard to judge the speed at which the researcher will digest the information, particularly if the extent of its relevance is questionable. If the office of the archivist is some distance from the storage of the records, as is so often the case, then it will be wise to discuss with the researcher the nature of the problem. From the archivist's point of view, the fewer the records produced, the lower the risks attaching to transit and use. On the other hand, it can be embarrassing to run out of material, perhaps stored a van journey away, when the researcher is two-thirds of the way through a one-day visit. The wise course of action is to have further material waiting in the wings, but to present the researcher initially with no more than the desk or table can comfortably accommodate.

A safe place should be arranged if the repository is distant, to store reserved documents between successive visits. Each document should be signed for and the number on the desk kept to a minimum. Tickets should always be used, even in a business archive with only one or two researchers a week. They allow some record to be kept of what was seen by whom and when, and can also prove a useful reminder for empty slots in storage areas when material is borrowed in the longer term.

Searchroom attributes

It is important that the searchroom is properly equipped and supervised:

- *Location*. If the archive is in an open-plan office, the confidentiality of information that might be discussed in adjacent areas should be considered.
- *Environment*. The temperature and humidity should not differ too greatly from conditions in the storage area, although plenty of light is required. The installation of ultra-violet filters should be considered.
- *Working area*. The table should be robust, with a wipe-clean surface and no sharp projections. A larger flat area should be available if outsize documents, such as maps and charters, might be consulted.
- *Equipment*. Book rests should be used to reduce damage to large volumes. Microfilm and microfiche readers should be available, or at least facilities arranged for access to such machines, if records are held in microform.
- *Supervision*. The supervisor should be able to see precisely what the researcher is doing at all times and desks should be positioned in such a way as to make this possible. A policy with regard to visitors' bags and coats should also be agreed.

Reproduction and loans

This section should be read in conjunction with that on copyright (pp. 391–3). Most of the comments below assume that copyright has already been considered before reproduction is implemented.

Photocopying

A practical issue which might well result from a researcher's visit is the question of reproduction of inspected material. The same question may of course arise without anyone having visited, but the problem is at its most intractable when the researcher confronts a page of finely detailed accounting, and there is a copier in the corner of the room. Knowing that the business world is less likely than central and local government to worry about the accountability of small runs of paper, the researcher may press for permission to photocopy as an alternative to taking notes. It can well be understood that from the researcher's point of view this is a great advantage in accuracy as well as speed. But the archivist has to remember that a whole document photocopied is one which has passed beyond the control of the organization that produced it. In other words, it might eventually be further reproduced, or even published, without permission or acknowledgement. Photocopying may also be damaging to tightly bound or cumbersome ledgers or to fragile paper, although it has a useful potential for making legible passages of fading ink. A copier with a flat, static platen is preferable.[10]

Both sides should be satisfied with an arrangement whereby photocopying is restricted to less than the whole extent of any one document (unless of course it is only a single sheet of no great moment) and to tables, or parts or tables, of accounts or statistics which are impossibly intricate to transcribe. It is possible to advocate a bolder policy of copying whatever is deemed suitable for production, putting faith in legal constraints against further copying or publication; but these constraints might not prevent such unauthorized reproduction abroad.

Pages may be flagged with strips of card or paper, bearing pencilled reference to folio numbers, or other identification. However, photocopying of archives should not become a substitute for note-taking by researchers, and some warning of restrictions on copying might well form part of the written searchroom rules. It is always good sense to stamp 'Copyright' on any product of reprography, if necessary making allusion to copyright being vested elsewhere than in the organization.

As copiers are such a commonplace of office life, it seems hardly necessary to charge for the service, unless the volume of copying is clearly excessive. Researchers should not expect photocopies to be made there and then, and they should be made by the archivist and not by the researcher. As many archives would have no other source of potential income, the establishment of a credit code for this purpose alone would seem hardly to merit the cost of its maintenance and audit. At some stage, however, accountants may think otherwise, and if written searchroom rules are adopted, some phrase such as 'charges for reproduction may be made at the archivist's discretion' allows for such charges to be introduced, should company policy dictate it.

Photography

Such wording in the searchroom rules also allows a charge to be levied for photography. Again, it might be the case that the demand for photographic copies is too infrequent to merit an income code, but the archivist has to weigh in the balance the high cost of the service against the goodwill or good publicity which the photograph might generate. It is also possible of course to have the bill sent straight to the customer, by-passing the machinery of internal accounting. This is often done when there is no in-house photographic service. The archivist must, however, be certain that a commercial photographic studio will take proper care of archive material.[11]

Other copying

Requests for documents, or series of documents, to be microfilmed for another repository accentuate the issues discussed above under photo-copying. That is to say, the archivist has to weigh the diminishing benefits of goodwill and gratitude against the increasing loss of control over the evidence. Furthermore, once one application is agreed to, the next one is the more difficult to turn down.

More acceptable in essence – if the subject matter does not militate against it – is agreement to the publication of an archive, *in extenso* or in extract, as some form of edited text. This can be agreed to on stringent conditions, such as having the company's name and logo clearly on the jacket and title page, and in this case there is little to lose and permanent publicity to gain, with clear legal redress against further unauthorized copying.

Loans

The loaning of original documentation is positively to be discouraged except when it is unavoidable in the interests of the business, e.g. in a legal enquiry or when the item is required for temporary exhibition. In the first of these cases the archivist does as he or she is instructed, but in the second there are almost inexhaustible considerations which will influence the decision. Among these are the following. Is the document fragile? Is it unique? Will it be insured? How will it travel? How long will it be away? Is the borrower reliable? Is there adequate security? Who captions it? What acknowledgement and publicity will there be for the business? All these are practical issues, which might well form the basis of a written agreement with the borrower, assuming there are no difficulties of a more abstract nature with the release of the information which the document contains.

As far as the archivist is concerned, the source of the request for the removal of material from his or her custody should have no effect on the documentation. In other words, the internal department borrowing or reclaiming an item(s) should sign the same form of receipt as an outsider, and the transactions should be entered equally in a register of loans. Those business archives which are subject to internal audit will know that the accuracy of the loan register is of no less interest to the auditors or inspectors than the accuracy of the petty cash account. The despatch of items on permanent loan to public repositories is of course a different question altogether, raising searching issues of confidentiality and authority upon which it is impossible to generalize. Such loans require a separate register, and receipts used in these cases will normally be the printed and *pro-forma* forms prepared by the accepting repository.

Copyright

The question of copyright follows naturally from the discussion of copying, and embodies the rights and restrictions implicit in the above paragraphs. Until recently the prevailing statute was the Copyright Act 1956, of which the anomalies and pitfalls have long been recognized. A new Copyright, Designs and Patents Act 1988 was passed on 15 November 1988, and sections were brought into force by statutory instrument during 1989. Although this Act repeals the 1956 Act as regards authorship and first ownership it does not affect copyright restrictions on existing material, which continue 'in accordance with the law in force at the time the work was made'. It is still necessary, therefore, to be aware of the terms of the 1956 Act. It can be construed that archives, in the sense of documents, fall within the definition of 'literary work' in both Acts.[12]

Copyright in business records

As far as business records are concerned, the traditional position, i.e. under the 1956 Act, has been that records created by employees in the course of their work are in the perpetual copyright of the organization – perpetual, at least, until published, in which case copyright runs for 50 years from publication. Definition of publication has always been difficult, as something which is printed is not necessarily published. A company's annual report and accounts, for instance, is not published by virtue of circulation to shareholders but by distribution to more than one outside enquirer. Under the 1988 Act there are no substantive alterations as far as unpublished material is concerned, although copyright in published material will now expire 50 years after the author's death, regardless of the date of first publication. For works where there is no identifiable author (for example, the annual report and accounts), copyright will cease 50 years from the end of the year in which they are 'first made available to the public'. Under the new Act, if a work is computer-generated, copyright will expire automatically after 50 years, regardless of authorship.

Copyright in letters and works of art

It has never been the case, however, that all records in a business archive are in the copyright of the organization. Letters, for instance, have an identifiable author, so correspondence with customers, say, or letters of application for jobs, are in the copyright of the writer and not of the recipient. It is always the form of words which is copyright, not the *contents* of the letter, although if the correspondence is of recent date the author might take legal steps to prohibit disclosure on the grounds of confidentiality.

The change under the 1988 Act is that copyright subsists for the author's life, plus 50 years. Where the author died before the Act came into force (1 August 1989), copyright will remain until 31 December 2039.

Many business archivists will have custody of works of art, particularly of portraits of former partners or chairmen. Under the 1956 Act, copyright lay in the commissioner of the portrait and not in the artist, although copyright ran for 50 years after the artist's death. On the other hand, the copyright in paintings, as opposed to portraits, lay with the artist. Now, however, the 'author' of an artistic work, of whatever kind, is the first owner of copyright, which lasts for 50 years after the artist's death. Similarly, if a photograph is commissioned, the first owner of copyright is now the photographer and not the commissioner. (However, if a photograph or portrait was commissioned before the commencement of the Act, but made after it, the commissioner will be the first owner of copyright.) Photographs will now have the same copyright period as any other artistic work, whereas under the 1956 Act the period was limited to 50 years. It must be emphasized again that existing material is not affected by the change, but archivists who keep, for instance, premises or public relations department photographs as soon as they pass out of currency will obviously wish to satisfy themselves as to the copyright position when batches are accessioned in the future.

'Prescribed library or archive'[13]

Fortunately for the business archivist, the more intractable aspects of copyright in archive repositories concern the copying of deposited material, as opposed to that of the organization itself. The problem therefore lies very much in the public sector, particularly in local government record offices where documents in private ownership are often held on permanent loan.

As far as literary and artistic works created on or after 1 August 1989 are concerned, business archivists benefit from section 43 of the 1988 Act, which allows, against certain safeguards, for works to be copied and supplied for research purposes without infringement of copyright. However, the provision in section 42 of the 1988 Act, allowing for the acquisition from another archive of a replacement copy of a lost work, without infringement of copyright, does not extend to archives conducted for profit – a definition which embraces most business archives.

Living with copyright

Given the fact that the business archivist is likely to be in consultation with a public relations department, or other internal unit, in questions of reproduction of the company's own material, the only problem likely to affect the archivist alone is how far copyright in material lodged in his or her care by subsidiary companies should be regarded as separate from the copyright subsisting in the records of the parent company. A lot will depend on the historical descent of the subsidiary and the degree of autonomy which it enjoys as well as the strength and personalities of its executives. But as a general rule any archivist would be ill-advised to consider that questions such as the reproduction of a boardroom painting from a subsidiary company, even if it is under the archivist's nominal control, are not matters for liaison with current management.

The business archivist can really do no more than act sensibly in any given case, giving notification of intention to all parties who might be concerned in questions of reproduction, and leaving it to them to make the legal running, should they wish to do so. In reality one can expect to work for years without difficulties of copyright ever arising, not because most organizations have no knowledge of the restrictions of the law, but because, in respect of their own records, the rationale of copyright legislation may be at odds with the mentality of self-centred goodwill which often encourages a business to run an archive service in the first place.

Notes

1 M. Cook, *Archives Administration* (Dawson, Folkestone, 1977), p. 6.
2 Companies Act 1948 (11 & 12 Geo. VI, c.38), ss.145, 146.
3 Banking Act 1979, s.19; Banking Act 1987, s.82.
4 Under the Medical Act 1969.
5 J. G. Bradsher (editor), *Managing Archives and Archival Institutions* (Mansell, London, 1988), p. 167.
6 1 K.B. 461.
7 That was the wording in the 1979 Act. The latest Act (1987), s.82, puts it the other way and prohibits disclosure of information 'without the consent of the person to whom it relates . . . .'
8 L. S. Pressnell and J. Orbell, *A Guide to the Historical Records of British Banking* (Gower, Aldershot, 1985).
9 L. Richmond and B. Stockford, *Company Archives. The Survey of the Records of 1000 of the First Registered Companies in England and Wales* (Gower, Aldershot, 1986).
10 Further advice is given in *BS 5454: 1989 British Standard Recommendations for the Storage and Exhibition of Archival Documents* (British Standards Institution, 1989), p. 16.
11 *Ibid*, p. 13.
12 For further discussion see M. R. Foster, 'Copyright and the business archivist', *Business Archives*, 59 (1990), pp. 1–18.
13 A definition introduced in the Copyright, Designs and Patents Act 1988.

Further reading

General
J. G. Bradsher (editor), *Managing Archives and Archival Institutions* (Mansell, London, 1988).
M. Cook, *Archives Administration* (Dawson, Folkestone, 1977).
A. Pederson (editor), *Keeping Archives* (Australian Society of Archivists Inc., Sydney, 1987).
A. A. H. Knightsbridge, *Archive Legislation in the United Kingdom* (Society of Archivists Information Leaflet 3, 1985).
J. Orbell, *A Guide to Tracing the History of a Business* (Gower, Aldershot, 1987).

Confidentiality
Banking Act 1979 (c.37).
Banking Act 1987 (c.22).
Official Secrets Act 1911 (c.28).
Official Secrets Act 1989 (c.6).
I. Morrison *et al.*, *Banking Act 1979* (Butterworth, London, 1979).

Copyright
Copyright Act 1956 (c.74).
Copyright, Designs and Patents Act 1988 (c.48).
M. F. Flint *et al.*, *Intellectual Property − The New Law. A Guide to the Copyright, Designs and Patents Act 1988* (Butterworth, London, 1989).
M. R. Foster, 'Copyright and the business archivist', *Business Archives*, 59 (1990), pp. 1–18.
J. B. Post, 'Copyright mentality and the archivist', *Journal of the Society of Archivists*, 8:1 (1986), pp. 17–22.

15

Supplementing the collection

Alison Turton

Until the essential work of the archive – acquisition, appraisal, arrangement and description, and proper storage and use of the records – is well in hand, it is unlikely that the business archivist will have the opportunity to consider ways in which the collection can be supplemented. However, the ultimate aim of the business archivist must be to build up as complete a record of the history of the firm as possible, plugging gaps in the surviving documentary material with oral history interviews and photographic programmes; the procurement or copying of material held in private hands and in other repositories; and the collection of textual and visual information from a wide range of sources. Such activities are often known as documentation programmes.

Supplementing an archive collection in a systematic way does, however, require a major commitment of time and resources. The programme must be carefully planned to ensure that the most useful material is sought and selected, that it is captured by means of suitable materials and techniques and that it is properly maintained and referenced. If this can be achieved, documentation offers almost limitless opportunities for the company to add to the understanding of its past and to involve staff, shareholders and customers in the process. It will provide vital information, often of the kind which could not be found among the documentary records generated by the company itself, and which may be needed at short notice for public relations activities.

Creating documentation

The creation of records which would never have existed had the archivist not intervened may be considered controversial and at odds with the archivist's traditional role as passive custodian. However, the business archivist, relatively well-resourced and with a finite and well-defined area to explore, is well placed to carry through a successful programme of ordered documentation. As long as the origin of the material is made clear, it is made available in conjunction with other records and its limitations are understood, there is no reason why created documentation should not add substantially to the information contained in conventional archive records.

There are many ways in which documentation can be created, and a few of the most accessible methods are discussed in detail below – oral history, photography and commissioning works of art.

Oral history[1]

Oral history is concerned with interviewing persons who were witnesses or participants in historically significant events to capture, with sound recording equipment, their personal memories or opinions for posterity. It is a type of documentation which can be particularly useful in reconstructing the 'atmosphere' of a place or time and in discovering facts which may never have been written down, such as the local reputation of a firm, the colour of the house livery, or the management style of a particular director.

The collecting programme must be planned, whether it aims to throw light on the routine business of a particular branch or factory during the Second World War or to record events of the previous year leading up to a take-over bid or new policy initiative. Appropriate informants must be found and the value of their evidence assessed. Interviewees may be identified and located through the house magazine, personnel department, articles in the local press in towns where the company traded, or on the advice of long-serving members of staff. There is, however, a need to define the area of investigation and to prioritize, as cost and time constraints will probably prohibit a comprehensive programme. Interview first those who may know most, such as senior staff, or those who may not be available long-term, such as the elderly.

The planning and preparation required for successful oral history interviewing should not be underestimated nor should the skill demanded of the interviewer. The aim is to elicit a frank, relevant and complete account of the events in question and to ensure that the information is clearly stated and the recording technically satisfactory. Some ideas on how to manage the practicalities and how to conduct interviews are given in Tables 15.1 and 15.2.

Oral recordings must be of high quality to merit permanent preservation and the cost of collection. Professional equipment is therefore essential. Although good cassette tape-recorders are now available, open reel machines are probably more suitable. They are sturdier, require less maintenance and, during the interview, make it easier to rectify tape jams and to check that the tape is moving smoothly. Two good clip or neck microphones will also be required, as integral microphones pick up the machine's own noise and are therefore not suitable. The venue should be checked before the interview to ensure that there is no continuous background noise, such as clocks or traffic. Bare- or hard-surfaced rooms should be avoided, as carpets, curtains and upholstery help to reduce echoes. When recording the interview, cushion the machine with a tablecloth or mat, to minimize vibrations. It should be placed close to the interviewer, so that its operation can be checked unobtrusively.

Polyester-based quarter-inch standard play tape should be used for long-term storage of masters in unit lengths of around 30 minutes. Less costly tapes may, however, be used for reference copies.[2] Tapes should be labelled and stored in accordance with the recommendations for sound recordings given in Chapter 8 (pp. 201–2).

Copyright of the information in the interview belongs to the interviewee and the archivist must secure a signed, dated statement allowing the tape to be copied or transcribed and made available to researchers, quoted in publications, broadcast or used in a public performance. It should clarify who owns the copyright, both initially and in the long term.

Each interview should be documented and the following information permanently retained:

- The interviewee's name.
- The duration of the recording.
- The date of the recording and subsequent copies.
- Technical information on, for example, the tape-recorder, microphone, speed of recording, etc.

The record itself must be properly listed. The information in the finding aid should include:

- Accession number.
- Full name and title of interviewee and any former names.
- Synopsis of contents.
- Interview date/location.
- Name of interviewer.
- Access and copyright arrangements.
- Number of reels.
- Associated documentary material.
- Index entries of the names, events, locations, products, etc.

A file should be maintained to hold correspondence, agreements, and other paperwork concerning each interview, along with any useful background biographical information.

Table 15.1 *Managing oral history interviews.*

- *Initial contact*. Define the overall aims of the project and general topics to be covered in the interviews. Identify useful interviewees and write explaining the scope and purpose of the project, why he or she has been chosen, and the use to be made of the recording.
- *Preliminary meeting*. Discover some biographical information, both career and personal, through informal conversation (unless the interviewee is eminent enough to research from other sources). Persuade the interviewee of the need to express personal experiences and opinions fully and candidly. Develop mutual trust and rapport by adopting a suitable appearance and showing appropriate interest, tact and respect. To avoid the meeting undermining the spontaneity of a later interview, deter the interviewee from recounting stories at length and allow a week or so to lapse before the recording.

- *Planning*. Research the interviewee and the subject of the interview thoroughly so that relevant information can be solicited. Prepare a brief list of questions to get the interview moving, but be prepared to add or abandon lines of enquiry as the interview evolves. Check that the equipment is working properly and practise operating it.
- *The interview*. Before the interview begins, chat informally with the interviewee for a few minutes and ensure that he or she is comfortable. Record a brief introductory statement, giving the name of the interviewee, the date, the location and the subject of the interview. During the interview make notes on points that might be elucidated later or on unfamiliar words or names, though avoid scribbling incessantly. Ensure that the interview is kept to a reasonable length (around 1½ hours maximum).
- *After the interview*. Make arrangements for second and further interviews should these prove necessary. Label the tape carefully. Ask the interviewee to sign a release form allowing research use of the tape and establishing copyright ownership and other rights.

Table 15.2   *Oral history interviewing techniques.*

- Questions should be brief, open, unambiguous, concerned with a single idea, match the interviewee's level of sophistication and be asked one at a time.
- Be neither coy nor confrontational, and save controversial questions until the interview is well under way.
- Allow the interviewee to do most of the talking, and avoid interrupting unnecessarily. Use leading questions to direct the interviewee away from irrelevancies.
- Use affirmation and reinforcement techniques to encourage appropriate responses, such as nodding in agreement and sympathetic eye contact.
- Do not worry about periods of silence, which allow both the interviewer and interviewee to gather their thoughts.
- Challenge inaccuracies tactfully, bearing in mind that the interview is a record of the informant's opinions and recollections and is not intended to be the sole factual account of particular events.
- If something is not clear, restate it in other words and make sure that the sense is clarified.

Taking photographs[3]

There will be many instances where visual evidence which would complement the information in the archive is not being recorded by the company in the course of its routine business. An old-established factory site or a current production process or social event may all merit the archivist's attention. In most cases the most accessible recording medium is the photograph.

Before new photography is initiated, however, it is important to establish whether a long-term programme of photography is required or whether there is simply a need for an occasional photograph to be taken. The size of the project will affect the way in which the work is commissioned and implemented. There are three main options available to the business archivist wanting to acquire new photography:

- Using professional photographers, operating either as self-employed individuals or as staff within a commercial photographic company.
- Approaching other organizations with a specialist interest in the subject being photographed.
- The archivist or another company employee taking their own photographs.

The use of outside commercial photographers requires an appreciation of the specialized disciplines within the profession, such as medical, wedding or industrial photography, each one requiring a different technique and approach. Photographers who specialize are capable of providing the very best record of any particular subject to be archived but they must be chosen carefully. A wedding photographer could be ideal for photographing a public relations event but might not fully understand the requirements for producing technical photographs of the latest company product. Specialist commercial photographers can be found from the directory published by the British Institute of Professional Photography.[4] Charges for professional photography are usually based upon a day rate, with the addition of expenses and material costs. The use of professional photographers will generally guarantee a good result in those cases where there is only one opportunity to take a photograph. There will always be times when the acquisition of a particular photographic record for the archive is so important that using the knowledge and experience of a specialist professional photographer is the least costly route.

Alternatively the archivist might approach other organizations with specialist interests which have such a demand for continual photographic recording that they have established an internal photographic department. For the Royal Commission on the Historical Monuments of England (RCHME), for example, photography is an important part of its work in surveying and recording archaeological sites and historic architecture. Archivists seeking to photograph old industrial buildings might be able to obtain the photography required from RCHME, if the subject fulfils the Royal Commission's criteria for recording and enhancing the national archive held in the National Monuments Record.

The archivist actively making his or her own photographic record can be both more cost-effective and more successful in obtaining the specific record. However, such work may require a major commitment of time and, if carried out to a high standard, a large capital expenditure. A qualified staff photographer may be employed with responsibility for setting up a photographic section, or more likely a member of staff with good photographic knowledge and a high level of interest used. Outside advice should be sought on the equipment needed. Professional camera equipment should be specifically suited to each type of record required by the archivist. Among these could be site location photography, copying or public relations photography. Each of these applications ideally require different equipment − a large format camera, with lens plane movements to correct distortion, supplied with a suitable range of lenses; a vertical camera arrangement in a fixed location with adjustable copying lights; and a small format portable camera fitted with a good quality electronic flash gun. In addition to this equipment, accommodation space will be needed, for darkroom facilities for developing and enlarging, with adequate water supply for processing. Not only will there be an initial capital expenditure, but forward budgeting will also be required for annual updating and replacement of equipment together with quarterly costings for chemicals, film and printing paper.

Where the archivist is able to indulge in photography, then a simpler approach may also be considered − undertaking photography in the archive to the limited degree of producing the negative only. This arrangement makes little demand on accommodation space and allows a range of contract photographic services to be bought in from other sources, rather than tying money up in capital equipment. Local contracts can be negotiated with specialist professional photographic laboratories for film processing and printing, using the high-street amateur processing services for the less demanding and less important work. The professional laboratory service will allow direct discussion with the contractor to enable processing to archive standards. Combining the use of external film and print processing with in-house photography can be a simple and highly cost-effective operation.

The equipment required for the production of the negative can be minimal:

- A good 35mm camera with a coupled exposure metering system, accepting a range of inter-changeable lenses.
- Lenses of focal lengths 28mm, 35–70mm zoom, and a 50mm macro lens for copying.
- A compact but sturdy tripod.
- A cable release.
- A thyristor-type electronic flash gun (and copying lights if copying is to be a main requirement).
- A notebook in which to write the subject information at the time of taking the photograph.

There is a wealth of literature available from good bookshops on how to compose and take good photographs.

The type of photographic materials used are of crucial importance to the archivist. The image recorded in the camera is primary source material containing the unique image, and every precaution must be taken to promote its longevity. Transparency or negative colour films are composed of fugitive dyes which will fade in light. However, colour film may have to be used where colour is an integral element of definition in the subject matter being archived. Permanence, however, is a proven quality of correctly processed silver halide black and white photographic emulsions, although some modern black and white films are chromogenic or dye-based, and will also fade with time and with prolonged exposure to light. It is therefore safest to use only the conventional and proven film types for new photography, enabling a single conservation programme to be evolved for recently acquired photographic material.

The photographic print is the secondary source, although the primary research item in seeking the visual information, and providing it can be replaced by the use of the original negative, standards of permanence can be less rigorous. The drawback of such a policy is the financial implication of a periodic and complete archive print replacement. Black and white printing is no longer done as a matter of course on archivally stable fibre-based papers, although these are still available as specialist items. Modern resin-coated papers are quickly processed but lack the degree of archival stability associated with fibre-based papers. Processing must be scrupulous so as to avoid chemical retention at the outer edge of the paper between the external layered coatings. The ideal mode of processing archive colour photographs would be the dye-transfer process, whereby colour images on paper are produced from a matrix made from individual black and white negatives. This is, however, extremely costly. Once processed both prints and negatives have to be stored in environmental conditions compatible with their long term preservation (see pp. 191–4).

A photographic programme must be properly planned. The archivist needs to visit the site and decide exactly what information must be included in the visual image and how this will best be achieved – the angle of the shot, the amount of detail which must be visible, whether people will be present, how many images are required of each subject, and so on. The photographer must know what equipment will be needed and at what time of day the photograph should be taken. In addition to short-term planning of this kind, it may be necessary to work out a programme for the rephotographing of particular products, sites or processes at regular intervals. Photography is costly and it is important that the work is not duplicated. Check with the public relations, sales, and other relevant departments that the company has not already commissioned the same photography elsewhere.

Finally, the photographic programme must be properly documented if the informational value of the images is not to be diminished. The date and location of the photograph and name of the photographer should be recorded. If the photographs are taken by other than a company employee, an agreement should be drawn up transferring both the custody of the image and its copyright ownership to the company.[5] Consent forms should also be signed by people who appear in the photographs, giving permission for un-restricted use of the image for an indefinite period if there is any likelihood that the image may later be used for advertising or published brochures.

Commissioning an artist[6]

For certain purposes a different kind of image than a photograph may be required. For an exhibition or printed book, for the decoration of the managing director's office, or simply for a more permanent and unusual pictorial record, the archivist may want to commission a work of art. Those who have no regular contact with the art world may have little idea how to go about finding an artist, it is therefore important to seek expert opinions. If the archivist wishes to commission an artist direct, there are several means of contacting one. Individual artists may be selected through reference to the Arts Councils and Regional Arts Associations, most of whom maintain slide libraries of work by artists in their area, or by approaching staff in a local art college who may be able to recommend a colleague or a recent graduate. Alternatively the archivist may be able to organize a project for a group of students by offering facilities or access to the company's building or working areas and secure an option to buy a selection of the work produced to the limit of the archive's budget. An exhibition of the students' work could then be arranged, which could not only provide publicity for the company but also foster good relations with the community. The selection of artists through competition would almost certainly be too costly for the sole purpose of supplementing a company's archival record.

The artist will need to be provided with relevant information about the history of the company, particularly anything of iconographical importance, but should be allowed sufficient freedom to select what he or she considers to be visually interesting. The artist should then report back to the commissioner on what he or she intends to do. A legal contract should be drawn up specifying the medium to be used, some idea of the size and quantity of the work and when it will be completed. The choice of medium and the conservation quality of the materials should all be discussed with the artist, and may be incorporated in the contract. The fee will probably be determined by the archivist's agreed budget, and should represent approximately the market value for the artist's work or the equivalent of a reasonable salary. The cost of paint, paper, photography and so on is normally drawn by the artist from his fee, but an additional grant may be requested if materials are especially costly. A quarter of the fee should be paid in advance, once the contract has been signed, to enable the artist to buy materials. Travel and accommodation costs should be borne by the client. Copyright in a commissioned work of art lies with the artist and lasts for 50 years after his or her death. If there is no commission as such, but the archivist buys work from the artist, the artist also retains the copyright.

Soliciting deposits

Few business archivists have the opportunity to undertake historical research on the company which is not directly related to the compilation of finding aids or to a public relations project, such as an anniversary exhibition or leaflet. It is, however, well worth seeking out those scattered records, both written documents and images, which are held outside the company itself.

Programmes designed to attract donations of records from the public or from the company's own staff and pensioners may prove particularly fruitful. The general public may be reached through brief articles in local newspapers in the town where the company is presently represented or has traded in the past. Articles which discuss some aspect of local history and which are accompanied by a photograph usually attract interest and solicit a response. Staff and pensioners may be contacted through the house magazine or the annual pensioners' party. Material which might be secured in this way includes photographs of premises or staff, product packaging, private diaries or correspondence, staff recreation club records, and so on. Senior staff may have taken away important records when they resigned or retired, and informal requests for help may provide an opportunity for material to be returned without embarrassment. It is important to provide accurate information on the kind of records that are sought so that donors are not disappointed when insignificant material is rejected. The archivist must, however, be selective and take only such records as will be useful. Once accepted, it will be difficult to dispose of the material without offence. As one donation often leads to others, it is important to deal pleasantly with donors and to make them feel confident that their records will be appreciated, used and safely preserved.

The archivist should also discover whether any of the company's own records are held in a local record office or other repository. If material was deposited on loan before the appointment of a company archivist and fills an important gap in the records held by the business, the archivist may wish to consider withdrawing the material so that it may be reunited with the company's other records. This is not, however, a course which should be undertaken lightly. The business archivist must be certain that the records can be catalogued, stored and retrieved at least as adequately in the company's collection, and that the long-term survival of the company's archive is assured. The local record office will understandably be loath to take back the records at a later date. It is also important to appreciate that the records, if not to be exploited intensively by the company itself, will almost certainly be more accessible to researchers and more used in the locality where they were generated than in the company's remote head-office archive. Records should therefore not be centralized on principle without weighing up these important considerations. The acquisition of microform, photographic or photostat copies may suffice.

Important records may also be held by the company's professional advisers – financial records with its auditors or accountants; title deeds and papers concerning registrarship and the company's financial transactions with its banker; partnership agreements, title deeds and other legal papers with its solicitors; advertising copy with its advertising agents; and so on. The business's advisers may of course have changed over the years, but names and addresses can usually be discovered by reference to other records, such as annual reports or minute books. Clearly the archivist will not be able to lay claim to the advisers' own records, however relevant, but rather to that material which has accumulated accidentally in their hands. In any case it is important to discover what exists and where, even if no accessions result.

Records *related* to material in the company archive may also exist elsewhere: for example, out-letters in the archive of another company or institution for which only complementary in-letters have survived in the company's own archive. Ideally reference copies of the records should be made up as photocopies or microforms. If this is not possible a copy of the relevant catalogue should be made and the existence of these related records referenced in the company's own archive finding aids.

Accepting deposits of private papers

If a decision is taken to solicit deposits of private papers from the public or former staff, it is important that the ownership of the records is established. It should be noted that ownership of the copyright does not necessarily pass with the ownership of the physical object. Once the archivist has decided which of the records that have been offered are worth preserving, an agreement should be drawn up setting out the terms of the deposit. If it is likely that a number of transfers will be made, a standard form should be developed. The agreement should protect the company against sudden withdrawal of the deposit; ensure reasonable terms of access (while observing legal restrictions, confidentiality and sensitivity); state whether reproduction, exhibition, or publication is allowed, and whether material can be weeded, reorganized, marked and conserved. Conditions of a possible deposit agreement are set out in Figure 15.1.

Terms of deposit may vary. A gift, outright and for all time, is clearly the simplest and most advantageous agreement. Material may also be acquired by purchase, bequest, loan, indefinite loan or temporary deposit. If the deposit is large, transportation of the material must be arranged and paid for and the time at which responsibility passes from one custodian to the other determined. Insurance cover may also have to be organized.

DEPOSIT AGREEMENT
Accession No.[   ]

[Description of records deposited]

1   Mr A Smith (hereinafter 'the depositor') will from . . . . day of . . . .
one thousand nine hundred and ninety . . . . . . place on deposit with the
Archives Department of ABC Company plc (hereinafter 'the Company') the
records listed on the attached schedule (hereinafter 'the records').

2   The records will be stored in the Company's archive repository and the
Company shall exercise towards the records the same care as it does to its
own archives but, subject to this obligation, the Company shall not be legally
liable or responsible for any loss or damage to the records whether such loss
or damage was caused by negligence of the Company, its servants, agents or
contractors or in any other way.

3   The records will be listed in accordance with the Company's current practice
and a copy of the list will be provided to the depositor. Copyright of such lists
will vest in the Company.

4   The Company reserves the right to return to the depositor any records
deemed to be of no historical interest.

5   The Company reserves the right to photocopy, photograph or microfilm the
records; to stamp or number them with finding references; and to undertake
conservation work if deemed necessary for the preservation of the documents.

6   The records will be made available to *bona fide* researchers on the
Company's premises in accordance with the Company's current terms of
access and in compliance with the Copyright Acts 1911 to 1988. The records
shall not, however, be lent to a third party or removed from the Company's
premises without the Company being satisfied that proper precautions have
been made for their custody and for indemnification against loss or damage.

7   The Company reserves the right to exhibit or publish, in compliance with the
Copyright Acts 1911 to 1988, the records without further recourse to the
depositor.

8   The depositors shall be entitled to call for the temporary return of all or part
of the records at any time upon reasonable notice in writing and the
depositor shall be responsible for the removal of such items and its/their
return to the Company and for any damage or loss arising therefrom.

9   This agreement may be determined at any time by either party giving to the
other three months' written notice. During the period of notice the Company
may copy the records and may exercise the right to charge the depositor for
the cost of listing, conserving and storing the records during the period of the
deposit.

SIGNED (on behalf of the Company):
NAME
POSITION
DATE

SIGNED (on behalf of the depositor):
NAME
POSITION
DATE

Figure 15.1   *Example of a deposit agreement.*

Collecting information

The collection of information is familiar to anyone who has undertaken original historical research, and calls for the transference of visual or textual information from one medium to another, more accessible, medium: for example, recording a factory foundation stone or old press advertisement as an illustrative or written record. At a simple level such activity could involve making a record of anything of interest which the archivist happens to stumble across or, if warranted, a more comprehensive research effort of the kind which leads up to the completion of a major history.

Conclusion

There is no doubt that, if time and resources allow, there are many ways in which a company archive can be supplemented. There is, however, no need to opt for a full-scale documentation programme. Local projects may be initiated in advance of a branch anniversary, or if an attractive opportunity arises such as the archivist's visit to a remote factory or contact with an interested photographer or informed pensioner. What is important is that the business archivist should remain alert to the possibilities of documentation.

Notes

1 This section is based on M. Brooks, 'A beginner's guide to establishing an oral history archive' in *Proceedings of the Annual Conference 1987* (Business Archives Council, London, 1988), pp. 52–82.
2 *Ibid.*, pp. 62–3.
3 Much of the information in this section was generously provided by Terry Buchanan, Chief Photographer, Royal Commission on the Historical Monuments of England, London.
4 British Institute of Professional Photography, Amwell End, Ware, Hertfordshire, SG12 9HN.
5 See *The Photographers' Guide to the 1988 Copyright Act* (British Photographers' Liaison Committee, London, 1989), available from The Association of Photographers, 9–10 Domingo Street, London EC1Y 0TA.
6 The information in this section was generously provided by Angela Weight, Keeper of the Department of Art, Imperial War Museum, London.

Further reading

M. Brooks, 'A beginner's guide to establishing an oral history archive', in *Proceedings of the Annual Conference 1987* (Business Archives Council, London, 1988), pp. 52–82.

T. Buchanan, *Photographing Historic Buildings* (HMSO, London, 1983).

D. Lance, *An Archive Approach to Oral History* (Imperial War Museum, London, 1977).

W. Moss, 'Oral history', in J. G. Bradsher (editor), *Managing Archives and Archival Institutions* (Mansell, London, 1988), pp. 148–60.

A. Pederson (editor), *Keeping Archives* (Australian Society of Archivists Inc., Sydney, 1987), pp. 281–310.

D. Petherbridge (editor), *Art for Architecture: A Handbook on Commissioning* (HMSO, London, 1987).

G. E. A. Raspin, *The Transfer of Private Papers to Repositories* (Society of Archivists Information Leaflet 5, 1988).

A. Seldon and J. Pappworth, *By Word of Mouth: Elite Oral History* (Methuen, London, 1983).

16

The public relations uses of business archives

Alison Turton

What is public relations?

Every company seeks good public relations, and business archivists should be aware of the many ways in which a company's archive can contribute to the public relations effort. Familiarity with the objectives of public relations and the jargon used by its practitioners will be helpful. According to the official definition of the Institute of Public Relations, public relations practice is the 'planned and sustained effort to establish and maintain goodwill and mutual understanding between an organization and its publics'. It is more than mere product publicity and should embrace all aspects of building up a creditable image for the company. Such goodwill is generated by informing and educating the public. The public in this sense would comprise not only the company's customers and users but also its employees, shareholders, suppliers, distributors, the media, the money market and the local community.

The creation of goodwill is, however, a long-term process, and the archivist must work with the company's public relations officer or consultant to ensure that his or her effort fits usefully into the company's broader strategy. If, for example, the company has recently spent vast sums of money on establishing a new company name and corporate identity or in emphasizing a forward-looking approach, highlighting the company's past may prove counter-productive and will have to be handled carefully. Similarly, if the company does not offer a product or service direct to the public, it will be more concerned to create a generally favourable image than to establish the pedigree of a particular brand name. Different sorts of company require differing public relations exposure – the needs of a breakfast-cereal manufacturer, for example, are quite different to those of a merchant bank.

The archive and public relations

The mere existence of a company archive is not in itself likely to generate goodwill. The information and material which the archive contains may, however, be used to present the company to its public in a sympathetic way. In order to direct ideas appropriately it is important for the archivist to find out about the organization of his or her own company's public relations division, and to understand the duties and responsibilities of its constituent departments. Time spent on making personal contact with departmental managers to explain the potential uses of the archive is rarely wasted. In general, public relations departments welcome creative input from the archivist, who is often the only person equipped to initiate historically based publicity projects. For the public relations officer archives boast some exceptional features. They emphasize longevity and thereby imply a quality of products and management which must recommend the company. They are a unique asset to which no competitor has access. They are generally uncontroversial, in that they do not relate to present business, and they are also often visually attractive.

In public relations terms a company's historical records should not, however, be seen simply as a decorative basis for an unusual promotion. A company's history, and the archives which substantiate it, can provide real protection and benefit in today's aggressive financial marketplace. They can create and reinforce a corporate image and, by making a business less anonymous, attract investors. Several companies have specifically commissioned histories with this in mind, and carefully used their past to assist in the achievement of current corporate objectives. In recent years brand names have become increasingly important, particularly with the advent of a single European market in 1992. The nurturing of a successful brand is a time-consuming, expensive and uncertain business, and their purchase off the peg is now a most attractive alternative. The prime prices recently paid for famous brand names reflect this trend, and British companies have now begun to include brands in their balance sheets as intangible assets. An archive can validate the pedigree of such brands and thereby enhance their value. Many companies have produced histories of their own profitable trade names, including the Oxo cube, HP Sauce, Sunlight Soap, and Lea & Perrins Worcestershire Sauce.[1] It is an optimistic company which trades on its past reputation, yet rejects the preservation of archives in the belief that its name alone is a sufficient advertisement for excellence.

In addition, an archive can furnish evidence about a company's historical links with particular countries, companies or individuals, which may help to solicit new custom and open new markets. It can also provide historical information for speeches, advertising copy and press releases, and ensure that such material is historically accurate and complete.

Answering enquiries

The company archivist's most immediate contact with the general public takes the form of historical enquiries, which may be addressed specifically to the archivist or redirected from a wide range of departments throughout the company. Enquirers can be immensely varied – children and students undertaking educational projects; genealogists pursuing the working careers of their forebears; academic historians researching specific industries or economic themes; owners of past products seeking detailed information from sales ledgers or catalogues; journalists and other writers requiring information and illustrations; or theatrical, film or television companies requiring the loan of period properties. Indeed the massive increase of interest in history as a subject in recent years has brought forth a wide range of specialized historical societies, devoted to architectural, furniture, family, gardening, design, transport, textile, construction and food and drink matters.

Techniques and systems for answering enquiries and managing a searchroom are discussed more fully in Chapter 14. It should, however, be remembered that one of the advantages of maintaining an archive is the goodwill which can be generated by demonstrating the company's awareness of the need to preserve its historical records and to make them available. A swift and helpful response is essential to make the most of such benefits. Replies should ideally be sent within a few days, and, if an enquiry will take some time to research, enquirers should be sent a holding letter as an interim measure. It is likely that there will be certain enquiries which crop up repeatedly, and it may be helpful to prepare broadsheets on popular topics. Otherwise common sense and local circumstances must dictate the amount of detail provided to enquirers, and whether they are expected to visit the company to undertake their own research.

In pure public relations terms enquiries from the media will be particularly rewarding, as pictorial material can be used to illustrate books, press articles and television documentaries. The provision of such material can be used to gain acknowledgement in a slot where the purchase of advertising space or time would be either impossible or extremely costly. It is important to ensure that acknowledgement is stipulated as part of the standard conditions for reproduction permissions of this kind.

Commissioning a history

Since the 1950s more British businesses have commissioned company histories than ever before, often as the focus of anniversary celebrations. The company history provides something worthy and tangible which will last long after the charity concerts, VIP receptions and other transitory celebrations are forgotten. It is an opportunity to set down a record of past events and to demonstrate a company's pride in its own achievements and an intellectual awareness of its roots in a local community or traditional product.

The published book

Recent years have witnessed a great variety of published company histories, ranging from lavishly illustrated coffee-table books, directed at customers and shareholders, to detailed analytical studies, providing both management and academic historians with some insight into past decision-making.[2] Many companies have also published biographies of founders or histories of particular brands, buildings, sites or advertisements.[3] All are to some extent seen as having a public relations function – whether as corporate gifts, prestige advertising, patronage of the arts or simply as a way of explaining and justifying continuity and change.

Few company histories in Britain have yet been commissioned wholly with a view to using history to inform present decision-making.[4] Studies analysing the functioning of a business and the development of its corporate culture, including contemporary histories, are more typical in North America, where business history is commonly seen as an integral part of business management.

A history produced for public relations purposes is no less laudable, but it must be well-designed and its content and format carefully targeted at its intended audience. The readership will certainly be limited, and a company history will rarely be a profitable venture. A few copies, depending on the nature of the business, may be sold through the ordinary book trade, but most will be distributed to shareholders, customers or staff on a complimentary or subsidized basis. Others may be given to trade-related or reference institutions as a long-term information source on the company's past.

The commissioning of a company history can be fraught with difficulties and many such projects have been wound-up prematurely, often because the original brief was not properly thought out. A history requires long-term financial commitment, and, providing it will not be counter-productive, a willingness to allow an outsider to produce a 'warts and all' account of the company's past. Finding the right author and publisher for the job is crucial, and the product has to be acceptable, relevant and completed to time. For the archivist the commissioning of a history provides an opportunity to raise awareness of the archive, both inside and outside the company. It may increase the resources earmarked for maintaining archives, allowing the appointment of extra staff or the initiation of new surveys of modern records. In the long term it will certainly provide information which can be used to answer future routine historical enquiries without recourse to the archivist. The project will, however, also generate a great deal of work for the archivist – retrieving documents for the historian, identifying useful illustrative material and undertaking research. It will therefore be helpful if a good working relationship can be built up between historian and archivist, and their respective authority and responsibility clearly defined.

The printed leaflet

The publication of a major company history is both costly and time-consuming, and it is not always necessary or possible to undertake such a large-scale project. Many companies have instead chosen to produce an illustrated historical brochure,[5] which can often be tackled in the same way as the company's routine public relations literature, and is thus more accessible than a commissioned company history. The archivist's role in such projects ranges from the provision of factual information and selection of illustrations to writing text and commissioning and administering designers and printers. It is important that all those engaged in the production – archivist, public relations officer, designer, printer and so on – liaise closely, and are absolutely clear about their respective duties.

From the outset it is important to determine the purpose of the publication and its intended market. Is it to commemorate the anniversary of the company as a whole, of the provision of a product or service, or of the occupation of a particular building or site? Will it form part of a new press or educational pack? Will it be used for staff recruitment or training? Will it be distributed to customers, shareholders, stockbrokers or staff, and at what level? Will it be useful if extracts on, for example, particular constituent companies or branches could be used as stand-alone broadsheets? The answers to such questions as these will help to clarify the nature of the required publication in terms of its format, size, content and print-run. It is also important, at an early stage, to work out both a total budget, to include writing, design, printing and distribution costs, and a realistic timetable for production, allowing for research and writing, editing, approval of format and content, typesetting, proof-reading, printing and distribution.

Leeway should always be allowed for contingencies; there are bound to be setbacks and unexpected costs. Considerable time will be required to research even a small brochure thoroughly. The archivist ought to be sufficiently familiar with the collection to direct research efficiently. If there have been previous historical pamphlets the facts which they contain should be rigorously checked, since they can often be misleading. There are also many sources of information and illustrations which might be tapped outside the company's own records.[6] Written authority should be secured from an executive at a sufficiently high level to secure access to all relevant records, both inside and outside the company.

The brochure must be written at an appropriate level for the intended audience. Illustrations, photographs, drawings and tables, are vital to relieve the text and to enhance its visual impact, and can in any case be a better way to express information. They must, however, be of a good quality and appropriately placed within the text. Pictures should always be carefully cropped to maximize their relevance, and supported by full and lucid captions. Permissions may have to be sought to reproduce illustrations acquired from outside sources. Colour is effective but can be costly to print properly, as it requires coated paper, which may have to be confined to specific folios. An alternative option would be the use of a single colour, such as blue, to lift a black and white text.

The organization of the text must be carefully considered, whether chronological or thematic. If the latter schema is chosen, it may be helpful to include a diary of major events, such as acquisitions, site moves, new products, executive appointments and so on, to provide the reader with some kind of sequential framework. At an early stage the designer should begin to produce ideas on page layout, considering such features as the dimensions of the brochure, the width of margins, the style of typeface, placing of page numbers, headings, photographs and captions, and the columnar arrangement of the text. All these factors will greatly affect the appearance of the final booklet, and the designer should be asked to produce a mock-up which, along with the text, can be approved by an executive. Major amendments at a later stage will be costly. The designer will then arrange for the text to be typeset and pasted up with the photographs. The final proof should be carefully checked by several people and submitted for approval.

It is important to ensure that the proof is seen by all those who generally approve material for publication – the archivist's line manager, the legal and marketing departments and the subsidiary company or branch for whom the leaflet is intended. If the use of the company's logotype and colours are carefully controlled, time should also be allowed for the minor adjustments which will probably be necessary. If the company has no printing facilities in-house, several quotes should be secured for the job, along with samples, of each printer's colour work. The printer will need to know the length of the brochure, the number of words to be typeset, the format, the paper quality, the number and type of illustrations, the cover quality, the nature of the binding, the print run, the production timetable, and any special delivery arrangements.

Using modern office equipment, such as word-processors, laser printers, quality photocopiers and desk-top binders, a good quality brochure can be produced cheaply in-house in small quantities. Facsimile copies of key documents, for example, could be reproduced by making clean photo-copies on to textured paper, and need only be prefaced by a general introduction and attractive title page. Leaflets put together in this way could be used for such occasions as a visit by a new corporate client or a small press launch. Similarly access to desk-top publishing software can allow ordinary word-processed text to be transformed by the employment of a range of different typestyles and sizes, and the facility to wrap text in columns or around graphics and logos. An imaginative use of the facilities available will multiply the opportunities for the archivist to contribute to the public relations effort without major expenditure.

Displaying archives and artefacts

Exhibitions

The use of business archives for temporary or permanent exhibitions has become increasingly popular in recent years. Such exhibitions can range from a small display in a head-office reception area or staff club to a major travelling exhibition in a busy public venue. All exhibitions, however small, require a substantial commitment of time and money in order to achieve the necessary high standard of presentation. They should not be regarded as an easy option, for the resources they demand will undoubtedly be disproportionately large. Exhaustive planning is essential. From the outset it is important to have a clear idea of the purpose and character of the exhibition. Is the objective to educate viewers about the history of the company as a whole, or about the development of a particular service or product? Is it to reinforce the company's corporate image, or merely to show off the range of material in the archives? It is also vital, at an early stage, to determine the venue, content, and likely audience, mindful of the fact that considerations of cost, conservation and security may constrain the type of items shown and the quality of the display medium.

The company archivist creating a major exhibition should seek the advice of a professional designer. Impeccable presentation is crucial in all public relations projects, and exhibition layout is exacting work. Indeed it may be necessary to consider the appointment of separate graphic and three-dimensional designers in order to achieve the best presentation. A designer knows the optimum length of captions and can plan space, scale, colour and textures effectively to create attractive and informative displays from a simple list of exhibits and accompanying text. A good designer can minimize wasteful errors by careful measurement and arrangement of materials, and can also manage contractors brought in to build cases and produce graphics. Design advice is, however, expensive and can only complement, not replace, the company's archivist and public relations department. Exhibits will have to be chosen, captions written and the designer's ideas appropriately channelled.

Table 16.1   *Guidelines on appointing and using a designer.*

---

1   *Find a designer*
- Visit other museums and exhibitions and discuss each designer's performance with the curator.
- Take advice from the Association of Independent Museums, Area Museums Councils and the Society of Industrial Artists and Designers.
- Invite a few designers to discuss your project in terms of content, budget and time-scale.
- Invite two or three of the most promising candidates to prepare some initial ideas (a fee may be demanded) and subsequently a full tender, to include design fees and other costs, design sequences and time schedule. Visit the designers in their own offices and introduce them to other staff engaged in the project.

2   *Appoint a designer*
- Select the most appropriate candidate with whom a good working relationship will be possible.

- Solicit 'letters of agreement' to protect the interests of both parties. Make sure all points are clear and acceptable, then reply with a letter of appointment.

3 *Compile a brief*
- Provide an initial statement on the aim of the displays, a list of possible exhibits and their groupings, and some provisional text.
- Refine this to create a detailed brief which includes a final list of exhibits (along with size and special conservation and security requirements), captions and graphic requirements.

4 *Produce designs*
- Close involvement in the work will allow the rejection of unsuitable ideas and acceptance of the inevitable compromises.
- The designer's general presentation should include a model, sample display sheets and design sketches.
- Detailed designs should include working/construction drawings, written specifications and a schedule for sub-contract work.

5 *Appoint a building contractor*
- Secure three tenders on the advice of the designer. Different contractors may be required for the graphics and general construction.
- Contracted on-site work should be supervised by the designer, who should certify all claims for payment.

6 *After-care*
- Ask the designer to provide a reference manual on how to clean and revise the displays, including addresses of suppliers.

If a display is very small, such as a single case or wall panel, it is probably not necessary to seek such professional advice. It is important to avoid amateurish presentation but if content and layout are carefully researched and planned, taking advantage of in-house typesetting, printing, photographic and other facilities, perfectly presentable results can be achieved. Most people can learn to write good captions, and the creation of satisfactory environmental conditions is relatively straightforward. The art of good arrangement and display is not, however, so easily acquired, and requires an ability to see what might work well both visually and technically. Local museums are often willing to advise, and archivists should not be afraid to seek specialist help on an informal basis, even if budgets do not allow for the engagement of design consultants.

Table 16.2 *Guidelines on how to create effective displays.*

---

1 *Display*
- Seek professional design advice.
- Formulate clear objectives and themes which dictate the exhibits on display.

- Use three-dimensional objects as well as documents and present them honestly.
- Displays may be aesthetic, evocative or didactic in character.
- Group material logically and without ambiguity or incongruity.

2   *Showcases*
- Select sturdy and secure cases, particularly for travelling displays or where supervision will be limited.
- The structure and finish of cases must complement the exhibits and work both spatially and aesthetically.
- Versatile cases can display material at various levels and in different planes, and may be used subsequently for other exhibitions.
- Tough, cleanable finishes are essential, particularly around the skirtings.
- Adults and children have different eye levels and showcase heights will necessarily be a compromise.

3   *Captions*
- Avoid over-labelling and too much supporting material.
- Use tiered captioning, i.e. brief identification, longer elementary description and definitive technical details, where space allows. Employ the same typeface in different sizes.
- Interpret the document in a way that will be meaningful to visitors with little or no knowledge of the company's history, and avoid being encumbered by the archival purity of documents.
- Encourage visitors to examine exhibits and relate captions to the display, both in content and in location within the showcase.
- Ensure legibility. Avoid coloured and fine typefaces with inadequate contrast. Remember that upper and lower case are more legible than capitals alone.
- Check factual and grammatical accuracy carefully at every stage. Mistakes will be costly to rectify.
- The order in which displays should be viewed must be easily apparent.

4   *Conservation*
- Seek expert advice.
- Avoid sources of ultra-violet light (including direct sunlight) and the heating effect of intense local illumination. Light levels of 50-200 lux are acceptable, depending upon the sensitivity of the material.
- Monitor and control temperature and relative humidity within showcases.
- Display originals for only a limited period and use facsimiles where possible.
- Use acid-free and reversible mountings.
- Support open volumes to protect bindings.

5   *Lighting*
- Select unobtrusive lighting, fully integrated into the design.

- Use lighting to create an atmosphere as well as provide illumination.
- Be aware of conservation implications.

6 *Audio visuals*
- Audio visuals are costly to create and maintain. Are they necessary?
- Slide and video shows must complement not reiterate the content of the exhibition itself.
- Secure professional design advice, eg. on the use of twin projectors and cross-fade techniques.

Good results require fine ingredients as well as thoughtful execution, and the important task of selecting documents and artefacts for display generally falls upon the archivist. The choice will depend upon the appropriateness of particular items for the proposed audience and display format, and upon considerations of security and conservation.[7] The archivist's knowledge and imagination, and the ease with which suitable material can be retrieved, are, however, equally important. It may therefore be useful to identify items with display potential during survey and listing operations. Such material might illustrate a particular aspect of the company's activities or may simply be attractive or memorable.

It is rarely helpful to display documents that are difficult to read or that require long explanatory captions. Archivists should also bear in mind that original documents are not always well-suited to display. They can cause great difficulties in terms of conservation, insurance and security, and may constrain the design of showcases and display panels. Indeed original documents may, on occasion, even obscure the purpose of a display, where enlarged extracts from records might clarify by focusing attention. The use of handmade paper and quality reproduction techniques can produce extraordinarily good facsimiles which are far more versatile than original records. The employment of large photographic panels is also a relatively inexpensive way of achieving a strong visual effect.

Finally it is also important to display a balanced mix of archives and artefacts. Three-dimensional material can lift an exhibition of documentary records by adding an element of variety. Most company archivists accumulate at least a small collection of artefacts, if only because there is no more appropriate custodian within the company. Otherwise material can be borrowed from museums or private collections, although acceptable terms will have to be agreed for the loan, and arrangements made for full insurance cover.

Once the production of the exhibition is in hand, the archivist should liaise with the public relations department to arrange for its promotion. Such publicity might include the production of an accompanying poster, catalogue or leaflet, the preparation of press releases and the arrangement of a launch party – a catchy title will make it easier to attract public attention. Promotion of this kind will require a substantial budget allocation.

Exhibitions may be shown on a company's own premises where there is sufficient space and a regular flow of customers or staff. They may be tailor-made for a specific location or circulated to branches or other sites owned by the company. A few years ago Midland Bank created a large exhibition as part of its anniversary celebrations which was shown in its principal banking halls throughout the country. Much of the information was re-used in a small exhibition for local display at sites where space was more limited. This second display was duplicated 18 times, thereby increasing the potential audience dramatically and at minimal cost.

A few companies have also sponsored travelling exhibitions for display in national and local museums and art galleries.[8] Ten years ago publicly funded institutions expressed doubt about the commercial implications of such shows, but today sponsorship is an economic necessity and company collections are welcomed. Travelling exhibitions do, however, present particular problems. Constant dismantling and re-erection require a high standard of construction and long-term administrative commitment. The displays must be flexible enough to fit different kinds of space, and be of a sufficient size to establish a presence and to justify the substantial origination and maintenance costs. In the light of these difficulties most companies have found it more palatable to sponsor one-off exhibitions in collaboration with museums or have loaned material for permanent or temporary display in ordinary museum galleries.[9] A presence in a museum not only suggests that a company has cultural interests but may introduce its name to an entirely new audience and create opportunities for media coverage.

Company museums

Museums are booming. Britain, where a new museum opens every 14 days, has in the region of 2,700 museums, entertaining around 80 million visitors each year. Several British companies have opened in-house museums, ranging from major enterprises, with several galleries, to small rooms set up as show places for customers, staff and important visitors. Museums on factory or head-office premises which are open to the public (some by appointment only) include those run by the Bank of England, Royal Doulton, Colman's of Norwich, Bank of Scotland, Twinings, C. & J. Clark, Bass Brewing, Bulmer, Royal Worcester, Wedgwood, Irish Distillers, Harveys of Bristol and Pilkington. The investment of these companies has been considerable and is indicative of their perception of the returns in terms of publicity and goodwill.

The Museums Association defines a museum as 'an institution which collects, documents, preserves, exhibits and interprets material evidence and associated information for the public benefit'. The nature and style of museums have, however, undergone dramatic change in recent years. The public expects more professional and sophisticated presentation than ever before. The vogue for participation prevails, and visitors are no longer content merely to peer into glass cases. This new approach, which began with the early open-air museums, at Singleton, Beamish, and Ironbridge, has of late become more pronounced with the opening of such museums as the Jorvik Viking Centre in York, using scholarship rather than objects to recreate history. At the Bank of England museum interactive video stations allow visitors to learn more about the Bank's history and present organization using the latest computer technology. The independent sector has thus set new standards in display and services of which every museum planner should be cognisant.

The decision to initiate a new museum must be more positively grounded than the mere availability of a suitable space and a collection of miscellaneous artefacts. Is a museum the right medium to meet the company's aims? Is there sufficient long-term commitment to management and funding? Is the display material sufficient and of consequence? If all these conditions are satisfied, and management enthusiastically supports the establishment of a museum, a feasibility study might be commissioned. It is important to plan the enterprise in some detail. The actual display of material has already been discussed in the preceding section on planning exhibitions, but some of the administrative issues which must be tackled at an early stage are set out below:

1 *Feasibility study*
- Define the purpose of the museum.
- Commission a feasibility study, preferably from outside consultants, to consider: (1) themes to be explored and how they can best be researched and presented, (2) suitability of the proposed site and building, (3) adequacy of the archive and artefact collections, (4) the likely market, (5) the nature and number of staff required, (6) projected capital and revenue costs, (7) range of activities to be undertaken, and (8) the relationship with other similar facilities.

2 *Legal status*
- Adopt appropriate legal status, such as independent charitable trust status, to protect the interests of both the collection (loan agreements, legal ownership, disposal upon liquidation of company) and the company (debt liability, tax advantages).

3 *Management structure*
- Compile a development strategy based on the findings of the feasibility study to include coherent and carefully considered business and financial plans.
- Set objectives for a 3- to 5-year period, with specific target dates for the accomplishment of particular tasks.
- Consider all aspects of the museum's work, including conservation, interpretation, research, marketing, finance, etc. Link all activities with a flexible development plan.

4 *Appoint a designer*
- See guidelines on p. 414.

It is not, however, sufficient merely to design and build displays and to open them to the public. A museum must have a development policy covering such key ongoing activities as collecting and documentation. A clear written statement on what should and should not be collected is essential. It provides a reference point for decision-making which will be helpful to both staff and donors, and should reflect the purpose of the museum. It should define acquisition by gift, purchase or loan, and may set out geographical, typological or period constraints on exhibits. Other factors which might impact on the collecting policy of the museum should be considered – for example, the ability to purchase, insure, conserve and store items; whether the donor has legal title or is imposing acceptable conditions on the gift; and whether a similar item is already held.

A museum collection must also be properly documented, in the same way as an archive, for purposes of retrieval, legal title, evidential value and security. This may be done manually or on a computer database. Special computer software, the Museum's Documentation System, has already been developed for this purpose and has been adopted in a slightly modified form, as Gos or Gosling, in some archives.

Archives in education

During the last 15 years the teaching of history in schools has been transformed initially, in the mid-1970s, by the Schools Council History Project and more recently by the introduction of the GCSE and National Curriculum. School history, once thought of as a series of facts bound by narrative within neatly organized and self-contained social, economic and political topics, is now widely taught as a balance between knowledge, skills and understanding,[10] with due consideration of its distinctive methodology and concepts. Consequently teachers have restructured, and are continuing to restructure, their syllabuses and reviewed their lesson planning in order to consider the nature of the past in a way that will be useful to pupils in adult life. Students are encouraged to acquire not only a body of facts and a sense of chronology but also to interpret and evaluate evidence and consider varying interpretations of the past. The teaching and learning of history is now about knowledge as understanding rather than knowledge as information, encouraging pupils to understand the processes of historical enquiry and to find out about the past for themselves.

National criteria for history in GCSE, which apply to all examining boards and all syllabuses offered for examination at 16-plus, state that 'all candidates will be expected to show the skills necessary to study a wide variety of historical evidence which should include both primary and secondary written sources, statistical and visual material, artefacts, text books and orally transmitted information'. Twenty to forty per cent of the GCSE is based on course work, and most of the examining boards continue to offer such business-related topics as industry, trade, urban society, transport, iron and steel, textiles and trade unionism as part of the post-eighteenth century British history courses. Indeed three of the most popular options offered by all the examining boards are the Schools History Project, British Social and Economic History and Modern World syllabuses. The first includes a compulsory 'History Around Us' unit, for which each school must devise a number of assignments, based on a variety of sources, which relate a local site to its historical context. Documentary sources often form the basis of this work. One school has founded an assignment[11] on a link with a local company and has successfully integrated industrial experience with historical teaching, involving not only the use of the corporate archive but also the inspection of buildings and processes and interviewing of staff.

GCSE history was first examined in 1988 and the syllabuses will cease to exist in their present form in 1994, following the phased introduction of National Curriculum history. The National Curriculum, prescribed by the Education Reform Act 1988, consists of ten 'foundation' subjects which all children must study at school. History is one of these subjects. For each subject there are objectives setting out what children should know and be able to do at each stage of their schooling, known as 'attainment targets', and 'programmes of study' describing what children should be taught. Children will be assessed at 7, 11, 14 and 16 years of age and organized in four stages, for different age groups, known as 'key stages' – key stage 1 for 5 to 7, key stage 2 for 7 to 11, key stage 3 for 11 to 14 and key stage 4 for 14 to 16 year olds.

The formulation of the National Curriculum for history engendered bitter controversy and prompted debate on the relative importance of facts and skills within the discipline. The final form of the history curriculum was settled, after the compilation of many consultative documents, in the Department of Education and Science's report *History in the National Curriculum (England)*.[12] This report covers key stages 1 to 4. Key stages 1 to 3 will be introduced for 5, 7 and 11 year olds from autumn 1991. The final form of the key stage 4 curriculum remains the subject of considerable debate. In order to help teachers it is vital that archivists should understand the precise requirements of the National Curriculum. The main demands of the programmes of study and attainment targets at each of the key stages are set out in Table 16.3.

Table 16.3 *National curriculum history: programmes of study and attainment targets*

PROGRAMMES OF STUDY

Key stage 1
'Pupils should be given opportunities to develop an awareness of the past and of the ways in which it was different from the present. They should be introduced to historical sources of different types.'

Pupils are to be helped to develop an awareness of the past through stories from different periods and cultures (including eyewitness accounts of historical events) and progress from familiar situations to those more distant in time and place looking at, for example, changes in clothing, houses, shops, diet, etc, and learning about the lives of famous people and about notable local and national events.

Key stage 2

'Pupils should be taught about important episodes and developments in Britain's past, from Roman to modern times. They should have opportunities to investigate local history. They should be taught about ancient civilizations and the history of other parts of the world. They should be helped to develop a sense of chronology and to learn about changes in everyday life over long periods of time'.

Pupils should be taught nine study units comprising five or six core study units, including:

- Victorian Britain.
- Britain since 1930.

and four supplementary study units, including:

- a theme over a long period of time, chosen from ships and seafarers, food and farming, houses and places of worship, writing and printing, land transport and domestic life, families and childhood.
- local history, involving investigation of an important historical issue, relating local developments to national trends and requiring detailed study of one aspect of a local community.

Key stage 3

'Pupils should be taught to understand how developments from the early Middle Ages to the era of the Second World War helped shape the economy, society, culture and political structure of modern Britain. They should have opportunities to study developments in Europe and the non-European world, and be helped to understand how the histories of different countries are linked. They should be taught about ancient Rome and its legacy to Britain, Europe and the world'.

Pupils should be taught eight study units comprising five compulsory core study units including:

- the making of the United Kingdom: Crowns, Parliaments and peoples, 1500 to 1750.
- expansion, trade and industry: Britain 1750 to 1900.
- the era of the Second World War.

and three supplementary study units including an in depth study complementing or extending investigation of the core study units relating to Britain pre-1920.

ATTAINMENT TARGETS AND STATEMENTS OF ATTAINMENT

Key stage 1: levels 1–3. Key stage 2: levels 2–5. Key stage 3: levels 3–7.
Key stage 4: levels 4–10.

Level:	Profile component 1 /attainment target 1:	Profile component 2: Interpretations of history and the use of historical sources	
	Knowledge and understanding of history	Attainment target 2: Interpretations of history	Attainment target 3: The use of historical sources
	Demonstrating their knowledge of the historical content in the programmes of study, pupils should be able to:		
1	a) place in sequence events in a story about past. b) give reasons for their own actions.	understand that stories may be about real people or fictional characters.	communicate information from an historical source.
2	a) place familiar objects in chronological order. b) suggest reasons why people in the past acted as they did. c) identify differences between past and present times.	show an awareness that different stories about the past can give different versions of what happened.	recognize that historical sources can stimulate and help answer questions about the past.
3	a) describe changes over a period of time. b)give a reason for an historical event or development. c)identify differences between times in the past.	distinguish between a fact and a point of view.	make deductions from historical sources.
4	a) recognize that over time some things changed and others stayed the same. b) show an awareness that historical events usually have more than one cause and consequence. c) describe different features of an historical period.	show an understanding that deficiencies in evidence may lead to different interpretations of the past.	put together information drawn from different historical sources.
5	a) distinguish between different kinds of historical change. b) identify different types of cause and consequence. c) show how different features in an historical situation relate to each other.	recognize that interpretations of the past, including popular accounts, may differ from what is known to have happened.	comment on the usefulness of an historical source by reference to its content, as evidence for a particular enquiry.

6	a) show an understanding that change and progress are not the same. b) recognize that causes and consequences can vary in importance. c) describe the different ideas and attitudes of people in an historical situation.	demonstrate how historical interpretations depend on the selection of sources.	compare the usefulness of different historical sources as evidence for a particular enquiry.
7	a) show an awareness that patterns of change can be complex. b) show how the different causes of an historical event are connected. c) show an awareness that different people's ideas and attitudes are often related to their circumstances.	describe the strengths and weaknesses of different interpretations of an historical event or development.	make judgements about the reliability and value of historical sources by reference to the circumstances in which they were produced.
8	a) explain the relative importance of several linked causes. b) show an understanding of the diversity of people's ideas, attitudes and circumstances in complex historical situations.	show how attitudes and circumstances can influence an individual's interpretation of historical events or developments.	show how a source which is unreliable can nevertheless be useful.
9	a) show an understanding of how causes, motives and consequences may be related. b) explain why individuals did not necessarily share the ideas and attitudes of the groups and societies to which they belonged.	explain why different groups or societies interpret and use history in different ways.	show an understanding that a source can be more or less valuable depending on the questions asked of it.
10	a) show an understanding of the issues involved in describing, analysing and explaining complex historical situations.	show an understanding of the issues involved in trying to make history as objective as possible.	explain the problematic nature of historical evidence, showing an awareness that judgements based on historical sources may well be provisional.

Note: This information has been reproduced from Department of Education and Science, *History in the National Curriculum (England)* (HMSO, March 1991) with the permission of the controller of Her Majesty's Stationery Office. Separate reports were published for Wales and Northern Ireland. For further details archivists are advised to procure a copy of the relevant report.

There is no doubt that the introduction of the National Curriculum represents a major opportunity for all archivists to become more involved in schools history. Attainment target 3 for all key stages involves the 'use of historical sources' and those specifically mentioned include written sources, pictures and photographs, artefacts, buildings and sites, computer-based material, adults talking about their own past and music. The need for suitable teaching material will be the more acute because many teachers have no foundation on which to build. A recent report showed that 80 per cent of primary schools were currently teaching no history or geography and teachers devising work programmes for key stages 1 and 2 will be particularly eager for support.

At key stage 1 simple illustrative material will be of most use. This could include a number of photographs of a familiar street, or pictorial advertisements or billheadings, ranging over a long period of time. These can be used to stimulate discussion and for exercises in chronological sequencing. At key stage 2 many business archivists will be able to compile material on aspects of the core study units on Victorian Britain and Britain since 1930. Teachers will also be interested in documents, and printed books, which could form the basis of a local study. Local history has always been popular in primary schools.

Unfortunately the local history option proposed in the original programme of study for key stage 3 did not survive. Teachers of 11 to 14 year olds are therefore more likely to be interested in material which can be linked to the core study units or to project work extending investigation of those units. At key stage 3 each core study unit will have to be taught within around 10 weeks and will therefore be impossible to approach chronologically. After stimulating pupils' interest and introducing the unit in a general way it seems likely that teachers will have to pose key questions which will provide a framework for an investigation from which useful conclusions can be drawn. For each stage of this process the business archivist may be able to provide useful source material or, indeed, create an information pack covering an entire study unit. How the National Curriculum is delivered is left entirely to teachers to determine and at key stages 1 and 2 assessment is initially to be based on the teachers' own judgement of classroom work, supplemented within the next two years by the administering of standard tests. For history these will be voluntary at 7 and 11 but compulsory at 14.

The way in which the National Curriculum links knowledge, understanding and skills promotes the teaching of good history (see Table 16.4) and archivists should seize the opportunity to become involved in the dissemination of an appreciation of the value of source material to a young audience.

For pupils over 16 many examining boards are currently piloting or operating A and AS Level syllabuses which feature course work and an emphasis on original sources. Some boards also include the option of an extended piece of work in the form of a local study. Associated Examinations Board 673 syllabus has proved very popular because of the inclusion of this sort of option. In addition, such skills and concepts as problem-solving, negotiation, motivation, group work and initiative, upon which the developing Technical and Vocational Education Initiative (TVEI) is based, are widely taught through the study of history.

However, an archive's educational service has to be properly planned and demands long-term and major commitment of resources. It also has to be relevant and must reflect teachers' real, not imagined, needs. Close liaison with teachers, teacher centres, museums and other local institutions offering a similar service is therefore essential. As a first step, it may be helpful to make contact with the local education authority adviser or inspector responsible for history in schools. These officials will be aware of locally based assignments currently taught in their areas and often arrange in-service training days for teachers which could provide opportunities for the discussion or launch of an archive-based initiative. Corporate archivists should also liaise with other local archive education services where these exist as jointly they are likely to be able to present a more attractive package and communicate more effectively with teachers.

Offering an educational service should not call for actual teaching of children – few company archivists have either the training or the facilities to cater for the potential demand. Instead it should involve advising teachers and providing ideas and materials with which they can link archive material on specific topics with their own mainstream teaching. These activities could include publicizing the range of documentary sources available; producing bibliographies on relevant topics; publishing archive guides specifically for teachers; suggesting other related sources of information (local record offices, museums, historical sites, etc.); reproducing individual or complementary collections of documents in facsimile or transcript; compiling displays; opening the searchroom at unusual hours to allow access to teachers; providing cheap photocopying facilities and allowing the circulation of material without copyright restriction on multiple reproduction for classroom use. Teachers may not be accustomed to using either archive repositories or original documents, and, more important, may be subject to extreme pressures of lack of time and resources. The company archivist may therefore have to take the initiative.

Archival sources may be particularly helpful in conveying empathetic understanding (i.e. in helping to reconstruct past attitudes and values and to demonstrate people acting in different ways to the same events) and in assisting in the evaluation of evidence (prompting questions on reliability, usefulness, completeness, bias and so on). It is important, however, before the archivist creates kits or assignments and selects records, to decide which sourcework or other skills they are intended to test (see Table 16.5). It is also necessary not to tackle too many issues with a single document. Facsimiles are particularly useful as they can be handled without danger of damage and can be used outside the repository. They can also be stored on a subject basis or incorporated in textual literature. Transcripts are even simpler to handle and use and are quite adequate as primary sources for both GCSE and National Curriculum pupils. Likewise printed documents, such as newspapers and catalogues, can be more successful than handwritten documents which may be difficult to read. Topic-based kits can be produced to include both facsimiles and information sheets. Meaningful selection and careful presentation of documents is more important here than lavish production.[14] All material should be adaptable so that it can be

Table 16.4   *Using archives to promote good practice in history teaching within the National Curriculum*[13]

1   Enquiry-based learning – through historical investigation.
2   Relevant to childrens' experience – incorporating a local dimension.
3   Developing skills and concepts as well as knowledge through planned aims and objectives, e.g. change and continuity.
4   Problem solving – addressing important historical issues.
5   Open-ended tasks – children pursuing a variety of directions and no necessary right answer, e.g. what was it like to live in Victorian Manchester?
6   Using a variety of sources – objects, pictures, buildings, etc.
7   Activity learning – children planning their enquiry, identifying key questions and working in groups.
8   Children coming to their own conclusions and offering their own explanations.
9   Opportunities to plan and present the results of an enquiry in a variety of forms.

pitched at the right level. Paraphrasing difficult words or phrases, editing out complex concepts or irrelevant detail and selecting appropriate tasks, can then be undertaken by the teacher according to pupils' needs.

Any material must be presented in a way which shows an awareness of the new approach which the National Curriculum and GCSE requires pupils to develop. It must make evident the range of source material and the selection process which has taken place; provide opportunities to compare and contrast information; look for evidence of change and continuity, similarity and difference, cause and consequence; foster

Table 16.5   *GCSE and National Curriculum history: sourcework skills*[15]

1   Comprehension of source.
2   Extraction from source.
3   Recognition of inference and implication.
4   Difference between primary and secondary.
5   Knowledge of a wide range of different kinds of sources.
6   Evaluation recognizing fact/opinion/assertion/prejudice; gaps; bias and pejorative and emotive language; and the vital importance of origin, context and motive.
7   How to establish reliability and accuracy using sources to corroborate other evidence.
8   Ability to compare sources in terms of differences and similarities and to understand contradiction.
9   Judgement and choice between various sources/opinions.
10   Formation of overview and synthesis.

awareness of political, gender, ethnic or class bias; allow analysis of the role of the individual and convey some sense of historical empathy.

The advantages of making school children and students aware of company and brand names are self evident. Several businesses have already pursued this line since the sixties by sponsoring school art and essay competitions nationwide. It is, however, important to keep a detailed register of school enquiries, both to justify the time and cost of developing educational uses for the collection and to prevent duplication of effort in answering numerous enquiries of a similar kind.

Opportunities for business archivists to become directly involved in school history are plentiful but it may also be fruitful to develop an involvement in further education. Undergraduate history is, for the most part, still focused on the acquisition of facts and assimilation of arguments from lectures and general textbooks. While undergraduates have neither the experience nor the time to handle large collections of business archives, individual documents or series of records may be used by the lecturer to illustrate a particular point. In addition, individual undergraduates, guided and directed by the archivist to useful source material and complementary secondary works, might undertake a specialized thesis based on selected records in a business archive. Clearly the latter exercise is more accessible to post-graduates engaged upon doctoral theses. Such research should be encouraged by the company archivist by building up good relationships with university and polytechnic business history departments. Regular researchers using the collection on a long-term basis may distract the archivist from other business but in the long run their detailed research will provide the company with a large amount of historical information which the archivist alone would not have time to compile from close analysis of the records.

Design, packaging and gift wares

During the last decade growing interest in, and nostalgia for, the past has been reflected in the re-working of historical designs, usually those relating to Victorian and Edwardian branded goods, for use in current advertising, packaging and product development. Company archives often include large collections of historical advertisements, labels and product samples which can be used to provide ideas for new design work. Food manufacturers have made particular use of such resources. Lea & Perrins, Frank Cooper and Colman's, for example, have based much of their regular labelling firmly on historical precedent. Others have reproduced old packaging for special promotional periods only. Jacksons, Kelloggs, Oxo and Cadbury's have all done so in conjunction with anniversary events.

Old designs are not only inherently attractive but their use can create a coveted and distinguished image for a brand, as well as considerably reducing expenditure on outside design consultancies. Coca-Cola, one of the world's most famous consumer products, boasts a bottle shape and trademark based firmly on historical designs preserved in the archive and harnessed to work for the corporation through massive promotional campaigns. Brands and their pedigree have indeed become increasingly important to food manufacturers in a fiercely competitive marketplace where supermarket 'own labels' abound. Other kinds of business, such as manufacturers of floor and wall coverings, textiles and china wares, tend to rework old designs as an integral part of product development. The design studio at Arthur Sanderson & Sons, for example, makes daily use of the company's archive collection, which comprises over 15,000 samples of nineteenth- and twentieth-century wallpapers and fabrics. Similarly old recipe books for food and drinks can provide a manufacturing formula for present-day preserves, beverages, spirits and beers.

A few companies have also used old advertisements or packaging to inspire a range of gift wares, including tins, trays, china, calendars, cards, posters, aprons, enamel signs, model motor vehicles and tea towels, most of which will have a long life around the home. Even if no directly reproducible art-work has survived, an old-fashioned look can be concocted by the clever use of photographs, catalogue illustrations and other pictorial material from the archive. The public appear to be surprisingly willing to buy nostalgic merchandise which advertises a particular company. Retailers, such as Harrods, Sainsburys and Marks & Spencer, and food manufacturers, such as Twinings and Colman's, have all successfully exploited the market for gift wares of this kind.

Advertising

The archive can also provide a rich resource for the company's advertising agency. The public's thirst for nostalgia has long been identified as a potent 'hidden persuader'. Illustrations and information from the archive can be used to conjure up nostalgia in both published and broadcast advertisements. Cinematographic film and sound recordings will be particularly useful for television and radio commercials. Longevity is itself an excellent recommendation, and a company's archive can furnish proof of establishment dates, early brand pre-eminence and original recipes or patterns. Old motifs, such as the Guinness toucan and the Bisto kids, can be revived and reworked, and are often as relevant and effective in today's marketplace as they were in the past.

Some companies have reproduced early advertisements in their entirety, although more often archive material is used to provide illustrations for new advertisements, particularly for those products, such as malt whisky or cruise holidays, for which the past can provide a marketable and sympathetic identity. Many early advertisements were of an extremely high quality and are now recognized as works of art in their own right. The purchase by Pears Soap of the rights to Sir John Millais' 'Bubbles' is well known, but many other firms have also commissioned designs from famous artists. Kodak, for example, used Claud Shepperson; Caley used Alfred Munnings; Nestlé used Alphonse Mucha; Guinness used John Gilroy; and Shell used Paul Nash, Duncan Grant and Graham Sutherland.

Even if advertisements do not use archive material, claims to be 'the first' or 'the oldest' may have to be researched by the archivist to furnish evidence demonstrating compliance with advertising codes of practice. Similarly the archive may be used to substantiate claims to ownership of particular trademarks where first use may be disputed.

Celebrating an anniversary

Historically based promotions are often the most popular way of making use of a company's archive for public relations purposes. A promotion exploits the archive in many of the ways described above as a concerted publicity campaign – the publication of a history, the holding of an exhibition, the revival of historical advertisements, the sale of nostalgic gift wares – all concentrated within a short space of time and linked by a single theme. A historical slogan or logo, to identify events with the promotion, may be devised for use on packaging, gift wares and stationery, and for postal franking. Such a promotion works best, and will be more readily embraced by the company's public relations department, if there is an obvious peg, such as an anniversary, upon which to hang it. The anniversary of an important technical invention, or of a local borough authority or chamber of commerce, many provide opportunities for company-based events, but the anniversary of a business's own foundation, incorporation, occupation of a building or launch of a particular product, is likely to be more potent.

Corporate birthdays have long been celebrated internally, with dinners, bonuses for shareholders, holidays for staff and the like, but during the last 20 years they have become major public events, with activities ranging from the publication of company histories and sale of commemorative goods to arts sponsorship and fun runs. Indeed the boom in public flotations during the 1880s has resulted in a wave of centenary celebrations during recent years. The enthusiasm in Britain's boardrooms for marking anniversaries in this way is difficult to explain. Motives may be complex and varied, with the reluctance to ignore a milestone set along aside an awareness of an opportunity to capture public attention, to reinforce a corporate image and to improve staff morale.

There are generally few people within a company who have any profound knowledge of its history. Occasionally managers at a sufficiently high level to initiate events will be aware of imminent anniversaries, but more often it will fall upon the archivist to draw attention to opportunities for birthday celebrations. Where there are a large number of constituent businesses or historic brands and buildings, it may be useful to create a bring-forward system for anniversary dates, either manually or as a computer database. Where a major exhibition or publication might be an appropriate option, at least 12 months should be allowed for planning and preparation. The business archivist often commands few resources and does not start from a position of strength in arguing the case for an anniversary promotion. It will be an uphill task and resistance will certainly be met with from the highly placed manager who cannot, and will not, see the relevance of the past. The archivist must not be deterred, and should seek the support of more sympathetic departments or individuals willing to confirm the value of such a project, or indeed to foot the bill.

The archivist's principal advantage is the time and expertise which he or she can devote to the promotion. Offering a total package, such as the provision of a leaflet and display, for which the archivist carries out the research, organizes a designer, secures approval and handles invoices and queries, can be more attractive than schemes which demand local involvement. Certainly the archivist should aim to play a major role in the anniversary celebration. Writing leaflets, inspiring gift wares, providing information for speeches and press releases and assuming a central administrative role in co-ordinating activities are important. If the archivist does not come forward, outside consultants will be brought in or the initiative seized by other departments, and a significant opportunity will be lost. The archivist will, however, need to be flexible. He or she may not always agree with the treatment of material, but a company archive must earn its keep, and commercial use of the collection will make the compromise of professional niceties inevitable.

Before a promotion is suggested, the archivist must verify the anniversary date, not merely the year but, if possible, also the day. It is likely that management will want to focus on a particular week or month, and the history of corporate anniversaries is littered with birthdays which were subsequently found to have been celebrated at the wrong time. The archivist will also have to determine, or at least explain, which is the appropriate establishment date to celebrate – the signing of a deed of partnership, the issue of a prospectus, the registration of the company, the laying of a foundation stone, the opening of doors to the public, the completion of construction work, the proposal to launch a new product, the first advertisement, the registration of a trademark – and must ensure that all published historical information is technically correct, or at least that a reasonable case can be made in support of all historical assertions. Where other departments and staff show an interest, efforts should be made to encourage broad participation, even if only at the level of undertaking some limited local historical research or dressing up in period costume.

The local context

Old-established businesses often have strong links with the local community and may, as major employers in a particular area, have dominated its social and economic history. The Halifax Building Society, still based in Halifax, West Yorkshire, claims that its cultural and historical links with the area are one of the main advantages of remaining there. Such companies as British Steel, British Coal and Pilkington, which have dominated local areas, have a responsibility to maintain archives which can explain and document the development and achievements of entire communities. Even where there is no long-established geographical connection, the maintenance of an archive provides the basis on which a company can play a part in the local community in an educational role. Company archivists may give talks to such groups as local history societies, women's institutes, rotary clubs, adult education classes and so on. Links might also be developed with local schools and further-education establishments to create opportunities for students to work on assignments relating to the development of their local firm. At an advanced level such research may provide the archivist with historical information which is not available elsewhere. Other local activities might include the instigation of displays in museums, articles in newspapers and appearances on radio and television, all of which can be used to underline a company's long-term commitment to a particular locality or community.

Skills and techniques

In the field of public relations the archivist cannot afford to become merely a keeper and fetcher of records. No other person in the company understands the kind of material available, and unless he or she suggests opportunities for historically based promotion of the business, it is unlikely that many such occasions will arise of their own accord. The business archivist must have a wide range of intellectual, managerial and practical skills in order to initiate and sustain a successful public relations programme. Some of these skills are set out below:

- Historical understanding of the development of the company and the significance of wider economic, social and political events.
- Familiarity with the historical material available, both within the company archive and elsewhere.
- Ability to undertake historical research.
- Ability to write in an appropriate, concise, lucid and interesting manner.
- Understanding of the technical processes of printing (typesetting, use of colour, paper qualities, binding methods); photographic reproduction; exhibition board production; etc.
- Knowledge of relevant suppliers of services and equipment, both inside and outside the company.
- Contacts with such experts as designers, printers, valuers, photographers, conservators and museum staff.

- Design acumen, to the extent of appreciating what might be visually appealing.
- Organizational skills.
- Interpersonal skills.
- Ability and willingness to come up with new ideas and to secure sufficient support to ensure their execution.
- Communicable enthusiasm for the public relations uses of archives.
- Competent public speaking.

An awareness of the historically based public relations projects devised by other companies will undoubtedly prove useful. Good ideas can be adapted to suit another company's needs or can provide samples to discuss during negotiations with designers or printers. The archivist must, however, also be receptive to feedback from inside the company, and be prepared to adjust ideas and compromise historical or archival purity in the interests of creating a relevant end-result.

Promoting the archive in-house

A company archive often functions in isolation, without other departments appreciating its role or even being aware of its very existence. At worst this might result in the company unwittingly spending a fortune on consultancy fees for a historical promotion, unaware that expertise was available in-house. At best it will certainly mean that the archive, as a resource, is under-used. Such an unacceptable state of affairs can be remedied by an integrated and carefully considered programme of activities and events aimed at raising the profile of the archive within the company.

A prompt, comprehensive and friendly response to historical enquiries received from colleagues in other departments is essential, as the reputation of the archive will largely be built upon opinions passed by word of mouth. At a personal level, the archivist's continuing and undisguised enthusiasm for the collection and its potential uses will pay dividends. Up-to-date copies of the main finding aid ought to be available, either in hard copy or on a networked computer database, in other departments which might make use of the collection. Such availability may prompt casual usage and will certainly raise levels of awareness. The archive can also be made more visible through small, changing exhibitions in staff areas, articles in the company magazine, a historical element in staff training courses or videos, and the circulation of leaflets on the company's history.

An archivist in business, if his department is not linked to an active records management function, can easily be left outside the company's mainstream commercial activities. This need not, however, ever become a problem if the archivist is prepared to take the initiative, not only in coming forward with ideas for historical promotions but also in assuming new and challenging responsibilities for their execution. Getting on the corporate map is important, and should be seen as a crucial element in any long-term plan for the development of the public relations potential of a company archive.

Conclusion

In the past public relations has been neglected by the archive profession. Purists have considered it to be irrelevant to the archivist's fundamental responsibilities, arrangement, classification and preservation, as defined by Jenkinson. In a company, however, an archive collection must also, to some extent, earn its keep, as few businesses can justify sustaining the considerable maintenance costs without some commercial benefit. Participation in public relations projects should, however, be structured so that the various activities are co-ordinated within a long-term development plan which reinforces the company's corporate image. The archive must create a clearly defined role for itself within the organization and attract sufficient resources and expertise to sustain its planned programme of public relations activities.

It is, however, inevitable that not all the public relations projects that may be devised by the company archivist will work well. There are bound to be problems, particularly for those with little experience in the field, as the public's response to historical exhibitions, publications and advertising is difficult to predict and measure. Public relations uses of business archives do, however, remain one of the few areas in which a company archivist can make a direct and visible contribution to a company's commercial activities. Indeed, without a public relations linkage, it is doubtful whether many important corporate archives would have been saved or business archivists appointed.

Notes

1   P. Vincenzi, *Taking Stock. Over 75 Years of the Oxo Cube* (Collins, Glasgow, 1985); D. Landen and J. Daniel, *The True Story of HP Sauce* (Methuen, London, 1985); and E. Williams, *The Story of Sunlight* (Unilever, 1984).
2   Recently published company histories include P. Bookbinder, *Marks & Spencer: The War Years 1939–1945* (Century Benham, London, 1989); K. Burk, *Morgan Grenfell, 1838–1988: The Biography of a Merchant Bank* (Oxford University Press, Oxford, 1989); L. Dennett, *Slaughter and May: A Century in the City* (Granta Editions, Cambridge, 1989); M. Moss and A. Turton, *A Legend of Retailing . . . House of Fraser* (Weidenfeld & Nicolson, London, 1989); J. St John, *William Heinemann: A Century of Publishing 1890–1990* (Heinemann, London, 1990); and P. Ziegler, *The Sixth Great Power. Barings, 1762–1929* (Collins, London, 1988).
3   For example, Anon, *John Spedan Lewis 1885–1963* (John Lewis plc, 1985); P. Vincenzi, *op. cit.;* D. Dow and M. Moss, *Glasgow's Gain. The Anderston*

Story (Parthenon Publishing, Carnforth, 1986), a history of the site of Britoil's new headquarters; B. Selby, *Guinness Advertising* (Guinness Books, London, 1985); P. Hadley (editor), *A History of Bovril Advertising* (priv. pub., 1971); and Anon., *The Advertising Art of J. & J. Colman Ltd. Yellow White & Blue* (priv. pub., 1977).

4 A few contemporary studies have been published in recent years but have rarely been commissioned by the companies concerned. For example, A. Pettigrew, *The Awakening Giant, Continuity and Change in ICI* (Blackwell, Oxford, 1985); S. Jefferys, *Management and Managed: Fifty Years of Crisis at Chrysler* (Cambridge University Press, 1986); and M. Reid, *Conversion to plc – the Inside Story of Abbey National's Conversion Flotation* (Pencorp Books, 1991).

5 *Recent examples include The Burmah Oil Company 1886–1986* (1986); *Charlesworth Celebrate 60 Years in Print* (1988); *'Pavement Glasgow': Scott Rae Stevenson Ltd 1838–1988* (1988); *The First 120 Years of Sainsbury's 1869–1989* (1989); *The History of Cox and Hicks of Ringwood* (1989); and *National Westminster Bank: A Short History* (1989).

6 See J. Orbell, *A Guide to Tracing the History of a Business* (Gower, Aldershot, 1987).

7 For further discussion of how to display archives safely, see *BS 5454: Storage and Exhibition of Archival Documents* (British Standards Institution, 1989).

8 For example, Colman's silver mustard pots and Harveys' wine glasses on tour during the early 1980s.

9 For example, the Twining Teapot Gallery opened at the Castle Museum, Norwich, in 1989.

10 Department of Education and Science, *National Curriculum History Working Group Final Report* (HMSO, April 1990). Chapter 3, 'The Essence of History'.

11 J. D. Clare, 'Eaton – An engineering firm since 1950 – An industrial liaison project', *Young Historian Scheme GCSE Projects*, Pamphlet 1 (Historical Association, London, 1989).

12 Department of Education and Science, *History in the National Curriculum (England)* (HMSO, March 1991).

13 Based on information supplied by Ian Coulson, Kent History Centre, Maidstone.

14 A useful series of National Curriculum key stage 2 studies has been produced by West Sussex History Unit as inexpensive, spiral-bound leaflets. These contain notes for teachers linking the topic to the requirements of the National Curriculum and copies of original documents suitable for further reproduction for classroom use.

15 *Op. cit.*, J. D. Clare.

Further reading

There are no books which specifically discuss the public relations uses of business archives, although there is a wealth of literature on all aspects of public relations practice, museum work, publishing, education and design. Specialist bibliographies should be consulted or further advice should be sought from experienced colleagues and such professional bodies as the Area Museum Councils and local education authorities.

The following may, however, be particularly useful:

A. Allan (editor), 'Business archives and education', *Proceedinigs of the Annual Conference 1988* (Business Archives Council, 1988).

T. Ambrose, *New Museums, A Start-up Guide* (Scottish Museums Council, HMSO, Edinburgh, 1987).

B. Dennis, 'Designers and the small museum', *AIM Guideline No. 8* (Association of Independent Museums, 1984).

J. Etherton, 'Record offices and the National Curriculum', *Journal of the Society of Archivists*, 12:1 (1991), pp. 51–62.

E. Green, 'Business anniversaries. The role of the company archivist', *Business Archives*, 57 (1989), pp. 63–9.

B. Stockford, 'Company archives in print. Producing a company brochure', *Business Archives*, 53 (1987), pp. 31–8.

K. M. Thompson, *The Use of Archives in Education: A Bibliography* (Society of Archivists, 1982).

N. Yates, 'Marketing the record office. New directions in archival public relations', *Journal of the Society of Archivists*, 9:2 (1988), pp. 69–75.

17

The business archivist as manager
Veronica Davies

Business organizations and structures : the position and role of the archivist.

The more rigid the organizational hierarchy of a business, the more the archivist can rely on rank and position to carry out his duties. With a clearly defined position on the management ladder, the business archivist has the power and status to see that his priorities are understood and met. In more unstructured organizations the personality and professional reputation of the archivist will tend to carry greater weight than position and grade. The archivist will have to convince rather than to instruct, and cooperation and liaison will become the hallmarks of his trade. Although much play has recently been made of the need for all businesses to achieve 'an unstructured environment', the level of business activity principally defines the structure of the company; larger and more established companies tend to have far more rigid and hierarchical lines of management than smaller and younger ones. With the possible exception of some of the newer 'high-tech' industries, it is hard to see how any business can avoid the rigidities of structure imposed by expansion and by a continued record of success. The position and role of the archivist within the organization is largely defined by the age and size of the business in which he is placed.

Corporate cultures

Regardless of whether the archivist is located in a medium or large organization, it will be the different atmospheres, different work methods, and the differing levels of personal responsibility and autonomy which will be the most striking. All organizations have their own 'cultures' – their different sets of values and beliefs – reflected in the systems, structures and types of employee. In all organizations there are some deep-rooted beliefs about the way the organization should work, about how authority ought to be conveyed, and about the way people should be rewarded. This culture often takes a visible form in buildings, in the type of employee selected for promotion, and in the presentation and marketing of the company's product to the consumer.

The culture of the organization cannot be precisely defined. It is more than just a perception; it is an ethos which pervades and affects every aspect of the business. Finding out what are the acceptable forms of behaviour is the key to mastering an organization's culture. The nature of the culture, however, is less important than recognizing what it is and understanding how it affects management and staff.

The approach the organization adopts will fundamentally affect the attitudes of all employees. It will of course also be reflected in the support given by the management team to the work of the archive manager. An organization whose culture is one of the naked pursuit of profit, and which gives financial results pre-eminence, is unlikely to give status to the archives unless its work can be marketed with a high return. By contrast, an organization which gives a high priority to providing services with humanitarian aims is more likely to give support and a recognition to the work of the archive manager. Whether the archivist is regarded as 'antiquarian oddity' or as a 'guardian angel' depends less on his personal qualities than on the the culture of the business in which he is employed. In consequence, a formal archive policy or mission statement should be developed and endorsed by the board of directors. This statement should include a precise definition of the relationship of the archives to the rest of the organization, as well as a definition of the main purpose and goals of the archival programme.

Formulation of a policy document

Of all the principles which define the role of the archivist and archives within an organization, the policy document has the greatest importance. The policy document defines the position and role of the archive department and, more significantly, of the archive manager within the organization. It should contain a statement of the purpose and direction of the department and a definition of the scope of work and its content. As a consequence it will be the mandate upon which the archive manager will base departmental plans of work and staffing structure (for further discussion see Chapter 4).

The planning process and planning framework

The effective implementation of the policy statement is achieved through the planning process, which is the key role of the archive manager. The creative planning process that results in the definition of objectives yields the framework around which the archive department is structured. It is this framework which provides the basis for the organization, personnel management and budget structure of the department. As a result of the planning process, tasks and activities for the department can be allocated in order of priority, budgets can be formulated and justified, and the best staff can be recruited. Planning provides a sense of purpose and an interim statement of direction. Archive managers who resist planning become 'fire-fighters', spending their time dealing with emergencies instead of preventing them. Planning is the best method for reinforcing the policy statement. It produces a routine for evaluating the performance of the archive department on a regular basis.

The activities of the archives department can usually be subdivided into the following:

- Aquisition and collection (to include compliance with procedural instructions).
- Selection and disposal.
- Arrangement and listing.
- Conservation and storage.
- Retrieval and access (to include answering enquiries and public relations activities).

Each archive manager will formulate a planning framework weighting each activity with a different priority according to the original policy statement. Identifying a list of priorities on the basis of the policy statement is the first step in the planning framework. Within each prioritorized activity, individual tasks and objectives may themselves then be defined; these tasks should also be ranked according to their importance to the activity under review. It is only at this stage that a departmental work-plan can be drafted, allocating personnel and financial resources to each identified task.

Organizing to meet task objectives is not difficult. The tasks should be divided among available staff, ensuring that the most important ones are timetabled to be completed first. If tasks and objectives are clear and well-defined, each individual should be able to relate his or her work to the achievement of the task and to how it impinges upon and supplements the rest of the work of the department. The following is a checklist of points to remember when drafting a planning framework:

- Objectives, targets and yardsticks should be clearly defined.
- Each part of the plan should be consistent with preceding parts.
- All who have to implement the plan should understand it.
- The plan must be seen to be workable.
- All those affected by the plan should be kept fully informed.
- The plan must be financially approved.
- The plan must be flexible: critical areas should be identified and contingency plans made.
- The resources available in terms of personnel, money, equipment, etc. should be taken into account.
- The skills required, any necessary training and expected standards of performance should be considered.

An equally important part of implementing any plan is the development of an effective control system – for tracking progress of the work-plans and evaluating the effectiveness of the work of the department. The first stage in the control cycle is the setting of standards, the second is the checking of performance, and the third and final stage is the correction of errors.

When drafting a control system for any plan remember the following points:

- Checkpoints must be clearly defined.
- The control system should be thought out and communicated to all those responsible before the plan is implemented.
- Delegated authority must be made known to all.
- Controls should be simple to operate.
- Clear standards of performance should be set.

The two main operational aspects of control are the organization of activities and the recording of statistics and other information. These two operations are particularly important in quality, quantity and cost control.

Achieving the plan should always be in the forefront of staff conciousness. Periodic briefings, well-prepared articles in the house magazine, and an annual report on the work of the department are all methods of communication and awareness to those outside the department. Senior managers should be made aware of efforts within the archive department, and briefings should not only report upon achievements but also highlight any difficulties encountered which may be obstructing the implementation of the archive policy statement.[1]

Time management

However well the archive manager plans the work of the department, an inability to manage his own time and work will prevent the team achieving its goals. Knowing where the time goes and how long it takes is the first step to using time effectively and to producing realistic plans. A starting point for the individual archive manager is to keep a detailed log of what happens each day. It often reveals that a comparatively small amount of time is spent on the key activities of managing the department and a disproportionately large amount of time is wasted. The telephone, drop-in visitors, uncontrolled meetings and personal disorganization all add up to a sense of frustration at the end of the working day.

Daily planning to organize the time available should become a habit. Its purpose is to 'unclutter' the desk as well as the mind. It allows the planner to see what has to be done and what is remaining. Daily planning is the bridge between what has to be done and the time available in which to do it. There are many techniques for 'getting organized', the most common of which are:

- *Appointment calendars*. These include wall charts and desk diaries – both paper and electronic. All should be designed to record daily activities by the hour.
- *'To-do' lists*. Listing action items that can be crossed off once achieved.

- *Weekly planning guides.* These keep track of both individual and department work, with formal checkpoints to review progress. It is often used as the basis for a weekly department meeting.

The following checklist is a guide to making the best use of the time available:

- Develop a daily work planning system. Do not rely on memory. Record where time is going.
- Plan ahead, using a weekly and monthly planning chart.
- Make the most of time available. Always allow a slot each day for reflective thinking.
- Learn to delegate as much as possible.
- Learn to say 'no'. Avoid overcommitment.
- Avoid clutter. Do not work in a state of personal chaos. Organize your own paperwork.
- Make the telephone and electronic mail systems work for you. Leave messages and learn when to accept or to ignore interruptions.
- Cut out unnecessary meetings and learn to control the ones that you do attend.[2]

Recruitment and appointment of staff

Without the right quality of staff, even the best designed plans are of no use. Archival work is labour-intensive; the selection and recruitment of staff is therefore an essential part of an archive manager's duties. The following section briefly describes all the activities and implications of the recruitment of a member of staff. It will in particular cover the cost of recruitment; job descriptions; the advertisement; the selection of candidates for interview; the interview itself, and the induction process.

So as to ensure conformity to established standards an archive manager should always be familiar with his particular company's personnel policy and practices. It may be that the archive manager does not play any part in the advertising and initial screening of applicants. The selection process itself will be intertwined with the corporate personnel policy for selection of employees. Patience and clarity of purpose will be required from the archive manager to ensure the selection of the best applicant for the position.

Cost of recruitment

Engaging a new member of staff is expensive. The costs incurred may be divided between *management costs* and *general costs*. Management costs will be in the areas of:

- Time spent in drafting the job description.
- Time spent pre-selecting interview candidates.
- Time spent interviewing.

General costs will be:

- Cost of advertising.
- Temporary cover during the vacancy.
- Interview expenses for the candidates.
- Administration costs, i.e. associated paperwork.
- Induction/training of the new employee.

The job description

The employment of a new member of staff is a two-way interaction. The new employee must feel comfortable with the organization and the organization most feel satisfied that it has chosen the best candidate. The key to a successful archive programme is the selection of the best applicant.

When a vacancy occurs, it is the ideal opportunity to review the work of the department. The vacancy allows the archive manager to manoeuvre staff around, to review work allocations, and to reconsider the skills profile of the department. It may be an opportunity for realigning responsibilities, for promotion, or indeed for a total reorganization.

Stage one of the selection process comprises a review of the operations of the department, analysing the job and drafting the job description. Performance in any job is directly related to the member of staff understanding exactly what his duties are. The following equation applies:

$$\text{Performance} = \text{ability} \times \text{motivation} \times \text{role clarity}$$

Role clarity is easily achieved through the formal, written job description.

A job description is a statement of tasks to be performed on a particular job, and should contain the following elements:

- Job title.
- Job summary.
- Identified relation to other jobs.
- Specific responsibilities and duties.
- Qualifications.

The level of detail will depend on the nature of the job and organizational house style.

Regardless of whether a professional archivist, clerical assistant or student helper is being employed, all will require some form of description of duties. Figure 17.1 is an example of a job description for an assistant to the Company Archivist of Nadir Consolidated Industries.

Nadir Consolidated Industries

Job: Assistant Company Archivist
Department: Company Secretary's Department
Section: Company Archives
Reporting to: Company Archivist
Subordinates: 2 staff, 1 clerical assistant, 1 part-time typist.

Job summary
The incumbent with the assistance of a small team is responsible for the day-to-day administration of the company archives. This includes the intake, arrangement and retrieval of material as well as answering external enquiries.

Statement of duties
The incumbent is expected to assist the Company Archivist in the management of the company archives programme.
  The duties of the incumbent are specifically:

- Appraisal of records for inclusion in the company archive and ensuring their safe transfer.
- Arranging and listing the archives in accordance with established procedures.
- Preparation of finding aids to assist in the retrieval of archival material.
- Answering both internal and external enquiries concerning the subject matter of the archives.
- Maintenance of administrative records and statistics for all aspects of the work of the department.
- Supervising and co-ordinating the work of the clerical assistant and part-time typist in relation to the carrying out of the above duties.
- Assisting with any other archival and administrative work of the department as and when necessary.
- Deputizing for the Company Archivist in his absence.

Date of description

Figure 17.1 *Example of job description.*

The job advertisement

It is the review and analysis of the work of the department and the job description that will form the basis of the advertisement for the vacancy. It is the responsibility of the archive manager to ensure that the vacancy is advertised in all appropriate professional journals.

To prevent an overload of applications, the advertisement should allow potential employees 'to select themselves out'. The language used should satisfy any legal requirements and avoid discrimination of any kind. Conditions of employment will obviously relate to the salary package offered by the company.

An advertisement for a vacancy should attempt to include the following elements:

- Identification of the company.
- The job title.
- The geographical location.
- The status of the job, whether temporary or permanent.
- Brief summary of the work.
- Required qualifications.
- Approximate salary band (although some company policies are that this should not be advertised).
- Benefits (variable according to company).
- Closing date for application forms/CV to be submitted.
- Contact address for further information.

Figure 17.2 is an example of a job advertisement for the assistant company archivist of Nadir Consolidated Industries.

On receipt of application forms, a selection of possible interview candidates should be made. In the case of a large number of applications it is necessary to establish a grading system in order to sort which candidates should be interviewed. Applicants may be evaluated on their technical expertise, personal qualifications, experience, and training.

The interview

Once a group of potential candidates has been chosen for interview, the following preparations should be made:

- A check that all members of the interview panel will be available at the right times should be carried out.
- A quiet room in which to hold the interviews should be booked.
- All members of the archives unit should be made aware of the interviews and prepared for introduction to the candidates.

Nadir Consolidated Industries – London
Assistant Company Archivist

A vacancy has arisen for an archivist within the Archives Section of the Company Secretary's Department of the above company.

With the assistance of a small team you will be responsible for the selection and processing of archival records. You will be required to give advice to other company departments on such matters and so good interpersonal skills will be needed. You will, in addition, be required to deputize on occasions for the Company Archivist.

You will be a graduate with a Diploma in Archive Studies, aged ideally between 24 and 30, and have 3 years' experience in a modern company archives. An interest in the management of modern archives, and in systems and procedures to handle such records, is essential.

A salary in the range of £xxxxx is being offered, depending on age and experience.

Please write or telephone for an application form to:—
The closing date for the submission of completed forms is:—

Figure 17.2 *Advertisement for assistant company archivist.*

- All relevant documents should be circulated to the interview panel.
- All your own duties should be covered by another member of staff.
- An interview checklist should be compiled, to include all necessary questions and all information to be given to the candidates.

The style and formality of the interview will depend upon the physical surroundings as well as the personality of the interview panel. Regardless of formality, the interview should be regarded as a two-way exchange of information and impressions.

The archive manager will wish to know that:

- The applicant can demonstrate the expertise claimed on the application form.
- The candidate's temperament will suit the department.
- The applicant's real interest is the job vacancy and that he/she understands the duties and responsibilities of the job.

The candidate will wish to know:

- Exact details of the job.
- The conditions of work – hours, restrictions, holidays, etc.

- Where the work is to be carried out and in what physical conditions.
- Welfare facilities, salary, pension arrangements, promotion prospects.
- Starting date.

In the interview always establish when a candidate is free to take up employment, and outline the progress of a job offer as well as the notification procedure in the event of being unsuccessful.

Induction

First impressions are very important. The new employee will be testing the atmosphere and making judgements on the environment. As for the archive manager, it is the first opportunity to set standards and indicate what is required. It will make assimilation of the new team member that much quicker and more effective if the organization's expectations are made clear, and the new employee equipped to satisfy them.[3]

Managing the team

Effective management is the key to a successful archive programme. The archive manager will need to combine the technical expertise of archival skills with the management techniques of business in order to be an effective and efficient leader. The ability to get members of the team to give of their best is an important skill. The archive manager is first and foremost the head of the team, and acceptance of this leadership role is vital to the success of the archive programme.

Management qualities

An archive manager should inspire a team to be both efficient and effective. Quite what is meant by effective is difficult to define. When the question 'What makes a good manager?' is posed, a long list of desirable qualities is produced: judgement, fairness, decisiveness, approachability . . . the list is endless. Most of the qualities listed are subjective and cannot be easily measured. Furthermore qualities cannot be taught; only skills can be acquired.

Management skills

Management skills can be developed by analysing the functions of management i.e. what managers actually do rather than what they are. This type of analysis is referred to as action-centred leadership, because it concentrates on the skills needed by a manager to be effective. The archive manager is leading a department that is a service-provider which is never noticed, until something goes wrong. The team will need regular encouragement and motivation if a sense of achievement and of team spirit is to be maintained. There are three main action areas:

- Achieving the task.
- Building the team.
- Developing the individual.

It is a management skill to ensure that tasks are completed at the same time as building the team in such a way that group work and group identity are maintained and developed. It must be recognized that each person in the team is an individual with needs, hopes and ideas which must be fulfilled if the individual is to be effective.

Achieving the task

In order to achieve the task the manager must:

- Clearly define the task.
- Understand how the task fits into the overall objectives of the archive programme.
- Plan the task to be accomplished.
- Define and provide the resources, i.e. staff, time, equipment, etc.
- Ensure the team structure allows the task to be achieved effectively.
- Control progress.
- Evaluate the results.

Building the team

The difference between a collection of individuals and a cohesive group or team is that in a team individuals co-operate. If the team has a say in the defining of objectives, the choosing of work methods, the drafting of the work-plan, and in problem-solving and decision-making, it has a good chance of being bonded.

The following checklist illustrates an effective method of team-building:

- Gather the team together regularly for briefings and discussions.
- Use the collective 'we'.
- Help resolve conflicts when they occur.
- Speak up for the team when necessary.
- Organize the team in such a way as to use the talents of individuals.
- Establish common standards and stick to them.

Developing the individual

In order to bring out the best in an individual it is important to have some understanding of what interests and motivates that individual. The more the individual can be motivated, the more he will give better and more productive work. People work for many reasons: to attain high levels of material comfort, for recognition and prestige, for social service and for work itself, if it is sufficiently interesting and challenging.

Some factors motivate the individual at work, while others are known to demotivate or to exercise a neutral effect. Those factors which motivate include peer-group recognition; recognition by superiors, often in the form of enhanced remuneration or promotion; job content; and a sense of belonging to a winning team. Demotivating factors include lack of clear goals; boring or overly testing work; poor communications; and a failure to recognize individual or team achievements. Physical conditions and welfare facilities are essentially neutral in their impact, unless they are perceived as indicators of regard.

The manner in which the archive section is managed is a starting point. Delegation plays an important part in developing and motivating individual team members. Delegation of the right job to the right individual gives him or her a sense of satisfaction which is reflected in the way he or she performs. Delegation gives a better quality of work, greater interest and more variety; it rarely fails because of lack of time. Delegation is one of the best ways of training staff and developing skills that they did not know they had.

The following are ways of developing the individual:

- Recognizing all team members as individuals.
- Delegating according to individual strengths and weaknesses.
- Letting individuals get on with the job.
- Showing the team the sum of the individual contributions.
- Thanking individuals for doing a good job and always sharing praise.
- Taking an interest in the individual.
- Providing adequate training for individual fulfilment.

Appraisal

Whatever the role of the individual, appraisal of performance is important. Most organizations have some form of annual staff reporting system by which performance is measured, and the archive manager and his department will not be exempt from this system. In theory the use of appraisal systems is excellent, since every member of the team wishes to be noticed for the good job he is doing. In practice it may be a more contentious issue, for where success is measured, failure can also be highlighted. However, appraisals which take the form of a list of achievements to be praised or failures to be criticized are of little use. The appraisal system should be a time for constructive reflection and positive forward planning. The appraisal system should:

- Allow the subordinate time to discuss his own feelings on performance; to raise major and minor work problems; and to recognize strengths and weaknesses and assess future priorities.
- Allow the archive manager to comment on the subordinate's assessment, and add his or her own observations and any other indicators which will contribute to the success of the subordinate.
- Allow both to agree on what can be done as regards training, personal development and promotion prospects.

The formal appraisal system should strengthen the contribution made by an individual to the work of the team.[4]

Resolving conflict

The archive manager will not be immune from having to resolve conflict within the team, or between himself and a team member. A genuine difference of opinion can be of value in thinking through work schedules. However, disruptive behaviour, open antagonism or discontent must be dealt with; to avoid the issue is to damage the team. The archive manager should seek the cause of the conflict and then seek a solution. Emotional involvement in the conflict must be avoided. Should the conflict remain unresolved, or worsen, then formal disciplinary action may have to be taken.

The formal framework of codes and procedures is normally acknowledged and maintained by an informal agreement from the team. Conflict that remains unresolved will grow and disrupt the working procedures. The archive manager can attempt informal action as his authority allows, or embark on formal action based on the written code. Formal procedures usually call for one or two verbal warnings, followed by one or two written warnings leading to eventual dismissal. The procedure for this formal disciplinary action will be clearly defined in each organization's personnel procedures. It is essential that the archive manager is aware of these procedures and that they are followed. As this procedure leads eventually to the dismissal of the individual, the emphasis must be upon the archive manager to resolve conflict before disciplinary action becomes necessary.

Conflict between a subordinate and manager can arise as a result of a feeling of lack of direction, indecision and poor communication. In order to eliminate this basic source of conflict, the archive manager should manage the team assertively.[5] The effectiveness of this will depend on the archive manager's ability to understand himself, to communicate successfully, to get the job done and to handle problems in such a way as to encourage the team to work together.

Planning the budget and monitoring expenditure

The costs associated with equipping, operating and staffing an archive section cannot, by the usual company cost-accounting methods, normally be 'charged back' to specific departments who use its services. The archive department is usually regarded as a central service, absorbing the budget of its parent department and only rarely producing revenue.

The allocation of a budget to the archive manager is therefore all the more important insofar as it ensures support for and justification of the work-plan and defines the services of the department. In effect a budget legitimizes the position of the archive department in the hierarchy of the company, and endorses the implementation of the archive policy statement.

Budgets are usually prepared on an annual basis. They are divided into categories for administrative convenience and are usually based upon what has been spent over the previous year and the projected expenditure for the forthcoming year. Two budget headings are used in categorizing the expenses of any company section. First, the *capital expenditure budget* deals with the large-scale investment in equipment, and so on, which, according to the accounting methods used, is offset against the balance sheet over a defined number of years. Second, the *operating budget* deals with the everyday expenses of the department.

Capital expenditure items normally require individual itemized justification at budget time, to convince the management team of the necessity of investing, say, in a particular specialized piece of equipment. In an archive department mobile shelving for a storage facility would be an example of a capital expenditure item. The operating budget consists of the costs normally associated with the routine administration, day-to-day commitments and staffing of the department.

The following is a breakdown of a typical company archive operating budget:

- Staffing.
- Training for personnel.
- Supplementary/temporary help.
- Confidential waste disposal.
- Archive stationery and conservation equipment.
- Travel and fares.
- Subscriptions to professional associations.
- Subscriptions to technical publications.
- Health and safety, to include equipment maintenance and safety wear.
- Sundries

The largest expense in any archive section is that of staff. Quite how high this percentage is will vary according to company, to accounting methods, and to the proposed work-plan of the archive section for the coming year.

What has not been included in the profile is the expenditure on storage space. If a charge to the archive operating budget is made, then this of course will form a significant amount on the budget profile.

The preparation of the budget and the receipt of funds is only half the financial cycle. Expenditure needs to be monitored. This is as important as the preparation of the budget. Quarterly reviews should be held to ensure that the budget target is as expected. Invoices and receipts should be kept and passed through to the accounting department for auditing purposes. The preparation of a financial report at the end of the budgeting period is another way of communicating with management about the work of the department.

Communication: presentation and publication of the archive programme.

Careful planning, good team management and adequate funding all contribute to the success of the archive manager in implementing the company archive policy. However, organizations expand and contract, and staff join and leave. It is a major responsibility of the archive manager to communicate the services offered, the archives policy, and the achievement of objectives to members of the management structure and to other company employees.

In order to secure the decisions required, and retain the continued, active support of the company management team and flow of funds necessary, the archive manager must be a skilled communicator. It is important that the message conveyed should be presented as effectively as possible.

Spoken presentation

A spoken presentation should always aim to be objective; short, no longer than 20 minutes; and positive, in its presentation of the argument. Effective speaking comes with practice. The three stages of preparation for making a spoken presentation are the following.

- *Stage 1 Preparation of the talk* First, define your purpose. Is the intention to communicate results or to request a decision? Second, clarify your topic. You must know your facts, and have examples and proposed supporting documentation ready. Third, recognize your audience; you must be aware of their attitudes, knowledge and attention span. Finally, check your time limit. How long have you got?

- *Stage 2   Shape of the talk*   First, state your proposition, then the subject. It is important to arouse interest; and to do this you must show enthusiasm. Next evaluate the options, weigh them up and anticipate objections. To prove your case, you must then select and highlight strong points. You may end by summarizing your main points.
- *Stage 3   The presentation*   It is important to be natural and to be confident. Show your evidence with handouts and overhead illustrations, but remember not too much paper. Enthusiasm and friendliness are likely to endear you to your audience during a presentation.

Written presentation

A written communication of results or the report of a completed project may be composed in a variety of styles. An archive manager should always conform to any established 'house style'. The communication may come in the annual report of the company, in the 'house journal', or in a pamphlet describing the services of the archive department. Regardless of form, the written communication should be presented in a logical sequence.

The following suggested headings could be used when preparing a case requiring a management decision:

- Title sheet and contents page to include the formal circulation list.
- Management summary of no more than one page in length – in effect a précis of the report.
- Introduction, providing background to the report.
- Factual summary of the existing situation.
- Analysis of the situation, commenting upon merits and disadvantages, and introducing possible solutions.
- Recommendations: a statement of the preferred course for remedial action.
- Proposal for any new system, to include a description of the implementation phase.
- Acknowledgements.
- Appendices, with supporting statistics and paperwork.

Managing a line manager

Presentations to the management team and effective communication of information to the rest of the company are only two aspects of the archive manager's role. 'Managing' your superior is the other aspect of effective communication of information to achieve results. Often the archive manager is reporting to a superior who knows little of archives. In order to secure necessary decisions, effective communication is required. Managing your line manager falls into four main parts:

- Understanding and exploiting his or her preferred working style.
- Representing the team's interests and concerns in communications up the management ladder.
- Being sensitive to his or her position in the organization, and, by extension, to the wider company policy and interests, if these should be potentially damaging in the narrower working environment.
- Showing on all occasions a mastery of one's professional task and of the work of the department.

Mutual respect and understanding should be the goal and confrontational exchanges should be avoided.

In order to establish a successful relationship with an immediate superior, the archive manager will need more than just a narrow technical expertise. The archive manager must have a firm understanding of his or her department's role within the organization of the business, and of its goals, ethos and development pattern. He or she should display a sense of financial responsibility, prove a capable leader and team-builder, and an effective communicator. Once the archive manager has gained the confidence of his or her superiors by demonstrating these essential management qualities, the status and reputation of his or her department will increase and the manager's position in the hierarchy be all the more firmly established.

Notes

1 For discussion of policy statements and planning, see C. Newton, *Strategic Planning for Records Management and Archives* (Society of Archivists Records Management Group, 1984).
2 J. D. Ferner, *Successful Time Management* (John Wiley & Sons, New York, 1980).
3 For the discussion of the recruitment and retention of staff, see J. Reay, *The Supervisor's Handbook* (Northwood Books, London, 1981), pp. 86–98.
4 T. Philp, *Making Performance Appraisal Work* (McGraw-Hill, New York, 1983).
5 M. Burley-Allen, *Managing Assertively* (John Wiley & Sons, New York, 1983).

Further reading

J. Adair, *The Action-Centred Leader* (The Industrial Society, London, 1988).
J. Adair, *The Effective Supervisor* (The Industrial Society, London, 1988).
C. Blaazer and E. Molyneux, *Supervising the Electronic Office* (Gower, with Philips Business Systems, Aldershot, 1984).
J. G. Bradsher (editor), *Managing Archives and Archival Institutions* (Mansell, London, 1988).

C. Handy, *The Age of Unreason* (Business Books Ltd, London, 1989).
C. Newton, *Strategic Planning for Records Management and Archives* (Society of Archivists Records Management Group, 1984).
A. Pederson (editor), *Keeping Archives* (Australian Society of Archivists Inc., Sydney, 1987).
T. Peters, *Thriving on Chaos: Handbook for a Management Revolution* (Macmillan, London, 1987).

Index